Competition Law and Development

Global Competition Law and Economics

Thomas K. Cheng, Ioannis Lianos, and D. Daniel Sokol, editors

Competition Law and Development

Edited by D. Daniel Sokol, Thomas K. Cheng,
and Ioannis Lianos

STANFORD LAW BOOKS
An Imprint of Stanford University Press
Stanford, California

Stanford University Press
Stanford, California

Printed in the United States of America on acid-free, archival-quality paper

Library of Congress Cataloging-in-Publication Data

Competition law and development / edited by D. Daniel Sokol, Thomas K. Cheng, and Ioannis Lianos.
      pages cm.—(Global competition law and economics)
    Includes bibliographical references and index.
    ISBN 978-0-8047-8571-6 (cloth : alk. paper)
    1. Antitrust law.   2. Restraint of trade.   3. Law and economic development.
I. Sokol, D. Daniel, editor of compilation.   II. Cheng, Thomas K., editor of compilation.
III. Lianos, Ioannis, editor of compilation.   IV. Series: Global competition law and economics.
  K3850.C653   2013
  343.07'21—dc23   2013011217

Typeset by Westchester Publishing Services in Bembo, 10.5/14

Contents

Contributors   vii

Introduction   1
    D. Daniel Sokol, Thomas K. Cheng, and Ioannis Lianos

1. Economic Development and Global Competition
Law Convergence   13
    David J. Gerber

2. Is There a Tension Between Development Economics
and Competition?   35
    Ioannis Lianos, Abel Mateus, and Azza Raslan

3. Who Needs Antitrust? Or, Is Developing-Country
Antitrust Different? A Historical-Comparative Analysis   52
    Aditya Bhattacharjea

4. Competition Law and Development: Lessons from the
U.S. Experience   66
    Thomas C. Arthur

5. Competition Law in Developing Nations: The
Absolutist View   79
    George L. Priest

6. Resource Constraints and Competition Law Enforcement:
Theoretical Considerations and Observations from
Selected Cross-Country Data   90
    Vivek Ghosal

7. Competition and Development: What Competition
   Law Regime?   115
   Abel Mateus

8. Prioritizing Cartel Enforcement in Developing
   World Competition Agencies   137
   D. Daniel Sokol and Andreas Stephan

9. Contracts and Cartels: Reconciling Competition
   and Development Policy   155
   Barak D. Richman

10. Your Money and Your Life: The Export of U.S.
    Antitrust Remedies   167
    Harry First

11. Rethinking Competition Advocacy in Developing Countries   182
    Allan Fels and Wendy Ng

12. Domestic and Cross-Border Transfer of Wealth   199
    Ariel Ezrachi

13. The Patent-Antitrust Interface in Developing Countries   212
    Thomas K. Cheng

14. Embedding a Competition Culture: Holy Grail
    or Attainable Objective?   228
    David Lewis

15. India's Tryst with "the Clayton Act Moment" and Emerging
    Merger Control Jurisprudence: Intersection of Law,
    Economics, and Politics   249
    Rahul Singh

Notes   271

Index   309

Contributors

Thomas C. Arthur is the L. Q. C. Lamar Professor of Law at Emory University School of Law.

Aditya Bhattacharjea is professor of economics at the Delhi School of Economics, University of Delhi.

Thomas K. Cheng is associate professor at Hong Kong University Faculty of Law.

Ariel Ezrachi is the Slaughter and May Professor of Competition Law at the University of Oxford and a fellow of Pembroke College, Oxford.

Allan Fels has been dean of ANZSOG since July 1, 2003. Prior to taking this position, he was chairman of the Australian Competition and Consumer Commission (ACCC) from 1995 until 2003.

Harry First is Charles L. Denison Professor of Law and director, Competition, Innovation, and Information Law Program at NYU School of Law.

David J. Gerber is the distinguished professor of law and co-director of the Program in International and Comparative Law at IIT Chicago-Kent College of Law.

Vivek Ghosal is professor at the School of Economics at Georgia Institute of Technology.

David Lewis is executive director of Corruption Watch. He chaired the Competition Tribunal for a decade from its founding in 1999. In 2009 Lewis was appointed an extraordinary professor at the Gordon Institute of Business Science. A year later, the University of Cape Town awarded him an honorary doctorate in economic sciences.

Ioannis Lianos is the City Solicitors' Educational Trust Reader in European and Competition Law at University College London. Ioannis was awarded a Gutenberg Research chair at the Ecole Nationale d'Administration in November 2011. He has also been a visiting professor at the Faculty of Law of the University of Chile in Santiago since December 2011 and a fellow at the Centre for Law and Economics at the Australian National University (ANU). Since September 2004, he has been a visiting professor in competition and intellectual property law at the Centre for International Industrial Property Studies (CEIPI) of the University of Strasbourg.

Abel Mateus is professor of economics at New University of Lisbon. Previously, he served as the first president of the Portuguese Competition Authority, deputy governor of the Banco de Portugal, member of the Monetary Committee, and member of the Economic Policy Committee of the European Commission.

Wendy Ng is a PhD candidate, Melbourne Law School, University of Melbourne.

George L. Priest is the Edward J. Phelps Professor of Law and Economics and Scholar in Law, Economics, and Entrepreneurship at Yale Law School.

Azza Raslan is a PhD candidate at University College London Faculty of Law.

Barak D. Richman is professor of law at Duke Law School.

Rahul Singh is assistant professor at National Law School of India, Bangalore.

D. Daniel Sokol is associate professor at the University of Florida Levin College of Law.

Andreas Stephan is senior lecturer in competition law at the University of East Anglia.

Competition Law and Development

Introduction

D. Daniel Sokol, Thomas K. Cheng, and Ioannis Lianos

One may be forgiven for asking what exactly is the purpose of this book. What exactly is meant by competition law and development? There are a few possible answers to this question. The most obvious answer is that it is about competition law in developing countries. Given that the vast majority of the countries in the world are developing countries—after all, there are only thirty-four OECD (Organisation for Economic Co-operation and Development) countries—there is a serious dearth of attention to developing countries in the international and comparative competition law scholarship, much of which has been preoccupied with the United States and the European Union.

Competition law is a regulatory tool to improve societal well-being. Competition law is a regulatory response to a market-based organization of the economy. As such, competition law is the backstop to correct market malfunctions. The market malfunction central to competition law is the exercise of monopoly power. Competition law and policy work within the larger development context to create a more competitive environment.

Competition law and policy has the potential to play an important role in greater economic development through the creation of competitive markets in the developing world. Competition law enforcement promotes higher economic growth. As competition reduces entry barriers, incumbent firms can no longer be supported through monopoly rents.[1] As a result of competition, firms become more efficient.[2] As trade and regulatory liberalization reduce some of the most obvious government barriers such as tariffs, the remaining government barriers—mixed government and private anticompetitive behavior—become more important concerns. These factors have made the implementation of effective competition law and policy more pressing. However, competition law does not operate within a vacuum. Competition law enforcement and broader competition policy that includes competition advocacy is a function of the prevailing economics and politics of any country at any given time.[3] In other areas of law the role of transplants and their effectiveness has been studied at great length. One question that this book asks is whether or not the competition law and policy transplant from Europe and the United States can "take" in the developing world or whether the developing world experience suggests a need for a different analytical framework.

There are reasons that developing countries may require a different analytical framework. The political and economic environment of developing countries often differs significantly from that of developed countries in ways that may have serious implications for competition law enforcement. The competition authorities and courts may lack the expertise or the resources to undertake sophisticated effects-based analysis. The importance of informal economy in these jurisdictions may challenge the usual understanding of the role of market definition and the assessment of market power. The business community may desire more clear-cut rules to facilitate compliance; such a need may be augmented by the lack of expertise in competition law in the domestic private bar. Corruption may be more prevalent in developing countries, which may undermine the impartiality of the enforcement agency and the courts. The domestic political system may be structured in such a way that independence of the enforcement agency from the executive branch of the government may be undesirable or perhaps unattainable. These considerations may bolster the case for legal rules that allow for less discretion and hence less room for arbitrary and politically influenced decision making by the enforcement agency.

The need to devote greater attention to developing countries is also justified by the changing global economic reality in which developing countries, especially China, India, and Brazil, have emerged as economic powerhouses. Together with Russia, the so-called BRIC countries have accounted for 30 percent of global economic growth since the term was coined in 2001.[4] China overtook Japan to become the second-largest economy in the world in 2010.[5]

According to the International Monetary Fund, China is expected to over-take the United States as the largest economy in the world in 2016.[6] In this sense, developing countries deserve more attention not because of any justifi-able differences from developed countries in competition law enforcement, either in theoretical or practical terms, but because of their sheer economic heft. The role of state-owned enterprises in their economies also adds a fur-ther complication to the conceptual apparatus of competition law.[7]

It would be a gross omission in international competition law scholarship to ignore how competition law is formulated and enforced in jurisdictions accounting for such a significant share of the global economy. The impor-tance of these markets may also impact the enforcement of competition law as these jurisdictions can hold up mergers or potentially have a different set of priorities for single-firm conduct. With greater resources, these countries may become more active in the provision of technical assistance to other countries in their respective spheres of influence. Already Brazil provides antitrust technical assistance to other agencies within Latin America.

What has attracted the most attention in particular is merger control in India and China and the treatment of the interface of intellectual property and competition in China. Given the importance of the Chinese and the Indian markets, nearly every multinational corporation has a substantial presence in both countries. This in turn means that every merger or acquisi-tion involving these corporations that exceeds the notification thresholds under their respective merger control regimes must be reported to and ap-proved by the Ministry of Commerce (MOFCOM) in China and the Com-petition Commission in India. In 2008, soon after the Anti-Monopoly Law came into effect, China's nascent merger control regime flexed its muscles when MOFCOM rejected Coca-Cola's proposed acquisition of Huiyuan, which was one of the largest fruit juice manufacturers in China. The treat-ment of the intellectual property–competition interface in China has simi-larly been subject to close scrutiny given the size of the Chinese domestic market and the country's weak record in enforcing intellectual property pro-tection. Multinational corporations have expressed concerns that China will use competition law to encroach upon intellectual property rights.

What might the emerging competition regimes learn from more estab-lished ones? One would think that after 100 years, the goals of antitrust would be clear both in the United States and around the world. Unfortu-nately, this is not the case. Competition law systems (including the United States) may have a number of complementary or even contradictory goals.

Although for developed countries the main driving force of their competition law is the efficient allocation of resources, this is not always the case in developing countries where efficiency concerns may in more fundamental ways be at odds with goals such as employment, poverty alleviation, and the empowerment of previously marginalized groups. The transplantation of competition law to a developing country setting may raise challenges to the traditional understanding of competition law and its role/function in public policy.

A first-order question is whether competition is the best way to promote economic development. Some assert that productivity is the key to economic growth and poverty alleviation and that distortions and inefficiencies in product markets are the most significant impediment to productivity growth. It is through competition in open markets that economies attain gains in productivity and hence the best growth prospects. The key to economic growth is to get government out of the markets and let businesses do their work. If this view is correct, competition law enforcement and competition policy reforms will play a pivotal role in any growth strategy.

Detractors of this competition-primacy view argue that there are other strategies that are equally, if not more, effective in promoting economic growth. A number of academics point to the experience of the Asian tigers as examples of the successful deployment of industrial policy to achieve phenomenal economic growth.[8] The implementation of industrial policy in most cases will require a de-emphasis of competition law enforcement, as attested to by the experience of Japan between the 1960s and the early 1990s. The resolution of this debate and the role of competition in economic development in general have important implications for competition law development in developing countries.

The terms "economic growth" and "development" have been used interchangeably thus far. Not every development scholar, however, believes that the two are the same. Economic growth refers to an increase in GDP per capita. Its focus is on output or income growth. Development is generally given a broader meaning. Nobel laureate Amartya Sen famously argues that economic development should not be parochially focused on growth in income, but should aim to increase human capability so as to allow individuals to take advantage of life's opportunities and to fulfill their full potential.[9] Development should endeavor to increase the freedom of individuals to pursue their life goals. This freedom-based approach to economic development rejects the implicit premise of the growth-focused view that the best way to achieve broad-based improvement in living standard is to increase social welfare and let the benefits trickle down along the social ladder.

The freedom-based approach also deviates from the growth-focused view by emphasizing the importance of education and health care. It is only through education, which can only be achieved in good health, that the poor can improve their quality of life. A singular focus on growth in GDP per capita would not suffice. This debate between economic growth and economic development has important implications for competition law enforcement. The compatibility between the fundamental assumptions of competition law and the growth-focused view should be apparent. Implementation of the growth-focused view would probably require few adjustments to competition law as it is practiced in the United States and the EU. If one were to subscribe to the freedom-based approach to economic development, however, one might need to incorporate in competition law analysis special considerations about the impact of competitive behavior on the poor's access to education, health care, and other essentials in life.

This book grapples with these themes and provides a number of viewpoints of what competition law and policy means in both theory and practice in a development context.

Chapters 1 through 5 are, in a sense, stand-alone chapters in that they do not directly speak to each other. Yet we find that this is exactly a problem with how different groups within the competition law and development debate view each other—within various intellectual silos. One view suggests an organic growth of competition law that is country specific given political and economic history and path dependency. As such, if one can create a set of best practices, it is not clear how to move countries to these best practices.

An alternative viewpoint suggests that there is a singular economic model that leads to development—the embrace of the market economy. Those economies that have embraced the market the most have been rewarded with greater growth and development. However, if the neoliberal view of the supremacy of market economy is correct, then the development of antitrust in the United States is an odd choice of a standard bearer of the market view. As a matter of institutional design, it would be folly to recreate the American competition policy system elsewhere given the various malfunctions of the U.S. approach, but it is precisely this approach that many advocate.

The expectation of policy makers and many academics is perhaps that developing world countries should not repeat the same mistakes that developed competition regimes have made. Many in the developing world, however, take issue with this paternalistic approach. They wonder if it is even possible to hold such assumptions about the goals and practice of competition law and policy given that the larger political and economic systems of developing world countries differ significantly from developed world ones. Yet another approach is to think outside of the traditional competition law and industrial organization economics paradigm and to draw from development economics, a subfield of economics that historically has been marginal in competition law and economics debates. When taken holistically rather than as stand-alone chapters, this first set of chapters grapples with these tensions.

In Chapter 1, David Gerber addresses broad issues of competition law and development and convergence. Gerber examines the various assumptions behind the economics-based model of competition law. Two themes emerge in his chapter. The first shows that claims (primarily in the United States and in Europe) for some sort of convergence of competition law and policy lack well thought out and empirically supported assumptions about developing countries. The second notes a fundamental tension between the goals of economic development on the one hand and convergence as global policy on the other, given the state of play of competition law and policy discussions. In particular, the mechanisms for convergence are not well thought out given their inconsistency with domestic intentions and institutional realities.

In Chapter 2, a companion to Chapter 1, Ioannis Lianos, Abel Mateus, and Azza Raslan sketch a parallel intellectual history of development economics and competition. Their starting point is that the economic principles underpinning development policies have been different from those enshrined in competition law. Hence, traditional competition law and competition economics scholars have ignored so far the important theoretical and empirical contributions of development economics. Yet development economists have also viewed for some time the neoclassical price theory–inspired competition law as antithetical to the objective of economic growth they valued, with the consequence that their policy suggestions undervalued the importance of competition for economic development. However, the authors remark that the focus since the 1990s of both development economics and competition economics on growth and institutions opens the door to a more dialectical interaction between competition scholars and development economists that could greatly contribute to the emergence of a competition law paradigm that better fits developing countries' concerns.

In Chapter 3, Aditya Bhattacharjea questions also the assumptions behind today's competition law convergence by undertaking a historical analysis of the development of competition law around the world. He reviews the history of competition law in a number of jurisdictions to illustrate that the actual reasons for adoption of competition laws in most industrialized countries were rather different from some sort of efficiency standard, as were the objectives that influenced their interpretation and enforcement for several decades. The second part of his chapter examines how much the experiences of developing world countries are different from those of the developed world countries that preceded them in the establishment of competition law systems.

In Chapter 4, Tom Arthur suggests limits for competition law convergence around the U.S. model. His detailed account provides historical analysis of the developments that shaped the U.S. competition law system, a system that he argues is not something that should be replicated abroad, given a number of flaws of the U.S. institutional design. He suggests that a number of lessons could be learned from the U.S. experience. The first and most important lesson from this experience for a developing country is the adoption of a more efficient mode of competition law enforcement than the U.S. system. Second, the American experience with competition law is not a useful guide for keeping government interventions to a reasonable level. For developing countries that lack a mature legal infrastructure similar to the United States, the third lesson is that effective legal and political institutions must precede significant competition law enforcement. Indeed, he argues that without such institutional support a competition law regime may do more harm than good, as the competition law system may become yet another form of institutional rent seeking.

In contrast to the previous authors, George Priest (Chapter 5) offers what he terms an "absolutist" view of the importance of the market as the default institution for effective economic growth and development. The competition law absolutist view rejects multiple intellectual approaches and purposes with respect to competition law. Instead, Priest proposes that competition law should be harmonized substantively because there is a single best-defined competition law to improve societal welfare. This law is based on market-based principles that will not be overwhelmed by local political discontent with market-based policies. In this sense, the absolutist critique should have equal policy salience among "developed" countries in Europe and North America as among more developing countries.

Chapters 6 and 7 address some of the institutional issues at play in competition law and development. In Chapter 6, Vivek Ghosal examines three issues. The first is a question of institutional design: should a developing country establish a competition authority that covers the full range of enforcement activities or an agency with a more limited agenda, such as cartels? In answering, Ghosal draws upon the economics of production (scale and scope). Ghosal then addresses agency independence. In doing so, he uses models of regulatory behavior under political and interest group dynamics to address how and when competition agencies can achieve independence to reduce distortions of optimal enforcement-related decision making. In the final part of his chapter, Ghosal addresses optimal agency size, using data from a selected sample of developed and developing countries. One important conclusion of this chapter is factual—Ghosal has discovered a paucity of standardized data and important conceptual problems behind data definitions across competition agencies. These data limitations impact a number of assumptions regarding competition agency development.

Offering some empirical findings to go along with some theorizing on how to facilitate effective competition enforcement, Abel Mateus (Chapter 7) finds that a number of factors restrict the effectiveness of a competition enforcement regime: (1) vested interests that dominate economic policy making, either through legal means (party financing, lobbying, influence in the nomination of the government, senior officials, or the council of the national competition authority [NCA]), or illegal means (corruption, abuse of public authority, or cronyism); (2) inefficient public administration and regulatory systems that limit the capacity and effectiveness of public bodies, including the NCA; and (3) inefficient judicial systems that preclude the sanctioning of violations of the competition law.

Chapters 8 through 13 address particular policies that competition systems around the developing world undertake. Regarding cartel policy, D. Daniel Sokol and Andreas Stephan (Chapter 8) note that while enforcement of anticartel laws has the potential to benefit consumers in developing countries, enforcement has been spotty. They identify how developing world competition agencies can best prioritize cartel enforcement. With limited resources and institutional challenges that are distinct across countries, no one area of emphasis is without its risks. However, they suggest a mix of domestic cartel enforcement focused on high-impact sectors (in terms of media awareness) where cartel members are not politically powerful and a similar strategy involving government procurement. International cartel enforcement should play a lesser role, as should cartels with a lower media impact, as developing a procompetition culture is a building block to more successful cartel enforcement across the economy.

In Chapter 9, Barak Richman combines competition law enforcement with contractual rights. It has become conventional wisdom that effective competition policy is a necessary ingredient to economic development. But competition policy, he argues, should be secondary to the more pressing priority of securing contract rights, and sometimes competition policy is at odds with the priority of securing contract rights. This is because, in under-developed legal systems, cartels are sometimes necessary to enforce contracts. When courts and other public instruments are unable to reliably enforce contracts, private ordering systems often arise to mobilize a group of affili-ated merchants to direct coordinated punishments against parties who breach contracts. Yet such coordinated punishment is akin to a group boycott that normally invites antitrust scrutiny. His chapter focuses on this tension be-tween the well-understood harms of group boycotts as restraints on compe-tition and the unappreciated benefits of group boycotts as a procompetitive solution to court failures.

Cartel violations also require effective remedies. In Chapter 10, Harry First examines two parts of the U.S. competition system in the area of remedies—private treble damages and criminalization and incarceration of antitrust violators. First argues that, although most other countries do not embrace these remedies as fully as the United States, these two remedies would be useful in other countries. He offers some case studies of the export of these remedies abroad.

Competition advocacy plays a significant role in economic development as government-imposed restrictions on competition may be just as signifi-cant, if not more so, than private barriers. In Chapter 11, Allan Fels and Wendy Ng argue that general advocacy—the traditional method of competi-tion advocacy—has significant limitations, particularly in developing coun-tries. They propose an alternate approach to competition advocacy, which they term a "comprehensive national competition policy" approach. This approach (Australian in design) has been incorporated by the OECD in its Competition Policy Assessment Toolkit. They analyze the experience of na-tional competition policy in Australia and elsewhere and its relevance for developing countries.

In Chapter 12, Ariel Ezrachi notes that structural changes in competition law enforcement globally have broader impact for the developing world. The unilateral enforcement approach has been supplemented by cooperation across agencies at bilateral, regional, and multinational levels. These cooperative systems (whether binding or voluntary) have increased convergence and coordination of competition enforcement across national competition systems. Yet, as Ezrachi points out, cooperation cannot override the domestic nature of competition enforcement. In this sense, domestic enforcement may not properly account for the totality of effects. This in turn may lead to suboptimal enforcement. Ezrachi explores this phenomenon through the lens of "transfer of wealth." He suggests that unless remedied, under-enforcement may yield a transfer of wealth across jurisdictions. As such, Ezrachi argues that effective domestic competition enforcement along with long-arm jurisdiction may remedy under-enforcement elsewhere.

In Chapter 13, on the intellectual property–antitrust interface, Thomas Cheng argues that developing countries require different approaches from those commonly advocated. The nature of different approaches is not merely as between developed and developing countries. Rather, developing countries' approaches need to differ from each other based on their stages of economic development, per capita income, and technological capacity. Indeed, Cheng suggests that it may make sense to adopt industry-specific approaches within a single competition system.

Chapters 14 and 15 provide country-level case studies of how complex in practice competition law and development is. In Chapter 14, David Lewis offers a ten-year retrospective on the implementation of competition law in the South African context. The experience has been mixed but has had some significant positive developments. In the first decade the South African competition authorities focused on private anticompetitive conduct. To continue enforcement in this area, Lewis argues, the South African authorities must aggressively assert their jurisdictional exclusivity in the private sphere. Lewis also suggests that the second decade must focus on confronting public anticompetitive conduct. Yet, as he notes, the transition from combating the former to the latter is fraught with difficult political challenges.

The implementation of competition law can be messy given legal, economic, and political factors that come into play. In Chapter 15, Rahul Singh provides a case study of clashing interests that have been implicated in the rollout of India's merger control regime. He suggests that the economics of merger control regulation is a bundle of contradictions (partly due to interest-group lobbying). On the one hand are the relatively high jurisdictional monetary thresholds required for the applicability of the merger control, and on the other hand is the nascent government proposal to subject all pharmaceutical merger cases (irrespective of the jurisdictional monetary thresholds) to the Competition Commission of India's notification and approval process.

This case study of implementation of merger control in India illustrates the type of problems that many young competition regimes have in implementing not only merger control but competition law more broadly.

Overall, this book fills a gap in the extant literature by identifying conceptual issues with competition law and development, exploring areas for focus and change, and offering cautionary tales in both developed and developing world contexts on the limitations of existing institutions and enforcement for bettering the lives of consumers around the world.

We wish to acknowledge the support of our editors at Stanford University Press, Kate Wahl and Michelle Lipinski, and their staff, as well as two anonymous reviewers.

1

Economic Development and Global Competition Law Convergence

David J. Gerber

Global convergence seems to many to be the best, perhaps the only, available strategy for reducing the conflicts, costs, and uncertainties that the current transnational competition law regime imposes on global economic activity. The failed attempt to include competition law in the World Trade Organization in the early 2000s has led many to conclude that multinational coordination regarding competition law has little or no chance of success and that therefore convergence is the only available strategy for improving the legal framework for transnational markets. This convergence strategy is based on the idea that the countries of the world (or at least most of them) will voluntarily move toward a central model of competition law and that this process will reduce the costs, uncertainties, and risks associated with the current jurisdictional system.[1]

This chapter examines a fundamental assumption on which the global convergence strategy is based—namely, that a large number of countries outside the United States and Europe will voluntarily adopt a specific conception of competition law that we will here call the "economics-based model" of competition law (EBM).[2] This view of competition law relies on a specific form of economic analysis as the basis for competition law. The EBM has been developed primarily in the United States,[3] and thus the issue is whether a model of competition law created in a highly developed country with a large, open market can attract widespread acceptance and emulation by decision

makers in a large number of countries that are not highly developed economically and that do not operate in a large, open market. The entire convergence strategy is built on this assumption, because it can achieve its stated
goals only if there is widespread participation by developing countries. This
assumption has received little systematic attention, at least until recently,[4] but
its central importance calls for closer scrutiny of its conceptual and empirical
foundations.

The chapter reviews some of the support for this assumption. Specifically,
it explores the basis for expecting developing countries to converge toward
the EBM. It identifies some of the incentives for decision makers in developing countries to follow this model and some of the factors that may influence
those decisions.

Two themes are central to the analysis. The first is that claims for convergence as global policy are often built on inadequately supported assumptions
about the participation of developing countries. The second is that there is a
fundamental tension between the goals of economic development and the
strategy of global competition law convergence.

Concepts and Assumptions

Two concepts that are central to this analysis call for clarification. "Developing countries" refers here to countries in which levels of economic development are low by international standards. This definition is obviously loose,
but two factors sharpen its contours. First, my concern here is with *economic*
development, as distinguished from social, political, or other forms of development. And second, I use a country's level of per capita income as the measure of economic development.[5] There are other measures of economic development, and for many purposes they may be more appropriate than the
"growth" standard that I use here.[6] In most contexts, however, economic
development continues to be primarily measured by per capita income levels
and I follow that usage here.

Clarifying the concept of convergence is particularly important, not only
because it is the focus of this chapter but also because there is much confusion
about its use. The term "convergence" is often used loosely to refer to the
reduction of differences, but without clarifying which differences are involved, in what ways they are reduced, and between which actors they are
reduced, the term is too vague to be useful and it is often misleading. The
core meaning of convergence, and the one we will use here, refers to a pro-

cess that reduces the distance between individual points and a central point (the all-important *convergence point*).[7] Here the convergence point is a competition law model with a particular set of characteristics, and convergence is a process that leads other systems increasingly to resemble that model.[8]

As used here, convergence refers to a specific type of *process* with two main characteristics. The first refers to the "what" of the process. Our concern is with the *decisions* of state decision makers and with the *incentives* that shape those decisions.[9] "Decision" here includes not only or even primarily the formal decisions of legislatures or courts, but all decisions that relate to the enactment, application, and implementation of competition law. The second element refers to the "how" of the process. I include only decisions that are made *independently* and *voluntarily*—i.e., those that are neither the subject of an obligation (created by agreement or otherwise) nor subject to coercive pressures from external sources.

Convergence as Global Competition Policy

This chapter focuses on convergence as *policy*—i.e., as a strategy for achieving particular goals. Here the policy goal is to reduce law-based distortions on global markets, and the method for achieving it is to reduce disparities among the norms of competitive behavior on such markets. It is a response to the inherent weaknesses and limitations of the international jurisdictional system. That system and its inherent limitations frame thinking about competition law at the global level, and we need to review it briefly.

The current legal structure for dealing with transnational competitive restraints is jurisdictional. In it, public international law grants each state authority to take particular types of action with respect to private actors. These international law principles have evolved over centuries for the purpose of avoiding conflicts among states.[10] Our focus here is on one form of jurisdiction that is referred to as "prescriptive" or "legislative" jurisdiction.[11] It refers to the authority of a state to apply its laws to those who engage in certain forms of conduct. Note that this jurisdictional system authorizes *unilateral* state action. It does not provide for collaborative legal relations.

Many of the tensions and problems within the jurisdictional system are rooted in the evolution of these jurisdictional principles. Prior to World War II, international law principles generally authorized a state to apply its laws only to its own nationals (nationality principle) or to conduct that occurred within its territory (territoriality principle). In this arrangement, the potential

for conflicts over jurisdiction was limited. Individuals and corporations seldom had more than one legal "nationality," and relevant conduct seldom
occurred in more than one place. Since World War II, however, the so-called
effects principle has been added as a basis for jurisdiction. It authorizes a state
to apply its norms to those who engage in conduct that has *certain kinds of
consequences* within that state. According to it, any state that is significantly
affected by the conduct may be entitled to regulate it. This has greatly increased the potential for conflicts arising from concurrent regulation of the
same conduct by multiple states, and this, in turn, has increased the costs,
complexities, and risks of transnational business operations.

The globalization wave that began in the 1990s has brought the weaknesses and limitations of the system into high relief through the combined
effect of two forces. One is the increasing globalization of markets.[12] Markets
have become more global because geographical and political barriers to operating on many of them have eroded. The other is increased reliance on
competition laws to protect markets. The number of countries with competition laws has expanded dramatically, as have the resources supporting application of such laws, and this has further increased the probability of jurisdictional conflicts among states as well as the complexity, cost and uncertainty
of operating on transnational markets. This reliance has intensified pressures on
the jurisdictional system and focused attention on disparities in the rules of
conduct on those markets. It has become increasingly obvious that such differences create significant burdens and costs for businesses that may be subject to the laws of more than one jurisdiction.

Reactions to this burden on global economic activity have led in two
directions. One was initially centered in Europe, where in the 1990s leaders
of the European Commission seized on the opportunity presented by the
newly created World Trade Organization (WTO) and sought to include a
competition law regime in the WTO.[13] The effort received some support,
but many developing countries opposed it, although their reasons appear to
have had little to do with the merits of the basic idea.[14] U.S. representatives
also failed to support it.[15] After several years of discussions, the WTO decided not to put competition law on its agenda.

A second response has been a convergence strategy, which emerged during the WTO discussions relating to competition law and was seen by many
as an effort to provide an alternative to including competition law in the
WTO. It has been strongly supported by U.S. interests, who in 2001 gave
this support institutional form by sponsoring the creation of the Inter-

national Competition Network (ICN), which many view as a vehicle for convergence.[16] I have elsewhere discussed in detail the evolution of convergence as policy and there is no need to recount that story in full here.[17] The main point is that the turn to convergence as a global strategy has been conditioned by the specific circumstances of the period in which it emerged.

The process of convergence is inseparable from its content—the convergence point toward which the process is intended to lead. The content of the process shapes perceptions and evaluations of the process, just as perceptions and evaluations of the process shape ideas about its content. Those who have promoted convergence as a global competition law strategy have typically had a relatively clear picture of what they think the convergence point should be. In order to evaluate the relationship of developing countries to the convergence process, we must therefore look more closely at what that convergence point is assumed to be.

Convergence as global competition policy has emerged in a context in which the EBM is generally viewed as the only politically viable convergence point. The main reason is that the United States is a central player in international commercial relations and U.S. officials have made clear that they would not accept a different conception of competition law as the convergence point. In addition, the EBM appears to be the only well-articulated and clearly identifiable "model" for competition law. There are other conceptions of competition law and other practices, but they are seldom conceptualized and developed in ways that would allow them to serve as models for global convergence. According to this strategy, most countries will gradually move toward a conception of competition law that was created in the United States and has been propagated primarily by its institutions, scholars, and lawyers. The reference here is not to the specific institutional arrangements of U.S. antitrust law, but to the central idea that *economics should provide the normative framework for competition law*.[18]

The EBM posits that a specific form of economics should define the substantive content of competition law—i.e., it should provide the criteria for determining whether conduct is consistent with competition law.[19] There is some disagreement about the specific standards to be used in performing this function, but the key point is that neoclassical economics provides the standard for determining *whether conduct is anticompetitive* and also supplies the language and the methods necessary for that analysis.

This basic analysis has important enforcement implications. It insists that competition law should intervene in business decision making only if there is strong evidence that the conduct causes economic harm. It thus urges constraint in competition law enforcement and emphasizes the potential harms and risks from intervening in economic decision making. This leads to an enforcement focus on cartels (horizontal agreements among competitors) in part because the economic harm from such agreements tends to be demonstrable and quantifiable. It also discourages enforcement based on vertical relationships and unilateral conduct, because the harm from such conduct is often significantly more difficult to prove and far more dependent on the particular circumstances of the case involved. Economists can, with some confidence, identify the economic harm resulting from horizontal agreements, but the profession has less confidence (and sometimes even categorical denial) of competitive harm in other contexts.

Convergence as Global Policy: Standard Justifications

In order to analyze the incentives for a developing country to move toward this convergence point, we look briefly first at some of the standard claims for relying on convergence as the central strategy for global competition law development. We can then relate them to the concerns, incentives, and perspectives common in developing countries.

For purposes of this analysis, I distinguish between two types of claims supporting a convergence strategy. One refers to the *process of convergence* and disregards its content. The other focuses on the *content of the process*—the point toward which convergence is expected to move. These two types of justification are often intermingled, but failure to distinguish between them impedes analysis.[20]

Process-based justifications for convergence fall into three main categories. One identifies the potential value of standardization; a second relates to network effects—i.e., the impact of convergence on the relationships among the participants; and a third refers to the feasibility of such a strategy.

Standardization-based claims posit that, ceteris paribus, an increase in normative similarity among competition law systems leads to more efficient markets. Where the norms of competitive behavior on a single economic market differ, firms must take these differences and their implications into account in making business decisions. This necessarily distorts their decisions, requiring that they take *noneconomic factors* into account in making *economic decisions*. For example, it may lead a firm not to make an investment that it otherwise would have made if competition law differences had not fragmented the market. Similarly, it may lead a firm to invest in one political unit, even though it would be more economically efficient to operate in another political unit within the same market.

These distortions also entail compliance costs. Firms must pay for the information and advice needed to evaluate the implications and consequences of differences among the normative frameworks for competition. These factors represent obstacles to efficient market operation and thus reducing such differences should reduce these obstacles and lead to more efficient markets. According to standard economic analysis, well-functioning markets direct resources to their highest and best uses—i.e., where they produce the most economic benefit and generate the lowest amount of waste. This, in turn, enhances economic growth and may reduce prices to consumers.

A second justification refers to what I call "network benefits," those derived from participating in the process. The convergence process creates a common frame of reference for discussion and thus facilitates communication and encourages interactions among participants. This allows officials and others to learn from each other and may identify common problems and lead to agreement about "best practices" to deal with specific issues.

The third process-based claim refers to its low cost in relation to other strategies for responding to the limitations of the jurisdictional system. Participation requires very limited resources from the participants. They need not, for example, engage in long and costly negotiations. It also imposes limited opportunity costs, because there are no binding obligations that preclude a country from pursuing what its leaders perceive to be in their best interests.

A distinct set of justifications relates to the specific convergence point of the process, the point toward which competition law systems are expected to move. As noted above, it is widely assumed that the EBM is the only politically acceptable convergence point and thus its features provide justifications for the process.

One set of content-based claims posits that the EBM is just a better form of competition law.[21] It is portrayed as a more rational and more clearly articulated model that is also less prone to creating economic harm, because it minimizes competition law interventions in market processes. If all states move to a "better" form of competition law, this change will benefit all participants and lead to a more efficient framework for international commerce.

The EBM also tends to support the convergence process. Economics is highly standardized throughout the world, and it provides a widely known set of concepts and methods that may facilitate communication and interaction among competition officials and others involved in competition law. This can be expected to foster similarity in both the goals and methods of competition law and thereby reinforce the standardization effects of convergence.

The above justifications are framed in universalist terms—they refer to benefits to the market and thus to *all* participants. This perspective does not take into account the distribution of benefits among participants. It is about the size of the "pie," not about the benefits that particular participants may derive from an increase in its size. Yet these benefits are not shared equally by all, and each state and group of stakeholders in the process has a different relationship to the process and derives varying levels and forms of benefits and costs from it.

Relating Convergence to Development

We can now examine the incentives for decision makers in developing countries to participate in the convergence process as currently conceived. In this section the perspective is particularistic rather than universal. It shifts from evaluating the benefits of convergence for "the market" in an abstract sense to identifying incentives for a decision maker in a particular context and with a specific objective—namely, supporting the economic development of her or his country. The shift is of central importance to thinking about the issues. As we shall see, the abstract, market-level perspective on which most claims for convergence are based produces images of convergence that may differ sharply from those foregrounded in developing countries.

The following analysis starts from the assumption that the primary incentive for a developing country's decision maker is to develop the state's economy. Other factors such as political and personal gain may influence decisions, of course, but they are not our focus here. This assumption allows us to isolate and identify individual components of the relationship between convergence claims and development policy.[22] It is important to emphasize that the process of economic development is case specific.[23] No two states have the same components in the same relation to each other over the same time frame. My objective is to identify incentives that are common to this group of decision makers, but I pursue this with the understanding that there is much diversity among the specific contexts in which competition law decisions are made.

Process-Based Incentives

From the perspective of a developing country's decision maker, process-based benefits depend on many factors, including in particular the relationship of the state and its economy to global markets. Five categories of potential benefit from participating in a convergence process are prominent: (1) efficiency effects associated with standardization, (2) network effects, (3) status enhancements, (4) investment–attraction advantages, and (5) cost minimization.

As we have seen, one set of justifications for convergence is based on the potential value of standardization itself—the idea that reducing law-based distortions within markets improves their efficiency and may generate economic growth. To a decision maker in a developing country, however, the question is: How much of this larger "pie" can we/I expect to get? Increased market efficiency has disparate impacts, affecting various interests and groups in differing ways.

Consumers as a group can be expected to be the primary beneficiaries of standardization. More efficient markets are associated with lower prices and improved quality. These consumer benefits tend, in turn, to spur economic development by increasing demand and inducing investment. Benefits to consumers are likely, but they tend to be difficult to identify and quantify.

The effects of standardization on domestic producers are similarly difficult to identify. Some producers may benefit from greater uniformity in competition norms, because it reduces the compliance costs of entry into foreign markets and is likely to be of greater relative benefit to developing country producers than to their typically larger and better-capitalized counterparts in developed countries. For other domestic producers, however, standardization may be harmful, because it is likely to favor stronger performers who may be in a better position to seize market opportunities and take advantage of economies of scale in areas such as distribution.

The relationships between producers and consumers are thus central to this analysis.[24] In developing countries those links may be closer than in more developed countries. For example, the relative dearth of many kinds of employment opportunities may give consumers in developing countries incentives to support local employers from whom they expect the best prospects for employment and with whom they may have familial or other social relationships. Similarly, the informal markets that are common in many such countries typically depend on the existence and viability of local producers, whose competitiveness may be threatened by larger foreign entrants. In general, they may be less concerned with prices than with jobs and accessibility.

The second category of potential benefits is network effects. They may be substantial, but their impact is difficult to assess. For example, convergence among competition laws tends to increase the potential value to each participant of exchanging information about experiences with those laws.

Competition officials, attorneys, and judges in each country know that their counterparts in other participating countries have the same reference points in thinking about competition law issues. They can discuss, for example, how particular language has been interpreted or particular forms of conduct have been evaluated. The ability to refer to the same or similar language and concepts facilitates contacts and may enhance the potential value to each of engaging in such exchanges. This may be particularly valuable for developing countries, because experience in those countries is typically limited. These network effects may provide significant inducements for a country to participate in a convergence process, regardless of the content of the process.

Convergence as a process may also enhance status—both domestically and internationally. For example, it makes participating states and institutions "part of the international game." They become "players." As such, their officials are more likely to be included in international meetings on competition law issues and more likely to be in a position to make their voices heard in such meetings. Decision makers in developing countries often want to play on the international level, and convergence enhances their opportunities to do that.

On the other hand, domestic leaders may doubt the potential status benefits to their countries or themselves, because they are so difficult to assess. Moreover, in some countries, international status may also lead to resentments and political risks on the domestic front. The relationship between international and domestic status is often highly complicated and opaque.

A fourth type of potential benefit from participating in a convergence process is that it may assist in attracting foreign direct investment (FDI). In developing countries, decision makers typically view FDI as critical to the development process, and there is evidence that capital exporters from the United States and the European Union (EU) often prefer investing in countries that have a competition law. It is taken as a symbol of support for a market economy and an endorsement of the process of competition. This attraction may be limited, however, to situations in which the potential investor believes that the competition law will not significantly interfere with its own operations. It also assumes that investors have confidence that competition law enforcement decisions can be predicted with reasonable confidence.

Finally, a major attraction of a convergence strategy in comparison with others is that it imposes few costs and constraints. This may be particularly attractive to developing countries, given their typically limited budgets. Its leaders can merely state that they are interested in developing a Western-style competition law. With that they are automatically viewed as part of the convergence process and they may be in a position to partake of some of its benefits.

This does not mean, however, that there are no costs in the economic sense. Opportunity costs can be as important as financial costs. If a developing country decides to participate in a convergence process, it limits its options to pursue other paths. It forgoes or at least disadvantages other opportunities that might be more valuable. The extent and degree of pressure to remain on the convergence course will vary, but decisions inconsistent with that course will inevitably entail some status loss or other costs for the country and for its decision makers and representatives.

This situation points to an irony of convergence as global policy: it is in one sense a top–down process. If a country is not in a position to influence the content of the convergence point, it has no "voice" in the process. It either follows or does not follow what the leaders of the process favor. It is in a yes/no posture. Developing countries typically and almost by definition have limited, if any, influence on the convergence point, which means that they may have little or no voice in shaping the process.

Taken together, these process–based benefits provide incentives for developing countries to participate. They are likely to be limited, however, and they will always be evaluated in the context of the content of the process— the proposed or expected convergence point.

Content-Based Incentives

In reviewing the incentives for decision makers to move toward an EBM, it is important to emphasize that responses to incentives are inevitably shaped by perceptions of economics and of the consequences associated with its use. Identifying incentives is a valuable tool for explaining and even predicting behavior, but the key issue is *how decision makers respond to those incentives.* Economics is often perceived quite differently in developing countries than it is in the United States and Europe, where it plays different roles and is associated with different events, groups, values, and relationships.[25] For many developing countries' decision makers, it may seem to be a specialized science that primarily serves the interests of those who have created and developed it. Its language and methods may seem alien and unrelated to developing country needs.[26] From here it is an easy and common step to assume that its use represents a theoretical justification for "exploitation" and "dominance." At the very least, there is often a tinge of distrust.

In specific contexts such as the WTO's Agreement on Trade-Related Aspects of Intellectual Property Rights (TRIPS), economics-based arguments have been seen by some as camouflage for "Western" or "developed country" interests. U.S. and European representatives there used economics-based claims in arguing that developing countries should commit themselves to increased intellectual property protection, but dissatisfaction with the application of the TRIPS Agreement in developing countries has often led leaders there to see those arguments as disingenuous.[27] The main point here is that in discussing the EBM, perceptions of economics and its uses may differ, depending on the interests and experience that shape those perspectives.

We look first at some of the potential benefits of the EBM and then identify some of its potential costs. Two types of incentives are particularly prominent. One derives from the EBM's value in supporting and facilitating the convergence process; a second is based on the "quality" of the EBM.

One set of potential benefits for developing countries from specifying the EBM as the convergence point derives from its capacity to support the convergence process. For example, as we have seen, the EBM may increase the benefits of standardization and enhance the potential network benefits to the participants, and some of these may be particularly valuable for developing countries. The potential benefits for a specific country from enhancing standardization will depend, however, on factors such as how competitive its businesses are and how attractive the national territory is to potential foreign entrants.

The EBM's potential to enhance network benefits may be particularly attractive to developing countries, because those benefits tend to be direct and immediate rather than derivative and long term (as is the case with standardization benefits). The conceptual precision of the language and its widespread acceptance provide a clearly defined reference framework for communication that can make interactions among participants more effective and productive. Participants can know what the convergence point is and what its basic implications are likely to be. This allows them to more effectively learn from each other, and it provides incentives for them to communicate and participate, because all participants share this common framework and can relate their experiences and criticisms to it. This can also illuminate some of the differences between systems and indicate the kinds of decisions that can be expected to reduce those differences. A reference framework with less clear characteristics and implications would be less likely to engender productive discussion and, therefore, it may provide less incentive for discussion and mutual learning.[28]

The "neutrality" of the EBM can further enhance communication, trust, and coordination and thus provide potential incentives for developing countries to participate in a convergence process. Its abstract and scientific language provides a standard for evaluating competition law decisions that is applicable to any competition law system. The issues can thus be discussed in abstract terms and assessed without supporting or criticizing any particular country's competition law model. This can, in turn, increase incentives for cooperation and for confidence in the value of participating. A reference framework that represented a particular country's laws would necessarily involve political relations and be likely to have ideological overtones. The issue would then be: Do you know and like what that particular country does? Moreover, the country's representatives would have strong incentives to defend it. The EBM tends to avoid this structuring of the relationships and discussions around convergence. The fact that the United States developed the model and is, therefore, closely associated with it reduces its "neutral" posture but does not eliminate it. The model itself is still couched in scientific terms and draws support from scholars and officials outside the United States.

In some cases, however, the EBM may also reduce network benefits. For example, the specificity and narrowness of focus of the EBM tend to reduce the "voice" of developing countries. The convergence point is fixed and the standards for evaluating whether decisions conform to it are well defined. Moreover, it is anchored in developed-country experience and leaves less room for developing countries to tailor competition law to their own needs.

The central issue in analyzing incentives for developing countries to move toward an EBM is whether that model is itself attractive. It has proved attractive to many in the United States and, less consistently, in Europe, but in other areas there has often been considerable resistance to it.[29] In many developing countries there is limited experience with competition as a policy concept and even less with using law to combat restraints on that process. As a result, the issues tend to be little known and poorly understood, and thus predictions about the attractiveness of the EBM are preliminary at best. Nevertheless, we can identify several potential benefits that are associated with the model's "quality."

The status of economics as a science provides one source of value. Even in regions that have had considerable experience with competition law, such as the United States and Europe, there is often much skepticism about the reliability and effectiveness of the methods used in making competition law decisions. This can inhibit the development of competition law and reduce support for its application. Using economics as the basis for decision making associates competition law with science, which typically enjoys relatively high status. It has a methodological framework and, presumably at least, mechanisms for self-criticism. As such, the association with science suggests higher-quality decision making and may provide support for those who seek a greater role for competition law. This may have significant value, regardless of the extent to which it actually provides a firmer basis for decisions. A convergence process built on a "scientific" basis is likely to have greater appeal than one in which the convergence point is more amorphous.

Independent of this status effect is the potential for economics actually to improve the quality of competition law decisions. It provides a basis for decisions that is—or at least appears to be—more rational, neutral, predictable, and transparent than alternative bases for competition law. Those who seek to promote competition law in a developing country can point to the potential value of the following attributes and may attract political support.

Rationality   The EBM is rational and internally consistent, and these attributes may be attractive to some developing countries' officials. Its basic principles can be clearly articulated—e.g., that competition law violations can occur only where it is clearly shown that the conduct has increased price above a competitive price or can be expected to do so. It possesses a systematic and well-developed conceptual language that can be deployed consistently in the institutional settings of any legal system. Its methods provide a basis for quantifying claims of harm and benefit, and its goals are based on this methodology. This framework thus provides a cogent basis on which competition officials, courts, and others can defend competition law decisions.

Neutrality   Decisions based on economics are neutral in an objective sense. If the methodology is deployed according to its own rules, there is limited room for subjective evaluation of conduct. If the goals and standards are clearly articulated, corruption and outside influences are more difficult to conceal and all firms are at least promised equal treatment. To the extent, of course, that decision makers prefer such external influences, the EBM will not attract their support.

Predictability   These factors can be expected to enhance predictability in decision making. Use of the EBM at least reduces the range of decisions that can be defended within the conceptual framework of the model. The degree of predictability that can be expected may be difficult to articulate, because numerous factors in the institutional context of a legal system can influence enforcement decisions, but the model's potential for enhancing predictability is significant.

Better Facts and Fact Interpretation Tools
The model also provides richer and more effective tools for acquiring and analyzing data, and it calls for extensive examination of the factual basis for competition law claims. This in itself may be expected to lead to better decisions, because it requires decision makers to enquire more fully into the data being used to support claims. Moreover, it employs sophisticated tools for assessing and interpreting such data and assigns the assessment of data to professional economists who are (hopefully) well trained in assessing those consequences.

Reduction of Overbroad Intervention in the Economic Process
Finally, the EBM may support higher-quality decisions by insisting that the law should intervene in the economic process only where there is a clearly articulated and economically justified basis for doing so. It is designed to reduce enforcement that is not supported by sound economic evidence and analysis. It claims that public interference in the economic process should be undertaken only when the potential value of doing so is sufficiently well identified and outweighs potential harm from such interference. To the extent that this methodology is implemented, it can be expected to align competition law decision making with economic development.

We have discussed several ways in which the EBM may indirectly support development policies, but it also impacts such policies directly. Given the many facets of economic development and the variety of policies used in responding to them, generalizations are particularly hazardous in this area, but we can at least identify factors that are likely to be relevant to the incentives of developing countries' decision makers.

On a general level, the EBM may support domestic development policies, because it is designed to improve the functioning of the economic system. To the extent that development policies are intended to improve the functioning of domestic markets, the EBM aligns with and supports these objectives. In theory at least, this serves the interests of both consumers and producers. Development policies tend, however, to have more specific objectives relating to one or both these groups of interests.

The presumed general efficiency value of competition law is closely associated with benefits to consumers. The microeconomic concept of "consumer welfare" is the acknowledged standard for assessing competitive harm in the EBM in the United States and the EU.[30] It is closely related to the concept of efficiency, although the term is used by economists in ways that are often misunderstood by others. The basic goal is to eliminate economic waste, to direct resources to their highest and best uses, and thus to make consumers as well off as they can be, given the demand and supply of goods on the market. This tends to support general economic development policies. Where consumers have leverage over decision makers (through voting or other means), their influence on development policy decisions tends to increase. Consumers in developing countries tend to have relatively limited political weight, however, and thus their interests may not be well represented in development policies.

National economic development is typically understood more as an issue of supporting domestic producers rather than benefiting consumers, and thus relevant decision makers are likely to focus on the impact of the EBM on domestic producers. On a general level, the EBM's general efficiency benefit improves the conditions of competition on a market and should tend to make producers more competitive, more innovative, and thus more likely to succeed.

Another general benefit for producers is that the EBM tends to constrain governments from interfering in the competitive process. Competition law regimes are sometimes accused of harming competition because they may distort market incentives without considering whether the interference is economically justified.[31] The EBM seeks to avoid this kind of unjustified interference with the competitive system because the criterion for assessing conduct is whether the conduct is economically justified. An EBM generates a narrower scope of enforcement, which tends to produce fewer burdens on business than other forms of competition law that are broader in scope.

In addition to these general benefits for producers, use of the EBM is likely to have several specific benefits. In order to assess them, it is necessary to recall the patterns of enforcement that have resulted from use of the EBM in the United States and, to a less well-defined extent, in Europe.[32] The main effect of the EBM on enforcement has been a marked tendency to focus on cartel conduct. Agreements among competitors are universally recognized as creating general economic harm. Hard-core cartels—those that directly or indirectly target key competitive parameters such as price—are widely acknowledged as harmful, because they increase price above a competitive price or create similar effects. Moreover, these effects can typically be quantified by economists. Horizontal mergers are generally understood to have similar harms. Other forms of anticompetitive behavior tend to receive far less attention. Vertical agreements, vertical mergers, and abuse of a dominant position have economic effects that depend very much on particular market conditions. As a result, economic modeling for these types of conduct is more difficult and less certain. They may have economic benefits; they may produce economic harm; it depends. In any event, vertical agreements and dominant firm conduct have received significantly less attention in jurisdictions where the EBM has been implemented.

With those patterns in mind, we look at the likely impact of the EBM on development goals specifically related to domestic producers. One important category of producers includes relatively large firms that either compete on both domestic and foreign markets or have the capacity to do so. For them, low levels of enforcement against dominant firms have two kinds of consequences. On the one hand, it is likely to reduce their competition law compliance costs and increase the range of business strategy options available, thereby enhancing their profitability and growth. On the other hand, however, this more limited scope of enforcement also provides fewer constraints on the conduct of their foreign rivals, allowing them opportunities to abuse their (often greater) market power to the detriment of domestic firms. It may also encourage foreign firms to enter local markets, where they may be in a stronger competitive position than their domestic rivals.

Another category of large firms in developing countries includes "protected firms"—those that are state monopolies or otherwise supported by the state. They are often protected from stringent enforcement of regulatory laws, and thus lax enforcement against dominant firms may have little direct impact on them. Low levels of enforcement may, however, benefit stronger and more efficient foreign rivals, allowing them a better competitive position than they would have if there were significant enforcement against dominant firm conduct. This gives governments an incentive to formally adopt a stricter standard of enforcement but to enforce this standard more aggressively against foreign rivals than against domestic firms.

Development policies often focus on small and medium enterprises (SMEs), and these may be adversely impacted by EBM enforcement patterns.[33] These patterns may allow dominant firms to engage in conduct detrimental to SMEs. In particular, foreign dominant firms may be in a position to impose particularly onerous supply and purchase conditions on local firms or innovation-restricting grant-back clauses on local licensees. Moreover, these enforcement patterns focus enforcement efforts on cartel arrangements, but cooperative arrangements among SMEs are often a significant feature of development policies, because such arrangements are often viewed as necessary to foster the growth of smaller domestic firms. Such cooperation may be deterred where there is a significant threat of enforcement against horizontal agreements.

Attracting FDI is often a prominent goal of economic development strategies. It brings jobs, resources, and often technical and managerial skills. This is especially important for reducing infrastructure bottlenecks in areas such as ports, rails, telecom, electricity, and financial institutions. Low levels of enforcement against dominant firms may attract large firms that can provide such benefits. Not only does it reduce risks and compliance costs but it also signals the government's commitment to providing a "level playing field" and reducing possible favoritism for local and politically connected firms.

These potential benefits must, however, be measured against cost factors, several of which suggest the need for caution in making assumptions in this area. One set of costs includes actual expenditures. Implementing an EBM necessarily imposes significant financial costs. It calls for reliance on forms of analysis that are expensive. In it, economics is the basic tool for determining whether competition law has been violated, and thus it requires highly trained economists to conduct the analysis. In order to apply this standard effectively, decision makers (whether in courts or administrative offices) must possess the capacity to interpret the results produced by these forms of analysis. This type of expertise is seldom readily available in developing countries. Either it must be imported or competition authorities must have sufficient resources to purchase it locally (presumably at a premium). These costs are likely to be particularly high in early stages of competition law development, a time when much needs to be learned quickly, but also when the need for political support is usually highest. These learning costs are necessarily high and they may be incurred at all levels of competition law operation—from policy to organization to specific enforcement decisions.

Actual costs may be particularly onerous in the context of implementation. Use of the EBM imposes significant enforcement costs because the economic effects of conduct must be investigated in justifying enforcement action and because assessing economic benefits requires sufficient factual data to enable economists to apply their analytical tools effectively. Such data is often difficult and costly to acquire. Procedural rules often severely restrict access to data, further enhancing the need to acquire the limited data that is available.[34] Other implementation costs such as educating business about competition law norms are necessarily also high. Officials cannot merely specify rules of conduct that businesses must follow. They must explain that a finding of violation depends on the effects of conduct and that this will depend on market structures and conditions. These cost-raising factors tend to reduce incentives for implementing competition law.

These costs are significant in absolute terms, but they are even higher in relative terms. In a developing country, the expenditures called for to assess a particular form of conduct are likely to be roughly comparable to costs imposed for performing such an analysis in a country such as the United States, but developing countries, by definition, do not possess the kinds and levels of public resources that are available in the United States and Europe for such implementation. As a consequence, the relative burden of the financial expenditures for the same level of enforcement may be far higher for a developing country than for a developed country.[35] This may be particularly true for merger control.

A second set of potential costs includes the opportunity costs imposed by participation in an EBM-based convergence strategy—i.e., the opportunities to obtain benefits that are lost as a result of taking a particular action. When decision makers in a developing country accept the EBM as their goal, they implicitly accept constraints on their decisions. Decisions they make will be measured and assessed with reference to the model. The model dictates goals and methods and it establishes a range of variation within which decisions should be located. Decisions that fall outside that range will be considered "wrong" with respect to the convergence process. To the extent that moving toward the convergence point is established as a serious objective, the country's decision makers forfeit the opportunity to pursue other options. Moreover, it excludes from attention perspectives, issues, and problems that lie outside the target range. For example, it precludes consideration of fairness in the application of competition laws. The cost of missed opportunities to respond to specific issues and situations can be significant, especially given that the capacity to experiment and adapt is often considered critical to economic and political development.

In both the United States and Europe, competition laws were developed with a far broader range of goals than those currently deemed consistent with the EBM. This allowed significant adaptation and response to specific problems. Pursuing the EBM would preclude this broader conception of competition law. The point here is not that the multiple-goal option *is* more valuable but that from a developing country's perspective it *might* be more beneficial, and whatever value it could bring may be lost to the extent that a country pursues the EBM.

Opportunity costs may be particularly significant in two areas relating specifically to economic development. First, the EBM may interfere with structural policies intended to generate wealth and jobs. For example, its focus on cartel enforcement may interfere with a government's efforts to promote cooperation among small and medium-sized domestic firms. Such efforts are often seen as critical for economic development. Even where the risks of enforcement are small, the mere threat of enforcement may deter firms from cooperating and thereby reduce the effectiveness of development policies. Second, the EBM's lower level of enforcement against dominant firms may encourage foreign dominant firms to engage in anticompetitive conduct that stifles the growth of domestic firms and the economic development potential associated with that growth.

One response to concerns about opportunity costs is that the convergence strategy does not have an enforcement mechanism, so there are no real constraints and thus no opportunity costs. This claim has two major flaws. One is that while convergence does not provide *formal* enforcement mechanisms, it generates informal pressures for compliance from other participants, business interests, and institutions such as international organizations that promote the convergence model. More fundamentally, however, convergence as a global strategy is a sham if it is not taken seriously, and taking it seriously means narrowing the range of decisional options.

Viewing these potential benefits and costs together suggests that decision makers in developing countries may have limited incentives to pursue convergence toward the economics-based model. There are potential benefits from adopting an economics-based form of competition law, but it necessarily also imposes significant costs and risks, and the potential costs may appear to outweigh the benefits.

There may be means of reducing the costs and increasing the benefits of the strategy. For example, the regionalization of competition law in developing countries may reduce financial costs to participating countries by providing a mechanism for distributing those costs among the members. This potential may help to explain the very recent movements in this direction in Africa and elsewhere.[36] Moreover, if effectively structured, regionalization has the potential to reduce corruption and other interference costs. Similarly, developed countries could share some of the financial burdens of adopting the EBM, and this may also be an important tool for reducing obstacles to convergence.

.   .   .

This brief review of incentives for developing countries to participate in a strategy for global competition law convergence reveals the fragility of some of the assumptions on which the current strategy is based and highlights the need to examine those assumptions more closely. The assumption that developing countries are likely to adopt the EBM in its present form is too facile to be a sound basis for global policy. The incentives for developing countries' decision makers to do so are likely to be weaker and more mixed than is sometimes supposed.

This should not be surprising. The EBM is based on conceptions of economics, law, and the relationship between the two that have been shaped by Western intellectual traditions and by experience in highly industrialized countries. Moreover, the model is promoted primarily by U.S. and European economic and political interests. It may not, therefore, accurately reflect the concerns of decision makers in developing countries. To the extent that it fails to reflect these concerns, it will reduce incentives for decision makers to move toward this model of competition law.

This suggests a fundamental tension between the goals of economic development on the one hand and current conceptions of convergence as global competition policy on the other hand. Little attention has been paid in the competition law literature to reducing this tension, in part at least because of excessive reliance on assumptions about the benefits of convergence. Until this tension is more clearly recognized, however, progress toward addressing its consequences is unlikely.

This chapter suggests some ways of analyzing tensions in the relationship between convergence and economic development. There are undoubtedly others. Critically important, however, is the recognition that assumptions about the convergence process in the United States and Europe are based on the experience of developed countries (whether or not abstracted into theory) and that these assumptions may well be misleading when applied to developing countries.

This tension poses two particularly serious risks. One is that convergence efforts devised and promoted primarily in developed countries will generate what I call "bi-level conduct" among developing country representatives—addressing one set of messages to international audiences and another to domestic audiences. Language on the global level may indicate acceptance of convergence objectives, but that language may not reflect a serious intention to take corresponding action on the domestic level. Discussions of convergence on the global level may, therefore, *appear* to represent participation in a convergence strategy, but there may be little or no actual movement toward convergence in the operative norms of domestic legal systems.

A second and related risk is that global competition policy may become (or remain) a phantom policy. The naked claim that there is such a strategy imposes few direct costs, and a state's claim that it is participating in it requires few, if any, commitments. The strategy may, therefore, drift on a mythical terrain of rhetoric that may produce little value. Moreover, this rhetorical drift may be harmful not only to developmental interests but also to the goal of developing a more effective transnational competition law regime. The potential value of developing a more effective means of protecting against competitive restraints on the global level is too important to allow this to happen.

2

Is There a Tension Between Development Economics and Competition?

Ioannis Lianos, Abel Mateus, and Azza Raslan

Competition law was born and framed in the developed nations of the West. The economic thinking it has relied upon is based on industrial organization, a subdiscipline of neoclassical price theory. Despite the existence of various intellectual traditions, neoclassical price theory emphasizes the importance of markets, not economies, the latter depending on a broader series of variables such as the rate of wages paid, the demand and supply for all goods, and the supply of money in society rather than the interplay of supply and demand in a specific product market. Competition economics also assumes that there is in fact a market economy with some competition. Development economics, on the contrary, focuses on the broader picture, that of the economy.

In Chapter 5 of this volume, George Priest challenges the position that "because the economic conditions in developing nations are different from those in developed nations, the competition law regime appropriate for developing nations must be different." According to his "absolutist" view, "competition laws of all nations should in principle be identical." Professor Priest goes as far as to contest the meaning of the distinction between "developing" and "developed" nations in competition law: according to him, "All nations are developing, in the sense that the economic output and the economic welfare of their citizens can be continuously improved." The same principles should apply to all.

Although we share Professor Priest's dissatisfaction with views advancing the alleged specificities of developing countries as an argument for a "light" touch or discounted competition law, without any proper empirical or theoretical backing, we consider that the "absolutist view" unfairly dismisses development economics from the competition policy canvas.

It might be appropriate here to refer to the opposition between the proponents of "monoeconomics," the claim that economics consists of principles of universal validity, and the proponents of the view that developing countries have particularities that require a different kind of economics.[1] The concept of the "underdeveloped country" that emerged out of this debate was instrumental in the flourishing of the separate discipline of development economics.[2] The rejection of the monoeconomics claim presupposed that underdeveloped countries shared a set of specific socioeconomic and institutional conditions that set them apart from the developed world, thus requiring the adoption of new economic strategies to promote development and growth.[3] The essence of the claim was that institutional differences between developed and underdeveloped nations affected not only the speed but also the path of economic development. A distinction was established between the concept of growth, an essentially quantitative process of expanding gross domestic product, and that of development, an inherently qualitative operation of generating a new equilibrium with higher productivity and changing socioeconomic structures.

Should one adopt the "monoeconomics" view, the concept of a "developing" country is no more meaningful in competition law than it is in any other policy field. From this perspective, the linkage between competition and development has no purpose, as long as this is not about how competition law promotes "development," the latter term being perceived as a synonym for economic growth. Yet, if one does not share the "monoeconomics" view, the concepts of "development" and of "developing" country become relevant for competition law, either at the level of designing appropriate competition policy regimes and/or at the adjudicative level in competition law, if some objectives of economic development, such as redistribution of wealth or the alleviation of poverty, become aims of competition law.[4]

This chapter aims to contribute to the cross-fertilization of the fields of competition policy and development economics. Competition policy, introduced by the antitrust movement in the late nineteenth century, was vaguely based on the Smithian notion of competition and had to wait until the second half of the twentieth century to be based on solid economic theory.

Development economics and policy was even more vaguely based on the Smithian notion of capital accumulation but appeared as an independent body of knowledge only in the second half of the twentieth century. Although tensions between the two fields had arisen already in the nineteenth century, it was only after the 1980s that economics had advanced enough to be able to rigorously contrast the two fields.

We consider that the disinterest manifested by the tenants of the "absolutist" view in the insights of development economics in competition policy may be explained by a perceived tension between the dominant intellectual tradition in development economics until recently, which highlighted the role of state intervention at the expense of markets and free competition, and the prior belief in competition economics on the superior efficiency of free competition. The recent evolution of development economics to the analysis of the microfoundations of growth, the focus on institutions, and the emphasis on empirical methods should nevertheless lead to a useful cross-fertilization between these two fields.[5]

The Rise of Development Economics as an Autonomous Discipline: A Challenge to the Competition (Market) Paradigm?

The Tension Between Development Economics and Competition

The concept of development is not absent from the writings of classical economists, whose aim was to achieve "material progress" or "economic progress."[6] Adam Smith was the first widely recognized economist to refer to the role of markets for economic development. Smith characterized the increase in productivity as the interaction of the division of labor and market expansion. This emphasis on the dynamic element was lost in the effort of neoclassical economists, on which competition economics is largely based, to address, primarily, issues of static allocation of given resources at a given period. Economic growth as a policy objective was ignored for several decades, from about the 1870s to the 1930s.[7] The concern of neoclassical economists was how consumer choice could be maximized (allocative efficiency) or producers' costs minimized (productive efficiency). In their standard model, interactions between producers and consumers are mediated through the price system, thus leading to a *unique* Pareto efficient equilibrium. If neoclassical price theorists examined interrelationships between different sectors of the economy, their analysis focused on a particularly short time horizon and the impersonal setting of a market for all goods and all periods. History and institutions did not matter and could not influence the choice of the equilibrium, and they were thus excluded from the analysis. The possibility that there can be *multiple* equilibria, inferior or superior, at a given point in time, which could be chosen because of historical, cultural, or institutional reasons or the distribution of wealth, was not seriously contemplated.[8] Schumpeter's theory of economic development attempted to break away from the concept of static equilibrium by emphasizing the dynamic aspects of change, the recognition of the primordial role of the entrepreneur as opposed to the secondary role of the consumer, and the neglect of consumer surplus, but his influence in the direction of neoclassical price theory was limited.[9]

The Walrasian general equilibrium theory, formalized by Arrow and Debreu in the 1950s,[10] assumed complete/universal markets for all current and future contingent commodities and perfect information (the first fundamental theorem of welfare economics). According to this theorem, every perfectly competitive economy in a state of general equilibrium is Pareto optimal. Wealth distribution is not a concern, as it is assumed that any Pareto-optimal allocation of resources can be achieved by means of a perfectly competitive equilibrium, once one makes an appropriate redistribution of initial endowments (the second fundamental theorem of welfare economics). Reinforced by the Coase theorem, which advanced that private bargaining might provide a solution to an inefficient redistribution of initial endowments in the absence of transaction costs,[11] the general equilibrium theory (as well as partial equilibrium theory) glorified the concept of perfect competition and confined the role of government to lump-sum redistributive measures.[12] The fact that partial equilibrium theory, developed by Alfred Marshall in order to resolve the conflict between the utility and cost theories of value by including both the costs of production (the supply curve) and utility theories (the demand curve) in a static analysis of equilibrium, serves as the foundation of modern competition law analysis may explain why growth has never been an explicit aim of competition law and policy.

The dominance of Keynesian economics post–World War II also led to a relative neglect of the price mechanism and the microeconomic foundations that were crucial for welfare economics.[13] Central government intervention was thought necessary in order to approach full-employment equilibrium. This argument, along with market failure theories, paved the way for a more active role for the state and legitimized interventionist policies from the 1930s. Although not concerned with developing countries as such, Keynes exercised an indirect intellectual influence on development economics, as manifested by the Harod-Domar growth models, which were used as the basis for planning models for developing countries following World War II.[14] Harod and Domar found that growth is proportional to the share of investment spending as a proportion of national income. The growth rate of national income is thus inversely related to the capital-output ratio. Although the Harod-Domar model was not concerned with underdeveloped countries and was initially formulated with the aim of addressing issues of chronic unemployment in industrialized countries following the Depression, one of its implications was that the principal strategies of development were thought to be the mobilization of domestic and foreign savings in order to generate sufficient investment to accelerate economic growth. These so-called two-gap models were extensively used by international organizations in the 1960s and 1970s to determine the need of foreign exchange (aid) required to achieve a given growth rate by the developing country.

The first phase of development economics as an autonomous discipline in economics, which covers the 1950s and 1960s, was dominated by a strong belief in the need for government intervention in the economy. This period was followed by a second phase, the return to the free market paradigm in the 1970s–1980s, and a third phase starting in the 1990s, when the emphasis shifted to institutional design.[15] Our claim is that while the first phase marked the departure of development economics from the neoclassical price theory framework that forms the theoretical backbone of welfare economics, in particular competition economics, the second phase was characterized by important ideological debates and tensions that led to a progressive embrace of the market/competition paradigm.

In the early post–World War II era, development economists contemplated that capital accumulation and technical progress were the main driving forces behind development. Development economists did not share the neoclassical economists' beliefs about the price system and markets in general, at least for developing economies.[16] Under the influence of the Harod-Domar model, the major obstacle to overcome was thought to be capital deficiency.[17] The suggested solution to this problem was foreign aid for planned investment and the adoption of import-substitution industrialization policies that would rely on central planning.

The theoretical underpinning of these theories was the "dual sector" model presented by Arthur Lewis in 1954.[18] Lewis's suggestion was that underdeveloped nations were characterized by the presence of two economies: a high-productivity one with high wages and a low-productivity one with low wages but surplus labor (essentially laborers, self-subsistence farmers, domestic services workers, small retailers). Capital accumulation will lead to the gradual transfer of these labor resources from the subsistence sector to the high-productivity one, as long as capital accumulation catches up with the surplus labor.

In *The Stages of Growth: A Non-Communist Manifesto*, Rostow also highlighted the crucial role played by investment in presenting his linear-stages-of-growth model as a road map for development.[19] Drawing on the historical example of Great Britain, Rostow identified the following five stages of economic development: traditional, transitional, takeoff, maturity, and high mass consumption. This evolutionary and linear path to growth was universally applicable (to both industrialized and nonindustrialized countries). Development was perceived as an evolutionary quantitative process led by the spread of the new technologies (steel, railways, textiles) that emerged in the Industrial Revolution. A common thread of these development theories was the active role advocated for state intervention in the economy in order to generate capital accumulation and the necessary investment for industrialization.

The "big push" theory, advanced by Rosenstein-Rodan in the 1940s, further emphasized the role of the state as an ex ante coordinator for economic activities.[20] The aim of state intervention was to take advantage of the increasing returns that could be realized from large-scale planned industrialization projects encompassing several major sectors of the economy simultaneously. Simultaneous industrialization of many sectors of the economy would be profitable on the aggregate, even if it would not be individually profitable to industrialize them separately, because of its domino effect on the economy. Yet the market mechanism alone will not be sufficient. Public investment and the simultaneous planning of several complementary industries were required.[21]

Nurske presented another variation of the "big push" thesis: the theory of balanced growth.[22] He argued that the problem with developing countries is their low capital investments capabilities, which affect their productivity levels and their overall per capita income, putting them in a "vicious circle of poverty." Mere individual capital investment efforts will not solve the problem. There is a need for creating a large-scale supply and a matching large-scale demand. The market economy is unable to achieve that: when an individual business or single industry alone attempts to raise its output level by increasing its individual capital investment, it runs the risk of not finding a market for its products because of the low level of overall average income.[23] Nevertheless, while Rosenstein-Rodan advocated a centralized solution to the development problem, Nurske thought of less interventionist approaches and emphasized the role of entrepreneurs in the development process.[24]

In the 1940s and 1950s a new wave of economic theories emerged to challenge neoclassical price theory from structuralist/institutionalist perspectives, at both national and international levels.[25] These heterodox economists did not believe that relatively minor changes, such as an increase in foreign aid or a sudden increase in investment, would be sufficient to create a "big push" or "takeoff" into sustained growth. In their view, "such limited changes, in the context of existing structures and institutions prevailing in less developing societies, might result in strengthening of the backward socioeconomic framework, consolidating adverse path dependence."[26]

In his work with Hal Singer, Raúl Prebisch was highly skeptical of Adam Smith's belief in the "international division of labor."[27] Prebisch distinguished between developed countries, self-sustained through technological progress, and the "periphery," suppliers of raw materials. The main thrust of the theory was that this center-periphery system was marked by a bipolar evolution favoring the technological development of the center, while for the periphery technical progress penetrated only to the degree that was necessary to generate exports of low-cost foodstuffs and raw materials for the markets of the center. Adam Smith's theory was thus flawed, because it was based on the assumption that the two systems are "strictly complementary"; yet, there are specific differences in the structure and functions among countries participating in international trade.

Neoclassical price theory was criticized for being disconnected from the realities of the periphery, in particular as it did not take into account their historical (political, economic, and social) background. Prebisch focused on the structure of export trade in underdeveloped economies, highlighting that the terms of trade based on comparative advantage put the developing societies in a less favorable position than that of the center, as the long-term trend of primary commodity prices would be negative. The solution proposed took the form of programmed industrialization via import substitution based on protectionist policies and the suppression of competition. This approach was widely adopted by Latin American countries until the 1960s, when it became obvious that it failed to fulfill its promises.

Beginning with the creation of a central planning commission by Nehru in 1950 in India, many other developing countries followed suit, believing in the efficiency of a national development plan that would determine priorities, set quantitative targets, and establish public policies to achieve the desired objectives. Governments of emerging nations turned to national planning as if this were a precondition for development. Yet China's success since the reforms of the 1980s proved that international trade can act as an engine for growth. The introduction of a market economy in the new special economic zones and the massive technological transfer that occurred, accompanied by foreign direct investment, has disproved the Singer-Prebisch theory in this case.

A different strand of the structuralist literature, the dependency theory,[28] argued that peripheral countries provide the center countries with the needed inputs and function as markets for their manufactured products. The under-development of poor nations was attributed to "monopoly capitalism,"[29] and colonization was the main "source of poverty" for developing countries. The center had an inherent interest in maintaining the status quo—the back-wardness— of peripheral countries. Dependency was the crux of this rela-tionship. These authors were skeptical about the role foreign aid could play in stimulating development, arguing that international monopoly capital would form alliances with precapitalist domestic oligarchies with the inten-tion to block progressive capitalist transformations in the periphery. The operation of multinationals would also have the effect of distorting the pro-cess of capitalist development in these countries. This theoretical framework was instrumental in the demand for a New International Economic Order in the 1970s,[30] and the increasing international regulation, through codes of conduct, of multinational corporations.[31]

With the government leading the development path, the default macro-strategies of the post–World War II period included state planning and state ownership of the main industries and banking facilities, import protection rules, restrictions on foreign investment, and industrial licensing.[32] These policies were in direct contradiction to the competition paradigm of the neoclassical economics school, leaving almost no room to envisage a compe-tition policy under such a state interventionist economic environment.

Development Economics Post–Washington Consensus

What is often referred to as the Chicago School of economics challenged the views of development economics of the past decades and adopted different assumptions: markets are usually efficient, there is no good alternative to the price mechanism, and government failure may be more serious than market failure.[33] According to Chicago economists, government intervention resulted in many price distortions in the market and provoked enormous allocative inefficiencies, curbing competition and increasing rent-seeking activities.[34] Through the lens of public choice theory, an intellectual neighbor to Chicago economics, governments are neither omniscient nor necessarily benevolent.[35] Empirical studies demonstrated the futility of state intervention in the economy: Ian M. D. Little's influential study of seven countries with Tibor Scitovsky and Maurice Scott showed that under import-substitution industrialization (ISI) strategies, consumers were forced to purchase commodities at a higher price, either imported with large surcharges or produced inefficiently domestically, while unprotected industries like agriculture and small and medium enterprises had low relative prices and profits were compressed due to high prices of industrial inputs.[36] These policies favored an industrial elite at the cost of rural and urban poor. Authors inspired by this paradigm provided empirical support for the importance of microeconomics in development planning.[37]

The recognized success of the Asian Tigers showed that an outward policy, based on export promotion, clearly taking advantage of the global trade, was far superior to the inward/autarkic policies of Latin America. The Chicago School and its insistence on minimal state intervention in the economy provided the required theoretical framework for a repositioning of development economics.[38] These policies based on markets and macroeconomic equilibrium marked a return to orthodox economics and were converted into a recipe appropriated by monoeconomics. The teachings of the Chicago School greatly influenced the policies of major international organizations, such as the World Bank and the International Monetary Fund in the 1980s.[39] The policy promoted by these institutions was coined the "Washington Consensus."[40] The Washington Consensus advised protection of property rights, market liberalization, deregulation, privatization, and specific fiscal policies.[41] Followers of the Washington Consensus focused their policy reforms on maximizing efficiencies through markets and integrating developing economies into the world economic order.[42]

The shift in development economics toward more market-oriented policies paved the way to a less conflict-prone position to mainstream welfare economics and thus to some degree of convergence with the theoretical framework of competition law and economics. However, the Washington

Consensus did not advocate the adoption of competition law frameworks, perhaps because of its belief in the superior efficiency of the market system.

Toward the end of the 1990s, multilateral agencies and policy economists suggested an adjusted approach (the "second-generation"), focusing on institutional reform and "good governance."[43] Now the Washington Consensus's list expanded to include other goals such as corporate governance, anticorruption, flexible labor markets, social safety nets, and targeted poverty reduction, leading the way to some state intervention in the economy. As Shapiro rightly observed, the "default policy recommendation is still the market"; however, "the emphasis of reform has switched to institutions that will allow the market to perform more efficiently."[44] This belief that markets work well only when they are founded on a sound institutional background challenged the Washington Consensus's one-dimensional focus on deregulation and highlighted the importance of adopting appropriate, market-friendly regulatory mechanisms, such as competition law.

This new approach is explicit in the final report of the Commission on Growth and Development. Released in 2008, the report highlights the importance of markets for the development process but also notes that "the task is to improve the effectiveness of government institutions rather than stripping them of their tasks."[45] The report's main message is that circumstances of each country are unique; hence, each should customize its own development plan.

The new consensus is that developing countries differ from developed countries "by much more than their level of capital—or even their human capital," and that "even a transfer of funds may not have a large effect on economic growth."[46] This marks a radically different insight into the evolution of the concept of development. As noted by Hoff and Stiglitz, "industrial and developing countries are on different production functions and are organized in different ways. Development is no longer seen primarily as a process of capital accumulation but rather as a process of organizational change."[47]

Economics of information, institutional economics, and the theory of coordination problems depart from the narrow assumptions of neoclassical price theory and provide new insights to development economics, offering the challenge for a more holistic, historically and culturally aware perspective.[48]

When contemplating a country's development path, one needs to understand that there are no given answers as both ends of the spectrum—state intervention and free market—come with their own limitations. Each country should thus find its own balance. Other variables, such as history and culture, also count. In his study on the causes of underperformance in continental Europe, Edmund Phelps found that various cultural values like competition and workplace attitudes are significant in explaining differences in economic performance.[49] The institutional context does matter.

The Emerging New Consensus

Despite the missing links between development economics and competition law and economics, it is important to acknowledge the need for the establishment of a sustained dialogue between the two disciplines. This is essential in light of the enactment of competition law statutes in several developing economies and the rising levels of competition law enforcement in the developing world, now seen in the light of institutional development theory.

The Role of Competition in Building Strong Institutions for Growth

Olson has made a prominent contribution in the recent theory of political economy models of development.[50] He applies his well-known theory of collective action[51] to explain why some countries grow and others stagnate. Olson uses the concept of a "distributional coalition," a group whose collective action can secure a larger share of the resources generated by the economy for its members at the expense of the population at large. The instruments used to redistribute income and wealth to these special interest groups are tax and subsidy policies, entry and mobility barriers, and tariffs and quotas on imports, among others. Encompassing groups have an incentive to promote growth because their interests do not differ substantially from society's goals.

Nonetheless, coalitions can trap a society into a stagnant economic state. Economists have developed various formal models capturing the idea that insider groups that operate with a given technology may oppose the introduction of innovations and thus block economic growth.[52] This generates a cycle of growth and stagnation, depending on which group dominates. Some studies have attempted to explain why there are different protection rates in external trade by industries and sectors.[53] In these models, special interest groups, organized in lobbies, make contributions in order to bias the government choice of (mainly trade) policy in their favor. Others have shown that a greater inequality in income or wealth distribution leads to a higher rate of rent extraction from lobbies, thus lowering social welfare.[54] More concentrated industries with higher capital intensity and inelastic demand have been found to host stronger lobbies.[55]

Another strand of the literature links competition, rents, and corruption.[56] When the principal (the people) pursues multiple and diffuse objectives, state contingent contracts with the agent (government) are hard to write and rents have to be allocated to enhance performance.[57] The problem can also be set in the relation between the government (principal) and bureaucracy (agent). Efficiency wage theory may be used to determine the optimal level of corruption: when a firm under the influence of a bureaucrat enjoys rents, the value of his control rights is high. Bureaucrats can trade part of this control in exchange for bribes. In a regime of monopolies there would be a higher level of corruption when compared with a more competitive world, as the public (citizenry) would have to incur greater losses if they were to try to redefine the contracts with the bureaucrats or spend more resources controlling corruption.

It is thought that the level of development may increase with a government change in policy from an investment-based strategy, i.e., a strategy where low-quality firms (with low-quality entrepreneurs) invest and imitate, to an innovation-based strategy focused on self-selection of efficient firms through competition and on innovation (approaching the technological frontier).[58] However, the country can fall into a situation where vested interests incorporated in the investment-based strategy can buy out the political power. In this case, societies are trapped with "inappropriate institutions" and relatively backward technologies. Some studies have empirically investigated the relationship between high barriers to entry/low competition and growth rates across a sample of developing countries and have found that high barriers are more harmful to growth close to the technological frontier, with growth rates slowing as they approach it. Such a trap is more likely in societies with weak institutions (which are more corruptible).

Another implication of this theory is that there may be a need for more government intervention at the beginning of a nation's development in order to solve coordination problems. However, the country ultimately *must* switch to a more competitive environment in order to approach the technological frontier, though this might prove difficult due to the capture of politicians by groups that benefited from the initial interventions. Cases like Brazil, Mexico, and Peru come to mind, contrasted with some East Asian economies like Hong Kong and Singapore. These studies emphasize the role of competition in the process of building stronger institutions for growth.

In conclusion, the political process is endogenous and should be taken into account in designing appropriate competition policy institutions. Contrary to Chicago School theorists who believe that neither institutions nor wealth distribution matter for efficiency, new theories of economic development argue that both institutions and distribution of wealth matter.[59] The common thread in this literature is the role of coordination failures, such as rent seeking, inefficient institutions (formal and informal), and underinvestment in human capital in developing nations.

The Positive Correlation Between Competition and Development

The role of competition law in development is linked to the prevailing economic policy: the greater the government intervention, the less significant competition law is and vice versa. Thus, competition law has featured in development economics only fairly recently.[60] Yet competition and industrial organization literature has long argued for a positive correlation between the level of development and competition and the importance of institutions for an optimal enforcement of competition law.[61]

The main link in today's industrial organization models between competition and growth is the relation between competition and dynamic efficiency.[62] The earliest Schumpeterian models predicted that, through the operation of the appropriability effect, competition reduces the prospective monopoly rents spurring innovation and therefore growth. New models insist on the non-linear relationship between competition and growth: although the increase in the intensity of competition will tend to reduce the level of profits of a successful innovator, it will reduce the profits of an unsuccessful innovator even more, thus having an overall positive effect on the rate of innovation.[63] The management of the firm will also be forced to innovate more.[64] There are generally four channels that have been corroborated empirically.

First, competition creates a larger number of opportunities for benchmarking, so the market can monitor firm management.[65] Second, innovations tend to increase productivity and reduce costs, thereby generating a higher level of profits in a competitive environment where demand price elasticities are higher. Third, higher levels of competition increase the probability of failure, which is an incentive for management to be more efficient.[66] Fourth, because workers share in rents, higher competition also leads to a higher productive effort.[67]

The Schumpeterian models arguing that monopolies are necessary to generate innovation[68] have been subject to challenge. Both Aghion and Howitt[69]

48 *Chapter 2*

and Grossman and Helpman[70] have produced models showing that firms that innovate are new entrants that had zero profits before entering the market. But there is an inherent contradiction. Where are the deep pockets to finance R&D? The Schumpeterian models assume that all firms have access to the same R&D technology and enter the market with the same productivity, which is contradicted by the large distribution of productivity and costs among firms, even in the same industry. Focusing on the different channels through which competition influences innovation, we can distinguish, among others: (1) the Darwinian effect introduced by Aghion[71] and Porter;[72] (2) the "neck-and-neck" effect;[73] (3) the Arrow effect;[74] and (4) the mobility effect.[75]

Competition may lower the preinnovation rents by a larger margin than it does postinnovation rents and increase the postinnovation profits, especially for new low-cost firms in oligopolies with not-too-dissimilar firms, thus eliminating the Schumpeterian effect. Empirical evidence on patents and other intellectual property rights shows that the impact of patenting is beneficial only in some intensive R&D subsectors, like pharmaceuticals or heavy chemicals. In these cases, the Schumpeterian effect is important as there are industries with very unequal firms in terms of costs, and the laggards have to catch up with the technological leader before innovating. These different cases may lead to the empirical finding of a U-shaped curve by Aghion et al.,[76] relating market structure to innovation.[77]

There is now important empirical evidence that competition is linked to growth in developed countries. Disney and coauthors conclude that competition increases productivity levels and the rate of growth of productivity.[78] Bloom and van Reenen's empirical research concludes that good management practices, which improve as competition increases, are strongly associated with productivity.[79] Finally, an efficient market for corporate control with open rules for takeovers reinforces the impact of competition on productivity.[80]

Research in developing countries has also shown the importance of the link between competition and growth. Dutz and Hayri find, in a cross-country model explaining growth rates, that competition policy has a positive impact on growth, even after taking into consideration trade and institutional policies.[81] Reviewing a large number of studies in the 1990s, Tybout concluded that there is evidence that protection increases price-cost margins and reduces efficiency at the margin and that exporters (firms that succeed in the international market) are more efficient than nonexporters.[82] Using a new data set for Latin America, Haltiwanger and coauthors confirm that trade liberalization and competition lead to higher levels of efficiency at the firm level and also to reallocation of resources to more productive sectors.[83] Using data for Colombia, Eslava and coauthors show that trade and financial reforms of the 1990s were associated with productivity increases resulting in reallocation from low- to high-productivity firms.[84] Similar evidence has been shown for Chile following trade liberalization[85] and for India due to the elimination of the Raj licensing scheme.[86] Aghion and coauthors provide evidence that increasing competition in South African manufacturing should have "large productivity effects."[87] Carlin and coauthors have been using survey data to examine the relative importance of infrastructure and competition in transition countries and have found some evidence that institutions and competition play a distinctive role in growth beyond their impact on innovation.[88]

It follows that, since development is a dynamic process of entry and competition is central to productivity increases and innovation, competition policies should be as important as other major development policies. Competition policies are also essential for developing a solid institutional framework for markets, and competition law is only one of the tools for these policies.[89] To be successful, competition policies have to permeate all policies of the government and be part of a culture practiced by the executive, legislative, and judicial branches.

The discussion has, most recently, moved to examine the kind of competition policy and law that would be suitable for developing economies.[90] There is almost a consensus that these policies/laws must account for the "special attributes" of developing countries, thus rejecting a mere transplantation of competition laws from developed countries.[91] Gal discusses the preconditions of enforcement of competition law in developing countries, noting that the challenges facing developing countries, such as a low level of economic development, institutional design problems, and complex governmental regulation and bureaucracy, create real-world challenges which should be taken into account in the early stages of the adoption of competition law,[92] thus warning against a copy-and-paste approach.[93] Fox suggests six different models (including the U.S. and European Union model) for developing countries to choose from, noting that what is important is the "knowledgeable choice."[94] Singh asserts the significance for developing countries of having a competition policy that takes into consideration their level of development, in conjunction with the objective of long-term sustainable economic growth.[95] There is an increasing consensus that jurisdictions at different levels of development and governance capacities require different types of competition policies than developed ones.[96] In a recent cross-country study using a sample of 101 countries, Ma shows that until a country reaches a certain threshold of institutional development, competition law will be idle: it is clear that in the least developed jurisdictions, competition law will have no effect on the country's economic growth. Once that threshold is reached, without an "efficient enforcement scheme," competition law may have an adverse effect on growth.[97] Along the same lines, Fox and Mateus advocate a targeted application of competition law for practices that have a significant impact on the most vulnerable, the poor, thus integrating development economics concerns in competition law.[98] The seclusion of competition law and economics from the macroeconomic level is ending.

.   .   .

The preceding analysis has brought to the fore the limitations of traditional approaches. Development economics of the 1950s relied on an all-pervasive state intervention to start growth and industrialize, substituted market allocations by planning mechanisms and external protection. History has shown that governments and administrations do not have enough information (and the required economic knowledge) and agents may lack adequate incentives, resulting in large distortions and huge waste of resources. But it has also been shown that the idea of a benevolent government acting to maximize welfare is far removed from the reality of developing countries—governments are too often captured by large interest groups and corruption may be rampant, so their actions and policies may instead block economic growth. By emphasizing markets, more recent economic theories were not only reintroducing the role of the price mechanism and market incentives but also trying to limit government intervention in general. What experience has shown is that this is a chimeric approach: by simply containing government intervention, governance problems, rampant in developing countries, will not be resolved. Contrary to the "absolutist" view, it is important to integrate insights from development economics, in particular the broader characteristics of an economy, in the design of appropriate competition law regimes for these jurisdictions.

The rebalancing that occurred after the 1990s toward a more eclectic economic and institutional and also a more "clinical" approach suited for each country, abandoning all-country recipes, may be more productive for a fruitful interaction between development economics and competition policy.

Moreover, recent empirical research[99] has also shown that we have to be more humble on what may be achieved with development policies. Within this more limited agenda we think competition policy can contribute to improving market efficiency in developing economies and can also be used for some cases of poverty alleviation. Competition law should nowadays always be part of the instruments of development policy.

3

Who Needs Antitrust?

Or, Is Developing-Country Antitrust Different?
A Historical-Comparative Analysis

Aditya Bhattacharjea

Most economists see the objective of competition/antitrust policy as protection and promotion of competition, which is desirable because it promotes allocative, technical, and dynamic efficiency, better quality, and greater product diversity. The first part of this chapter will review the history of antitrust in several jurisdictions in the nineteenth and twentieth centuries to show that the actual reasons for adoption of competition laws in most industrialized countries were rather different, as were the objectives that influenced their interpretation and enforcement for several decades. The second part of the chapter will examine whether and how things are different in the early twenty-first century for developing competition regimes, making the history of present-day industrialized countries irrelevant. This assessment will be made on two fronts. First, has antitrust changed? The answer is obviously yes. But I argue that it has changed in ways that make it more difficult to implement for new competition agencies. It now involves far more sophisticated economic analysis (e.g., a regime of simple per se prohibitions and exemptions being supplanted by the rule of reason) and new issues where the economic understanding is still evolving (e.g., the economics of network industries and two-sided markets). The cost of wrong decisions could be very high. Second, has our understanding of "development" changed? Undoubtedly it has, from a focus on aggregative growth plus structural change, to one based on the expansion of human capabilities.

These observations suggest that if antitrust is to be promoted in developing countries, it should be doubly selective. First, interventions should be limited to those based on robust and uncontroversial economic principles that make some kinds of conduct unambiguously reprehensible. Second, priority should be given to addressing these competition issues in sectors that directly impinge on the well-being of the poor, in particular essential consumer goods, agriculture, and health care. More ambitious enforcement efforts can evolve as antitrust agencies acquire expertise and legitimacy based on early successes with this limited agenda. Meanwhile, emerging antitrust regimes should try to share experiences with their peers in other developing countries instead of relying exclusively on advisers from developed countries.

The Historical Record

The modern world's first antitrust statute, Canada's 1889 Wallace Act, was widely regarded by contemporaries as an empty political gesture by the politician who had pushed for it. The act proscribed behavior that "unlawfully" restricted competition in various ways. However, this amounted to deferring to the common law of restraint of trade, which allowed most combinations. The federal government did not create an agency to enforce the act, and provincial governments were not interested in enforcing a federal statute that threatened local interests.[1] The act was replaced successively by three other competition laws: the Combines Investigations Act in 1910, which was used only once; the Combines and Fair Prices Act in 1919, which was struck down the very next year by the judiciary as ultra vires of the Canadian constitution; and then the second Combines Investigation Act in 1923.[2] According to one Canadian scholar, "In the earlier days of antitrust there were many pressures to use the law in the service of several goals, sometimes simultaneously—for example, as a weapon to fight big business, or to protect domestic firms from international competition, or simply to attack large firms for being large."[3]

Cartel prosecutions were increasingly successful after the 1930s, but even in the 1960s and 1970s, Canadian courts imposed requirements that made it almost impossible to take action against cartels and mergers that did not virtually eliminate competition, as well as conspiracies in which anticompetitive intent could not be established.[4] In 1986, after nearly two decades of failed attempts, a modern Competition Act was passed with a clear focus on efficiency. However, it retained some of the earlier legislation's problematic language, which continued to hamper enforcement and required two subsequent rounds of amendments (in 1999 and 2009) to extirpate. These misadventures did not prevent Canada from becoming an industrial power with a high standard of living.

The 1890 Sherman Act in the United States was similarly motivated by "populist" political concerns about the power of big business and in particular about cartels and large firms that charged prices that were either too low (thereby endangering small business rivals) or too high (which was regarded as objectionable on wealth-redistributive rather than allocative efficiency grounds).[5] The motivation for the enactment of antitrust in the United States was thus multifaceted and at times contradictory:

> The Congressional debates leading to passage of the Sherman Act reflected a number of differing and inherently conflicting goals: promotion of healthy competition, concern for injured competitors and distrust of large concentrations of economic and political power all make appearances in the debates over the bill. These differing goals have continued to surface in its application ever since.[6]

According to some scholars, "the Sherman Act was a harmless way of appeasing public demands for regulation and at the same time allowing members of Congress to garner support for and deflect criticism regarding the protective tariff legislation."[7] It was regarded as harmless because under the then prevailing view of congressional authority, it required state-level legislation to make it effective, and the states were not keen on antitrust.[8] Although price-fixing came to be treated as per se illegal after the Supreme Court's 1897 judgment in *United States v. Trans-Missouri Freight Association*,[9] in 1933 the Court endorsed a cartel formed to avoid distress sales during the Depression.[10] Indeed, the federal government also pushed industry to cartelize during the New Deal as part of national policy.[11]

The Clayton Act of 1914, too, was used for decades to address concerns other than efficiency. Its condemnation of price discrimination in section 2(a), inserted by the 1936 Robinson-Patman Act, was motivated by the need to protect small retailers from large discount stores. As one author notes, "The initial title of the Act reflected the particular interest group that sought protection—'Wholesale Grocer's Protection Act.'"[12] The "failing-firm defense" of a merger is described as a "judicial gloss on section 7 of the Clayton Act," preserved by congressional desire "to protect the creditors, employees and shareholders of failing companies if necessary at the cost of permitting monopoly pricing."[13] In its 1962 *Brown Shoe* decision, which blocked a merger that would have had a negligible effect on competition, the Supreme Court cited congressional intent behind the Clayton Act, in support of maintaining numerous small, independent businesses, even if this resulted in higher costs and prices.[14]

Only with the ascent of Chicago School antitrust thinking in the 1970s did the courts and antitrust agencies abandon the other objectives in favor of efficiency. It became widely recognized that the multiple legislative goals that found expression in the antitrust laws were incoherent and could not provide workable guidelines for enforcement. Efficiency, as defined in mainstream economics, has emerged by default as the only alternative in the eyes of most American judges and economists. Thus, according to Judge Richard Posner:

> No doubt most of the legislators whose votes were essential to the enactment of these statutes cared more about the distribution of income and wealth and the welfare of small business and particular consumer groups than they did about allocative efficiency, especially since the economics profession itself had no enthusiasm for antitrust policy. But these legislators did not succeed in writing into the statutes standards that would have enabled judges to order these goals and translate them into coherent, administrable legal doctrine without doing serious and undesired damage to the economy. For guidance the courts perforce turned elsewhere. After a century and more of judicial enforcement of the antitrust statutes, there is a consensus that guidance must be sought in economics.[15]

And from the editor of the authoritative *Handbook of Antitrust Economics*, an equally clear statement:

> This *Handbook* has been written under the assumption that what makes a conduct competitive, or anticompetitive, does not depend on how the legislator phrased the prohibitions and with the conviction that the economic science is the only body of knowledge that provides the rational foundation for the proper interpretation of any substantive antitrust rule.[16]

Antitrust became respectable even later in Europe and then, too, very slowly; the efficiency paradigm is still not fully accepted. In the late nineteenth and early twentieth centuries, cartel agreements were legal in Britain and France and sometimes enforceable through the courts in Germany.[17] Anti-cartel laws began to be more strictly enforced only from the 1950s, but with room for exemptions. Rationalization and specialization cartels could be exempted under Germany's Act against Restraints of Competition. Section 10 of the U.K. Restrictive Trade Practices Act of 1956 permitted restrictive agreements to be defended on various public interest grounds, including the protection of employment and exports, although these provisions were sparingly used. Cartels were swiftly and effectively tackled, but concerns were expressed until the 1990s about the act being excessively form based in listing types of registrable agreements, the cumbersome procedures for evaluating them, and the absence of real competition assessment in most cases.[18]

With respect to U.K. policy on monopoly and mergers in its early decades, a detailed study by Wilks is illuminating.[19] The governing principle was not public enforcement but rather self-regulation by industry, as part of the "post war settlement" between capital and labor, based on accommodation and mediated by political and bureaucratic discretion. According to Wilks, it is important "to appreciate that the machinery of government was designed as much to restrict competition as to encourage it."[20] Efficiency was not a major objective; other goals that were given greater priority at various times included export promotion via building "national champions," full employment, balanced distribution of industry, technical improvement, and price control. "Economists have been critical of the politicization of competition policy, the diverse criteria allowed by the public interest test, the apparent incompatibility of the reasoning on different reports and the divergences from the prescriptions of welfare economics."[21] But these criticisms, Wilks argues, are beside the point. Until the late 1970s, "[T]he policy more or less did what it was intended to do. It allowed government to address episodic problems, it provided a façade of control and it allowed industry, on the whole, freedom to operate in a context of reasonable self-regulation. It did not deliver economic efficiency or consumer welfare, but then it was never intended to."[22] It "has made a minor contribution to the efficiency of the economy, but a major contribution to the legitimacy of the market."[23] The market having been legitimized by the Thatcherite revolution of the 1980s, Britain passed a modern Competition Act in 1998.

Antitrust violations with a "community" dimension are dealt with supranationally in the European Union (EU). Integration of the European market has always been a paramount objective, trumping economic analysis of price discrimination and vertical restraints. In the 1970s, decisions of the Commission and Community courts "were not based on economics or consumer welfare . . . they were based on the protection of the economic freedom of market players as well as on preventing firms from using their economic power to undermine competitive structures."[24] As Alison Jones has recently argued, it is still not clear that procompetitive efficiency arguments will temper the prohibition of what are regarded in the EU, despite its "modernization" program, as hard-core horizontal and vertical restraints. Even for cartels, as late as the 1980s and 1990s, the European Commission was prepared to exempt "crisis" cartels designed to bring about orderly capacity reductions in troubled industries, invoking employment concerns as well as the efficiency arguments provided in earlier incarnations of Article 101(3) of the Treaty on the Functioning of the European Union (TFEU).[25] When illegal cartels are successfully prosecuted, agencies and courts in the EU (and even the United States) have accepted financial constraints as an argument for reduced fines, effectively increasing the incentive to collude in hard times.[26]

Moving to Asia, it is instructive to recall that during its rapid industrialization before the Second World War, Japan's highly concentrated industrial structure was untrammeled by antitrust. In the 1930s, hundreds of cartels were in fact mandated by the state. The 1947 Antimonopoly Law imposed by the postwar occupation authorities was not seriously enforced until the 1990s, and the economy was dominated by a handful of *keiretsu* business groups. Japan's competition law and its enforcement, according to one very critical observer, was heavily influenced by considerations of "fairness"—including fairness to competitors. This meant that established business practices were tolerated even at the cost of competition; aggressive competition in the form of excessive discounting was discouraged, and explicit cartels and tacit collusion were encouraged. Competition and growth were treated as possibly inconsistent goals. At the height of its economic miracle in the 1960s and 1970s, Japan exempted dozens of cartels, mainly for exports, imports, small and medium enterprises, rationalization, and specialization. Working closely with the *keiretsu*, the Ministry of Trade and Industry set production targets and encouraged industries to form cartels to implement this "administrative guidance."[27]

It might be argued that developing countries have an advantage in not having to repeat the mistakes of more advanced countries and should adopt an approach that has been "perfected" by more recent developments in economics and is manifested in current practice. But the economics of antitrust continues to evolve (witness the waxing and waning influence of first the Harvard structuralist and then Chicago approaches), and there remain fundamental differences in practice between Europe and the United States on matters such as crisis cartels, predatory and excessive pricing, and vertical restraints. Thus, adopting whatever approach is currently in vogue in the developed country that is funding capacity building or supplying advisers may lock in a possibly inappropriate model.[28] It might also be argued that shielding firms from the full blast of market competition has impaired European and Japanese economic performance in recent decades. But it would be a bold analyst who would extend this argument to the century before the Second World War, when these countries turned a blind eye to anticompetitive practices, or to the "Golden Age of Capitalism" (1950–1973), when their competition laws were riddled with cartel exemptions and (in Europe as well as the United States) informed by a per se approach to prohibiting most vertical restraints that is now regarded as wrongheaded.

A historically informed assessment of antitrust must also take account of the fact that today's developing countries, like developed countries a century ago, lack unemployment and social security benefits. Without such safety nets, it is difficult for policy makers and judges to privilege economic efficiency to the complete exclusion of concerns about unemployment, which is an inescapable consequence of vigorous competition. Active enforcement began in Europe only along with the establishment of welfare states in the mid-twentieth century, and rationalization and crisis cartels were permitted for decades thereafter.

Continuing in the historical-descriptivist vein but coming to more recent experiences that are more relevant for developing countries, we must consider the East Asian Miracle in the late twentieth century. Making his own disapproval very clear, one scholar traces the influence of Japanese "fairness"-based competition laws on those of Korea, Taiwan, Thailand, and Indonesia, where laws were enacted relatively late and antitrust agencies often protected competitors from vigorous competition, legalized cartels, and fixed "fair" prices and royalty rates.[29] Again, the argument could be made that the effect of the 1997 East Asian crisis was worsened by the insulation of firms in these countries from vigorous competition. But even if there is some truth in this argument, the decline in the gross domestic product (GDP) levels of the countries hit by the crisis was small in relation to their gains of the preceding decades, and their rapid recovery has occurred despite the continued weakness of their competition regimes; only Korea began enforcing its laws more seriously after 1997. Other Asian "tigers" like Vietnam, Singapore, and China, which were unaffected by the crisis, have only recently enacted competition laws that were brought into effect in 2005, 2006, and 2008 respectively, after decades of rapid growth. Malaysia, which made a strong comeback from the crisis, enacted a competition law only in 2010.

India's dismal record with competition law also takes on a different complexion in the context of the country recording a growth rate second only to China's between 2003 and 2009. It was precisely during this period that enforcement of India's largely ineffective Monopolies and Restrictive Trade Practices (MRTP) Act of 1969 (whose merger review clauses already had been deleted in 1991) slackened even further with the enactment of the Competition Act of 2002. Enforcement of some sections of the new legislation began only in 2009, and merger review commenced only in mid-2011. In its first seventy-five decisions, the Competition Commission of India had established violations in only two cases, imposing token fines in one of them.[30]

It would be hard to argue that the absence of modern antitrust laws, or their weak enforcement, has impeded development in any of the countries discussed above. Even the presence of a modern competition law is of little avail if the institutional and political climate is inimical to its enforcement. Studies of various developing countries show that the enactment and enforcement of competition law is often stalled by political economy factors such as business opposition, regulatory capture, anticompetitive government policies and "public interest" considerations, lack of coherence with sectoral regulation, threats to the independence of the regulators, lack of accountability, dilatory procedures, inadequate funding, and the absence of a competition culture.[31]

Although these examples are numerous, they might be regarded as "cherry-picked" in order to serve my argument. The same cannot be said of an ambitious econometric exercise recently undertaken by Ma.[32] Earlier attempts to establish a statistically significant impact of antitrust on growth used a dummy variable to distinguish countries with and without such laws, controlling for the standard macroeconomic determinants of growth (the investment rate and the growth rate of labor force adjusted for changes in efficiency). Ma goes much further. He attempts, with data from 101 countries at various levels of development, to establish a relationship between the growth rates of their GDP per worker between 1990 and 2004 on the one hand and the *scope* of their antitrust laws (where present) on the other, also controlling for government effectiveness and the rule of law, as measured by widely used indexes. He finds that antitrust laws have no effect on growth of poorer

developing countries until they cross a threshold level of institutional development, captured by the rule of law index. Almost half the countries fall
below this threshold. Even for those above the threshold, the more generally
effective the government is, the stronger is the relationship between growth
and the scope of antitrust law. The idea that there is a simple relationship
between enactment of an antitrust law and subsequent economic performance is not supported by the cross-country evidence. Neither, for that matter, is the idea that competition is necessarily stifled in the absence of competition laws. Despite higher industrial concentration in developing countries,
standard measures of firm turnover, mobility, and persistence of profits (based
mainly on data from the period before the recent rush to adopt such laws)
show that competition is at least as intense as in developed countries.[33]

How Are Things Different Now, and What Should Developing Countries Do?

I referred above to the evolution of antitrust in order to caution against lock-
ing developing countries into whatever happens to be the current consensus
in the developed country that is supplying advisers. It is true, of course, that in
one sense antitrust has evolved unidirectionally. There has been a decisive
move away from simple per se condemnation of certain kinds of behavior to
a nuanced application of the rule of reason to the facts of each particular case.
But this makes life especially difficult for new competition agencies, with
little or no experience or expertise to draw upon. Further, the coverage of
antitrust in the United States and Europe was expanded in stages. Merger
review commenced decades after the basic provisions against anticompetitive
agreements and monopolization ("abuse of a dominant position" in the EU)
had been enforced, interpreted, and refined.[34] But most developing countries
have enacted full-spectrum laws, telescoping this process and imposing on
their new agencies the complete range of enforcement activities. These burdens will severely stress their limited resources and governance ability, which
would probably be better deployed in enforcing more fundamental laws and
regulations in relation to taxation, public health, property rights, and contract enforcement.

　　Moreover, recent years have seen the emergence of completely new areas
of antitrust law and economics, where there are no settled principles even in
the rarefied world of theory, let alone administrable standards for messy real-
world cases. This poses difficult problems even for mature antitrust jurisdic-

tions. Examples are the behavior of two-sided markets and network industries. As regards the latter:

> [T]he economic theory of networks is so incomplete and unsettled that there is no commonly accepted body of knowledge on market structure with network effects. . . . The bottom line is that as things stand today, there are many areas of antitrust law where there is significant uncertainty on how to apply the law in network industries and when to judge various practices as legal or illegal.[35]

Thus, in relation to a range of economic activities that are becoming increasingly important in modern economies, including relatively underdeveloped countries, economics does not yet provide the clarity that could dispel the incoherence that Posner and others deplore in the antitrust statutes.[36] Even for other sectors, the efficiency criterion of standard economics assumes that market prices accurately measure society's "opportunity costs." This assumption does not hold if greater competition causes unemployment or generates externalities, such as pollution.

Be that as it may, given that most developing countries have adopted antitrust laws, how should they proceed? I would suggest two principles. First, enforcement should be initially confined to the basic offenses where the principles are clear and robust: hard-core cartels, merger to monopoly absent a credible failing-firm defense or verifiable efficiency gains, and predatory pricing with bright-line standards for costs and an assessment of entry conditions. (Establishing probable recoupment of lost profits is probably too ambitious for new agencies and is not required even in the EU. Besides, dominant state-owned firms, facing private-sector competition unleashed by market-oriented reforms, may not need to recoup profits.) Even this limited agenda will require infant agencies to learn the intricacies of market definition and evaluating effects on competition; these skills can gradually be extended to a wider range of competition offenses. Other exclusionary abuses and non-monopolizing mergers can be taken up subsequently, subject to clearly stated market-share thresholds for presumptive anticompetitive effects as well as safe harbors.

The second principle to be kept in mind is that the competition regimes should be locally rooted in order to gain political traction, instead of being seen as foreign transplants. Recall that it was the populist packaging of antitrust laws in the United States, Canada, and Europe that made them politically viable even when they were ineffective. Nowadays, however, with many developing countries emerging from decades of state ownership and control of business and the failure of socialist models worldwide, anti-big-business sentiment is not something that can be banked upon.[37] Also, without effective labor legislation, the populist rhetoric of protecting small business (usually conjuring up the image of mom-and-pop retail stores) will not work in developing countries where small enterprise often takes the form of sweatshops employing workers (including child labor) who toil for a pittance under appalling conditions.

But this kind of populism is not required. Agencies in developing countries can deploy standard antitrust analysis without the intention of restricting the growth of big firms or protecting small ones, by concentrating their limited resources on anticompetitive acts that directly impinge on the standard of living of the poor. Several scholarly articles on competition law and policy in developing countries, collected in a recent anthology edited by Eleanor Fox and Abel Mateus, between them offer several examples of such competition abuses.[38] These include seller cartels in goods and services that are basic necessities, including dietary staples, building materials, petroleum products, and local road and waterborne transport; buyer cartels and cartels in trucking and shipping that depress the prices received by small farmers; and anticompetitive practices by dominant firms in telecommunications and financial services.

Focusing on such activities requires an agency to be proactive in initiating inquiries and seeing them through to a successful conclusion, instead of simply investigating complaints from the "public." The latter approach will embroil the agency in consumer protection issues, contractual disputes, and business torts. India's erstwhile MRTP Commission was overwhelmed by such complaints, and something similar seems to be happening to its new Competition Commission.[39] Even otherwise, genuine competition issues may be raised by individuals and consumer associations who may not be able to afford the consultants and lawyers required to make a convincing case, especially against powerful corporate interests who can deploy far better resources.

One can prune the list of priorities even further. In the preceding section of this chapter, I quoted several historical examples of weak or absent antitrust regimes being compatible with economic development. That discussion employed the traditional definition of development: growth of per capita income accompanied by a shift of the labor force from agriculture to industry and services. But just as perspectives in antitrust have changed, so have those in development studies. Thanks largely to the work of the Indian Nobel laureate Amartya Sen, we are now concerned much less with production or command over goods and more with what he calls individuals' capability to achieve "functionings" that they have reason to value. This so-called capabilities approach is articulated in very general terms, privileging functionings such as the ability to live a long and healthy life, gain access to knowledge, achieve a decent standard of living, participate in the life of the community, and appear in public without shame.[40] These are poorly correlated with income or wealth, depend crucially on individual circumstances, and span a wide range of social and economic rights. In practical terms, however, adherents of this approach assess countries and regions on the basis of multidimensional indicators that incorporate measures of health, longevity, and education along with income.[41]

This change in orientation suggests that antitrust enforcement should pay particular heed to markets that have a direct bearing on such capabilities. While the market for educational services in most developing countries, to the extent that the state allows it to function, is highly competitive, the same is not true of the health care sector. Here we need to consider giant pharmaceutical firms participating in international cartels and cross-border mergers, while exploiting strengthened patent protection under the World Trade Organization's (WTO) Agreement on Trade-Related Aspects of Intellectual Property Rights (TRIPS) and the even stronger "TRIPS-plus" protection increasingly being pushed into bilateral and regional trade agreements. With poor state-provided health care and limited spread of health insurance in most developing countries, these actions adversely impact the capability of a very large number of vulnerable people to lead a long and healthy life. The same applies to antitrust abuses by multinational firms producing agricultural inputs such as seeds, fertilizer, and animal feed.

However, confronting such activities requires transborder enforcement, which is difficult for inexperienced and underresourced antitrust agencies in developing countries. And although Article 40 of the TRIPS Agreement allows WTO members to use national legislation to regulate anticompetitive licensing conditions, it provides an illustrative list of practices that conspicuously omits the more serious ones.[42] It is too much to expect new antitrust agencies to employ the kind of sophisticated rule of reason analysis that has replaced the "Nine No-Nos" that used to be applied in U.S. patent licensing cases. Therefore, instead of being stampeded into passing antitrust laws, extending their scope, or enforcing them in the way that they have come to be

enforced after decades of evolution in mature jurisdictions, developing countries should, first of all, insist on retaining the right to award compulsory li-
censes and to permit parallel imports for patented products. This can be implemented in TRIPS-consistent patent laws, and does not require antitrust.
Developing countries should also fight for a supranational agency to which
cases involving international cartels, mergers, and intellectual property rights
abuses could be referred. Alternatively, they could insist that national agencies and courts in developed countries be given jurisdiction when domestic
firms inflict antitrust injury on foreigners, treating the victims as if they were
domestic residents.

    Of course, the first of these alternatives would be too much to hope for in
light of industrial countries' hostile attitude to anything more than selective
voluntary cooperation during the debate over a possible international agreement on competition at the WTO. And the U.S. Supreme Court's 2004 judgment in *F. Hoffmann-La Roche Ltd. v. Empagran S.A.* (542 U.S. 155) effectively
foreclosed the second approach, at least in the United States.[43] But these arguments can still be made if the issue of competition law comes up in negotiations over regional trade agreements or in the WTO. Instead of scrambling
defensively to enact and enforce such laws to impress their richer trading
partners, developing countries need to be more assertive in proposing institutional changes to address the kind of antitrust abuses that really matter to
them.

    That said, developing countries also need to share their experiences with
each other instead of relying exclusively on advisers from developed countries. Apart from uncovering domestic cartels whose activities directly impacted the lives of their poorest people, the young competition agencies of
South Africa and Zambia have taken on cartels and abuse of dominance by
large foreign corporations,[44] while Brazil and South Korea have successfully
prosecuted some international cartels.[45] These could be mentors to other
countries. Stand-alone regional antitrust arrangements between developing
countries—rather than competition chapters shoehorned into trade agreements between developed and developing countries—could be one way to
proceed. As Eleanor Fox has recently argued, such arrangements would allow pooling of resources and experience, enforcement in line with development priorities, and greater leverage against firms located in developed countries (and against competition agencies in those countries that may be
reluctant to cooperate with an agency in an isolated developing country).
Without glossing over the problems such a supranational authority would

face, she also argues that it could provide a counterweight to local interests that may suborn national competition agencies or induce national governments to adopt policies inimical to competition.[46] The recently formed Latin American Competition Network should be closely watched by developing countries on other continents.

Summary and Conclusions

I have shown in this chapter that for several decades, present-day developed countries adopted and implemented competition laws with various objectives, stated or unstated: legitimizing the growing role of big business by giving the impression that its worst features would be controlled; protecting small firms, or employees or investors in bigger firms that were in danger of failing; building "national champions"; controlling prices; or integrating the European market. The idea that greater competition promotes economic efficiency had an impact only in the late twentieth century, and is itself problematic. I also provided evidence that antitrust laws in developing countries are ineffective unless they are embedded in a congenial institutional context of the rule of law and effective governance.

Nonetheless, given that most developing countries have (reluctantly) passed such laws in recent years, I argued that they should limit themselves to enforcing a few basic principles and that they should take up investigations and cases that have a widespread impact on the poor. In this context, I suggested agriculture and health care as priority areas. Developing countries should also learn from each other, rather than relying exclusively on transplanted frameworks and ideas from advanced countries that persisted with very different antitrust regimes when they were at a comparable stage of development.

4

Competition Law and Development

Lessons from the U.S. Experience

Thomas C. Arthur

Although developing countries can learn much from American competition doctrine, they should not copy U.S. antitrust institutions. Created when modern economic regulation was nascent, the American competition regime is unique in two ways. First, no single body is in charge of antitrust. Only the U.S. Supreme Court can establish a consistent interpretation of the generally worded U.S. antitrust statutes, but it lacks the resources to do so. Developing countries should avoid this. Second, American antitrust is almost completely limited to the prevention of private restraints on competition. It does not include competition advocacy to address the problems presented by former state enterprises or by central direction of the economy.[1] For developing nations dealing with these issues, the American experience has little to teach, other than to suggest that a moderate degree of government intervention can be consistent with the development of a market economy. Finally, the United States by 1890 had already developed mature and stable legal and political institutions, which are necessary for regulation of a modern market economy. The first task is to develop this legal and political infrastructure. Without them any competition law regime may do more harm than good. This may be the most important lesson from the American antitrust experience.

This chapter will first briefly describe the founding and early development of the U.S. antitrust regime, explaining how it came to take the unique form that it did. It will then describe how, and how well, the regime works and conclude with lessons for developing countries from the American experience.

The Historical Background of U.S. Competition Law

The United States was a developed country in 1890, when the American competition law institutions were created. Politically, it was a liberal democracy.[2] Both the national and state constitutions limited government powers and protected individual rights, and an independent judiciary enforced contracts and protected property rights.[3] But the country was just beginning to experiment with business regulation by administrative agencies.[4] Modern agencies did not exist. The proper role of the federal and state governments in the economy was, after slavery, the most contested question in nineteenth-century America. Significant interventions into the economy were opposed, often successfully, by a large portion of the Democratic Party, so that while there were significant governmental interventions in the economy, the average citizen had little contact with any federal institution other than the post office.

Economically, the United States was on its way to being the leading economic power in the world.[5] A "transportation revolution"[6] and a "communications revolution"[7] in the first half of the nineteenth century had provided the infrastructure for a national economy. The Industrial Revolution in America began early in the century in New England,[8] and by 1900 the United States was the leading manufacturing nation in the world. Historians debate whether the colonial economy was market based or there was a "market revolution" after the American Revolution,[9] and whether Americans were coerced into labor and commodity markets or willingly embraced them.[10] But they agree that the economy was market based.

The state and national ("federal") governments did promote economic development, however. The national government soon established the patent and postal systems,[11] built lighthouses, and improved harbors. Both the national and the state governments built or subsidized roads, bridges, canals, and railroads. The "transcontinental" railroads to the Pacific Coast were subsidized by federal land grants.[12] In 1869 Massachusetts created the first modern commission to regulate railroads,[13] and the first federal administrative agency, the Interstate Commerce Commission, was established in 1887 for the same purpose, although the regulation was not very extensive at either level.[14] Both governments chartered banks, and state and national banknotes became an important part of the national money supply.[15] State and local governments operated public schools and colleges, and the federal government in 1862 began subsidizing "land grant" colleges to support subjects, especially agriculture and engineering, that were important to economic development.[16] The national government sold its vast holdings of public land cheaply and later provided 160 acres for free to any "homesteader" who would cultivate the land for five years.[17]

The most disputed government intervention was the federal tariff policy. In the first half of the nineteenth century, when the agricultural South had a larger degree of political power, tariffs wavered between revenue and protection, depending on the balance of political power between the protectionist Whigs and antiprotectionist Democrats.[18] But after the Civil War the dominant Republican Party made protectionism one of its main objects, and tariffs generally remained high until the Democrats reduced rates substantially in 1913.[19]

Nonetheless, the economy was predominantly market based. Of the five interventions listed above, three—money and banking, education, and transportation—are government functions in virtually every developed country. Some sort of federal land policy was unavoidable in light of the vast public domain, and the predominant policy of cheap land was basically a privatization policy that distributed public land to small landholders. Even high tariffs left plenty of room for competition, as the U.S. internal market became the largest in the world.[20] Beyond these specific areas, government regulation in the nineteenth century was minimal, and the only state-run enterprises were public schools and universities and the postal system. Socialism never achieved political success in the United States.[21]

Moreover, each of these intrusions in the economy was contested, often successfully, by substantial political and judicial forces. Significant constituencies in the Democratic Party opposed high tariffs, national banks and paper money, and federal "internal improvements," i.e., infrastructure investments, believing that they favored one section over another, promoted only special interests, or would lead to government-sponsored monopoly, especially in the case of the Bank of the United States.[22] At the same time, the Supreme Court protected the internal market from trade barriers imposed by the states by striking down state laws that trenched on the federal government's exclusive legislative jurisdiction over interstate commerce.[23] Late in the century the Court began to use the due process clause of the Fourteenth Amendment to strike down state regulations that it deemed "unreasonable" restrictions on private economic activity.[24]

This strong tradition of political opposition to governmental interventions into the economy sharply limited the need for another institution devoted even partially to competition advocacy. Instead, the three basic American competition laws, the Sherman, Clayton,[25] and Federal Trade Commission (FTC)[26] Acts, were directed at what was called the "trust problem,"[27] the combination of competitors in so-called loose combinations (cartels) or tight combinations (monopolistic mergers) in the 1880s.[28]

The trust problem quickly proved too big for state courts and legislatures to curb, although they tried,[29] and it became one of the biggest issues in national politics. Although there was irresistible pressure for a federal antitrust law, there was considerable disagreement as to what to do, from doing nothing at one extreme to breaking up all large corporations at the other.[30] Congress in 1890 tried to strike a balance, permitting "combinations in aid of production" and proscribing those designed to create monopoly power; banning cartels, monopolistic mergers, and predation by dominant firms while permitting productive associations by competitors, most mergers, and even dominant firms resulting from superior efficiency.[31] These decisions still constitute the core of American antitrust.

Congress was less successful, however, in its efforts to implement these decisions. The drafters of the Sherman Act did not even consider creating a national competition authority. They instead tried to write their choices into law, to be enforced by civil and criminal cases in the federal courts.[32] Congress attempted to federalize the common law doctrines that state courts had used against the trusts in section 1's proscription of "contracts, combinations in the form of trust or otherwise and conspiracies in restraint of trade."[33] While these statutory terms had emerged in common law cases, they proved difficult to apply. Neither these cases nor contemporary economics provided much help in drawing the distinction between the trusts and "combinations in aid of production."[34]

Notwithstanding these difficulties, the Supreme Court by 1911 had implemented the statutory policies against cartels and monopolistic mergers.[35] But its vague statements of the "rule of reason" provided little guidance. Lower courts cited the Court's words while deciding cases by analogy to the results in prior Supreme Court cases. This produced tolerable results, although the courts struggled with hard cases.[36] The vagueness of the law led to calls for new antitrust legislation. Enemies of the trusts feared the vague rule of reason would condone restrictive practices. Businesses feared the uncertainty of the law and began to call for a federal administrative agency that could provide guidance. What to do about the trusts became one of the predominant issues in the 1912 presidential campaign.[37]

After the election, Congress tried to provide specifics in the Clayton Act, which forbade local price-cutting, exclusive dealing and tying, horizontal mergers, and interlocking directorates so long as they "substantially lessen[ed] competition" or "tend[ed] to create a monopoly." Even before the act was passed, many realized it would be ineffective, due to the uncertainty of this qualifying language. This led to the creation of the FTC,[38] which could have become a modern national competition authority. But Congress did not repeal or amend the Sherman or Clayton Acts when it passed the FTC Act. The nation now had two antitrust authorities with largely overlapping jurisdictions.

Congress amended the merger provisions of the Clayton Act in 1950 to close a loophole that had rendered the original provisions ineffective. Seeking a more restrictive antimerger provision than the Sherman Act, which covered only very large mergers, perhaps only monopolistic ones, Congress amended the statute to close the loophole and extend its scope to vertical and conglomerate mergers.[39] But Congress failed to specify what kind of merger "substantially lessened competition," and the legislative history provided nothing more than the hope that the amended statute would somehow deal with the problem of oligopoly.[40] Although the FTC had played a vital role in promoting the new legislation, it was not given exclusive jurisdiction to enforce it, and the leading cases on mergers in the next quarter century were brought by the Justice Department.

American Competition Law Institutions Today

As the previous section has shown, the shape of U.S. antitrust is due to its historic evolution. Had the American antitrust experiment begun just twenty-five years later, the FTC almost surely would have been the sole national competition authority, operating much like the European Commission and most national competition authorities. Instead, America's competition law institutions differ from those in four very significant ways.

First, antitrust law is not only applied by the federal courts, it is made by them. There is no single federal antitrust agency authorized to develop competition law and policy.[41] The primary federal competition agency, the Antitrust Division of the Department of Justice, adjudicates no cases, issues no orders, and propounds no regulations. Its core function is to bring civil and criminal enforcement actions in federal court.[42] While it issues guidelines and policy views,[43] they bind no one; courts follow them only to the extent they find them persuasive.[44] The Federal Trade Commission[45] can issue orders to cease and desist from "unfair methods of competition," but the Supreme Court has interpreted the scope of the Sherman and Clayton Acts so broadly that this phrase in the FTC Act[46] adds little or nothing to those statutes, despite language in a few Supreme Court decisions suggesting that the Commission's authority is not limited to prohibiting violations of the "letter or the spirit of the antitrust laws."[47] The federal courts therefore see no need to defer to the Commission's view of appropriate competition policy, although they must defer to the policy decisions of the other regulatory agencies that issue orders in formal agency adjudications.[48] The FTC in its competition jurisdiction is almost unique among federal agencies in the *lack* of deference the courts give its policy views.[49] Both the Antitrust Division and the FTC influence the law with their policy statements, enforcement guidelines,[50] and amicus curiae briefs,[51] but neither has the statutory authority to bind the courts.[52]

In the American competition law scheme, then, the role of the judiciary is not, as it is in the typical regulatory regime, merely to ensure procedural regularity, reasoned decision making, and faithfulness to the regulatory agency's governing statute, while deferring to the agency's policy judgments.[53] It is not even the application of legal standards developed by the national legislature.[54] Instead, substantive federal antitrust law is entirely judge made. The antitrust statutes are very generally worded.[55] Although its general words can be given, and for over forty years were given, a far more limited interpretation using traditional methods of statutory construction,[56] the U.S. Supreme Court gradually came to interpret the Sherman Act as a standardless delegation to the federal judiciary to make American competition law.[57]

This point cannot be emphasized too strongly. Under the Court's modern view, the Sherman Act, "[a]s a charter of freedom, has a generality and adaptability comparable to that found to be desirable in constitutional provisions"[58] and thus affords the federal courts unfettered discretion to make antitrust policy.[59] As noted by a leading antitrust scholar and former head of the Antitrust Division, as "the courts refine antitrust law . . . *they act much like Congress* (at least in principle) *when it updates statutory law.*[60] In the words of a prominent American political scientist, the "antitrust decisions of the Supreme Court . . . are not basically judicial decisions, but law-making decisions based both immediately and ultimately on the Court's vision of what the economy is and should be."[61] Congress could alter this by enacting detailed antitrust legislation but has not.[62]

Second, because it is made by the federal courts, antitrust law often is applied inconsistently across the nation. Only the Supreme Court can assure certain and consistent antitrust law, and often it has proven unequal to the task.[63] To the extent the Supreme Court leaves the law unsettled, each of the thirteen intermediate appeals courts[64] is free to adopt its own view. Thus the law often varies among the circuits on important questions, such as the proper definition of "below cost" pricing in monopolization cases, to name a significant example.[65] Even within the circuits, inconsistent adjudication can result from the continued use in private damage actions of lay jurors to decide difficult questions of fact, e.g., whether defendants have market power, as vaguely defined by the federal courts.[66] Juries almost surely do not understand these complex questions and must decide cases on factors they think they do understand, such as their attitudes toward big business, or the credibility of opposing counsel and witnesses.[67]

Third, the American competition law regime is extremely decentralized. No one is in charge of it, not even the Supreme Court. Federal courts may not issue advisory opinions; they may act only by deciding concrete "cases or controversies" brought to them by adverse litigants. Their law-declaring function, then, is ancillary to their dispute resolution role; they declare law only as necessary to decide the cases before them.[68] No federal court may express an opinion on any antitrust issue until a case raising it is first brought to it by an appropriate public or private plaintiff, and the Supreme Court cannot resolve any antitrust issue until an appropriate case reaches it on appeal. On the other hand, the courts must address contested antitrust issues if necessary to resolve cases properly before them.[69] In short, the federal courts cannot choose the antitrust cases and issues they must decide. They do not control the antitrust agenda.

A single federal agency with the exclusive power to bring cases would control the antitrust agenda, but there are two antitrust agencies, and except for the Justice Department's exclusive right to bring criminal antitrust cases, its jurisdiction and the FTC's overlap almost completely.[70] Private parties also may bring civil actions for damages and/or injunctions to redress injury to their "business or property."[71] The definition of private party includes the fifty American states, whose attorneys general may bring civil actions for overcharges to state purchasing agencies or, as *parens patriae*, to redress actual injuries or prevent threatened injuries to natural persons (but not business associations) residing in their states.[72] The state attorneys general have been extremely active in recent years.

Significantly, the decision of the Department or the FTC not to proceed against a company does not bind the other agency, any state attorney general, or any private party who can allege injury. While the federal antitrust enforcers seldom disagree,[73] the states often disagree with them over antitrust questions, favoring more intervention in private decision making. The National Association of Attorneys General has issued its own guidelines setting forth more interventionist policies for vertical restraints[74] and horizontal mergers.[75] Nineteen states were coplaintiffs with the Justice Department in the *Microsoft* litigation, so that the primary federal antitrust authority could not control the most significant antitrust case of this generation. The Department could not even settle it. There are two Microsoft consent decrees, one with the Department and some states and the other with a "California Group" of holdout states. The states' participation added little but cost much. According to the authors of the definitive work on the case, it "could have been terminated five years earlier, on similar terms and at far less cost, had the states never been involved."[76] Further, even if all twenty plaintiffs could agree, an aggrieved competitor or customer could bring its own case alleging the same violations and the courts would be free to uphold the view of that private plaintiff, despite the contrary views of the state attorneys general and the Justice Department.[77]

In sum, responsibility for the implementation of American competition law is fragmented. While the United States Supreme Court can conclusively establish substantive antitrust doctrine, it can do so only if a case is properly brought before it. Once the parties settled the *Microsoft* case, the Court had no power to determine the important unresolved legal issues that case raised. As a court, the Supreme Court cannot issue binding regulations, nonbinding policy statements or guidelines, or informal advice. The Justice Department, the FTC, and the state attorneys general may issue guidelines and give informal advice, but their views do not bind the federal courts. Thus an American antitrust counselor cannot obtain an authoritative ruling shielding her client's transaction. As Judge Easterbrook has written, in antitrust the American legal system "contains dozens of institutions that can say 'no,' but not one that can say 'yes.' "[78]

Merger control is the one significant exception. The 1976 Hart-Scott-Rodino Act[79] drastically altered the administration of the Clayton Act.

Premerger notification and the availability of preliminary injunctions have drastically altered the balance of power in merger litigation. Companies cannot afford to litigate an acquisition that cannot be consummated until the case concludes. Consequently, the Supreme Court has not decided a merger case on the merits since 1975, and the relative handful of lower court decisions have come in preliminary injunction cases. As many have noted,[80] the premerger notification process has turned the merger law into a de facto regulatory regime at the Department of Justice and FTC, which divide the cases between them. In the merger area, then, U.S. antitrust practice has come to resemble that of other countries and the European Union. Most cases are resolved by agreement between the companies and the agencies, and the very few litigated cases are in effect resolved by the preliminary injunction litigations. But in these injunction cases, the lower courts are not obliged to defer to the agencies' views. And they receive no supervision by the U.S. Supreme Court.

On the other hand, businesses now receive far more guidance. The FTC and Justice Department revised their merger guidelines in 2010 to more accurately reflect their actual analysis.[81] And in this area there are almost no other actors than the federal agencies. While private plaintiffs can challenge mergers directly in court, at least in theory, it is extremely hard for these actions to succeed.[82]

Finally, competition advocacy is a minimal part of the mission of the Justice Department and FTC. Less than 2 percent of their combined budgets is devoted to competition advocacy. Neither agency played any part in the debates surrounding either the new health care or financial regulation legislation. This is not a real problem, however. Political opposition to government interventions in the economy remains a major part of the American political tradition, in evidence in the recent struggles over health care and financial regulation and also in the deregulation of the airline, trucking, and telephone sectors in the last third of the twentieth century.

Performance

American antitrust law has been notoriously indeterminate. Not all of American antitrust law is unsettled, of course, and competition law has made a substantial contribution to American economic life. The Court's long-standing, unambiguous per se prohibition of hard-core cartel price-fixing and market division,[83] has enabled the Justice Department to prosecute cartelists without

due process concerns.[84] Here the law is so clear and simple that other enforcers, especially private treble damage plaintiffs, are a positive benefit, providing additional enforcement resources.[85]

But there have been substantial uncertainties in every other major antitrust area.[86] That has been less true in this generation, due to more consensus
about antitrust goals and antitrust economics. But there is no guarantee that
this consensus will hold,[87] and policy disagreements have been particularly
fierce over the law governing dominant firms.

The traditional uncertainty in American antitrust flows inevitably from
the nature of the antitrust lawmaking task and the comparative *dis*advantage
of the federal courts as the national competition authority of the United
States. First, consider the nature of the task. To provide consistent and clear
rules, the Supreme Court must definitively resolve two great policy debates
that have long divided antitrust lawyers: the basic goals that antitrust law
should further and the proper economic analysis to be applied.[88]

The goals question is whether courts in antitrust cases should only attempt to further economic efficiency or should instead balance the maximi-
zation of allocative, productive, and dynamic efficiency against noneconomic
social and political goals, such as the preservation of small, locally owned
businesses.[89] Absent legislative direction,[90] this basic policy question turns on
the judges' own preferences and can be resolved definitively only by the Supreme Court, which has never addressed it squarely.

The economic question concerns the correct analysis to be applied to
ambiguous business conduct that may simultaneously injure competition and
produce efficiencies.[91] This may appear to be less political but in reality is
not. Prominent economists can be found on both sides of many disputed
antitrust policy issues.[92] In these cases, the question becomes whether to err
on the side of regulation, on the theory that erroneously prohibiting ambiguous business practices is less dangerous than erroneously permitting them, or
vice versa. This question ultimately is political.[93]

Next, consider the institutional limitations of the courts. First, with almost a thousand federal judges, consensus is unlikely on either issue.[94] Only
the Supreme Court can impose a consistent national policy, but competition
regulation is just a small portion of the Supreme Court's workload. It cannot
address all the contested policy issues that a national competition authority
routinely resolves, nor can it issue regulations or provide informal advice.
It can only guide by issuing decisions in actual cases,[95] whose precedential
value often can be disputed by skilled counsel and judges, not to mention

subsequent Supreme Court justices. And the lower courts often get around Supreme Court cases with which they disagree.[96]

The question of fidelity to precedent presents a more fundamental flaw with competition regulation by courts. Competition law must be sufficiently flexible to adapt to new learning and new conditions. Strict fidelity to precedent, at least by the Supreme Court, would enshrine doctrines based on discredited economic premises. Yet fidelity to precedent is a fundamental premise of legitimate judicial decision making in common law jurisdictions, and Supreme Court justices have cited precedent to preserve discredited legal rules.[97] This tension between precedent and flexibility has caused the Court to exhibit multiple personalities in antitrust, sometimes a traditional Anglo-American court and sometimes an administrative agency.[98]

Even if the Supreme Court could produce clear doctrine, it is unlikely that the lower courts could apply it consistently, unless the Court forbade only naked cartels, monopolistic mergers, and obvious predation. American courts cannot administer any more ambitious policy consistently, especially in private treble damage actions where disputed fact issues must be left to lay jurors. Even without jurors, all but the simplest antitrust cases can tax the decision-making capabilities of an otherwise capable federal judge.[99] American judges are not career civil servants who have been trained for their jobs. They are generalists;[100] few have any business or economic background. Their primary qualification for appointment is almost always political.[101] Nearly without exception, American federal judges have been active partisans of the political party of the president who appointed them, often as officeholders.[102] Their views on controversial American political issues— abortion and criminal procedure especially—are far more important in the appointment and confirmation process than their views on business regulation.[103] Few judges come to their offices having practiced or taught antitrust law, and those who have are hard-pressed to keep up with new developments in antitrust economics.[104] And they have no staffs of lawyers and economists to assist them.

Consider just one example: the market power inquiries increasingly required in American antitrust law, not just in monopolization and merger cases. As the authors of one of the leading antitrust texts state, "[i]n theory and practice, relevant market definition is as difficult an undertaking as any in antitrust."[105] Assessing the defendants' power once the market is defined is no easier. Market power is a matter of degree, not kind; almost every seller in the real world has some. The Supreme Court has never satisfactorily explained how much market power is enough to justify judicial intervention, and the results in litigation are notoriously inconsistent.[106] It is hard to fault the Court for this failing. Questions of this complexity are beyond the capacity of generalists. They are difficult enough for the experts.

Implications for Developing Countries

As this chapter has shown, American antitrust institutions are a product of the era in which they were created, a period when modern regulatory institutions were just beginning to be developed, antitrust economics was primitive, and a developed, predominantly market economy had already evolved, supported by a strong tradition of political support for free markets. This history accounts for the uniqueness of American antitrust, both its relative insignificance as a force against government restraints on competition and the radically fragmented antitrust system in which the federal judiciary creates the bulk of competition law.

While the American experience is generally instructive on the questions attending the attempt to stimulate economic development by creating a predominantly market economy, the American antitrust tradition is relevant only for the control of private restraints. As for these, the institutional lessons from the United States are largely negative: what not to do. An ambitious competition law cannot be efficiently made and implemented by generalist judges, no matter how able. Specialist courts and administrative agencies with their resources of specialist expertise, greater political accountability, rulemaking powers, and general flexibility are far superior. Generalist courts should be used only for a simple policy against obvious cartel restraints, enforced by criminal and damage sanctions, and for deferential judicial review of competition agencies.

To be more specific, the American experience with competition law and policy provides four lessons for developing countries. First, the American economy developed in a political context of limited government and liberal democracy, featuring an independent judiciary at both the federal and state levels that enforced contracts, protected property rights, and otherwise upheld the rule of law. Creating such institutions should be the first priority for a developing country. Indeed, until these institutions are fairly well developed, any competition regime may do more harm than good, regardless of its design.

Second, the creation of a predominantly market economy does not preclude governmental efforts to promote economic development. In the United

States both the state and local governments played significant roles in creating the necessary transportation, communication, and educational infrastructure needed for a national, developed economy. For much of its history the United States has protected its industries and farmers from foreign competition. It can be argued that American manufacturing needed this protection, at least in the early years of its development. In any event, American tariffs did not prevent the development of a predominantly market economy.

Third, there has always been significant political opposition to government intervention in the American economy, which has limited the role of government and kept the economy primarily market based. It has also obviated the need for the American antitrust agencies to engage in serious competition advocacy. Where this type of political support for free markets is lacking, as it is in many countries, competition advocacy must be a significant part of the national competition authority's mission. But the United States experience provides little or no guidance in this area.

Fourth, generalist judges are poorly suited for either the development of competition rules or their enforcement, with the single exception of a per se prohibition of obvious cartels. Private parties and state enforcers should be limited to prosecution of these simple, clear-cut prohibitions. For everything else, the far better system is either (1) a single national competition authority with power to both make and enforce policy, reviewed by generalist courts employing a deferential standard of review, or (2) a single expert enforcement agency that brings cases to a specialized competition court staffed by experts. If a developing country lacks the resources to create such an administrative agency or specialty court, it would be wise to limit its competition policy to a simple anti-cartel policy that can be effectively implemented by a capable and independent judiciary.

5

Competition Law in Developing Nations

The Absolutist View

George L. Priest

Much of the discussion of the introduction or application of competition law in developing nations is importantly influenced by the view that, because the economic conditions in developing nations are different from those in developed nations, the competition law regime appropriate for developing nations must be different. According to this view, competition law within developing nations must be adapted to the unique conditions developing nations face, perhaps to the unique conditions *each* developing nation faces.

This chapter seeks to sharpen the discussion of these issues by presenting what I will call an "absolutist" view: that, after a century of study and application of competition law, there is widespread agreement that there is a set of competition law principles that if appropriately implemented will maximally improve consumer welfare, enhance economic growth, and aid those with low income in any society. If this view can be supported, then there is little value in debating how different economic conditions in different countries compel differences in competition law. The competition laws of all nations should in principle be identical.

The ambition of this chapter is purposely provocative and, as will be explained, conflicts with one of the central theses of a number of the chapters in this book. I believe, however, that there is value to the provocation. Of course, economic conditions and institutional conditions (probably more important) differ across countries. These differences will affect the implementation of any competition law and cannot be discounted.

Nevertheless, I believe that there is value in presenting the absolutist view as a template against which explanations or proposals of competition law departures from the template can be more seriously considered and addressed. There is a long history of this approach in scientific study. Over a hundred years ago, Charles Lyell proposed a theory according to which changes in world geography progressed at essentially an identical pace over many thousands of years, called uniformitarianism. Darwin built on Lyell's theory to propose his theory of natural selection. Today, no one exactly believes that Lyell's theory explains all of geological or biological change— Stephen Jay Gould was the most prominent modern opponent, claiming that many geological and biological developments in world history are inconsistent with Lyell's predictions. But Darwin's and Gould's scientific demonstrations would not have been possible without Lyell's theory of uniformitarianism, which served as a template for understanding geological and biological change.

The ambition of this chapter is similar. Perhaps there are good reasons, idiosyncratic to a given culture, to depart from optimal competition law. This chapter seeks, by defining an ideal, to sharpen the focus in order to force proponents of a competition law designed for a country at a particular level of development to more carefully articulate what those reasons are.

Initially, the chapter contests the distinction between "developing" and "developed" nations. All nations are developing, in the sense that the economic output and the economic welfare of their citizens can be continuously improved. The chapter will argue that those ends can be achieved through the implementation of a rigorous competition law, as important in currently higher-income as in lower-income economies. Competition policy can be improved in any society. In the United States, we regard the Sherman Act as a high statement of principle of the values of enhanced competition. Its implementation in the United States, however, would benefit from substantial redefinition, especially with respect to state and federal market regulation.

The approach of this chapter implicates the issue of the harmonization of antitrust policy across the world. Harmonization of competition law, as well as of other areas of law, has been widely promoted on grounds of reducing transaction costs as well as on the humanitarian embrace of principles of comity, including the respect of other nations' laws, with which laws of other nations should seek compromise. The competition law absolutist view rejects these grounds for harmonization and proposes that competition law should be harmonized around the world not by compromise allegedly among separately valid approaches to competition law, but harmonized substantively because there is a single best-defined competition law to improve societal welfare. Thus, all nations of the world should adopt a similar competition law because that single policy will benefit the consumers of each nation and thus, by definition, the world in the aggregate.

Finally, the chapter will address the relationship between optimal competition law and the Washington Consensus. In recent years, the Washington Consensus—put briefly, governmental policies of privatization, low taxation, free trade, and a balanced budget—has been widely disparaged and generally abandoned by the World Bank and the International Monetary Fund as conditions for assistance to developing countries.[1] A recent article by the distinguished antitrust scholar Eleanor Fox claims that the Washington Consensus has "failed" and that the promotion of a competition policy with similar aims should not be supported.[2] This chapter rejects that view. Although a detailed analysis of the implementation of the Washington Consensus is beyond the scope of the chapter, the Washington Consensus did not fail but was overwhelmed by local political forces. Indeed, the policies recently implemented by the European Union with respect to the financial difficulties of Greece, Portugal, Italy, and other member nations are very similar to those of the Washington Consensus. Further, if the United States itself had conformed more faithfully to Washington Consensus policies, it would not be facing the extraordinary financial difficulties it does today. This chapter argues that it is important for the ideal competition policy discussed below not to be overwhelmed, as was the Washington Consensus, by similar local political forces. The proposition that competition law be designed to be responsive to the individual economic conditions of developing nations poses exactly that threat.

The Modern View: Differential Competition Law by Level of Economic Development

Most modern discussions of competition law in developing nations presume that such policies must be defined to take into account the differing economic positions of each developing nation. As an example, a recent publication of the Organisation for Economic Co-operation and Development (OECD) addressing, among other subjects, competition policy for developing nations concludes:

Modern regulatory regimes for private sector development should include competition policy regimes. . . . The design of the law should reflect the level of economic development of the country concerned, the structure of its economy and its constitution and culture. A competition law should not simply be transplanted from a developed country, or even from another developing country.[3]

An often-cited article on competition policy and development makes the identical point: "It is important for developing countries to have a competition policy which is designed to take appropriate account of their level of development and the long term objective of sustained economic growth."[4] Indeed, the editors of this book appear to hold a similar view. The Conference Program on which this book is based announces:

The starting point of the workshop is the idea that institutions and laws cannot be transferred blindly and need to be experimented and adapted to the institutional level of the country. It has three objectives:

1. to characterize rigorously the institutional development level of a country with regard to market efficiency, by using present theories of economic, political and social development;
2. to think of a model competition law system, according to specific categories of institutional development;
3. to identify what are the most important characteristics that determine what is the optimal competition law regime for a specific level of institutional development.

As a consequence, many chapters in this volume elaborate different competition law policies argued to be appropriate for the given countries addressed.

The belief that countries at different levels of economic development should implement different competition policies most commonly is simply presumed and has not been adequately explained. There have been some efforts to articulate a theory. For example, the prominent Brazilian antitrust scholar, Calixto Salamao, has argued that the implementation of competition laws must differ across developing and developed countries because of legacies of colonialism that have entrenched power elites whose control over an economy is not easily broken.[5] This is more an empirical than a theoretical point. Certainly, institutional structures deriving from colonialism that distort current markets should be dismantled. Those institutions or structures may differ across countries because of differential historical experience during or after the colonial period. But the existence of different postcolonial structures does not affect the general competition law policy of removing impediments to the operation of markets, the absolutist position.

As another example, Eleanor Fox has emphasized systemic economic differences as between developed and developing nations as justifying differential competition policies. Developing nations have different economies:

> Common and defining characteristics include scarce human and financial capital, sluggish markets, especially sluggish capital markets, high barriers to entry and expansion, pervasive state or parastatal ownership and privileged privatized business, an extensive informal economy, pervasive corruption and often a marginalized majority shut out of participation in the economic life of the community.[6]

These are important descriptive points and surely valid. But do they dictate differential competition or regulatory policies across nations? All countries suffer "scarce human and financial capital" compared to greater human and financial capital. The question is how to increase those forms of capital. "Sluggish markets," including "capital markets," "high barriers to entry," and "pervasive state or parastatal ownership and privileged privatized business" are problems for any economy that must be addressed by facilitating capital markets, removing barriers to entry, and restricting state and parastatal ownership (discussed below, a serious problem in developed nations including the United States). But, again, do these economic characteristics require differential competition policies? The details of policy implementation, country by country, may differ. But the general policies themselves seem clear.

A third argument for differential competition laws is that competition law in the abstract does not deal with distributional issues within a country and may impair redistributive goals. This point, of course, was the principal argument against implementation of the Washington Consensus, which constrained redistribution (modestly) by encouraging privatization, low levels of taxation, and balanced budgets.

Concerns over redistribution are likely to be the most serious challenge to the absolutist view of an optimal competition policy. Put conversely, most departures from an optimal policy are likely to be motivated by (though not always explicitly defended by) redistributive ambitions.

An example of this point is a passage cited by Eleanor Fox describing the effect of enhanced markets for tourism in the Caribbean, based on work of Taimoon Stewart. Stewart explains that "competition among . . . big hotel/

leisure/travel chains [leading to] exclusive contracts . . . might assure a competitive product to consumer/travelers" but "shut out local independent hotels, drivers and others."[7]

It is accurate that the optimal competition policy described in the next section does not address political efforts to *re*distribute wealth among citizens. Thus, Stewart and Fox are correct that maximizing competition may benefit "big hotel/leisure/travel chains" at the expense of "local independent hotels, drivers and others." Maximizing competition, however, even at the expense of some members of the citizenry, will increase the wealth of the country more generally. In the Caribbean example, to prohibit exclusive contracts with big hotels in order to subsidize independent hotels will reduce wealth by increasing costs and prices to "consumers/travelers," whose custom in the Caribbean represents a form of direct foreign investment.

An optimal competition policy increases the aggregate wealth of the citizenry by facilitating market exchange. But the implementation of that policy distributes wealth—better, income—according to the productive services provided by each citizen, not according to political choices of redistribution from one set of citizens to another. As will be explained, the optimal competition policy is not without effect on the distribution of resources: its implementation will enhance the position of the less well-off in the society by rewarding them for the talents and services they bring to the economy, which, for many reasons, they might not otherwise be able to exploit.

A final defense of differential competition law and policy derives from nationalism: according to this view, to impose a competition policy from abroad is as imperialistic as imposing a foreign religion. Some argue that a country should be entitled to develop its own industries and the policies necessary to facilitate them without regard to competition laws of other nations.

This argument is generally indefensible. First, there is no question of imperialist imposition. Certainly, a sovereign country may adopt any policy—competition or otherwise—that it believes aids its citizens. The question is the content of such a policy.

Second, the idea that governments can select policies that differentially aid industries, sectors, or individual firms within a country and also aid the country in the aggregate is largely a myth. Following World War II, many developing nations adopted import substitution policies to aid domestic industries and firms, which all now agree served to impoverish, rather than enrich, those nations as a whole. It is difficult to distinguish calls for a nationalist competition policy from discredited import substitution policies.

Finally, each of the arguments for differential competition policies mis-understands the normative basis of an optimal competition policy. An optimal competition policy is a set of principles for the operation of an economy, based on principles of economic science and a long history of real-world application. As a set of principles, it is comparable to basic principles and norms of democracy such as one person, one vote, fairness and equality and impartiality in governmental decision making. There is a closer connection. An optimal competition policy is designed to disperse economic power in society, just as the principle of one person, one vote is designed to disperse political power. The advocacy of these broad principles of social organization can be defended under any moral system and is not imperialism.

The Absolutist View Expounded: Optimal Competition Policy

There is a well-defined set of competition law principles that most accept will enhance competition and, as a consequence, economic welfare for the consumers of any society. These principles are economic, not social or cultural, and will apply across societies. Differences among societies in levels of competition and economic advance surely exist, but they exist because of departures from these economic principles, typically because of historical or institutional reasons that should be targeted for change in the modern world.

Optimal competition law and policy enhances societal welfare because, at base, it seeks to free up the talents and resources of the society for maximal aggregate advantage. The most basic principle of an optimal competition law and policy is to maximize market participation by limiting all constraints on the market that do not generate consumer benefit. The principle of comparative advantage establishes that any individual has the possibility of contributing efforts to aid the production of the society. The greater the opportunity available to individuals (and, by extension, to groups of individuals through firms), the greater the incentive to invest in developing talent to boost the productivity of the society. As a consequence, competition policy, by maximizing market opportunities, aids the least well-off in any society.

Policies addressing competition, of course, are only part of a set of market-enhancing policies that will lead an economy to grow to the benefit of its citizenry. Trade policies (eliminating tariffs and internal protectionism); financial policies (stabilizing the currency and freeing up financial markets); regulatory policies (limiting economic regulation to natural monopoly industries and limiting other forms of regulation to the correction of externalities); governmental policies (limiting government activities in the market by privatizing state and parastatal organizations)—all contribute to maximizing aggregate production. Basic competition policy, however, suffuses and informs each of these other policy areas, both in terms of policy implementation itself and as providing guiding principles to inform the design of related policies.[8]

The endorsement of these principles is not simply theory. There is strong empirical support informing the analysis. The absolutist approach is confirmed by the great economic advance in recent years of China and India (though economic advance in these countries would be even greater if they had adopted fully open competition policies), as well as of other previously less developed countries, such as Brazil, Chile, and Peru, which have adopted market-facilitating policies, plus the economic decline of modern countries that have rejected these economic principles, such as Venezuela, Bolivia, Ecuador, Zimbabwe, and, for a depressingly long period, Cuba.

The principles of a well-defined competition policy are as follows:

1. Prohibit price-fixing and market division among competitors, as well as any other form of cartel activity.

2. Prohibit mergers to monopoly. There are many industry-specific issues here, in particular determining optimal scale and scope under different market conditions. The principle is clear; the implementation involves judgment.

3. Prohibit exclusionary practices through contract or, more typically and harmfully, through governmental regulation.

4. Adopt policies of free entry to all industries by removing regulatory restrictions and tariffs, as well as all other forms of protectionism. Though counterintuitive, smaller developing nations are in a superior position to benefit from free entry policies since such policies allow established competitors from other nations to enter markets and reduce prices. The ambition of an optimal policy is to maximize industrial competition. Opening borders to encourage as much global competition as can be supported contributes to this end.

It is well established that these simple policies will enhance competition and improve economic welfare for a country as well as for its poorest citizens.

There may be serious institutional concerns in many countries with respect to the implementation of competition policy. In many countries, corruption or the influence of economic interests might impair effective implementation.

Note, in this respect, the experience with implementation of the Washington Consensus. These are not problems of principle—the economic principles are clear—but of determining how to effectively implement the principles. As a historical example, on the basis of economic principle, immediate privatization (shock therapy) in former socialist countries such as Russia could be predicted on economic grounds to best increase national economic wealth. Nevertheless, as we have seen, in the absence of correlative policies protecting property rights, rooting out corruption, and prohibiting market domination, the expected economic gains could not be achieved.[9]

The Implementation of an Optimal Competition Policy

As defined, the optimal competition policy is appropriate both for what are conventionally known as developed and as developing nations. Again, I do not believe that there is any helpful content to this conventional distinction. As discussed, all nations are developing, in the sense that refinements to their economies remain available; economic progress can continue in economies at any level of development. There are no limits, theoretical or empirical, to economic growth. Hopefully, if the appropriate policies are adopted, future generations will look back on economic conditions in the richest countries today, like the United States, and be amazed at what appears a relatively primitive level of economic development.

Although the United States possesses the longest historical experience with the implementation of a competition policy, dating at the federal level from enactment of the Sherman Act in 1890, with earlier state experiments, the United States is far removed from having adopted an optimal competition policy.

The principles adopted at the federal level for interpreting the U.S. antitrust laws, the Sherman and Clayton Acts, have matured; disputes remain, but at a relatively minor level. Further, in the United States at the federal level there has occurred over the past thirty years a substantial reduction in the extent of governmental economic regulation; the deregulation movement, dating from the 1980s, has generally enhanced competition in previously regulated industries. In recent years, there has been some resurgence of regulation, in particular in the context of financial industries, in response to the 2008 collapse of many property markets. These new regulatory institutions remain unproven; their adoption might well be shown eventually to have been counterproductive and to have dampened economic recovery. The dominance of the parastatal organizations Fannie Mae and Freddie Mac in guaranteeing home loans played an important role in creating the housing bubble. As in other countries, these parastatal organizations should be dismantled.

In addition, for historical and political reasons, there remains in the United States a very peculiar divide between federal and state economic regulation. Economic regulation at the state level has oddly been protected from general antitrust review. Indeed, the principal legal authority for the proposition acknowledges individual U.S. state sovereignty over economic regulation, even where it serves an openly anticompetitive end.[10] Policies of this nature are largely incomprehensible in a legal environment in which the federal—interstate—effects of all industrial activity are well recognized. These policies should be reformed.

As has been argued with respect to less developed economies, however, these historical and political anomalies in the United States are not reasons to argue for different competition law principles or particular competition law rules. The basic principles of an optimal competition law remain clear—in the U.S. case, dismantle the parastatal organizations and end state protectionism through economic "regulation," among other reforms. The means of implementation may be specific to the United States context; the principles are universal.

The adoption of the principles of an optimal competition law is even more important in the context of less developed economies. Less developed economies mean poorer economies. Any policy that will increase the income or wealth of citizens of those economies should—must—be adopted. The principles of the optimal competition policy do so.

Many efforts to justify deviations from an optimal competition policy derive from empirical examples where clear benefits can be shown to a local industry, or to an economic sector, or even to a set of local firms though some form of subsidization. As all economists know, however, gains to some through subsidization can only be supported by losses to a greater number. As a consequence, an economy with a lower level of overall wealth should be more demanding than a richer economy, not less demanding, of adoption of principles of optimal competition policy.

This is also the reason that less wealthy nations should be more aggressive, not less aggressive, in pursuing policies of free trade in order to take advantage of our increasing global competition. It is a deep and ultimately tragic irony that the countries most vigorously advocating free trade in the modern world are the richest nations, rather than the poorest, which would benefit from global competition the most. Irony is perhaps the wrong word—there are reasons that rich nations are rich. One of those reasons is that they have embraced and encouraged competition, including global competition. Indeed, the greater the embrace, the richer the countries have become.

Optimal Competition Policy Considered

It is a fair characterization of what I have described as the optimal competition policy that it is unobjectionably optimal because it has been defined at a very high level of generality. I view that to be a strength of the point. Those who advocate or defend more specific rules or regulations that depart from the general points described above should be called upon to justify the departures. The invocation of historical dependence, institutional incompatibility, or, the least defensible, "culture" should not be generally acceptable as grounds for departure.

Again, the normative goals are clear. Every society benefits as it becomes richer. Although economic growth is sometimes identified as relating solely to commercial activity or what to some appears to imply the promotion of materialistic as opposed to spiritual or philosophical values, there are strong moral grounds to defend it. Most obviously, economic growth is responsible for the most basic improvements in the quality of the lives of citizens, such as increases in life expectancy and reductions in infant mortality, among others. With the exception of peculiar examples, every moral system must endorse policies that lead to a general increase in life expectancy. Economic growth generates that increase. Experience is clear and dramatic. On a comparative basis, citizens in richer societies enjoy longer life expectancies than citizens in poorer ones. There are many sources of relative advantage across societies that enhance average life expectancy—better nutrition, better medical care, greater safety of consumer products and machines used in employment, cleaner air, and so on. Whatever the combination of these factors, *all* are made possible by an increase in economic growth and made increasingly possible by further increases in growth. These broader grounds for promoting economic growth are shared by all humanistic value systems. They transcend historical experience and differences in culture.

Adopting principles of an optimal competition policy will increase wealth similarly. As a consequence, these broad humanistic objectives can best be achieved by adopting the most rigorous competition policy possible.

6

Resource Constraints and Competition Law Enforcement

Theoretical Considerations and Observations from Selected Cross-Country Data

Vivek Ghosal

Developing economies face considerable challenges related to establishing competition law and enforcement programs and institutions. Historically, competition law enforcement was primarily confined to a select set of relatively advanced economies. In more recent years, however, there has been a remarkable spread of competition agencies and enforcement activities across the globe.

There are many economies in Asia, Africa, South America, and Eastern and Central Europe that have a history of mixed economic systems and varying periods of colonization. Relatively recently, these economies started undertaking reforms to open up their markets and integrate better with the global economy. In most of these countries, there has been little history of competition culture, a prevalence of publicly owned firms, relatively small markets, and a general lack of vibrant private enterprises and sophistication of markets. In these countries, how to structure a competition agency ("Agency") and enforcement institutions, how to determine the allocation of resources to the Agency given the government's scarce resources, and how to determine the optimal size of the Agency and the range of areas of enforcement the Agency should focus on pose a challenging set of questions.[1]

A very basic question is: Should a (developing) country have an Agency and enforcement regime? In some countries, many do not see the need for one given the pressing economic and social problems that need to be addressed first. In other countries they argue that their economies are small and open, hence there is less need for one.

The example of Singapore is illustrative, as until recently it did not have an Agency. The reason for having no agency was that Singapore believed that as a small, advanced, and open economy, this openness imposed competitive discipline. But even an economy like Singapore's needs competition enforcement. This is because while Singapore is an open economy, there can be significant competition-related problems in specific markets. These can include, for example, services markets such as real estate, various areas of banking and finance, grocery stores, pharmacies, and other local services.

More generally, every economy has markets that fall into the relatively nontradable category and hence there is a need for an Agency to oversee and discipline anticompetitive behavior of market participants. In some countries, local and regional issues could arise in, for example, agricultural and natural resources markets, depending on the nature of the economy and international trade flows. Therefore, irrespective of the specific structure of the economy, it will pay dividends in the longer run to establish and enforce competition laws, as the overall benefits of competition are myriad. While there is a tendency to focus on price as the key variable due to its link to consumer welfare, competition can provide numerous benefits such as a greater variety of goods and services; a wider spectrum of product quality offerings; fostering of technological change, innovation, and entrepreneurship; and overall growth of markets. Since a culture of competition takes time to instill, it is best to start early and have a clear direction.

The challenges faced by a relatively new Agency can be daunting. Some of the issues relate to the following:

1. The legal system may not be prepared to handle complex competition cases. While many aspects matter, the efficiency of the legal system, time lags in processing cases, and sophistication of judges and legal staff in competition-related matters are very important.[2]

2. Human capital may be lacking, both legal and economic. In an advanced jurisdiction like the United States, with over 120 years of enforcement history, development of the necessary human capital has been extensive. In the newer jurisdictions this will take many years to develop, affecting their ability to enforce competition laws.[3]

3. Effective administrative procedures and sophistication of the Agency's organizational structure vary enormously across countries. How

investigations are conducted and procedures handled, for example, determines the effectiveness and efficiency of an Agency's operations.

4. The Agency may lack competition case development and fail to use contemporary methods for investigations.

5. Civil service systems, prevalent in many countries, that rely on relatively frequent rotation rather than more stable staff and professionals may pose considerable challenges in establishing consistent enforcement.

6. Scarcity of monetary resources—funding for the Agency, experts, and additional funding as cases progress through trial—poses severe constraints on enforcement.

Against this backdrop, I examine three issues in this chapter. First, I examine whether a (developing) country should establish an Agency that covers the full range of enforcement activities (e.g., merger control, unilateral conduct enforcement, anticompetitive horizontal and vertical agreements and cartel enforcement) or should establish a restricted agenda, such as cartels. I draw on the economics of production and use concepts related to economies of *scale* and *scope* to shed light on this.

Second, independence of the Agency is a widely discussed topic and a desired feature of governmental oversight and enforcement agencies. However, I note that genuine independence from political and interest group effects is relatively difficult to attain. I draw on models of regulatory behavior under political and interest group dynamics to examine the extent to which we can realistically achieve independence. This is important, as political and interest group effects can distort optimal enforcement-related decision making.

Third, I attempt to assess the optimal size of the Agency. This has implications for allocation of scarce resources and the efficiency and effectiveness of the Agency and enforcement. I use data from a selected sample of developed and developing countries and conduct a benchmarking exercise to obtain relative rankings.

I conclude by noting the paucity of standardized data and important conceptual problems lurking behind data definitions. The lack of good data across countries limits the inferences drawn by scholarship on competition law and development about optimal competition policy in a development context. Based on this I comment on a desirable design of Agency and enforcement data and record keeping. I end with a recommendation that international organizations such as the International Competition Network (ICN), the Organisation for Economic Co-operation and Development (OECD), and the World Bank, among others, should launch initiatives to harmonize both collection of relevant data for national Agencies and the definition of variables for which data are collected. This will go a long way toward attaining consistent international standards for data and facilitating important research on cross-country comparisons, as well as within-country analysis of enforcement patterns. Apart from the obvious value to academic researchers in competition policy and law enforcement, it will also be useful for national policy makers.

Competition Agency Enforcement Areas and Efficiency of Operations

In the more advanced jurisdictions, Agencies cover all the major areas of enforcement related to merger control, unilateral conduct enforcement, and cartels. For developing economies, however, there are important monetary and nonmonetary constraints.

Given the constraints, an important question to ask is: *Should the Agency in a developing country devote its investigative and enforcement efforts to all areas or restrict its activities to a subset?* In addition to having little (and sometimes no) experience in investigations and enforcement in some of the key areas, resource constraints potentially can pose daunting barriers to how rigorous and expansive the investigative and enforcement activities can be. Here I examine how to conceptualize an Agency's structure and operations and what might be a meaningful answer to the above question, with an eye toward administrative, operational, and enforcement efficiency.

I use the analogy of a production function in economics to characterize the functioning of an Agency and highlight how to think about the tasks it needs to accomplish and the allocation of scarce inputs and resources.

To accomplish its tasks related to investigations and enforcement, the Agency is expected to use multiple "inputs" such as lawyers, economists, paralegals, interns, and administrative staff, and potentially external specialists and consultants. Let us denote the four broad categories of inputs as: x^{Legal}, x^{Econ}, x^{Admin}, and x^{Expert}, where x's are the respective quantities of the inputs.

We can think of the various tasks that need to be accomplished as the "outputs" of the Agency, which can be classified narrowly or more broadly. The outputs can be conceptualized as follows:

1. Relatively narrow measures such as actual "cases" related to mergers, abuse of dominance, and cartels. The term "cases" may encompass actual litigation matters, investigative matters that have reached an advanced (near-litigation) stage, as well as settlements. In combination, these can be thought of as the "final products" of the Agency.

2. Somewhat broader measures that would include all of those noted above, as well as various preliminary stages of "investigations" related to mergers, abuse of dominance, and cartels. For a more visible final action, such as blocking of a merger or prosecution of a cartel, the initial or preliminary investigations can consume significant resources. In addition, the broader measure can include competition *advocacy*. All of these items constitute important aspects of the Agency's operations.

Given the above characterization, it is best to think of the Agency as an entity that produces multiple services and bears a resemblance to a *multiproduct firm/organization*. For the purposes of the discussion below, I consider the "broader" output measure noted above.

To get a better perspective of the operations, think of an Agency's outputs by the category of violations: that is, anticompetitive mergers, abuse of dominance, and cartels. This is in contrast to considering the aggregate, which would be the sum of all investigations and cases for all the categories. Given that the individual categories cover different types of anticompetitive conduct, we can distinguish between different types of violations when measuring the Agency's output. Previous work vividly illustrates the widely differing time paths of merger, monopolization, and cartel court cases and investigations, and it highlights the perils of assessing competition enforcement actions as a single aggregate.[4] Thus, let us denote four important outputs of the Agency as: $q^{M\&A}$, $q^{Monopolization}$, $q^{Cartels}$, and $q^{Advocacy}$, where q's are the respective quantities of output by category of violations, and advocacy reflects the more general noninvestigative and non–litigation output.

Having defined the broad categories of *inputs* and *outputs* of the Agency, we can now think about a production function that describes the link between various inputs and outputs. My objective here is not to provide a comprehensive analysis of an Agency's production structure, but only to highlight specific issues that shed some light on the areas of operations and allocation of resources. As an example, consider merger control as the enforcement category we are interested in. The merger control production function can be written as:

$$q^{M\&A} = f(x^{Legal}, x^{Econ}, x^{Admin}, x^{Expert}),$$

where, as noted earlier, q is the relevant output (measured by the number of investigations and cases) and x's the respective inputs.

Similarly, we can write the production functions for the other outputs $q^{Monopolization}$, $q^{Cartels}$, and $q^{Advocacy}$. The right-hand side variables x^{Legal}, x^{Econ}, x^{Admin}, and x^{Expert} are the same as in the merger control production function. Of course, each output's production function will have different coefficients for each of the inputs. For example, the role of economists in an internal cartel investigation that includes forensic elements is quite limited, while economists generally have a more significant role in merger evaluation, which can require sophisticated economic analysis of markets in order to predict the competitive effects of a transaction. This would imply that the coefficient attached to x^{Econ} would likely be higher in the $q^{M\&A}$ production function as opposed to the q^{Cartel} one. Beyond this basic understanding, I omit other details here.

Economies of Scale and Scope

There are at least two important considerations when examining the production and cost structure of the Agency. First, if we examine a single category such as merger control, there are input-indivisibilities in that the Agency will need to hire a minimum quantity of inputs (legal, economic, and administrative professionals and staff) to operate. As the number of merger investigations increases, however, the inputs do not have to increase in the same proportion, as the existing legal and economic staff can handle some additional investigations without the Agency necessarily having to hire new staff. This implies that there are *economies of "scale"* in the Agency's operations.

Second, many of the inputs in merger investigations can also be used for other categories of outputs: $q^{Monopolization}$, $q^{Cartels}$, and $q^{Advocacy}$. In other words, the legal, economic, and administrative staff inputs can be *"shared"* across the production of different Agency outputs. This implies that there are likely to be *economies of "scope"* in the Agency's operations. Before examining the implications of these for an Agency, I briefly present a formal description of the above concepts.

Scale economies are defined to be present when a k-fold proportionate increase in every input quantity (the x's) yields a k'-fold increase in output (the q's), where $k' > k > 1$. For a multiproduct firm or organization, strict economies of scale exist in the production of N outputs if for any initial input-output vector $(x_1, \ldots, x_r, q_1, \ldots, q_n)$ and for $z > 1$, there is a feasible input-output vector $(zx_1, \ldots, zx_r, v_1q_1, \ldots, v_nq_n)$ where all $v_i \geq z + \sigma$, with $\sigma > 0$. In our context, this implies that a doubling of all the input quantities x^{Legal}, x^{Econ}, x^{Admin}, and x^{Expert} would lead to more than doubling of the outputs $q^{M\&A}$, $q^{Monopolization}$, $q^{Cartels}$, and $q^{Advocacy}$.

   Scope economies can be defined as follows.[5] Let there be n different outputs under consideration. While I noted four different outputs for the Agency, this can be generalized to include a wider set of outputs. Let q_s denote the vector of respective quantities: $q = (q_1, \ldots, q_n)$. The function $C(q_s, w)$ denotes the cost of producing the products, at the quantities indicated by the vector q. $C(q, w)$, therefore, is a multiproduct cost function and w is the vector of input prices; in the case of the Agency, these would be the prices at which they hire the respective inputs related to legal, economic, and other staff noted above.

   Now consider a set $T = \{T_1, \ldots, T_m\}$, with $m > 1$, to denote a nontrivial partition of the output set q_s noted above. There are economies of scope at q_s and at factor price w with respect to the output partition T if:

$$\sum_{i=1}^{m} C(q_T, w) > C(q_S, w).$$

The economies of scope are weak if the inequality is weak (rather than strict) and diseconomies of scope if the inequality is reversed.

   To interpret this in terms of an Agency's operations, the cost of only producing outputs, say, q^{Cartel} and $q^{Advocacy}$ could be greater than, equal to, or less than the cost of producing the full output vector $q^{M\&A}$, $q^{Monopolization}$, q^{Cartel} and $q^{Advocacy}$. If it is greater, it indicates existence of scope economies, implying that the Agency is better off producing the full range of outputs as opposed to a restricted set.

   To put it differently, the degree of economies of scope at q_s relative to the product set T can be measured by:

$$SC_T(q) \equiv \frac{[C(q_T) + C(q_{n-T}) - C(q)]}{C(q)}.$$

The degree of economies of scope, therefore, measures the relative increase in cost that would result from a splintering of production of q_s into production lines T and $n - T$. Such a fragmentation of the production increases, decreases, or leaves unchanged the total cost as SC_T is greater than, less than, or equal to zero, respectively.

Implications for the Competition Agency and Enforcement

Scope economies critically hinge on the presence of *sharable inputs* and an interdependent production process with allocatable inputs. An interdependent production process leads to economies of scope through local cost complementarities. For example, if the multiproduct cost function can be represented as $C(q_1, q_2)$, where q_1 *and* q_2 are two different outputs (for example, $q^{M\&A}$ *and* $q^{Monopolization}$), cost complementarity occurs if $\Delta MC_1/\Delta q_2 < 0$. This means the *marginal cost* of producing output 1 (say, $q^{Monopolization}$) actually declines as more of output 2 ($q^{M\&A}$) is produced.

Overall, the lumpiness of various inputs, the reuse of an input by more than one product, internal economies of sharing and networking, and the high cost of gathering and managing information are all determinants of local cost complementarities.

As noted earlier, the critical inputs for a Competition Agency relate to the broad categories x^{Legal}, x^{Econ}, x^{Admin}, and x^{Expert}. If we focus on any one category, say economists, there are clear synergies in training. Developing the competition-related human capital in areas such as market definition, barriers-to-entry, understanding and estimating market demand and costs, assessing technological parameters, and case development can all be costly and time-consuming. But training staff in the above areas for, say, merger evaluation also provides significant spillovers into assessment of market dominance (monopolization) related anticompetitive behavior. Identical reasoning applies for the Agency legal professionals.

The above conceptualization of an Agency's inputs and outputs reveals the likelihood of significant local cost complementarities and economies of scope. This, in turn, implies that for operational, administrative, and enforcement efficiency, an Agency should cover all aspects of operations, which include matters related to merger control, unilateral anticompetitive conduct, problematic horizontal and vertical restrictions and contracts, cartels, and advocacy. This has particular relevance for developing countries that either have a nascent Agency or are just establishing one. Splintering the Agency's output set to enforce only a restricted set of violations, say, only cartels, would imply forgoing the benefits of economies of both scale and scope.

Administrative Structure and Independence
of the Competition Agency

It is commonly argued that the Agency should be "independent." Typically this refers to the political arena and the concerns relate to the distance between optimal economic and legal decision making and political interference that may cloud judgment and outcomes. In a broader sense, independence can be linked to political as well as interest group effects. However, aside from possibly monetary policy and central banks of selected countries, it is difficult to imagine that a regulatory or market-oversight agency can be truly independent of political or interest group influences. It is therefore important to examine what this means in practical terms and the relative degree of independence.

There is an influential literature that provides insights into the functioning of government regulatory or oversight agencies by considering both political and interest group effects. Here I briefly highlight two important papers that provide useful insights and then spell out implications for the structure of the Agency.

In a classic article, Peltzman models a *vote-maximizing* regulator who faces a trade-off between producer (firms) and consumer interests.[6] While Peltzman's model applies to regulatory settings in general, there are clear parallels to our focus where the Agency head has to make decisions on whether or not to challenge competition cases and often faces a complex balancing act related to economic and legal factors. In Peltzman's framework, the group interests are captured by two variables: the commodity price p for consumers and profits π for producers (firms). Consumers prefer lower p, which increases consumer surplus, and producers prefer higher π, which increases producer surplus. The regulator's objective function is given by $M = M(p, \pi)$, with $M_p < 0$, $M_{pp} < 0$, $M_\pi > 0$, $M_{\pi\pi} < 0$, and $M_{p\pi} = 0$. $M_p < 0$ ($M_\pi > 0$) implies that as prices (profits) increase, consumers (producers) are worse (better) off and this affects the regulator negatively (positively). The negative second-order effects imply diminishing political returns to higher π or lower p. The constraint is given by the profit function $\pi = f(p, c)$, where c = production costs and $c = c(q)$ with q = output. This yields an equilibrium condition $-\left(\dfrac{M_p}{f_p}\right) = M_\pi = -\lambda$, which states that the marginal political product of a dollar of profits equals the marginal political product of a price cut that also costs a dollar of profits. This aspect of Peltzman's model implies that equilibrium will *not* result in protection for only one group (consumers or producers), and the regulator will perform a balancing act.

To provide additional clarity to political and interest group aspects of the model, consider the following. Rewrite the regulator's objective function as $M = log[\pi^\kappa (A-p)^\varphi]$ or $M = \kappa log\pi + \varphi log(A-p)$, where κ and φ are the weights attached to the relevant group's (producers and consumers) interests and A is an arbitrary constant with A > p, satisfying the optimality conditions in Peltzman's model. Elections produce change in political parties and ideologies (e.g., relatively more versus less probusiness) and these could be conceptualized by changes in κ and φ, with κ being higher under a more probusiness regime with less vigorous enforcement.

Peltzman's model reveals the important forces related to political and interest group effects that may influence the Agency's enforcement patterns. Peltzman's model, however, does not directly address the structure of the agency. For example, how is the head of the Agency appointed and what are the effects of this appointment mechanism on enforcement? Some insights into this can be obtained by examining the article by Faure-Grimaud and Martimort.[7]

Faure-Grimaud and Martimort link the institutional structure of the agency with policy implementation across political principals. To state it differently, here the political party in power may or may not have direct control over who to appoint as the head of the Agency. As an example, the head of DG (Directorate General) Competition at the European Commission (EC) is not appointed by a single political principal, but the head of the Department of Justice Antitrust Division (DOJ) is a presidential appointee. The political principal P delegates the task to regulatory agent R and one of the results relates to the extent to which R can be captured by the firms it is entrusted with regulating. The principal P_i puts weight ψ_i on the firm's utility, with $\psi_i < 1$ indicating that all principals dislike giving up rents to firms. Let P_1 be more concerned with rent extraction and less by efficiency than P_2; $\psi_1 < \psi_2$. They interpret the gap $\psi_1 - \psi_2$ as the degree of polarization. The regulatory agent R can be one of the following:

1. *Independent*, implying that R stays as P changes. In general, this politically independent regulator can span several political principals, is longer lived and has greater scope for capture by firms. Here the principal can change without significant changes in enforcement.
2. *Affiliated*, implying that R changes as P changes. The politically affiliated regulator, in contrast, is shorter lived, has less scope for

being captured by firms, and can be dismissed by the principal if
there is deviation from the desired political policy stance.

The Faure–Grimaud and Martimort framework is richer and provides more
detailed insights into the complex world of regulatory decision making. We
note a central aspect for our purposes. If an Agency has an *affiliated-regulator*
setting, we potentially expect a distinction in enforcement between more
probusiness versus more proconsumer political parties due to the direct link
between party preferences and the appointed head of the Agency.

One aspect not explicitly addressed in the above model relates to the issue
of "term limits." That is, we can have the above two settings, but with no
explicit term limits built in. We can also have two additional scenarios: (a)
independent-regulator with term limit and (b) affiliated-regulator with term
limit. While term limits do not really affect the political polarization aspect
as political principals may be able to directly affect the Agency's head position, it does limit the potential for longer-term capture by competing interest groups.

Competition Agency and Independence

Against the above backdrop, I briefly examine the institutional and administrative settings in some countries/jurisdictions. In the European Union, the
competition commissioner is appointed for a four-year term. Given the supranational and term-limits characteristics of EC's DG Competition, this is
an exceptionally different administrative setting and most likely fits the
independent-regulator setting in Faure–Grimaud and Martimort where, at
least a priori, we expect little political or interest group influence. The commissioner's own characteristics, however, may matter. For example, the tenure
of European Commissioner Mario Monti saw unusually proactive and reactive
enforcement. But this is a different issue from the affiliated- versus independent-
regulator considerations discussed in Faure–Grimaud and Martimort.

The U.S. Federal Trade Commission, with five commissioners, also has
regulatory agents who span different political principals (presidents), but the
mix of the commissioners shifts over time and with the political party in
power. This has elements of both the affiliated-regulator and independent-
regulator settings. In contrast, the assistant attorney general who heads the
DOJ Antitrust Division is an executive appointee, and here the relationship
is akin to a *principal-agent* one and fits the *affiliated-regulator* setting; in this case
we can expect marked variations across the U.S. political regimes.[8]

The above three examples provide a useful backdrop. The EC model appears ideal as, one can argue that it is likely to be relatively free of external political and interest group effects. However, this model is typically not possible to emulate due to the unique supranational nature of the Agency and the institutional structure. The two U.S. agencies offer an interesting contrast in the appointment processes and institutional setting and may serve as useful comparison points for developing countries.

Implications for the Structure of the Agency and Enforcement

In many countries, including many developing countries, the competition commissioner is part of the national civil service corps and is appointed by rotation. In this "civil service" model, who actually gets appointed to a particular agency chair or director position, and for how long, is related to a variety of factors that may include the individual's areas of specialization as well as political connections. Not uncommonly, a minister may have a direct role in a particular appointment at this high level. Typically, the duration of these appointments is not long but can vary considerably across alternative arrangements in different countries. It is also not uncommon for the Agency head to be rotated out to a different ministry or agency if he or she falls out of favor with the minister. There are many different scenarios that could lead to this, including pressure from particular business or consumer groups.

The civil service systems that exist in many (developing) countries are a bit difficult to directly relate to either the affiliated- or independent-regulator settings described in Faure-Grimaud and Martimort. The commonly observed civil service model is best treated as a mixed model containing features of both affiliated and independent regulators due to the appointment process and the variation in tenure. Without knowing exactly how a country's Agency is set up, it is difficult to identify the economic and legal biases that may creep into the decision-making process.

To embed elements of independent decision making in such systems, rather than direct ministerial oversight a preferred structure may be to have a bipartisan oversight committee to monitor the Agency. Apart from allowing for better decision making by the Agency, such a bipartisan oversight committee would be in a position to weed out biased dismissals of professional staff and rotation of the head of the Agency. Overall, this structure stands a better chance of increasing the distance between optimal economic and legal decision making and political and interest group effects.

Agency and Enforcement Statistics

The previous two sections examined specific theoretical issues related to an Agency's operations and structure. In this section I examine Agency and enforcement statistics for a selected group of developed and developing countries. Agency data related to nonmonetary and monetary resources convey important signals of a jurisdiction's commitment to competition. Enforcement statistics are vital indicators, as one can have the best-drafted laws in the books but tepid enforcement can render them inconsequential.

The countries I examine are the United Kingdom, Finland, Australia, Czech Republic, South Africa, Taiwan, Hungary, Ireland, and Poland. They represent an interesting mix with a diverse history of economic systems, colonial rule, and developmental paths, as well as current levels of economic development and sophistication of markets.

There are interesting differences across these countries. At present, all of them appear to have sound laws and institutions to pursue competition law enforcement, and some are active in reforming their laws and improving enforcement to bring them on par with international standards.[9] But there are important differences in other dimensions, which become clear when we examine the data. First, the strength of enforcement appears to vary considerably. Even among the up-and-coming competition law jurisdictions, we see significant differences between, say, Ireland and South Africa. Second, the monetary and nonmonetary resources allocated to pursue enforcement vary considerably.

Given that my sample generally consists of small to medium-sized countries, I begin by examining data on the United Kingdom to set the stage for comparison across the countries. While the United Kingdom is an advanced economy, its current competition laws and enforcement regime are relatively new and in the process of change yet again (now as the Competition and Markets Authority). Of the other alternatives for a reference point, using European Commission data would not be meaningful due to its supranational characteristic, and using U.S. data as a benchmark is probably not appropriate due to its 120-year history of competition law enforcement.

In Table 6.1 I present data from the U.K. Office of Fair Trading (OFT).[10] Before describing the data, it is useful to keep in mind that the 2008–09 data are likely to be influenced by the severe economic downturn that affected the economies from 2008 onward. Row 1 presents data on the staff devoted to competition enforcement activities. The numbers are relatively stable but fall off toward the end. Row 2 data, which presents the OFT's expenditures on competition enforcement, are relatively stable other than a spike in 2006–2007. The resources data present a mixed picture, with staff levels tapering off but budget allocation being relatively stable. Row 3 shows a significant decline in merger proposals evaluated, and this is likely attributable to the economic downturn. To take a closer look at mergers, row 4 notes mergers that raised complex issues. These are relatively stable between 2003 and 2006, increased dramatically in 2007, and remained high in 2008 before falling off in 2009. While part of this pattern may be attributable to the market boom and bust, from the details provided by the United Kingdom's submission to the OECD I was not able to get a clear picture.[11] Finally, there is a secular decline in cartel enforcement activity (row 6). Unfortunately, the OFT data do not contain information on abuse of dominance cases. Noting the caveat that I was unable to obtain data on the United Kingdom's Competition Commission (CC), the data presented for the OFT in Table 6.1 provide a useful look at their resource base and enforcement activities.

Next, I present Agency and enforcement statistics from the other countries. I encountered significant difficulties in my attempt to collect comparable Agency resources and enforcement data. As noted above, even for an advanced jurisdiction like the United Kingdom, I was unable to obtain data

Table 6.1 U.K. Office of Fair Trading data

	2003– 2004	2004– 2005	2005– 2006	2006– 2007	2007– 2008	2008– 2009
1. Staff	261	243	242	310	188	177
2. Budget (in millions)	£17.7 ($29.9)	£18.3 ($33.7)	£19.8 ($35.4)	£51.0 ($96.6)	£21.5 ($43.2)	£20.3 ($34.8)
3. Total M&As and proposals evaluated	267	257	248	131	112	96
4. M&As with complex competition issues	26	35	36	103	98	18
5. M&A complexity ratio (percent) (Row 4/Row 3)	9.7	13.6	14.5	78.6	87.5	18.7
6. Cases for possible cartel activity	46	27	23	20	12	n/a
7. Cases for abuse of dominance			- N/A -			

NOTES:
1. I compiled these data from United Kingdom's submissions to the OECD as part of their annual reports for each of the fiscal years (April to March) noted above. The data on *staff* refer to "the OFT dedicated staff to competition enforcement activities." The *budget* data are for "the OFT expenditure on competition enforcement work" and were provided in millions of UK£. I converted these data to US$ values (in parentheses) using the published official exchange rates. The budget and staff data for 2006–2007 are markedly higher than other years. The reason for this was not clear from the details provided in the OECD report. One possible explanation relates to a note in the OECD document that "the OFT embarked on a program of radical change inside our organisation"; such a restructuring may have contributed to the higher resources used and the reported numbers. Another explanation could be that OFT had relatively more mergers that raised complex competition issues (103 cases) during that period, leading to additional use of monetary and human resources. This higher percentage of mergers with complex issues is also true for 2007–2008, but the budget and staff for that year is much lower and roughly consistent with other years.
2. Statistics on abuse of dominance investigations were not available from U.K.'s (OFT) OECD report.

on abuse of dominance cases (see Table 6.1). For the other countries, the reporting of statistics by the Agencies seemed rather idiosyncratic, with several countries presenting information based on what appeared to be their internal needs. While this is acceptable from a domestic standpoint, it creates obstacles to meaningful cross-country comparisons. Even if a particular country's objective is simply to have its Agency present the number of investigations under the various provisions of the law, there is considerable value in producing statistics for the sake of comparisons and benchmarking to other jurisdictions.

Table 6.2 presents the country-specific Agency resources and enforcement data. Finland, Australia, and the United Kingdom, relatively the more broad-based, diversified, and advanced economies in the set, serve a useful purpose for the benchmarking exercise I conduct in the next section.[12]

It is clear from Table 6.2, which presents the available statistics, that several countries have missing data for the key variables. Particular problems were the abuse of dominance and cartel statistics. To be fair, some countries, for example Turkey, present data in a more complex form with significant details based on their own competition acts. But distilling those data and information and presenting them in a more standardized form for international comparisons proved challenging, and it was not clear to me whether it could be easily done.[13] There were similar problems with data from Ireland. As a check, I attempted to collect data for several other developing countries, but data constraints were quite severe, especially for the purposes of making cross-country comparisons. Hence I do not present them here.

Aside from the problem of missing or hard-to-interpret data, there were other important conceptual problems. For example, it was sometimes not clear whether some of the data related to just preliminary investigations, more advanced cases, or actual court cases. This distinction is rather important for the purposes of examining the enforcement activities within a country as well as making cross-country comparisons. When measuring staff numbers, precisely what is being counted appears a bit uncertain. For example, in some cases the Agency also had a mandate to examine consumer protection issues. While to the best of my ability I tried to obtain and report staff numbers for those engaged in competition enforcement activities, I wonder to what extent the multiple functions of the Agency result in sharing of competition staff with, say, consumer protection activities. Thus even when data are available and "seemingly" comparable, the underlying conceptual and definitional issues raise obvious concerns.

Table 6.2   Selected competition agency data

	Staff	Budget	Merger investigations	Abuse of dominance investigations	Cartel investigations
Finland	68	€5.0 mil.	56	17	6
Australia	295	AU$54 mil.	323	7	33
United Kingdom (OFT)	237	$45.6 mil.	185	n/a	26
Taiwan	217	NT$354 mil.	59	n/a	21
South Africa	98	Rand 74 mil.	397	5	13
Turkey	321	US$ 13.3 mil.	n/a	n/a	n/a
Poland	284	PLN 42.7 mil.	267	240	n/a
Hungary	116	HUF 1692 mil.	70	25	n/a
Ireland	55	€5.7 mil.	75	n/a	n/a
Czech Republic	119	€5.36 mil.	59	3	9

NOTES:

1. These data were compiled from various country-specific sources by contacting the respective competition authorities directly for information and annual reports of some of the competition authorities. The data cover the period from 2004 to 2008. Part of the reason to stop at 2008 relates to the current financial crisis, which from 2009 onward resulted in significant distortions of economic and other metrics. The numbers above denote the average number per year for the five-year period. For some countries data were missing; in these cases I calculated the average based on the years for which the data were available (for example, data for Turkey were available only for 2006–2008).

2. An important shortcoming is that the data do not seem to be available in a systematic manner for most countries and that the data definitions vary across countries. Therefore, I had to rely on multiple sources to compile the information. Without an in-depth examination, it is difficult to make a judgment on how comparable the data are across the countries due to issues related to reliability of the data as well as the definitions used.

3. The U.K. data are from the OFT only. I was unable to obtain data from the Competition Commission (CC). As noted in the description of the United Kingdom's competition institutions in the text, the OFT and CC have different functions and investigative powers.

4. Staff data: In some instances, the competition agency's functions are commingled with consumer protection and related activities. Sometimes these functions within the agency are not clearly separable as staff may be asked to do multiple tasks. Based on available information, I tried my best to separate such data, but a high degree of refinement is beyond the scope of this chapter. The United Kingdom has two agencies, OFT and CC. Without more detailed information, a basic conversion would be to double the OFT's staff number to get the U.K.-wide total. Admittedly, this is a crude conversion.

5. Budget data: The data are in millions of local currency. Due to averaging over the five-year period and complications arising from currency conversion, I have not converted the budget numbers to U.S. dollar or euro equivalents. The reader can take this next step if desired.

6. Merger investigations: There is a sharp difference between merger investigations and merger cases challenged by the competition agency. It seems difficult to believe that South Africa had more mergers investigated than the United Kingdom. Part of the differences in the reported data must be due to differences in the definitions.

7. Dominance investigations: In some cases the relevant competition agency did not disaggregate the pure abuse of dominance cases and cartel cases. This makes it difficult to compare enforcement actions by specific category. Abuse of dominance and cartel activity are fundamentally different and need to be separated.

From Table 6.2 we can see significant differences in Agency staffing and enforcement statistics related to mergers, abuse of dominance, and cartels. The staff numbers I report in the table relate to the Agencies' competition enforcement activities. The size of the Agency staff varies widely with lows of 55 and 68 for Ireland and Finland, to highs of 284 for Poland, 295 for Australia, and 321 for Turkey. Merger investigations also show large differences. Abuse of dominance investigations for Poland numbered 240 per year over the 2004–2008 period, which is a very large number and reflects my concerns above as to what these reported statistics might be measuring.

Table 6.3 Selected cross-country economic statistics

	Finland	Australia	United Kingdom	Taiwan	South Africa	Turkey	Poland	Hungary	Ireland	Czech Republic
GDP per capita (a)	42.06	37.98	40.87	16.15	5.39	8.03	9.72	12.28	53.07	14.87
GDP(b)	221	791	2,479	357	257	556	371	124	226	153
GDP growth	3.54	3.51	2.11	4.08	4.92	5.99	5.42	2.19	3.60	5.24
Population(c)	5.27	20.76	60.62	22.89	47.73	69.07	38.14	10.07	4.25	10.29
Foreign direct investment (b)	5.18 (2.34)	23.19 (2.93)	136.88 (5.52)	n/a	4.48 (1.74)	14.91 (2.68)	16.31 (4.39)	34.91 (2.81)	−7.72 (−3.41)	7.86 (5.13)
Internet users	77.72	65.61	70.87	69.53	8.15	22.94	42.83	45.54	51.33	45.64
Market cap (percent)	107.85	120.89	124.83	141.75	236.09	29.90	33.68	28.27	53.15	31.56
Market cap ($) (b)	238	956	3,095	506.05	607	166	125	35.05	120	48
Time to start business	14	2	13	23	32	6	31	30	15	28

NOTES:

1. The data are from the World Bank country statistics and are the averages over the period from 2004 to 2008. As noted in Table 6.1, part of the reason to stop at 2008 relates to the current financial crisis, which from 2009 onward resulted in significant distortions of economic and other metrics.

2. Data denoted by (a) are measured in thousands of current USD ($); data denoted by (b) are measured in billions of current USD ($); data denoted by (c) are measured in millions of current USD ($).

3. The variables are as follows: GDP per capita, current USD ($); GDP current USD ($); GDP growth (annual percent); Population (total); Foreign direct investment, net inflows, current USD ($) (the numbers in parentheses are FDI as a percentage of GDP); Internet users (per 100 people); Market capitalization of listed companies (percent of GDP); Time required to start a new business (days).

Examining "raw" Agency resources and enforcement statistics, such as those in Table 6.2, can be misleading as the size and characteristics of the countries and the sophistication of their markets are very different. To get a perspective on this, in Table 6.3 I present selected cross–country economic data. Finland's population is roughly 5 million, whereas South Africa's is 48 million. Finland has a per capita gross domestic product (GDP) of about $42,060, whereas South Africa's is only $5,400. The market capitalization of publicly listed companies varies from a low of 28 percent (of GDP) for Hungary and 30 percent for Turkey, to highs of 236 percent and 125 percent for South Africa and the United Kingdom. South Africa's market capitalization number looks too high relative to its level of economic development and is likely due to its colonial past, with large European multinationals skewing this number.

In terms of sophistication of the economies, one proxy is Internet usage. This varies from lows of 8 percent and 23 percent for South Africa and Turkey, to highs of 70 percent and 77 percent for the United Kingdom and Finland. Another measure of the vibrancy of the economy and markets relates to the flows of foreign direct investment (FDI). The United Kingdom, Poland, and the Czech Republic have relatively high flows, as measured by percentage of GDP. South Africa, in contrast, has rather low inward FDI flows. In regulatory and bureaucratic characteristics, the time to start a new business varies a lot, with highs of 31 and 32 days for Poland and South Africa, and lows of 2 and 6 days for Australia and Turkey. Overall, we see dramatic differences across the countries in their size, wealth, economic and business characteristics, and overall sophistication of markets.

These wide-ranging differences across the countries imply that we need to examine the Agency and enforcement statistics after controlling for their economic and related characteristics.

Cross-Country Benchmarking of Agencies

By examining different countries, can we make a meaningful determination about whether a particular country appears to be at the right point on its Agency resources and enforcement frontier? Or does the country need to devote more toward Agency resources and boost its enforcement activities? This exercise is an obviously important one. It is unfortunately also one that is rather challenging due to the significant data problems I noted above, as well as the considerable differences in the economic profiles and sophistication of markets across the countries.

To shed some light on such relative comparisons and obtain a benchmark, I examined Agency resources and enforcement statistics, along with country-specific economic data, to reach some conclusions. The differences in size and characteristics of the economies imply that we need to find a way to normalize and compare size-or-characteristic adjusted Agency metrics. The purpose here is not to conduct an extensive analysis but to highlight some important issues and identify shortcomings in data that limit our ability to benchmark the activities of Agencies from different countries and make cross-country comparisons.

From Table 6.2, the only Agency variable for which we have consistent data is staff. Staff data are meaningful to use for benchmarking as they indicate the country's commitment of core resources toward its Agency and enforcement efforts. For merger control, abuse of dominance, and cartel enforcement there are missing observations and/or problems interpreting the numbers due to variations in definitions across the countries. These problems unfortunately rule out using any of the enforcement data for comparisons and benchmarking.

As I noted earlier, we need to adjust staff data, since characteristics of the countries vary dramatically. A simple way to conceptualize Agency staff levels across countries is to consider the following relationship:

$$Staff_{jt} = g(Economic\ activity_{jt};\ Sophistication\ of\ markets_{jt};\ Trade\ orientation_{jt})$$

where j and t denote country and time and g represents an appropriate functional form. The relationship indicates that, ceteris paribus, a country with a higher level of economic activity may need a larger staff for the Agency to oversee a potentially larger number of mergers or more cartel activity that may occur. Similarly, a high international trade orientation may mean the presence of more multinational firms, which again calls for greater scrutiny of markets.

In this chapter I do not have a wide enough cross-section of countries to carry out formal statistical analysis. Instead, I implement an alternative strategy and normalize the staff numbers. I choose three alternative deflators:

1. *GDP* measures the level of overall economic activity in the country. A problem with GDP is that while a country can have a large GDP in absolute size (for example, due to large population), it might still be a rather less developed economy lacking advanced technological and business development and sophistication of markets.

2. *Market capitalization* is a proxy for the size and vibancy of business. Given the above issues with GDP, I use the market capitalization of the publicly listed companies.

3. *GDP per capita* can be thought of as a proxy for the sophistication of the economy in the sense that high GDP per capita signals high wages and incomes, and this generally occurs due to superior technological and business development and sophistication.

While all three measures are likely to offer useful insights, the market capitalization and the GDP per capita measures have the ability to parse out countries somewhat better than the absolute GDP number. In the absence of a large cross-section of countries, deflating the Agency staff with the above measures is a simple way to address the issues raised in the equation above and allow for comparisons across countries.

The last three columns of Table 6.4 present data that allow us to examine cross-country differences. Within each column, a higher number indicates a relatively larger staff. Using *GDP* as the deflator, Hungary, Poland, and the Czech Republic have relatively high ratios. In contrast, Finland, the United Kingdom, and Ireland have relatively low ratios, implying much lower staff relative to their GDPs. Using *market capitalization* as the deflator, we see broadly similar patterns, but there are some important changes in where the countries end up, relatively speaking. Finally, using *GDP per capita* as the deflator, we see considerable reversal of the positioning of each country.

Given the different interpretations of each of the three deflators used in Table 6.4, it is difficult to directly interpret the numbers across the three columns. To facilitate an easier interpretation, in Table 6.5 I report the *within*-category ranks for each ratio and, in the last column, report the average rank. There are some meaningful ranking reversals across the three categories. For example, Hungary is ranked number 1 on GDP and market capitalization ratios, but drops to number 5 using the GDP per capita measure. I find the reverse trend for Turkey. Focusing on the average ranking in the last column, we see that Turkey, Poland, Hungary, and the Czech Republic have high rankings, implying a larger allocation of staff-based resources relative to the indicators of economic activity and status. South Africa and Taiwan fall somewhere in the middle. The three advanced countries, Finland, Australia, and the United Kingdom, are ranked low, implying a much smaller allocation of staff-based resources relative to the indicators of economic activity and market sophistication. Ireland is a bit of an oddity as it is ranked close to

Chapter 6

Table 6.4   Relative benchmarking of competition agencies

	CA staff	GDP ($ billions)	Market cap. ($ billions)	GDP per capita ($ thousands)	Ratio 1 (Staff/ GDP)	Ratio 2 (Staff/ market cap.)	Ratio 3 (Staff/ GDP per capita)
Finland	68	221	238	42.06	0.307	0.286	1.617
Australia	295	791	956	37.98	0.373	0.308	7.767
United Kingdom (OFT)	237	2,479	3,094	40.87	0.095 (0.190)	0.076 (0.152)	5.798 (11.597)
Taiwan	217	357	506	16.15	0.607	0.428	13.436
South Africa	98	257	607	5.39	0.381	0.161	18.182
Turkey	321	556	166	8.03	0.577	1.933	39.975
Poland	284	371	125	9.72	0.765	2.272	29.218
Hungary	116	124	35	12.28	0.935	3.314	9.446
Ireland	55	226	120	53.07	0.243	0.458	1.036
Czech Republic	119	153	48	14.87	0.778	2.479	8.003

NOTES:
1. The staff numbers are from Table 6.2. GDP ($ billions), Market cap. ($ billions) of publicly listed companies, and GDP per capita ($ thousands) are from Table 6.3.
2. Ratio data: These columns present data that are the ratio of a competition agency staff to the respective deflator. Following up on note 4 in Table 6.2 (related to the U.K. structure having OFT and CC), a crude way to approximate a U.K.-wide number would be to double the reported ratio to get 0.19; I report these values in parentheses below the U.K. OFT number.

the bottom based on GDP and GDP per capitabenchmarks but is in the middle of the pack based on market capitalization.

With a broad brush and without trying to interpret each number, the less developed countries generally have a higher ranking and the more developed countries a lower ranking. The three relatively advanced economies in the sample, Finland, the United Kingdom, and Australia, all have low rankings— that is, low staffing ratios relative to the underlying economic characteristics noted in Table 6.4. South Africa and Taiwan are in the middle, with Ireland, as noted earlier, being somewhat of an oddity.

So what does all this mean? Are the more advanced countries devoting too few resources, or are the less developed countries devoting too many? The answers are potentially complex and most likely combine a mix of each country's history and institutional settings, as well as underlying theoretical issues I discussed above. I list the following four factors that may contribute to differing relative staff levels:

1. For the Eastern European countries, part of the explanation for their high rankings—that is, high staffing ratio relative to the underlying economic characteristics noted in Table 6.4—may be their former centrally planned economies with large state-owned enterprises and the need to dismantle and convert this structure to a more

Table 6.5 Benchmarking ranks

	Ratio 1: Rank (Staff/GDP)	Ratio 2: Rank (Staff/ market cap.)	Ratio 3: Rank (Staff/GDP per capita)	Average rank
Finland	8	8	9	8.33
Australia	7	7	7	7.00
United Kingdom (OFT)	10	10	8	9.33
Taiwan	4	6	4	4.66
South Africa	6	9	3	6.00
Turkey	5	4	1	3.34
Poland	3	3	2	2.67
Hungary	1	1	5	2.34
Ireland	9	5	10	8.00
Czech Republic	2	2	6	3.34

NOTES:
1. For each of the ratios reported in Table 6.4, this table notes the within-ratio rank of the countries. A high rank indicates a high staff level relative to the deflator used. For example, using GDP or market capitalization as the deflators, Hungary has the highest staff ratio, but Turkey has the highest staff ratio using GDP per capita as the deflator.
2. The last column reports the average of the three individual ranks.

market-oriented economy. Since this process of privatization, deregulation, and dismantling of the centrally planned economy required significant oversight, resources, and analysis, and the respective Agencies were part of this process, a high number of staff were necessary, which may explain their high staffing ratios.[14]

2. The degree to which bureaucracies are entrenched tends to differ, in their relative proportions, across countries. Australia, the United Kingdom, and the United States, for example, have undertaken significant reforms over the years in trimming staff and engaging in paperwork reduction, among other changes. Some of the less developed countries appear likely to have less efficient bureaucratic structures.

3. Because of the economies of scope and human capital arguments I noted earlier, it is likely that the more advanced economies, due to their deeper and more extensive legal and economic human capital and productivity of staff, are able to operate more efficiently with relatively much lower numbers of staff.

4. The more advanced economies potentially have better institutional and organizational structures and better management of professionals, tasks, and staff and are better able to reap economies of scope, which allows them to operate more efficiently with relatively lower staff levels.

In this context, it would be interesting to see how the relative staffing levels change over time for the developing countries in the sample. Based on the above arguments, if the level of efficiency, economies of scope, and bureau-cratic processes improve, the relative staffing ratios may fall for the develop-ing countries.

.   .   .

Many developing countries either have a nascent competition agency, or are considering establishing one, or are considering significant expansion of the Agency's scope and activity. There are even developed economies, such as Singapore and Hong Kong, that fall into this broad category. For such coun-tries, several important questions must be answered. Below I note some of the complex issues they need to grapple with.

First, should such a country establish an Agency that covers the full range of enforcement activities ,or should it focus on a restricted agenda, such as cartels only? In this chapter I examined the structure and functioning of an Agency and conclude that to reap administrative, operational, and enforce-ment efficiencies, it is best if designed to cover the full range of activities. The primary reason for this answer lies in the Agency being able to reap economies of scale and, more importantly, scope due to the lumpiness of various inputs, sharable inputs, internal economies of sharing and network-ing, and the potentially high cost of gathering and managing information.

Second, how do we conceptualize independence of the Agency? The fac-tors that may distort optimal legal and economic decision making relate to political and interest group effects and interference. Aside from a suprana-tional organization like DG Competition at the European Commission, it is difficult to have genuine independence from political and interest group ef-fects. I commented on various observed organizational forms of the Agency and how civil service institutional structures, which are commonly found in many countries, along with bipartisan oversight committees, can ensure at least a reasonable extent of independence.

Third, how large should the Agency be? I used a selected sample of devel-oped and developing countries and conducted a benchmarking exercise to obtain relative rankings. Based on my exploratory exercise, it appears that the less developed countries in the sample have disproportionately large staff-ing ratios relative to the size of the economies and the sophistication of their markets. I attribute this to a mix of historical, institutional, organizational, and bureaucratic aspects. Based on my illustrative evidence, I argue that these countries are probably not operating on an efficient resource-allocation frontier. Overall, my benchmarking exercise, along with considerations of economies of scale and scope, allows policy makers and competition agencies to rethink their institutional structures and move closer to optimal size and allocation of resources.

Fourth, how should the Agency maintain its resources and enforcement statistics? I analyzed selected countries and noted the paucity of available Agency data for many countries. Equally important, some of the data may "look" similar in terms of definitions or concepts, but countries often appear to have different interpretations. This poses considerable problems for cross-country comparisons and potentially also for the country's Agency to meaningfully benchmark its activities to international standards.

In principle, in terms of an Agency reporting its enforcement activities, it is important that at least certain core statistics be reported. These could include, for example,

- mergers, total number investigated;
- mergers, total number blocked;
- mergers, total number approved with conditions (e.g., divestitures);
- abuse of dominance cases, total number;
- cartels, total cases investigated; and
- cartels, total number prosecuted.

This basic list of enforcement data can be meaningfully expanded to include more detailed statistics related to, for example,

- mergers: whether the mergers blocked or remedies applied were for horizontal, vertical, or conglomerate types;
- abuse of dominance: information on specific types of behavior investigated and prosecuted; and
- cartels – the extent of fines imposed, number of individuals and firms prosecuted.

Finally, these data items should be augmented by data on the Agency's

- staff numbers, with disaggregation into legal, economic, and other support staff;
- core funding for the year; and
- expenses incurred in hiring of external experts and related professionals.

The last set of items provides a glimpse of the resources allocated and utilized.

The above data are not difficult to compile, as the Agency is already engaging in various activities and, in principle, should have these data ready to report. It is a matter of institutionalizing the process. Apart from recording these data, the definitions need to be consistent with international standards, for example, definitions used by the EC and the United States. In some of my examination of data from various countries, the definitions used seem far from transparent or consistent with international standards.

My strong recommendation is that organizations such as the ICN, OECD, and World Bank, and bilateral exchanges between the more advanced competition law jurisdictions and the developing countries, all undertake concerted efforts to harmonize agency activity and enforcement statistics in terms of the relevant variables noted above and consistent definitions across countries. This will go a long way toward facilitating comparisons and offering benchmarks on what may be some of the parameters of optimal size and enforcement based on the country's economy and its business and technological characteristics.

7

Competition and Development

What Competition Law Regime?

Abel Mateus

At international gatherings, competition authorities usually refer to the fact that now more than 100 countries have a competition law. However, have competition laws really been effectively implemented in so many countries? If not, why not? Even among developed countries and even within the Organisation for Economic Cooperation and Development (OECD), enforcement of competition law has encountered major obstacles. Moreover, only a small number of countries have endowed their competition authorities with enough resources. What role should competition law enforcement play in different policy regimes? What role should international organizations play in the larger framework of competition policy? How should the European Commission push for a spread of the *Acquis communautaire* in competition policy around its neighbor countries? These are some of the questions we will try to address.

We have identified elsewhere the set of factors that limit the effectiveness of a competition law regime from a law and economics perspective.[1] The following factors restrict the effectiveness of a competition enforcement regime: (1) vested interests that dominate economic policy making, either through legal means (party financing, lobbying, influence in the nomination of the government, senior officials, or the council of the national competition authority [NCA]) or illegal means (corruption, abuse of public service power, or cronyism); (2) inefficient public administration and regulatory systems that limit the capacity and effectiveness of public bodies, including the NCA; and (3) inefficient judicial systems that preclude the sanctioning of violations of the competition law. This chapter undertakes an empirical exploration of these factors.

What is the role of competition policy? Different instruments should be used according to the level of institutional development. For developing countries with weak institutions, priority should be given to improving business environment and setting up efficient markets. If a competition authority is set up, priority should be given to competition advocacy and to pushing the role of competition policy in external trade, privatization, and industrial policies.

What is the role of international organizations? International organizations could play a major role in supporting the independence of NCAs, advocating that governments supply NCAs with enough resources and emphasize the role of competition policy in overall economic policies. Moreover, international organizations should contribute to protecting developing countries from cartels formed by firms originating in developed countries. For example, the European Commission has had a major role in the spreading of competition law regimes among accession candidate countries and under the European Neighborhood Program but has encountered significant limitations due to the institutional weaknesses of these countries.

The following section of the chapter uses a law and economics model of competition enforcement, based on the regulation theory of Glaeser and Shleifer,[2] which argues that competition law regimes should be designed according to the level of institutional development of the country. Below a certain level of development there is little support for a competition law regime because it requires a high level of information in the implementation of the regulatory system and a high level of enforcement capacity by the judicial system. It also requires a certain balance of power among economic agents, which is usually absent. Once those prerequisites are satisfied, the model specifies at least two regimes of enforcement that are distinguished by the level of institutional capacity. The highest level of enforcement is similar to the regime found in the United States or the most advanced jurisdictions of the European Union (EU).

The third section uses a "revealed preference" approach in conjunction with a model of an efficient competition law regime to characterize empirically different regimes. It starts by characterizing the efficiency of the enforcement regimes using three types of indicators: competition authority

capabilities in terms of the competition act, personnel, and financial resources. It then uses these indicators to study the properties of their statistical
distributions. The fourth section analyzes the factors that influence competition law enforcement using statistical and econometric analysis, and the fifth
section specifies the policy implications from the theoretical and empirical
models.

A Law and Economics Model of Competition Law Enforcement

The basis of a market economy is the operation of the markets and the process of rivalry that sets markets in motion (competition). The new microeconomics of development has shown the central role of the mechanism discovered by Adam Smith regarding the link between the division of labor and
market dimension. The second strand of the recent literature is the dynamics
of firms that shows the importance of the turnover of firms, entry and exit,
and the growth and success of these firms in successive waves of technological growth. This is, to some extent, the Schumpeterian process of "creative
destruction." There are two processes operating at the micro level—the shift
of resources from less productive to more productive firms and the expansion
of the more productive firms by technological improvements. These two
mechanisms, (1) the division of labor with market expansion and (2) the dynamics of firms that lead to productivity increase, are largely driven by competition. The main link in today's industrial organization models is between
competition and dynamic efficiency, as illustrated in Spence's seminal paper.[3]

There is now important empirical evidence that competition is linked to
growth in *developed countries*. Disney and his coauthors[4] conclude that competition increases productivity levels and the rate of growth of productivity.
Recently, Bloom and van Reenen[5] show that good management practices
are strongly associated with productivity, and those practices are better when
product market competition is higher. Finally, an efficient market for corporate control with open rules for takeovers reinforces the impact of competition on productivity.[6] Other studies by Blundell et al.[7] and Aghion and
Griffith[8] also confirm the above results. A study about Australia shows that
competition-enhancing reforms in the 1990s contributed to an increase in
gross domestic product (GDP).[9]

Research in developing countries also has shown the importance of the
link between competition and development. Dutz and Hayri[10] find that

competition policy has a positive impact on growth, even after taking into consideration the contribution of trade and institutional policies. Reviewing a large number of studies in the 1990s, Tybout[11] concludes that there is evidence that protection increases price–cost margins and reduces efficiency at the margin, and that exporters (firms that succeed in the international market) are more efficient than nonexporters. Using a new data set for Latin America, Haltiwanger and his coauthors[12] confirm that trade liberalization and competition lead to higher levels of efficiency at the firm level and also to reallocation of resources to more productive sectors. Using data for Colombia, Eslava and her coauthors[13] show that trade and financial reforms of the 1990s were associated with productivity increases resulting from reallocation from low- to high-productivity firms. Similar evidence has been shown for Chile[14] and Brazil[15] due to trade liberalization and for India due to the elimination of the Raj licensing scheme.[16] Aghion and his coauthors[17] show evidence that increasing competition in South African manufacturing should have "large productivity effects." Aghion and Schankerman[18] even found situations where countries can find themselves in a competition trap that blocks growth. Those most vulnerable situations are when the initial level of competition is low, the initial degree of cost asymmetry among firms is low, and politicians are less driven by social welfare concerns.

The theoretical and empirical work establishes the importance of competition in the development process. However, in order to study the role of competition policy we need to build a model with endogenous policy, i.e., where the formulation of economic policy depends on the institutional characteristics of the country. But competition policy is a broad set of policies. Its domain contains the competition law and enforcement regime and the set of policies that influence market structures and the intensity of competition in the markets: external trade policy, industrial policy, privatization, procurement and licensing policies, regulation, and policies regarding entry to and exit from the market, among others.

We now focus only on the antitrust regime, i.e., the competition law and its enforcement. For each level of institutional development there is an optimal degree of differentiation in the competition rule that minimizes costs of information and transaction. But these rules also vary with the level of institutional development. Individual fines imposed by the law and actually enforced have to be higher than the per case subversion costs (legal costs, bribing, lobbying costs plus political costs). Moreover, the probability of being detected multiplied by the unit costs of subversion has to be higher than the opportunity cost to the firm that is restricting competition. Thus, if the level of capture of the government is high and the costs of subversion are rather low, it is doubtful that any competition statute would ever be enforced. In fact, antitrust can even be used for favoring interest groups and extortion.

We define three regimes based on the Glaeser and Shleifer regulatory state.[19] In Regime I there is an environment of weak law and order. Introducing competition law enforcement is difficult because it would elicit extortion at a higher social cost.[20] Due to the importance of vested interests in the economic policy, the main role of competition law is in advocacy to influence the formulation of external trade and industrial policies.

In less developed countries, there are a large number of markets that are either nonexistent or inefficient. There might be a serious lack of physical infrastructure, and the information and legal networks for market operation are lacking. Thus, informal arrangements predominate. In this case, competition policy should concentrate on building the foundations of a market economy and physical infrastructure. By reducing tariffs and quantitative restrictions, external competition penetrates into the country, eliminating inefficient industries and firms and reallocating resources toward the sectors where the country has competitive advantages. However, since a large number of these developing countries are major commodity exporters to the world market, issues of monopoly in the domestic and international markets may cause restrictions in production and affect incentives for farmers. For the nontradable sectors, naturally protected from competition, privatization policies are usually major determinants of market concentration in telecom, energy, transport, and other service sectors. Equally relevant is the influence of procurement and licensing policies for shaping market competition levels. Regulatory barriers to entering and exiting markets as well as other business policies also may condition competition by restricting entry and thus promoting monopolization.

Regime II corresponds to a lower-intermediate level of institutional development where the country already has a minimum level of democracy (see infra). In this regime, the country already has surpassed a minimum level of education, mainly at the secondary level, that reflects on the maturity and efficiency of operation of its institutions. More specifically for a competition law regime, the country needs to have an administrative and judicial system with a minimum level of efficiency. In this case the country may adopt a simplified system of law enforcement, where rules play a major role.

Once the country has climbed up the institutional development ladder to an upper middle level, it enters into the first window of Regime III where it can attempt to resolve disputes based on negligence and private litigation. As we will see below, only developed countries (in the sense used by the World Bank) should enter this regime. The country already needs to have a well-developed institutional system in terms of law and order. These attributes include administrative and judicial capabilities that reflect the independence of the regulators and courts from the influence of the executive branch and major businesses. Empirical observations suggest a two-tiered system in Regime III, with two levels of fines and requirement of information in the procedural aspects of competition law.

In the last window of Regime III, the country has strengthened institutions in such a way that the political, administrative, and judicial systems are subject to checks and balances and largely immune to capture by vested interests. In this case, the country can introduce strict liability as the rule, with private litigation functioning as the main instrument of law enforcement. High fines have a high dissuasive effect. In this regime, societies can reap all the benefits of modern competition law enforcement.

What Characterizes an Effective Competition Law Regime

As in so many fields of economics, we are going to take a "revealed preference approach" in characterizing competition law regimes by exploring statistical data to determine competition law regimes and infer what characterizes them.

The first element of a competition law regime is the introduction of the competition law itself. However, no two competition laws are exactly alike. They differ in both substantive and procedural matters. We classify competition laws according to the following criteria:

- *Coverage.* Does the law apply to all sectors of economic activity, including public enterprises and public entities, when performing commercial activities?
- *Substantive law.* Does it explicitly prohibit cartels and coordinating practices? Does it prohibit abuses of dominant position, in particular predatory practices, and maintain an open access to essential facilities? Does it control mergers that may lessen competition substantially?

- *Procedural law.* Does it safeguard the rights of defense and due process? Is the process transparent, but does it protect commercial secrets and allow the parties to access information? Is there judicial control of the NCA decisions? Does it sanction violations of the law and establish fines, and are the fines significant?

The classification is from 1 = weak competition law to 5 = strong competition law. To get the maximum points the competition law has to fulfill all the above criteria in full force.

The second element is the creation of a national competition agency. The starting point to assess a regime is simply to measure the capabilities of the agency and its resources. The legal, human, and financial capabilities of the agency are the most important. The competition law and its statutes establish the legal capabilities of the agency. The human capabilities are given by the number of professionals (economists and lawyers or sector specialists). Ideally we should also consider their qualifications in terms of academic aptitude and experience and the leadership and independence of the executive council.[21] The financial resources are given by the annual budget of the NCA. All the indicators for resources and performance, as discussed below, refer to the activities of an NCA with regard to competition enforcement. Thus, it excludes state aid, consumer protection, or any other function that the NCA may perform.

Our index of NCA capacity is given by a weighted average of professionals and financial resources divided by the population of the country in thousands. We can raise the issues of whether there are economies of scale in NCAs or there is a minimum number of professionals to become effective. We leave these questions for future research.

Thus far we have examined the institutional infrastructure of the competition law. The next step is to measure its effectiveness. The measure of effectiveness has to be taken in relation to the aims of the NCA. What are the roles of a competition authority? They usually comprise investigatory and sanctioning functions relative to the administrative enforcement of the competition law, supervisory and regulatory functions, and advocacy and advisory functions.

The most important role of an NCA is undoubtedly to investigate unlawful behavior or practices and to sanction undertakings to deter market participants from engaging in anticompetitive behavior or practices. Thus, first we should look at restrictive practice cases by collecting the number of competition cases decided by the NCAs in a given year. We should be careful not to confuse decisions with the number of cases pending or reported, or the number of complaints, which usually exceeds greatly the number of cases opened by the NCAs. However, there is a large differentiation in the importance, coverage, and complexity of cases. For computing our index of enforcement, we considered only the number of cases that had a substantial impact on the economy, judged by national impact and relevance of the industry. We consider only cases that implied some relevant sanction.

Most of the NCAs with modern statutes control mergers that have an impact on the domestic economy. We do not consider relevant to enforcement the number of mergers processed by the NCA, since it depends on thresholds and specific merger activity in the country for a given year. We considered the most relevant is the number of mergers that were either prohibited or had major remedies imposed.[22]

The law and economics movement has made it very clear that the level of deterrence of a legal regime depends on the expected losses imposed on the violator of the law. One of the variables is related to the number of cases decided by the NCA;[23] the other is the amount of fines imposed. We collected this data from the reports of the NCAs. We measure the level of enforcement of the NCA by an average of the three above indicators divided by the population (in thousands): number of restrictive practices cases, number of mergers prohibited or cases where major remedies were imposed, and the amount of the fines in millions of USD.

However, it is not enough to have a measure of the level of enforcement related to the activity of the NCA. All competition authorities are subject to judicial control. What effectively counts for undertakings is the final decision of the court. In fact, even in relatively developed countries a nonnegligible number of decisions of NCAs are annulled, or sometimes fines are substantially reduced by courts. In developing countries and with younger authorities, NCAs have many difficulties in having their decisions upheld by courts. We collected data on the proportion of decisions that have been upheld by courts, usually available in the annual reports of the NCAs. But courts, like NCAs, also make mistakes in applying the law. We measure how effective in general the judicial system is by using several indicators available in databases like the World Bank Governance Database.[24] This indicator varies from 1 = worst to 5 = best system. By averaging the NCA effectiveness and the judicial control indicator, we have a final indicator of the effectiveness of the competition law regime.

How Competition Law Regimes Have Spread
Around the World

We have studied 101 countries. The data collected for each country centers on 2006, and when data was available, our estimate is the average for three or four years. The data was collected from the annual reports of activities published on the websites of the NCAs and from OECD and United Nations Conference on Trade and Development (UNCTAD) peer reviews. In our sample there are eighty countries with a competition law, and sixty-seven countries have an active competition law regime, i.e., have instituted an NCA.

We started by studying the NCA capabilities, which measure the human and financial resources of the authorities. A country without an NCA with a minimum level of resources can hardly be considered as having a competition law enforcement regime. Figure 7.1 plots the Index of NCA capabilities against the GDP income per capita (gross national income or GNI, Atlas method, for 2005, from the World Bank databases).

As we can see from Figure 7.1, in our sample of 101 countries there are thirty-eight countries that either have no NCA or have an NCA with extremely limited resources. Of the remaining sixty-three countries, there are thirty-three countries that have NCAs with very limited resources and some of them are from highly developed countries.

According to our experience, there is a rule of thumb for the capabilities of an NCA in order for it to be fully effective. The rule is that it should have about five to seven professionals (economists and lawyers, mostly case handlers) per 1 million population.[25] For small economies there may be a minimum scale of an office of no fewer than eight to ten professionals; otherwise it would be difficult to fulfill all the functions normally given to an NCA. Obviously, the financial resources depend on the wages of public servants in the country. However, the required qualifications of the lawyers and economists of an NCA are among the highest in the country, since they are confronting the best lawyers and economists that would be hired by the most powerful firms in the country. This benchmarking would give an index of capabilities of around 1. Only twelve NCAs satisfy these more exigent criteria.

Among EU countries, and given their populations, Belgium,[26] Germany, Austria, Spain, and Slovenia were understaffed and underresourced for the period under analysis.[27] The countries with the best-endowed NCAs are

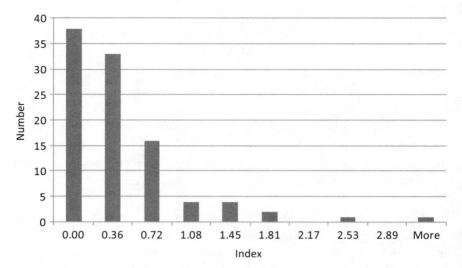

Figure 7.1 Distribution of NCAs by their capabilities
DATA SOURCE: National Competition Authorities' annual reports, OECD and UNCTAD Peer Reviews.

New Zealand, Australia, Denmark, and Norway. Only twelve countries with an NCA placed in the upper 70 percent of the range of the distribution. Thus, a major conclusion of this chapter is that governments around the world have not placed competition law enforcement among their highest priorities and have generally not endowed their NCAs with sufficient resources for effective enforcement.[28] No country with a GDP per capita below 13,570 USD has a competition authority that is well resourced.

Next we looked at the level of NCA competition enforcement. Figure 7.2 gives the histogram of the NCAs by enforcement level according to the methodology described above.

The first thirty-eight authorities were not active, as we saw above. However, there are some authorities that with rather limited resources are able to have a substantial level of enforcement. Germany, Ireland, Netherlands, Hungary, and Slovenia were the authorities with the highest level of enforcement per resource available.

Figure 7.2 plots the Competition Enforcement Index against GDP per capita.[29] The first comment is that the level of enforcement increases with the level of GDP per capita. The second is that below the GDP level of 7,800 USD, corresponding to Turkey, there are only twenty-one countries with a competition law regime out of forty-four and that the average index is 0.4.

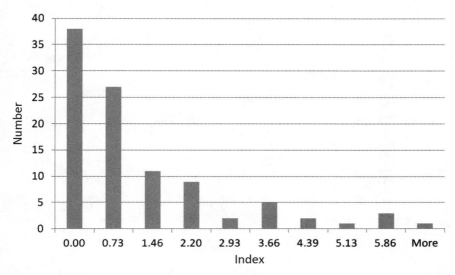

Figure 7.2 Distribution of NCAs by enforcement level
DATA SOURCE: National Competition Authorities' annual reports, OECD and UNCTAD Peer Reviews.

No country below that threshold has an index above 1.6. This seems to be our first threshold, in terms of GDP, that a country has to cross in order to have a regime of competition law. Using the terminology of the World Bank, only countries in the high end of upper middle income[30] have the capability to have a competition law regime.

On the opposite end of the scale, all the countries with an income per capita above 13,570 USD have an enforcement index above 1.6, with an average of 3.[31] This seems to be a threshold for a Type III Regime. However, as we shall see, other indicators of institutional infrastructure are also required. Notice that these are countries well above the threshold of high income used by the World Bank.[32]

The figures below show the histograms of the overall level of competition enforcement around the world (Figure 7.3) and restricted to countries that have a GDP per capita above 13,570 USD (Figure 7.4). The first shows a two-peaked distribution, excluding the zero observations, which may be due to the fact that some countries with a low level of resources dedicated to competition enforcement are able already to make an impression in terms of enforcement and countries with a higher level of resources may do a less than impressive job in terms of enforcement. By comparing distributions of NCA competition enforcement with overall competition enforcement in Figure

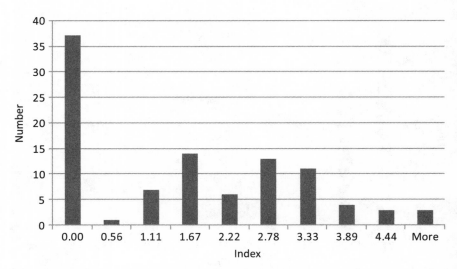

Figure 7.3 Distribution of overall competition enforcement by level of enforcement
DATA SOURCE: National Competition Authorities' annual reports, OECD and UNCTAD Peer Reviews.

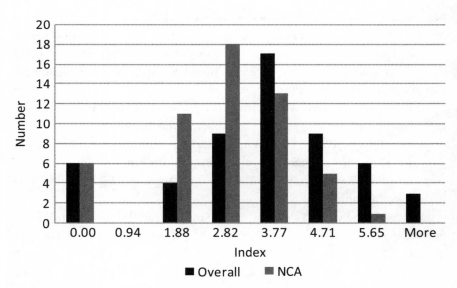

Figure 7.4 Distributions of overall and NCA enforcement levels for developed countries
DATA SOURCE: National Competition Authorities' annual reports, OECD and UNCTAD Peer Reviews.

7.4 we see that for low levels of NCA enforcement, courts in general contribute to an even lower level of enforcement. However, for high levels of NCA enforcement the opposite holds. This is related to two factors. First, in countries with weak NCAs the overall institutional environment is rather weak, including judicial control, which further undermines the work of NCAs.[33] However, in countries with a high level of institutional development, the competition regime may be strengthened by judicial control that corrects procedural and substantive mistakes of weak NCAs.

We started the econometric analysis by regressing the overall level of enforcement, for countries with a competition regime, with GDP per capita. Figure 7.5 shows the estimated values and the residuals of the regression.

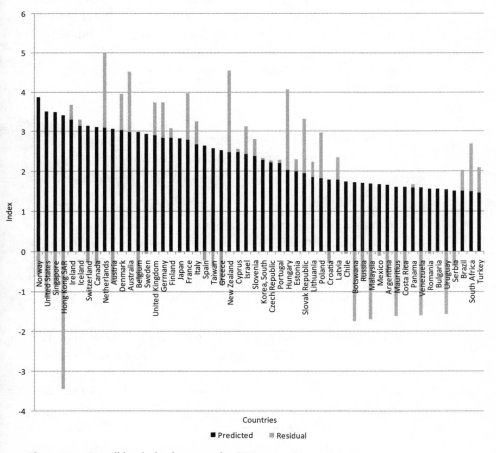

Figure 7.5   Overall level of enforcement by GDP per capita
DATA SOURCE: World Bank, Social and Economic Indicators, 2011 and author's estimates.

The highest positive residuals, meaning that countries are doing more than would be expected given their GDP per capita, are found for the Netherlands, Denmark, Australia, New Zealand, Hungary, Slovak Republic, France, and Poland. At the end of the scale of GDP per capita are three notable contributions: Brazil, South Africa, and Turkey.

The analysis so far refers only to public enforcement. In most of the countries private enforcement was rather weak at the time of our analysis. But if we include private enforcement, the United States jumps to number one by far in terms of level of enforcement.

The highest negative residuals are for Hong Kong, Botswana, Malaysia, Mauritius (where a competition regime was recently introduced), Venezuela, and Uruguay, which have no de facto competition law regime. Among the higher income levels the largest residuals are for the United States, Austria, Belgium, and Greece. As we just referred, the low level of public enforcement for the United States is complemented by private enforcement. If we distribute the enforcement levels of the European Commission by member state, considering the territories of each case, our analysis is not significantly affected.

Factors That Contribute to a Successful Competition Law Regime: An Econometric Analysis

The social infrastructure required to have a regime of competition law involves the following dimensions:

- A state and political system with, at a minimum, a functioning democratic regime[34] with a separation of powers, checks and balances among the three branches of the state, periodic general elections with political parties representing the spectrum of society, and sufficient political stability and peace.
- Public administration and a regulatory system with at least a minimum level of efficiency and nondiscretionary control and without a high level of corruption. This is required for the business environment to operate in terms of licensing, taxes, and subsidies. Bureaucratic interferences and control of business activity should be fair and in the public interest.
- The rule of law to establish the following institutions:
    i. Protection of property rights: This is required for a firm to operate in a market economy.

ii. Contractual enforcement: All transactions in the market are based on formal or informal contracts.

iii. Judicial system with an adequate level of efficiency: The system must be able to enforce (i) and (ii) with some level of predictability and in a timely manner, respecting due process.

The first dimension of the social infrastructure is a general requisite for the functioning of a society and the basic system for the economy. A stable and peaceful environment is essential for the functioning of the economy. Although a democratic regime may not be a sine qua non for development, we think that the exceptions only confirm the rule that a democracy, with the three branches of government and checks and balances among them, is the basis of a well-functioning market economy with the rule of law.

Since antitrust law enforcement is only a part, and sometimes a small part, of the economic law and is also embedded in the regulatory framework, it requires a minimum of efficiency of public administration and regulatory quality. One part of the law is usually enforced through administrative bodies and law, so it is intrinsically part of the public administration. The other major role is played by courts that control decisions of these administrative bodies and by private litigation, so the judicial system is also a major part of law enforcement.

The law and economics model we want to test is a linear combination of these factors:

$$ENF = \alpha_0 + \alpha_1 DEM + \alpha_2 CEI + \alpha_3 ADM + \alpha_4 JLEI + \varepsilon$$

where ENF refers to the level of competition enforcement, DEM is the level of democracy, CEI is the index of corporate governance that measures the legal capture index plus the illegal corruption level in the country, ADM is the level of efficiency of public administration, and $JLEI$ is the quality of the judicial system. Other variables that could be additionally tested are the level of education, EDU, since the efficiency of institutions is higher if the human resources have a higher level of education, and GCR, an indicator measuring the business environment or the quality of the market economy.

We used several databases for our research. First, we used the database assembled by Kaufman and in the World Bank Governance data. Second, we used the database on institutions and policy from the Inter-American Development Bank. Third, we included the World Bank Doing Business database. Fourth, we used the data published in the Global Competitiveness Report of

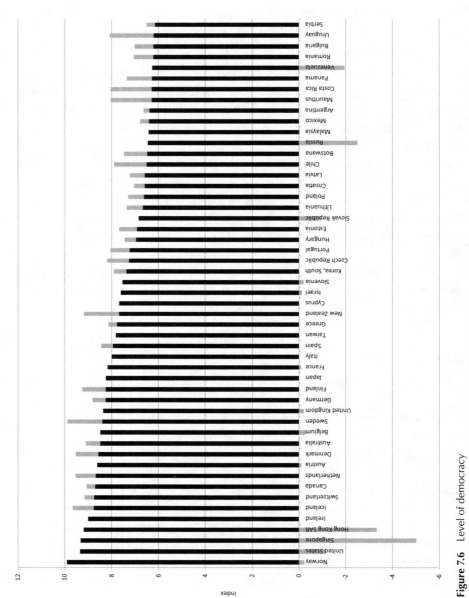

Figure 7.6 Level of democracy

DATA SOURCE: World Bank Governance Indicators, endnote 33, and author's estimates.

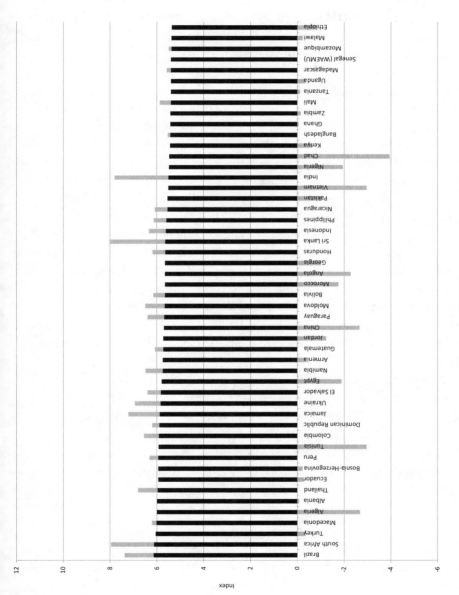

Countries

■ Predicted　■ Residual

the World Economic Report for 2010–2011. Finally, we used data from the World Bank for GDP per capita, population and level of education.

There are a number of indicators available to measure the democratic regime (Freedom House, Economist Intelligence Unit, Polity IV). We took the Economist Index of Democracy for 2008[35] because it has reasonable variance and seems more appropriate for our analysis.

Figure 7.6 plots the Democracy Index against GDP per capita. By correlating this index with the index for overall level of competition enforcement, we conclude that no country has a Democracy Index below 7.3, with the exception of Singapore and Slovakia, for a Regime III type. And Turkey, which is the borderline case for a Regime II type, has a Democracy Index of 5.7. If we take the estimated values, which are a better cut-off point since they are based on the overall estimation, we obtain the same thresholds.

We carried out the same exercise for the following variables (Table 7.1): Education level = percentage of active population with at least secondary education; Business environment = Global Competition Report Index of Competitiveness, which measures quality of infrastructure, credit availability, extent of taxation, distortion by subsidies, burden of regulation, efforts to improve competitiveness, and informal sector; Institutional level = average of several institutional variables; Corporate Governance = legal and illegal capture plus corruption index; Quality of Public Administration and Quality of Judicial System are indices collected from the Governance site of the World Bank.

In general, a country has to cross the lower 43rd percentile of the cumulative distribution of institutional and educational levels, worldwide, in order to be able to have an enforceable competition law regime (Regime II). And only when it reaches the top 20 percent class of the distribution is it ready to have a developed competition law enforcement system (Regime III).

We then proceeded to estimate the factors that contribute to successful competition law enforcement using econometric models. Because part of the

Table 7.1 Thresholds by competition regime

Variable	Regime III	Regime II
Democracy	7.3	5.7
Education level	23.9	17.9
Business environment	40.8	30.7
Institutional level	47.4	39.0
Corporate governance	41.0	33.4
Quality public administration	39.5	30.0
Quality judicial system	45.1	35.6

sample has no competition law, we have to use a censored data model of estimation, also known as a Tobit model. We tried several variables, but because of multicollinearity only a few variables explain most of the variance of the enforcement level (ENF).

Model 1 (in Table 7.2) explains the level of enforcement of the competition law regime by the Corporate Governance Indicator (CORP), Educational Level (EDU) and Level of Democracy (DEM). All variables are significant and the overall estimators of the equation have a good adherence. Model 2 is not very different from the first one, and the enforcement level is explained again by the Level of Education and Level of Democracy and the third factor is an overall Institutional Indicator (INST) that includes Corporate Governance and the quality of Public Administration (ADM) and the Level of the Judicial System.

A variable representing the efficiency of the Judicial System (JLEI) always has a negative sign. Our interpretation is that in most of the countries in our sample the judicial system acts on enforcement by reducing its impact, either by annulling decisions or by reducing fines, usually curtailing its deterrent power. We rarely see legal systems where courts increase fines or take on themselves the power of enforcing competition law. There are two reasons for this. The first is the lack of competition law and economics knowledge by judges on these matters. The second, due to either lack of competition culture or the dominance of vested interests, is that violation of economic laws is not regarded as particularly serious.[36] A variant of the model with a Censored Logistic instead of a Censored Normal improves the results very marginally. Model 3 includes ADM and JLEI separately.

Table 7.2 Models explaining the level of enforcement

	Model 1	Model 2	Model 3
Corporate governance	0.012676 (.007233)		
Education level	5.939956 (1.15617)	5.5716 (1.1219)	
Democracy	.30637 (.09578)	.2610 (.0957)	.4920 (.0957)
Institutional level		.01742 (.00677)	
Quality public administration			.0732 (.0154)
Quality judicial system			−.0394 (.0136)
Log likelihood	−120.35	−118.71	−123.76
Left censored observation	38	38	38
Uncensored observation	63	63	63

It is interesting that acceding to the EU is no longer a certification for entering into Regime III. The accession of Romania and Bulgaria and even some of the institutionally weaker Eastern European countries has brought into the EU countries that on a substantial number of dimensions are not yet able to fully enforce a competition law regime. These countries need special support and a broader approach to institution building than just introducing the *Acquis communautaire*. Even the OECD has now expanded its membership to countries that are not yet ready for Regime III, requiring broader support for its institution building and reinforcing law and order within the context of democratic institutions.

Policy Implications

In *Regime I* there is an environment of weak law and order, and imposing a heavy legal and regulatory system would elicit a high social cost without measurable benefits.[37] Competition policy should concentrate on building a market economy. First, emphasis should be put on building institutions for law and order, since there is no easy substitute for this requirement. A crucial part of competition policy relates to external trade policies. Reduction of tariffs and in particular quantitative restrictions (QRs) can increase competition in the tradable sector by subjecting exportables and importables to a higher level of competition from international trade. Another important policy is to eliminate export and import monopolies that sometimes control the most important commodities in developing countries and extract rents from farmers. In fact, a large number of these developing countries are major commodity exporters to the world market, and issues of abusing market power, sometimes on the buying side, are important.

Regime II corresponds to a lower-intermediate level of institutional development where the country may adopt a simplified system of law enforcement. The country should enact a simple competition law and establish an independent competition authority. High-powered incentives (rule based) should be the basis of market regulation. Competition law should use simple per se rules covering the core areas of prohibiting cartels and prohibiting refusals to supply by large firms. Such regimes should establish "bright lines" for merger control. These include high levels of turnover for merger notification and prohibition of mergers above a set of simple criteria. The country should also establish a competitive system for procurement with clear rules, supervised by a national auditing court. Based on the historical experience of the United States in the Progressive Era, the following systems are important: the introduction of regulation of inputs, basic labor and social laws, safety regulations in work, buildings construction, sanitation, medicines and transportation. More important than antitrust and probably easier to implement is regulation of natural monopolies with high-powered incentives (e.g., a price cap is preferable to cost-based systems) and interoperability and access to basic infrastructure: telecommunications, electricity, gas, water, and transportation. It is also very important to introduce regulation of the financial sector to avoid systemic problems like supervision of depository institutions, insurance, and capital markets.

Once a country has crossed the upper-middle of institutional development it is ready to adopt a more sophisticated judicial system, based on negligence and private litigation. This would mean in terms of antitrust, first of all, raising the amount of the fines to an intermediate level. Second, it would entail the introduction of the "rule of reason" in a number of areas of competition law and the introduction of a merger control regime based on the principle of "lessening the competition." However, the legal regime would retain some "bright lines" like per se prohibition in extreme cases of concentration.

Finally, we arrive at the last window of *Regime III*, where the country has strengthened institutions in such a way that the political, administrative, and judicial systems are almost immune to extortion. In this case, the country can introduce strict liability as the rule, with private litigation functioning as the main instrument of law enforcement, with the possibility of high fines. In this regime, the government should reap all the benefits of modern competition law enforcement. The competition authority should be entrusted with prosecuting violations under public interest as an administrative body like the Federal Trade Commission or the Department of Justice in the United States or the Office of Fair Trading and the Competition Commission in the United Kingdom. The government should entrust the authority with sufficient investigative powers. The authority should set high fines in the law and also apply high fines in real cases. The model of law to follow is the standard antitrust law of the United States and the EU. The country is also ready to apply leniency programs to detect cartels, which would strengthen the investigatory capabilities of competition authorities.[38]

The best regime, for countries with this higher level of rule of law, is to combine an administrative and litigation system. Private enforcement is also essential to redress damages between parties, and to make antitrust more "democratic" and understood by citizens; it is also important to complement the legal system and check the inoperability of the administrative body.

· · ·

This chapter is mainly an empirical exploration of the factors that limit the effectiveness of a competition law regime, namely the level of democracy, which is an overall indicator of the institutional level; vested interests through either legal or illegal means; inefficient public administration and regulatory systems; and an inefficient judicial system.

The first conclusion is that countries around the world, including a substantial number of developed countries, have not provided enough resources for their NCAs to fulfill their basic duties (only twelve countries have met or surpassed our proposed high standards benchmark). Second, a GDP per capita above 3,500 USD[39] is in general required to have a competition law enforcement regime, and only countries with a GDP per capita above 13,500 USD have an effective competition law enforcement regime (our Regime III). Countries with a weak competition law regime are especially affected in their performance by the judicial system. Improving the judicial system, in particular in the competition area, is a priority for these countries.

We studied several institutional development indicators and the thresholds required for a Regime type II and Regime type III. The indicators used were the level of democracy, general institutional development, completion of secondary education, corporate governance, quality of public administration, and quality of the judicial system. All were highly correlated with the competition enforcement level.

Once again, only a country that has crossed the lower 43rd percentile of the cumulative distribution of institutional and educational levels, worldwide, is able to have an enforceable competition law regime (Regime II). And only when it crosses the top 20 percent class of the distribution is it ready to have a developed competition law enforcement system (Regime III).

Finally, our econometric results confirm to a large extent the theoretical model. They show that the most important factors for explaining the level of enforcement of a competition law regime are the overall level of democracy, the control of vested interests and corruption, and the overall level of education of the population.

8

Prioritizing Cartel Enforcement in Developing World Competition Agencies

D. Daniel Sokol and Andreas Stephan

Competition scholars, courts, and policy makers recognize hardcore cartel collusive practices such as price-fixing, market sharing, and bid rigging as the most unequivocally harmful breaches of competition law. For this reason, they tend to be the main area of enforcement for developing world competition agencies. These jurisdictions typically model their anti-cartel laws on Article 101 TFEU (formerly 81 EC) and adopt a European-style system of administrative enforcement. The implementation of an effective anti-cartel regime remains uneven across the developing world. The successful enforcement of anti-cartel laws has the potential to benefit consumers within the developing economy and to improve the competitiveness of domestic markets.[1]

The purpose of this chapter is to identify how developing world competition agencies can best prioritize cartel enforcement. Each jurisdiction will face a slightly different set of issues depending on their specific level of development and their socioeconomic, legal, and institutional endowments. Nevertheless, there are four key challenges facing most economies in transition: (1) an inability to challenge international cartels, which are potentially very damaging to developing economies; (2) obstacles to effective domestic enforcement, including the successful introduction of leniency, the imposition of penalties, and the creation of competition and compliance cultures; (3) the danger of firms in typically concentrated developing world markets colluding tacitly, so as to put their activities out of reach of anti-cartel enforcement; and (4) collusion in public procurement, which may be particularly widespread. The chapter concludes with a discussion of how developing world competition agencies can best prioritize enforcement in light of these key challenges. We suggest that with limited resources and institutional challenges, no one area of emphasis is without its risks. However, in terms of priorities, we suggest a mix of domestic cartel enforcement focused on high-impact sectors (in terms of media awareness) where cartel members are not politically powerful and a similar strategy involving government procurement.

International Cartels

Although generally positive in terms of growth, trade openness may have a negative impact on developing world countries as a result of international cartels. These hinder the growth of developing countries by inflating prices and preventing domestic firms from accessing international markets. There is some empirical evidence to suggest that less developed countries are disproportionately affected by international cartels, as these tend to involve upstream products and resources that are important to developing economies. Levenstein and Suslow analyze the effects of international graphite product collusion, noting the particular adverse consequences for developing economies.[2] While there has been significant progress in the United States, Europe, and elsewhere in tackling international collusion, enforcement by developing countries continues to be limited, further compounding this problem.[3] The multinational firms involved in cartels also tend to be based in developed countries and have shareholders there. Figure 8.1 illustrates how international cartels uncovered in the last decade involved firms based in Asia, Europe, and the United States. International cartels therefore often facilitate the illegal transfer of wealth from developing economies to shareholders in the developed world.

As enforcement in a limited number of developed jurisdictions intensifies, developing countries actually may become more tempting as a target for international cartels.[4] Foreign firms know that developing countries either do not have modern cartel laws or do not have the resources to effectively enforce them. Weak or nonexistent anti-cartel enforcement by developing countries results in an international deterrence gap, as fines and damages recovered in developed economies tend to be calculated according to domestic harm only. The use of criminal sanctions against individuals involved in in-

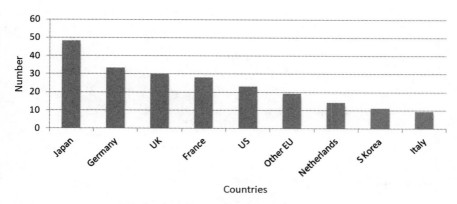

Figure 8.1   International cartel members by country of EU cartel cases
DATA SOURCE: Data taken from a sample of eighty European Union cartel decisions completed between 1974 and 2010.

ternational cartels is also very limited outside of the United States. If we assume that the decision to collude is motivated by a rational profit-maximizing strategy, global collusion's benefits outweigh its potential costs to cartel member firms despite the significant fines imposed by a handful of jurisdictions. Studies suggest these fines even fail to outweigh the illegal profits earned within those jurisdictions.[5] In any case, the United States and the European Union (EU) can never be expected to become global competition policemen, not least for reasons of comity and respect for jurisdictional sovereignty. The U.S. Supreme Court decision in *Empagran*[6] shut the door to foreign claimants seeking to use the United States as a platform for recovering damages for cartel harm caused in their home jurisdictions. International antitrust procedural issues aside as to who can be sued, we note that even damages awarded in U.S. courts are typically nowhere near treble the harm and are closer to single damages.[7] Single damages create underdeterrence, especially if we accept that many cartels are never uncovered. Export cartels, although distinct from other international cartels, create many of the same sort of enforcement problems for developing world jurisdictions.

   There is reason to be pessimistic about both developing economies' capacity to take on international cartel infringements and the relative value of such enforcement efforts.[8] One of the biggest challenges is gaining access to evidence. Institutions like the International Competition Network (ICN), the Organisation for Economic Co-operation and Development (OECD), and the United Nations Conference on Trade and Development (UNCTAD) have helped developing countries adopt anti–cartel laws, build capacity, and enter into collaborative agreements with other jurisdictions.[9] While such bilateral agreements do facilitate some information exchange, competition authorities are understandably unwilling to share evidence obtained through leniency programs. Firms are far less likely to self-report a violation if they know their dirty laundry will be hung out to dry, potentially exposing them to multiple prosecutions internationally. The use of plea bargains and other settlement mechanisms also serve to restrict the amount of information that becomes publicly available. Even if developing world agencies were able to access evidence, the valuable assets that could be seized to enforce a court order or an authority's finding of a violation of competition law would also usually lie overseas. Where the producers do have operations in the developing jurisdiction, there may not be an appetite for enforcement because of the jobs or investment brought by the firms' operations. There have been instances where foreign firms have threatened to exit a market when restrictions on their behavior have been imposed by developing world competition authorities. Focusing on international cartels also risks a populist antitrade backlash, as it highlights foreign firms exploiting developing markets after they have lowered their trade barriers. This enforcement-fueled trade backlash may create additional costs for country competitiveness and hurt consumers. It also may unleash a populist backlash against broader policies of openness to foreign direct investment. This could politicize competition law merger enforcement in developing world countries and would lead to less efficient outcomes.

The main argument against developing countries engaging in enforcement against international cartels is that this constitutes a poor use of resources. International cartels are at least punished (though not optimally) by the EU, the United States, and a handful of other jurisdictions. Moreover, the increasing use of criminal sanctions in developed countries should plug the deterrence gap. These foreign enforcement actions bring the infringement to an end, which allows the developing country to free ride on foreign enforcement. In this respect, international enforcement will represent a poor diversion of resources and secure only a small gain in terms of deterrence.[10] Having a very large number of jurisdictions actively enforcing laws against international cartels also risks undermining leniency applications. Detecting a cartel is no easy business, even given the relatively few jurisdictions a multinational firm currently has to worry about. Multiple leniency applications can be hard to coordinate, and it is notable that the firm enjoying immunity in one jurisdiction has sometimes been beaten to the prize in another. Even within the EU there is still no one-stop shopping for leniency, making it necessary for firms to file multiple leniency applications at the national level where their case may not be taken up by the European Commission.[11]

Domestic Enforcement

The limited benefits of international enforcement, in terms of added deterrence, suggest that developing world competition agencies should focus on domestic infringements of competition law that would otherwise go entirely unpunished. By purely domestic cartels, we mean cartels not just limited to domestic markets but firms that have domestic ownership rather than local subsidiaries of multinational companies. International firms that have acquired or via greenfield expansion have developed subsidiaries in developing world countries should conform to their international practices because they face compliance issues globally. Thus, they have incentives to ensure compliance at a high level globally.[12] This is not to suggest that multinationals are not active worldwide cartelists. Rather, for those multinationals that have effective compliance programs and knowledge of the illegality of cartel crimes, there may be some internal pressure to create credible compliance. This is less the case for local firms where the competition knowledge may not exist. That is, the same cannot be said of truly local cartels, which may lack international operations.

Domestic cartels are also distinct from international cartels because they occur in nontradable sectors and therefore will not be disrupted by trade liberalization. The pervasiveness and strength of domestic cartels therefore have a distinctive local flavor and are highly influenced by broader issues of business culture, social ties, levels of corruption, weak rule of law, and other factors. Levels of trust may, in particular, encourage the formation of local cartels, particularly in industries where coordination among competitors has been the norm.[13] Collectiveness and the cohesion of social groups within business may also serve to stabilize cartels and resist the incentives created by leniency, thus reducing the probability that a cartel will be detected.[14]

One limit to cartel policy is that effectiveness is predicated on a robust competition culture. This is particularly true of domestic and bid-rigging cartels, which rely exclusively on the developing country for detection. The lack of a basic understanding of competition law and of cartel violations has a number of repercussions. One is internal to firms. Without knowledge of cartels as a violation, compliance will be weak. Firm culture reflects in part the overall ethical and compliance culture of the country. A strong competition culture will create greater social constraints on such behavior, such as shaming penalties and negative publicity for companies involved in the cartels. There is an element to moral shaming for cartel activity. When competition authorities can frame cartel conduct as not merely illegal but unethical, this can impact the moral sanctions that cartel members will face and improve detection. These moral sanctions go beyond the profit-maximizing calculations made by individual decision makers. They may include being distanced by social business groups or finding reduced prospects for reemployment.[15]

To our knowledge, there are no studies on the impact of competition law and policy in developing world countries in terms of popular perception of such laws. In developed countries where there has been empirical work, it seems that the smaller the business, the less aware the business is of competition law and how to comply with it.[16] It would also appear that, while most members of the public understand that cartel practices are harmful, their negative perceptions of such behavior are still relatively weak.[17] If we assume that with older and better funded agencies there is little understanding of competition law in developed jurisdictions, we assume that the understanding in developing world countries is even lower.

Media coverage and the creation of a competition culture impact detection efforts. In weak competition cultures, purchasers of affected products will not be on the lookout for signs that there is cartel activity and will not be able to share this information with competition authorities in the first place. The role of the media is important as they can create legitimacy of competition law enforcement in cartels, while helping to educate and promote a competition culture.[18] This legitimating function creates increased awareness of cartels and hence leads to improved detection, as there are fewer information costs involved in detection. However, the media tend not to report on cartel cases because these are not "sexy." Also because the harm tends to be remote (where the cartel does not sell to final consumers), there are no easy visual aids to promote awareness. While there may be many good cases to bring, they might not increase the visibility of competition law in the country if the cartels do not involve basic consumer goods. An effective domestic cartel program requires case selection that takes newsworthiness into account. By ensuring the media are engaged in effectively communicating enforcement to the wider business community and public, the agency helps to create a robust competition culture. A cartel of supermarkets (Bulgaria), bread (South Africa, Panama), cooking oil (Indonesia), or toilet paper (Brazil) has a much better chance of significant media coverage than a cartel involving ball bearings or marine hoses.

Two developed world examples of cartel coverage in the media provide insight into the power that media may have to create a stigma for cartels. A postinfringement study of the construction sector by the United Kingdom's Office of Fair Trading found that more companies had heard about enforcement through media than through trade associations.[19] Many of the firms that relied on media as a source of information were not aware of codes of conduct for competition law, which had recently been adopted by their trade associations. In the Netherlands, though information about the Dutch construction cartel was already available in the market, one study found that after a television show about the Dutch construction cartel appeared, the stock price of firms mentioned in the television show fell by 10 percent.[20] One reason for this may be that investors believe that cartel offenses suggest a more general corrupt firm culture. The reputational effect on the firm of its illegality also may lead it to suffer or simply fuel concerns that the firm will be less profitable.

These press-related effects on competition culture may not be as significant in the developing world. In smaller markets there may be only rudimentary stock markets. Family-run firms may be the norm in these countries in which the ability to trade stock is limited.[21] These families also may be well connected politically.

Another method to create a better competition culture is through increased formal education.[22] This is a long-term process as it requires a change in the thinking of lawyers and businesspeople. That requires teaching competition law and economics in business and law schools. In many countries such courses are lacking. Hence, if the culture of the country is one in which cooperation on pricing is a norm, it will be difficult without the media and educational strategy to change this behavior. Formal education on the harms and illegality of cartels helps to build a competition culture more broadly within business and legal cultures.

A weak competition culture may undermine the success of a leniency program. Under leniency (either immunity or some form of discount for voluntarily reporting involvement in cartel activity), a firm will receive a reduced penalty if it self-reports cartel behavior to a competition authority and provides evidence necessary to prosecute the cartel. Leniency has the effect of increasing the likelihood of cartel detection, reducing cartel formation, and making enforcement significantly less resource intensive for the agency.[23] Because most cartels detected in the United States and Europe are found through leniency applications, leniency constitutes the central cartel enforcement tool. Without leniency, many cartels would never come to light. Moreover, in some systems leniency may be the only way to gather hard evidence, as some courts may view claims of tacit collusion with what the antitrust literature refers to as "plus" factors as ones that do not meet requirements under the penal code for the finding of guilt.

Leniency may be more difficult to implement in developing world settings. Many developing countries may have leniency programs on the books, but these often do not get implemented in practice. There may be cultural explanations for this. Social life may be based on familial relations and trust within social groups. Also, the need to underpin contractual relations with social ties may have developed over many years as a response to weak contract law or through an inherent distrust of public institutions.[24] Such factors conspire to make the act of "snitching," "ratting," or "dobbing" perceived as more deplorable than the illegal act itself. The building of a competition culture will help counter some of this effect, but it is also important that leniency be used consistently and effectively. It must convey the stark consequences of being beaten through the door to the immunity prize, with significant fines imposed on those who lose.

In many developing world countries, a small and tight-knit elite control large parts of the local economy.[25] In such settings, social ties are strong, and to stop colluding with family may be difficult. Strong social ties also may extend to the political arena. Many wealthy families either directly or indirectly may have significant political power. A competition agency may lose funding or an agency head if the agency enforces the competition law against a politically well-connected family firm. Thus, there may be significant public choice considerations that might lead to agency inaction against cartels in certain industries. "Independent" agencies may be less independent in case of potential funding cuts.[26] In other circumstances, the power to grant leniency can be misused to extort money or favor businesses owned by the well-connected family, or simply for the purposes of corruption.[27]

There are significant problems associated with promoting competition law compliance within firms. Some relate directly to developing economies. Cartel compliance needs to be part of the risk/reward analysis of doing business for a given local company. If the level of fines is not sufficiently deterrent (along with reputational loss or criminalization), then it is rational for firms to continue their cartel activities. In developing world jurisdictions, the penalties are often too low in practice to deter illegal firm behavior. It is rare in many countries for the judiciary to apply the maximum penalty as provided under the law.

An additional factor in developing economies is that compliance may be low because overall compliance with law is low. Recent empirical work suggests that corruption causes a lack of confidence in public institutions.[28] Not surprisingly, one might find poor cartel-related compliance where the rule of law is weak in other institutions, such as low level of tax enforcement, high incidence of bribery and corruption, and nonenforcement of contractual provisions.[29] This suggests that competition law and cartel work may need some basic political and economic development level in the country in order to succeed. Without meeting the minimum threshold for political and economic stability and growth, cartel enforcement against domestic cartels may be doomed because the population and businesses will see enforcement as the arbitrary use of power by the state. Under such a political economy backdrop, cartel enforcement may be perceived to be (regardless of truth) a payback against a particular industry for political purposes.

Other political economy factors play into compliance and cartel detection in the developing world. There is the possibility of extralegal criminal reprisals against leniency. The individual leniency applicant may be killed as a result of the leniency application. Moreover, where there are high levels of organized crime, violence may be used to enforce the cartel agreement.[30]

Compliance depends not merely on the larger political economy of a country but on the inner workings of firms as well. If we accept the premise that senior management is the management level that sets pricing, then middle level management is a group prospectively able to inform on potential illegal activity, provided they are aware of the types of activities that suggest illegality. Middle managers and employees might be able to monitor the corporation and more senior management for cartel activity. Though this sequence of events occurs in theory,[31] in practice corporate whistle-blowing occurs less often than theory would suggest. To inform presents significant risks. As Dyck, Morse, and Zingales note from a study of U.S. whistle-blowing:

> [E]mployee whistleblowers face significant costs. In 45 percent of the cases, the employee blowing the whistle does not identify him or herself individually

to avoid the penalties associated with bringing bad news to light. In 82 percent of cases with named employees, the individual alleges that they were fired, quit under duress, or had significantly altered responsibilities as a result of bringing the fraud to light. Many of them are quoted saying, "If I had to do it over again, I wouldn't."[32]

We suspect that the negative repercussions may be even larger in the developing world given country-level political, economic, and social realities. This suggests that employee incentives are not aligned with the firm in terms of compliance because employees or midlevel managers risk losing their job if they come forward with information on illegal activity.[33] This is especially the case where there is no competition culture or no stigma attached to cartel practices. Whistle-blowing is more likely to be viewed as an attempt to damage the firm and undermine those in charge, rather than "doing the right thing." The cost of informing outweighs the benefit of remaining silent. The misalignment of incentives between employees and firm replicate themselves in the cartel context. Perhaps the reason that whistle-blowing is particularly unlikely in developing countries is the stickiness of their labor markets. If one loses one's job over whistle-blowing, it may be very difficult for one to find another job because of the general weakness of the employment market. In addition, there may be only a handful of firms in each industry, which means that the whistle-blower's reputation may spread quickly across the industry, making it yet harder to find a job.

Another element of whistle-blowing is that it occurs more often in organizations where employees feel empowered by their work environment.[34] Social context matters when employees decide to blow the whistle or to participate in illegal behavior. Some people violate laws because they do not understand them rather than because they actively seek to do so. The creation of symbols for what constitutes bad behavior and giving such symbols normative cultural values affect law compliance. Institutional and organizational forces thereby constrain individual decision making.[35]

Creating an ethical compliance environment suggests that individuals have internalized the procompliance social norm.[36] An environment of compliance will not be created until there is a credible threat of enforcement and acceptance within the business community of competition rules. This means that individuals will factor the social cost of noncompliance into their risk/reward calculations of cartel participation because noncompliance will be internalized as deviant behavior. Yet business may become paralyzed if managers fear that every possible decision might subject them to discipline internally or from antitrust authorities. Even competition rules can be made clear in creating an ethical compliance environment, as compliance paralysis can ensue when enforcement is arbitrary or the law is unclear. This suggests a need for established case law and guidelines on corporate compliance in a competition law setting.

Providing rewards for information may improve cartel detection—a so-called bounty for enforcement.[37] This may overcome some of the problems inherent in leniency in a developing world context. Bounties may be the only way to create financial incentives great enough to have people inform on cartels given that the consequence of such informing may mean social shaming or potential death. A bounty would allow informants enough money to potentially leave their country and resettle elsewhere.

There are potential limitations to the introduction of a bounty for whistle-blowing on cartels. Cartel bounties have to be high in order to counter the dangers outlined above and may create high administrative costs due to overreporting by employees. Business may become paralyzed if managers fear that every possible decision might subject them to discipline internally or from antitrust authorities. However, such concerns seem unfounded, based upon the South Korean cartel bounty experience. In the short time the bounty has been offered, South Korea has shown it may be possible to change company culture in a countrywide context with increased fines and visibly large payouts. Moreover, the cost of compliance has not increased noticeably since the introduction of cartel bounties in 2002.

The Korean Fair Trade Commission (KFTC) offers a reward to informants based on a percentage of the cartel overcharge. However, the bounties did not prove successful until the maximum reward was increased from 100 million KRW (94,000 USD) to 1 billion KRW (940,000 USD) in 2005.[38] By providing such a high bounty, the KFTC wanted to convey a message that in extreme cases, even the most senior of executives could leave their job for a reward for information. To date, most rewards have not approached the upper limit. The lack of major bounties has limited the appeal of viewing the bounty as nothing more than playing the lottery (in the sense that a worker might make an excessive number of unfounded claims with the hope of retiring based on a big reward). The highest amount awarded has been 210 million KRW (approximately 198,000 USD), which the KFTC gave to informants on a sugar cartel in 2007. As rewards get larger, the payout is enough for midlevel executives to think about informing on a cartel to the KFTC.

Through 2008, there were fifteen cases in which the KFTC granted rewards to cartel informants. The amount of rewards totaled 333 million KRW (314,000 USD). In 2008 alone, the number of cases in which the KFTC granted rewards increased to six compared to a rate of one to two awards up through 2007. The significant payout from the sugar cartel seems to have caused drastic cultural change on being a cartel informant in Korea.

Many developing countries are characterized by comparatively small domestic markets in which there may be room for only a very limited number of firms. Cartels typically involve around five to seven firms, and it is less common for an infringement to involve two to three. Where there is a duopoly or oligopoly it will be easier for firms to reach a collusive outcome simply through a realization of their mutual interdependence.[39] This will be perfectly legal in the absence of a concerted practice (EU) or any plus factors (United States). After a period of heated competition, which could involve price wars, these firms may realize it is not in their interest to compete. They may do this independently by simply not undercutting each other or by failing to pass on the benefits of lower costs or greater efficiency to consumers. Alternatively, they may develop sophisticated ways of signaling an intention to increase prices, which is followed by other firms in the industry without any explicit or direct communication. The rise in the price of oil, metals, or other commodities can also be used as a collusive "focal point." Such outcomes are described as tacit collusion, conscious parallelism, coordinated effects, or parallel pricing.

Anti-cartel enforcement, in economies characterized by concentrated markets, forces firms to get smart. The exercise of monopoly power through the collective action of a cartel can be substituted by mergers and acquisitions between the colluding firms. While over 110 jurisdictions have competition laws, a smaller subset of these have merger control. Assuming a developing country enforces effective merger control alongside antitrust enforcement, firms may instead shift to tacit collusion. This poses a major problem for antitrust enforcement. Firms have the right to set prices intelligently. So long as they do this independently of their competitors (pure tacit collusion), there is no breach of anti-cartel laws. Under a European-style monopolization law (Article 102 TFEU) it may be possible to find an infringement by multiple firms on the basis that they abused their collective dominant position. However, collective dominance cases are very difficult to defend at appeal and are one of the main reasons the United Kingdom uses market investigation references.[40]

Cartels and tacit collusion are not two discrete conditions. Collusion is best understood as a sliding scale, which has explicit "hard-core" cartel agreements at one end and independent conscious parallelism at the other. While cartel laws are designed to capture behavior that falls short of hard core, it is very difficult to prosecute a case or defend a decision at appeal where the collusive conduct consists of indirect communication. These cases are particularly difficult for agencies in the developing world to win, as courts in those jurisdictions seem to prefer direct evidence.[41] The essential problem is that signaling—for example, announcing future pricing intentions—can be defended as having a legitimate economic justification. A European example of this is the *Wood Pulp* case, which involved an alleged concerted practice in the form of next-quarter price announcements. On appeal, these were found to have been justifiable, in part because they had been requested by buyers (paper producers), whose main cost was wood pulp. It would also be very difficult to justify the finding of an infringement based simply on a firm's announcements to the world. There are therefore serious constraints on what competition law can do to punish and prevent tacit collusion. A regulatory approach could be taken through controlling prices, but this would go against the movement toward liberalized markets and competition. If markets in the jurisdiction are characterized by concentrations only just outside those thought to be conducive to tacit collusion, it may be better for merger regulation to be given priority over cartel enforcement.[42] The government could also break up existing firms to introduce a new competitor or encourage new entry by foreign firms. This would in any case follow the privatization of state-owned enterprises. The problem is that many industries susceptible to collusion have high sunk costs, with a relatively high minimum efficient scale of production. If markets are small, with room for only two to three firms, it is less efficient to have more competitors.

The danger of tacit collusion does not render cartel enforcement a lost cause. Even if it is simply pushing industries from explicit to tacit collusion, firms will find it harder to successfully raise prices to monopoly levels and sustain them. The reason is that cartels have to contend with constantly changing conditions in the market and the temptation to cheat. Taking market conditions first, markets are subject to frequent cost and demand shocks that can make it hard for firms to coordinate their behavior without the reassurance of regular meetings. With regard to cheating, tacit collusion will not have the level of monitoring and threats of punishment that characterized many well-organized cartels.[43] The number of hard-core cartels that continue to be uncovered in the United States, the EU, and elsewhere suggests that direct communication is still necessary in many cases. In addition, countries without competition cultures may be characterized by habit, trust relationships, industry meetings, and social connections that all push collusive practices away from tacit collusion and closer to hard-core cartel behavior.

Bid Rigging/Procurement

Bid rigging involves collusion in public procurement. It may involve techniques such as bid suppression, complementary bidding, bid rotation, subcontracting as a compensating mechanism, and other forms of collusive activities.[44] Cartels in the area of procurement suggest both an important priority in a developing world competition agency context and an area where there can be an immediate impact. The public procurement portion of developing world budgets is approximately 20 percent.[45] Collusion may raise procurement by 20 percent to 30 percent above the competitive level.[46]

Creating an emphasis on developing world competition agency enforcement on bid rigging in procurement is not as simple as it first seems. Some procurement agencies will see the intervention of the competition agency as part of a turf battle and may not assist in coordination. This may be a serious problem, as some procurement agencies may be more powerful than the competition agency and may not want the assistance.

In many developing world countries, there is no single procurement agency. A large number of procurement agencies create coordination problems. In some cases, there are multiple procurement guidelines for central and local government. In situations in which there is no single procurement agency, it may be difficult for a competition agency to effectively reach all procurement officials to spread the message of effective mechanisms in procurement design to reduce the likelihood of collusion and to detect such collusion when it happens.

There are problems of information costs for competition agencies to focus on bid rigging. The problem is that competition agencies understand how to investigate and prosecute bid rigging in procurement while public procurement agents can best detect the bid rigging and design rules to reduce the possibility of bid rigging. In the case of Chile, competition advocacy work in bid rigging revealed significant problems of competition culture and knowledge of competition law. While most procurement officers were aware that bid rigging might be going on, they were unaware that such behavior was illegal and that such activity could result in significant penalties. In many cases, these procurement officers were not even aware that there was a competition law or an agency to enforce it.[47] Given that Chile has one of the most robust competition regimes in all of Latin America, we suspect that the problems identified in Chile are just as severe, if not more so, elsewhere.

The better the outcomes are in detecting bid rigging and creating better design of auction and tender rules, the more political capital the competition authority has for its other cartel (and noncartel) related activities. That is, the advantage of bringing procurement-related cartel cases is that it creates goodwill within the government and shows that competition law enforcement is worthwhile. This may have an impact on the very highest levels of government, where officials of ministerial rank may take notice of anticollusion efforts in procurement, given the monetary implications. Cartel-related efforts also can be linked to other forms of good governance such as anticorruption work. Indeed, in some cases bid rigging may result from corruption in the bidding process.

The Brazilian experience offers an example of how to make an effective effort toward competition in procurement. The Secretariat of Economic Law (SDE) began its efforts in 2007 in conjunction with the OECD on bid rigging in the country. The SDE also worked in conjunction with the Ministry of Planning. This collaboration was necessary to get buy-in for the competition efforts. The SDE was able to focus in an area where there was no action—where there were issues of bid rigging detection. Similarly, the SDE was able to assist in the area of data collection and analysis, given its experience in cartel matters.[48] In Brazil there is both a criminal and a civil cartel regime. The SDE created awareness among procurement officers of what bid rigging is, how to identify it, and how to contact the SDE to begin an investigation and potentially bring enforcement. SDE also created a media campaign and disseminated pamphlets to the population at large. Other efforts involved training programs for procurement agents from over forty procurement agencies. Successful programs created the invitation for the SDE to make presentations for other procurement agencies as part of a road show. Similarly, the SDE created guidelines to assist procurement agencies in anticollusion efforts. Bid rigging detection and enforcement increased as a result of these efforts.

Finding an Optimal Mix

This chapter has identified a number of challenges faced by developing world competition agencies enforcing cartel laws. These include the problem of international cartels, the difficulties associated with building a competition culture, introducing leniency, imposing penalties, and instilling a culture of compliance. Further challenges include the danger of tacit collusion and the problem of bid rigging in public procurement.

Strong institutions are a prerequisite for effective cartel enforcement. One institutional problem may be *pushback*. As cartel cases are challenged in courts and as agencies require additional powers to carry out investigations and to sanction offenders at an optimal rate, an understanding of the importance of competition by the legislature and highest levels of the executive is required. Essentially, the competition agency needs to have champions at the highest levels of government to ensure that the agency can undertake investigations into some of the most economically powerful actors in the country or large international investors. This problem will hold regardless of whether or not the cartels are international (where firms can threaten to exit a market) or domestic (where powerful families may be cartel members). A second institutional problem may be a *soft judiciary*. Judges may refuse to fine near the maximum levels permitted or, in an administrative system, may slash fines imposed by the competition agency at appeal. Slow appeals will also eat away at enforcement resources and can delay actual collection of cartel fines for a very long time. Judicial training in competition law may help address these problems, as well as a focus on cases involving direct evidence. Where institutional weaknesses still exist, resources committed to enforcement could be wasted or diverted from more important initiatives such as tackling corruption.

Once institutions are reasonably robust, any consideration of an optimal enforcement mix should begin with a country-specific inquiry that takes into account the factors outlined in this chapter. In terms of enforcement, developing countries should prioritize domestic cases over international ones. This is because of the difficulties associated with enforcing competition laws against foreign companies that do not have significant operations within the developing jurisdiction. There are also likely to be difficulties relating to trade interests, comity, and foreign investment. International cartels are detected and punished by the United States, the EU, and other developed jurisdictions, which increasingly are plugging the deterrence gap in international enforcement through criminalization and the imprisonment of individual executives responsible for cartel activities. By contrast, developing world domestic cases will go unpunished and continue to cause harm if the competition agency fails to act.

Concentrated markets make tacit collusion more likely and, although this generally lies outside the reach of competition law, it should not discourage cartel enforcement. Tacit collusion should not be as profitable or sustainable as a sophisticated explicit agreement between competitors. Nevertheless, some consideration should be given to whether it is appropriate for resources to be concentrated on cartel enforcement at the expense of other areas of competition and regulation. Competition agencies should undertake market investigations and impose structural remedies such as divestitures in order to promote competition. Where markets are very small, a more conventional regulatory regime may serve the interests of consumers better. Where merger activity is likely to act as a complement or facilitator to collusion, rather than as a substitute, it may be better to prioritize merger regulation over cartel enforcement.

Competition culture is central to the legitimacy and success of cartel laws, to normative perceptions (and therefore social constraints on such behavior), and to corporate compliance. In order to build competition culture, competition authorities must choose their cases carefully so as to maximize positive media coverage, information dissemination, and interest by ordinary members of the public. Bid-rigging cases may be a good place to start. Competition law abuses involving public procurement are more newsworthy because the harm is concentrated and affects the taxpayer. If the competition authority can create alliances with other parts of government and show that the agency is saving the government money in terms of overcharges, this will create political backing for the agency from a number of key government ministries. Competition agencies also should link the procurement emphasis within a broader country-level anticorruption campaign, as this will raise the visibility of the agency and its accomplishments. Creating political capital also holds in the case of domestic cartels and overall agency enforcement priorities. In such cases, the best way to build political capital is to identify domestic cartels in end user products where the firm owners are not politically powerful and then maximize press exposure of such cases to build political capital for the competition agency to take on cartels where powerful families own the firms.

.   .   .

Overall, building an effective competition culture and an effective developing world competition culture will take time. However, agencies should focus on the important building blocks of domestic cartels and bid rigging and on an effective media strategy and creation of a national compliance culture to combat cartels and benefit developing world consumers.

9

Contracts and Cartels

Reconciling Competition and Development Policy

Barak D. Richman

It has become conventional wisdom that an effective competition policy is a necessary ingredient of economic development.[1] A volume, such as this, that dedicates itself to examining global antitrust and competition policy in developing nations appropriately emphasizes the damage of local monopolies and cartels to regional economies, the utility of fostering competitive pricing in international markets, and the importance of prosecuting anticompetitive practices. This chapter offers a modest cautionary note against the call for greater antitrust—and specifically, anti-cartel—enforcement in the developing world. The reason is because, sometimes, cartels are needed to enforce contracts.

In the hierarchy of priorities for promoting economic development, securing contract rights is probably at the very top. No less than Nobel laureate Douglass North has advanced the strong claim that "the inability of societies to develop effective, low-cost enforcement of contracts is the most important source of both historical stagnation and contemporary underdevelopment in the Third World."[2] Yet sometimes, courts and other public instruments are unable to reliably enforce contracts. For some contractual settings, this type of "court failure" invites the emergence of private enforcement to secure transactions. Many such private ordering systems rely on mobilizing a group of affiliated merchants to direct coordinated punishments against parties who breach contracts, which in turn creates a group boycott that normally invites antitrust scrutiny. This chapter focuses on this tension between the well-understood harms of group boycotts as restraints on competition and the unappreciated benefits of group boycotts as a procompetitive solution to court failures.

This chapter first explores the literature on contract enforcement and economic development. It then highlights within this literature a species of merchant communities that self-enforce contracts by collectively punishing parties in breach of contractual obligations. The chapter then illustrates how self-enforcement mechanisms rely on cartel-like arrangements—mechanisms that effectively amount to concerted refusals to deal and coordinated group boycotts. Finally, the chapter offers its central argument: even though these enforcement mechanisms resemble instruments that traditionally inflict economic harm, they are better viewed as procompetitive collaborations because the cartels enforce contracts that state courts cannot. This leads to a rather modest policy conclusion, that there should be a general apprehension to eradicating coordinated boycotts in nations with weak contract law enforcement. Sometimes, cartel-like behavior, by enforcing value-creating contracts, promotes rather than impedes economic development.

Contract Enforcement and Development

The world has by and large listened to North's admonition. International agencies and external donors have invested heavily to promote the rule of law and law reform in many developing countries.[3] Even though North cautions that no one has convincingly demonstrated how to develop state institutions that exert the requisite coercion to enforce contracts and property rights without also risking abuse of that coercive power, development strategists have followed a formal "rule of law" recipe to promote economic development.

Michael Trebilcock and coauthors have called this prevailing strategy of pursuing legal development for economic development the "contract-formalist approach."[4] The international community has aimed primarily to develop state-sponsored, third-party contract enforcement mechanisms, along with sophisticated financial intermediaries, public administrations, and other hallmarks of a first-world government. Trebilcock observes, however, that an "alternative school of thought has emerged that downplays the need for a formal third-party mechanism for contract enforcement." He calls this

alternative school the "contract-informalist perspective" because it acknowledges that "extralegal, socially, or culturally determined norms can
and do provide the assurance of stability and predictability necessary to induce participation in private transactions."[5] In other words, this school rec-
ognizes that informal mechanisms can—especially during a nation's early
stages of economic development—serve the same roles in facilitating economic growth as conventional formal legal structures. Without diminishing
the central importance of securing property and contract rights, there appear to be informal substitutes for formal instruments of property and contract law.

Both law and society scholars and economic historians have long recognized that formal and informal mechanisms alternatively complement, crowd
out, and compete with each other in securing economic transactions. Thus
Trebilcock's recognition of alternative mechanisms has been similarly made
by an assortment of scholars. In the context of economic development,
however, Trebilcock and coauthor Kevin Davis remark that some aspects of
the informalist school are associated with a "radically skeptical" view of
whether legal reforms promote economic development.[6] Because informalists understand that social structures can usefully facilitate commercial exchange like well-functioning courts, informalists argue that "it would be
unwise for development practitioners to use the quality of a society's legal
system as a benchmark for development." In short, because informal mechanisms can thrive and relegate a nation's legal system to a marginal role in
informal capitalism, "substantial investments in legal reform are of dubious
value."[7]

Development practitioners debating the relationship between law and
development, according to Davis and Trebilcock, can thus be divided between optimists and skeptics. Optimistic formalists believe that contract
rights are advanced by building new legal institutions, and skeptical informalists believe that contract rights are secured through indigenous institutions. There is no disagreement, however, over North's identification of
contract enforcement as a foundational prerequisite for growth and prosperity. Thus, even formalists would have to concede that pockets of commerce that rely on informal contract enforcement institutions should not
be supplanted but instead should be left to prosper. In such circumstances
where commerce relies on informal institutions, all would agree that introducing laws that would unhinge those commercial institutions would be
counterproductive.

Contract Self-Enforcement and Cartels:
Peering into the Diamond Industry

The species of enforcement mechanisms articulated by informalists have been popularized most famously by recent Nobel laureate Elinor Ostrom,[8] as well as a star-studded list of institutional economists like Avinash Dixit[9] and Avner Greif,[10] development economists like Marcel Fafchamps,[11] and multi-disciplinary social scientists like Janet Landa.[12] Legal scholars long ago observed that agreements are secured through both legal and nonlegal mechanisms, often thriving "in the shadow of the law,"[13] but more recent legal scholarship has capitalized on the phenomenon of informal contract enforcement, concluding both that contract rights can be secured—even in the modern state—without any reference to formal legal entitlements[14] and that informal enforcement achieves many administrative and transaction cost efficiencies. [15]

The underlying mechanisms articulated by all of these scholars are essentially identical. Economic parties are expected to adhere to certain norms, specifically, to comply with the contractual obligations to which they voluntarily assent. Individuals that fulfill their obligations will be deemed to deserve the benefits of future transactions, but those that fail to comply with an obligation will be denied future opportunities. Thus, reputation mechanisms impose a penalty—in the form of lost future business—upon those who breach a contract that is sufficiently painful to induce forward-thinking parties to fulfill current obligations. In short, the promised benefits of maintaining a good reputation sustain commercial exchange.

Although the theory is both intuitive and relatively simple, there is a steep logistical challenge to developing institutions that can sustain reputation mechanisms. Lisa Bernstein has popularly identified one industry—the diamond industry—that relies on reputation mechanisms without invoking the coercive mechanisms of formal public courts.[16] Although the structure and mysteriousness of the diamond industry (which is explored in Bernstein's work and in some of my own[17]) might suggest its unusualness along many dimensions, its reliance on informal mechanisms is explained simply by the inability of courts—even the most sophisticated in the most developed nations—to enforce the most common and essential transaction in the industry: a sale of a diamond on credit. Because of diamonds' universal and extraordinary value and because of the ease with which diamonds can be carried undetected across jurisdictions, even sophisticated courts in developed economies cannot credibly secure a simple diamond credit sale. A merchant purportedly purchasing a diamond on credit can easily flee with the diamond to a distant and undetectable jurisdiction, leaving no secured assets for a court to reclaim. Informal mechanisms, however, are not limited by jurisdictional constraints, can rely on industry networks to invoke expertise for difficult evidentiary questions and to disseminate information, and most importantly can impose reputational harm that includes both monetary and nonmonetary sanctions. For these reasons, the diamond industry relies exclusively on informal enforcement, and the industry offers a concrete empirical window into the institutional foundations of a reputation mechanism.

The Institutional Foundations

The diamond industry's central nervous system—the mechanisms that enable the industry's use of reputations and support exchange—lies in its network of diamond bourses scattered throughout the world's diamond centers. These bourses serve as focal points for the industry, acting as ports or gateways to and from significant markets and production centers. For example, the Bharat Diamond Bourse in Mumbai, a twenty-acre, eight-tower complex adjacent to India's financial capital, is the world's largest diamond trading center. Nineteen out of every twenty stones in the world are polished in India, with Mumbai offering a passageway between the world market and India's thousands of diamond cutting factories in nearby Gujarat. Mumbai's diamond merchants serve primarily as middlemen between dealers in rough diamonds and agents of Gujarati factories, and then again between the factory agents and purchasers of polished stones. Similarly, the New York Diamond Dealers' Club (DDC), located in midtown Manhattan's diamond district on 47th Street, serves as the gateway to the American market. While India is chiefly a manufacturing center for diamonds, America is a consumer, with nearly half of the world's sixty-billion-dollar sales in diamond jewelry made in the United States. The DDC handles over 95 percent of the diamonds imported into the United States, and DDC members act primarily as middlemen between dealers of polished stones and diamond retailers who convert polished diamonds into jewelry.

Despite the diamond industry's geographical and cultural diversity, diamond bourses exhibit some important commonalities. Each bourse adheres to a minimal set of common guidelines established by the twenty-eight-member World Federation of Diamond Bourses, and they maintain many institutional linkages with each other. Moreover, since most diamonds are

bought and sold several times before they are ultimately purchased by a jewelry manufacturer, a bourse is home to a stable coterie of active traders who
transact with each other frequently. For this reason, diamond bourses are
more than mere arenas of commerce but also centers of information, where
merchants seek business partners, accumulate market information, and develop meaningful social connections. Many bourses also house restaurants,
social halls, and other areas where members congregate and socialize regularly, and because homogeneous ethnic and religious networks also play important roles in the industry, many bourses also contain prayer chapels, caf-
eterias with food that complies with assorted religious dictates, and other
services that accommodate religious practices. The integration of social,
ethnic, and commercial networks enables the rapid spread of valuable personal and industry information both within each diamond bourse and
throughout the international industry.

The Nonetheless, bourses also exhibit significant differences from each other.
New York's DDC, for example, operates with highly formal rules. It is organized as a voluntary association with extensive bylaws and mandatory rules
for its approximately 1,800 diamond merchant members. Each member must
agree to these rules for admission to the DDC, and failure to comply with
DDC rules would lead to a member's expulsion. The most important of the
DDC bylaws compels members to resolve all disputes before an arbitration
panel. Arbitrators are fellow DDC members who have earned the respect of
their peers and have abundant industry expertise. The panel abides by its
own set of procedures that limit testimony (and thus a trial's length) and enable arbitrators to ask questions and delve into fact-finding, thus empowering
arbitration panels to arrive at prompt and informed rulings. And critically,
arbitration is mandatory. Members are prohibited from bypassing DDC arbitration and bringing suit instead in New York state courts or any other system of dispute resolution.

The key to, and genius of, the arbitration panel is not its role as an alternative enforcement mechanism. To the contrary, the arbitration panel—like
public courts—cannot by itself return a diamond to a jilted seller or impose
fees or penalties on a breaching party. The true value of industry arbitration
is its role at the fountainhead of the industry's reputation mechanism. Once a
panel has reached a conclusion, it announces nothing more than its judgment, which amounts to identifying the merchant against whom the panel
issued a judgment, the date the judgment was decided, and the amount
owed. The individual found to be liable has an opportunity to pay his debt to

the merchant who brought the suit, and if he does so he remains a DDC member in good standing. However, if that individual fails to make payment immediately following the arbitration panel's decision, he is expelled as a member of the DDC. In addition, a picture of the individual in default is placed on the wall of the DDC's central trading hall with a caption that details his failure to comply with the arbitration panel's ruling. From there, the information network within DDC and its international partners is triggered. An individual's default thus becomes swiftly known to all DDC members, and news spreads rapidly throughout the global marketplace, as similar pictures and captions are placed in the world's other diamond bourses as well. This formal and informal dissemination of information supplements the transmission of news through the many informal information networks in the DDC and other bourses worldwide.

Mumbai's diamond bourse, on the other hand, rests on far less formal adjudication rules. There are no standing arbitration panels that play well-defined roles in resolving disputes. To the contrary, their dispute resolution process has been described as follows:

> AUTHOR: So what happens when merchants have a disagreement?
> MERCHANT: They resolve it. They always want to work things out.
> AUTHOR: But what happens when they can't resolve it themselves, when there was a genuine misunderstanding or disagreement that has no easy compromise solution?
> MERCHANT: Then they'll find a senior, respected person in the industry and that person will resolve it.[18]

The world's other bourses have their own distinct mechanism for resolving disputes. Israel's bourse is much like New York's: parties follow structured arbitration procedures, and elected arbitrators play major leadership roles in stabilizing trade. Antwerp's four bourses offer an interesting hybrid, where the bourses have formal bylaws and arbitration procedures, but most dispute resolution occurs informally.

Regardless of the dispute resolution mechanisms used, each bourse is organized to expeditiously identify and disseminate information regarding particular wrongdoings. Thus, both formal arbitration procedures and informal gossip ensure that news of an individual's default spreads quickly to future potential trade partners. This news substantially affects commercial opportunities. Merchants in default or otherwise expelled from a diamond bourse have tremendous difficulty obtaining further business and, conversely, maintaining a membership in good standing to a particular bourse becomes a signal to other merchants of a spotless past. Moreover, current DDC members will not transact with merchants who were expelled from the DDC, because their own reputations would be discredited by dealing with members who have failed to live up to previous commitments.

Therefore, following a formal ruling by an arbitration panel or an informal determination by an industry elder, the meaningful penalty is imposed collectively by the merchant community. Merchants who have defaulted become the object of a group boycott; thus collective and coordinated sanctions punish wrongdoing by denying future business, not by directly compelling compensation to victims of breach. Members who receive an adverse arbitration ruling can certainly compensate an opposing party without suffering additional sanctions, but those who refuse suffer foreclosure of business rather than a seizure of assets or other coercive mechanisms to obtain payment. This enforcement system is thus vulnerable to parties who leave the industry—a major concern for the industry—but is less vulnerable to gaps in enforcement that plague the state-sponsored civil and criminal justice systems, such as the failure to detect wrongdoing or the high litigation costs to initiate punishment. The information network at the foundation of the reputation mechanism responds quickly to reports of wrongdoing, imposes few costs on members who bring wrongdoing to the arbitrators' attention, and is available to the parties who are most familiar with and highly incentivized to report misconduct.

How It Works

It might be said that cheating in the diamond industry can be unusually lucrative. So much so, that even the foreclosure of all future business would be insufficient to deter a calculative thief from cheating once and remorselessly departing the diamond world. Well aware of the threat of would-be flight risks, the diamond industry employs a rich set of family and community institutions to dispense both rewards and punishments and thereby secure credible contracting.

A quality reputation is a prerequisite to obtaining business with a fellow diamond merchant. In other words, the industry rewards (only) those with good reputations, rather than waiting to punish a merchant who has earned a bad reputation. Entry is therefore largely limited to merchants who enjoy some reputational sponsorship and tacit insurance from existing industry players. The industry overcomes these enormous entry barriers by relying on family businesses, where senior merchants sponsor and support their junior relatives. Profitability becomes dependent on the quality of a family's reputation, which can be both inherited and bequeathed.

Thus, family connections create a valuable and otherwise hard-to-obtain entryway into the industry. Conversely, fulfilling contractual obligations and maintaining a good reputation not only secures a lifetime of business but also enables one to confer a good reputation, and the opportunity to secure future business, on one's heirs. Merchants are thus induced to fulfill their contractual obligations throughout their lifetimes, and the industry overcomes what game theorists typically describe as an end-game problem.

A merchant's reputation therefore has an enormous impact on his family's livelihood, where a quality reputation secures steady income for multiple generations, whereas a tarnished past forecloses an entire family's opportunities. This puts enormous pressure on the reliability of reputation information, not just its dissemination, both to ensure proper incentives to cooperate and to secure industry-wide credibility. Several forces work to ensure the veracity of industry information sources. The composition of arbitrators and adjudicators provides one guarantee of accuracy. The industry's arbitrators are experienced insiders who are extremely familiar with the nature of the industry and the difficulties involved in entering diamond contracts. Their expertise helps them understand the context within which disputes arise, distinguish meritorious from nonmeritorious claims, assess the reliability of proffered evidence, and, when appropriate, impose the proper damages. Additionally, the board may respond to misinformation and punish any party responsible for spreading inaccurate information about another's reputation. In a world where good reputations are so critical to commercial success and where gossip can be so damaging, these filters are important in discouraging the spread of information of questionable veracity.

This reliance on reputations and on the associated sanctions also means that the reach of the DDC arbitration board is limited to cooperating parties. Merchants comply with the DDC arbitration board, for example, not to avoid the brunt of the DDC penalties, which exiting merchants can simply ignore, but instead to reap the benefits of having good industry and community reputations. Thus, the industry sanctions and threatened boycotts will compel compliance only from those who have strong preferences to remain active in the industry and respected in their community. Accordingly, the role of the DDC's arbitration board is purely informational, and the power of its dispute resolution system rests solely on the degree to which it can disseminate information about merchant reputations and past dealings. In this sense, the DDC is a modern, though more effective, version of the private judges in the twelfth and thirteenth centuries in the Champagne fairs, whose power lay solely in their ability to publicize the individuals who shirked contractual obligations.[19]

In sum, the DDC's arbitrators identify merchants who have engaged in wrongdoing, and both formal and informal industry mechanisms disseminate the identities of those deserving of bad reputations. Industry and community norms then inflict coordinated punishment on wrongdoers by foreclosing future business to those who have failed to uphold their commitments in the past. This collection of industry and community institutions has sustained the reliability of a $60 billion industry that has avoided, has not required, and could not be supported by state court enforcement. Could the institutional foundations for the industry's procompetitive reputation-based enforcement nevertheless amount to a violation of competition law? Ought developing nations crafting their own competition laws aggressively prosecute industry-wide group boycotts when those arrangements may simply compensate for ineffective contract enforcement?

The Antitrust of Reputation Mechanisms: Carving Out Permissive Treatment for Development

Competition laws outlaw cartels and place limits on the degree to which competitors can cooperate. Informal enforcement mechanisms, however, rely on cooperation among competitors. Thus, a formal application of current antitrust law presents a number of arguments that might lead a court to conclude that diamond merchants and their coordinating trade associations are in violation of conventional competition law.

In other work, I have detailed the assorted legal possibilities in which the collaboration that enables reputation mechanisms in New York's diamond industry might run afoul of the U.S. antitrust laws.[20] Diamond merchants might be found, for example, to have orchestrated a group boycott with a competitive target,[21] created a joint venture with positive externalities that prohibit excluding competitors,[22] or engineered information-sharing mechanisms that trigger anticompetitive restraints.[23] A meaningful antitrust analysis can proceed only if there is recognition that the industry's collaborative restraints are necessary consequences of the transactional difficulties of contract enforcement. Or, put more starkly, just as competition law permits procompetitive collaborations that improve upon particular market fail-ures,[24] competition law also ought to permit collaborations that compensate for a court failure.

Note that these concerted enforcement mechanisms—wherein industry arbitrators disseminate information and merchants and community leaders coordinate punishment—is not merely a species of private third-party arbi-tration. Typical arbitration is a simple product of contract, wherein parties contractually agree on arbitration to reduce the collective costs of dispute resolution. But following an arbitration ruling, the victorious party then seeks enforcement in public courts, and state-sanctioned coercion, such as asset seizure and property liens, remains available to enforce the arbitration judg-ment. Reputation-based sanctions, therefore, are not merely a response to costly rules of litigation, and they would not evaporate even if legal proce-dural rules became more efficient or less costly. In short, whereas most com-mercial parties choose arbitration to reduce the costs of litigating in public courts, the diamond industry abandons public courts because they offer in-effective enforcement. And whereas the effectiveness of most commercial arbitration depends on ultimate state court enforcement, the diamond indus-try designs its own arbitration rules to harness its reputation mechanisms and coordinated punishments.

Competition law, therefore, ought to be sympathetic to the need for cer-tain concerted actions to compensate for the failure—or inherent limits—of public institutions, particularly so in developing world countries. This is true even if the concerted actions closely resemble group boycotts that tradition-ally have been deemed illegal per se. And even truer for developing nations, like India, whose thriving diamond industry has meaningfully contributed to the nation's economic awakening.[25]

Conclusion: In Defense of Cartels

The utility of informal contract enforcement in the context of development economics is rather straightforward: when public institutions are unable to credibly secure economic exchange, informal institutions have unquestion-able value. The persistence of informal private ordering in the modern state, where ostensibly efficacious public contract enforcement is available, reveals a far more powerful lesson: cartel-like arrangements that engineer reputation mechanisms can even be superior (i.e., more efficient) to public courts in developed economies. They therefore deserve favorable treatment from competition law and ought to be considered in the context of development objectives, not just in the short run but perhaps in the longer run as well.

The most immediate lesson for competition policy in developing nations is that concerted group boycotts can be a foundation for meaningful economic growth. Those advocating the spread of competition law to developing nations should recognize that meaningfully securing contract rights is a higher priority than combating cartels, and sometimes securing contract rights is best achieved by cartels. While a detailed antitrust analysis of an idiosyncratic industry with an odd structure and unusual features offers a relatively small insight into competition law, it also meaningfully reveals the proper role of the rule of law in bringing prosperity to the world's poorest nations.

10

Your Money and Your Life

The Export of U.S. Antitrust Remedies

Harry First

Substantive antitrust law has spread around the world. This has been a rather amazing turn of events in our post–Cold War era, with more than 100 jurisdictions now claiming some form of antitrust legislation.[1] Even though there is no global treaty framework for antitrust (similar, for example, to the Agreement on Trade-Related Aspects of Intellectual Property Rights (TRIPS) for intellectual property), there does now appear to be broad international consensus on the basic principles of competition policy.

Substantive antitrust law may be one of the United States' more popular legal exports, but how does the rest of the world view two very important remedy aspects of the U.S. antitrust enforcement system, private treble damages suits for antitrust violations and incarceration of antitrust violators? As is well known, in the United States we take your money *and* your life. Conventional wisdom is that other countries do not.

This chapter argues not only that these two remedies are in fact good exports, but that non-U.S. jurisdictions are increasingly coming to accept them, as shown in a study presented in this chapter. This trend should not be surprising because the policy arguments in their favor make good sense.

The chapter begins with a discussion of the history of the acceptance of these remedies in the United States. The next part presents a study focused on thirteen enforcing jurisdictions, representing a cross-section of large and small economies located in different parts of the world, examining the spread of these remedies. The chapter concludes with an assessment of the wisdom of adopting the two remedies, not only in the jurisdictions covered in the study but also in other jurisdictions.

The History of Incarceration and Private Damages in the United States

The case in the United States for incarceration in antitrust has generally been made on utilitarian deterrence grounds.[2] Commentators have argued that incarceration is a necessary criminal punishment in addition to corporate or individual fines because monetary payments can easily be perceived as prices—just another cost of doing business. Jail time, on the other hand, is hard to monetize, and few in the business world are willing to view it as a cost of doing business, to be traded off for higher profits. As one antitrust enforcer has said, violators may be willing to pay a larger fine to avoid jail, but they have never offered to serve a longer jail sentence in return for a smaller fine.[3]

The consensus view that imprisonment is an appropriate remedy was slow to emerge in the United States.[4] Criminal antitrust cases have been pursued from the earliest days of the Sherman Act,[5] but the first sentence of imprisonment was not imposed until almost twenty years after the act's passage.[6] For the first part of the twentieth century, the imposition of imprisonment was generally rare,[7] so much so that the thirty-day sentences of seven executives in the 1960s heavy electrical generating equipment price-fixing case drew national press attention.[8]

A consensus that criminalization and imprisonment are appropriate began to emerge in the 1970s, when Sherman Act violations became felonies and the maximum term of imprisonment increased to three years, and it took real hold in the 1980s. In 1980, fifty-five criminal prosecutions were brought (nearly double the previous year); in 1984, there were 100 criminal prosecutions; in 1988 there were eighty-seven.[9] Although these prosecutions could be criticized for focusing on "small fry"—for example, local road-paving and electrical contractors—nevertheless, the effort to use the criminal sanction and seek imprisonment was a serious one and furthered the shift in the moral judgment that price-fixing should be viewed as a crime.[10]

This shift in attitude was in keeping with a broader view that U.S. courts had been too lenient on white-collar criminals generally, a position that was reflected in the 1987 federal sentencing guidelines.[11] These guidelines required sentences of imprisonment for first-time white-collar criminals who in the past had escaped imprisonment. Judges were required to follow the guidelines except in certain exceptional cases, and the guidelines' requirements substantially altered sentencing practices in antitrust cases. Sentences of imprisonment for criminal antitrust cases gradually became common. Average sentences today are now approximately two years.[12]

The case for private damages rests on two grounds, compensation and deterrence, although commentators and courts in the United States today generally stress the deterrence rationale.[13] The treble damages multiplier can similarly be justified on both grounds, either as an incentive for injured parties to sue for compensation or as a (rough) way to ensure that defendants are appropriately deterred by forcing them to account not only for their injury to purchasers or competitors but also for the deadweight welfare loss their conduct causes.

Receptivity toward the private action was mixed in the early days of the Sherman Act. A small number of cases were filed early on, exploring the issues raised by the private action. Lower courts were generally skeptical of plaintiffs' arguments, although the Supreme Court was not.[14] As with incarceration, by midcentury the private treble damages remedy was generally considered to be ineffective.[15]

This view began to change in the 1960s. First, a well-publicized bid-rigging criminal prosecution against electrical equipment manufacturers led to successful follow-on private treble damages actions with large recoveries for plaintiffs and their attorneys. Next, the Warren Court showed particular willingness to see private actions as part of a system of antitrust enforcement, playing an important public enforcement role in addition to its core function of compensation.[16] Criminal antitrust enforcement actions and penalties were still relatively low (although both would soon increase), leaving it to private parties to fill the deterrence gap. As late as 1979, when the Supreme Court's composition had changed from Warren Court days, the Court still saw the private action as "a significant supplement to the limited resources available to the Department of Justice for enforcing the antitrust laws and deterring violations."[17] Finally, this period saw the growth of class actions and a sophisticated private plaintiffs' bar, making it easier to bring cases on behalf of large groups of injured consumers.

The result of these forces was a dramatic increase in the use of private actions. In 1960 there were 228 private antitrust cases filed in the United States; in 1980 there were nearly 1,500.[18] From the mid-1960s until 1980, there were approximately sixteen times more private cases filed than public cases. Although the ratio of private to public cases dropped in the 1980s, as did the number of cases, private filings increased again in the 1990s and they continue to be substantially higher than the number of cases the federal enforcement agencies file.[19] Recent monetary recoveries by private plaintiffs have also been substantial, with a number of settlements in the hundreds of millions of dollars and a few in the billions.

The reaction of courts and commentators to the private action, however, has come to diverge from their reaction to imprisonment. There is no indication today of retrenchment with regard to imprisonment, but there has been substantial resistance to private actions, with the courts resorting to various procedural devices to make it harder to win a private suit.[20] Commentators, as well, have expressed skepticism about the wisdom of the private action.[21] Nevertheless, Congress has not yet responded in any significant way to change the default view that private treble damages should be available to those injured in their business or property by antitrust violations.

The Spread of Remedies Outside the United States

To what extent have the remedies of incarceration and private damages suits been adopted in antitrust systems outside the United States? The study presented in this chapter examines thirteen enforcing jurisdictions with different-sized economies located in different regions of the world, in an effort to gain some insight into this question.[22]

The overall status of private damages suits and incarceration in the chosen jurisdictions is presented in summary form in Table 10.1. It illustrates three important points regarding the spread of the private damages remedy in these jurisdictions.

First, all the jurisdictions, with the exception of the European Union (EU) itself, have some form of private action but reject a damages multiplier for their private actions.[23] Although the lack of a Europe-wide private action is important, the failure to date of the European Commission to achieve this goal does not leave Europeans without this remedy. Member states can provide for private damages suits for breach of competition law in their domestic courts, which the two European jurisdictions in the study do (Germany and the United Kingdom).[24] Thus we can still conclude that there is a high degree of unanimity among the countries in the study on the two basic policy choices regarding private damages suits.

Table 10.1 Current status of remedies (13 jurisdictions)

Enforcement agency	Private enforcement			Criminal enforcement	
	Damages awarded?	Treble?	Level of enforcement	Imprisonment imposable?	Level of enforcement
Australia	Yes	No	Increasing	Yes, cartels	Too early
Brazil	Yes	No	Rare	Yes, under separate Economic Crimes Law	Increasing
Canada	Yes	No	Increasing	Yes	Increasing
Chile	Yes	No	Rare	No, potential Criminal Code fraud provision	Pending prosecution
China	Yes	No	Preliminary phase	No, potential Criminal Code provision	Unknown
European Union	No	No	N/A	No	N/A
Germany	Yes	No	Rare	Yes, under separate fraud and bid-rigging statute	Many cases, nearly all suspended
India	Yes	No	New Act	No	N/A
Israel	Yes	No	Increasing	Yes	Rare but increasing
Japan	Yes	No	Gradually increasing	Yes	Jail terms suspended
Korea	Yes	No	Gradually increasing	Yes	Jail terms suspended
South Africa	Yes	No	Rare	Yes	Too early
United Kingdom	Yes	No	Increasing	Yes, cartels	Too early

Second, the record for the imprisonment remedy is less unanimous than for private actions. Three important jurisdictions (the EU, India, and China) do not provide for imprisonment at all.[25] Three other jurisdictions (Brazil, Germany, and Chile) do not include an imprisonment remedy in their competition laws, but prosecutors have used (or are trying to use) other criminal laws with imprisonment remedies against cartel offenders.[26] Even with this somewhat mixed record, however, there is more overall unanimity than might otherwise have been expected—ten of the thirteen jurisdictions provide for imprisonment for core cartel offenses under some statute.

Third, the actual use of these remedies is generally weak. There is a recent movement toward an increase in private litigation, for example, in Australia, Canada, Israel, and, to a more limited extent, in the United Kingdom,[27] but private litigation is rarer in the other jurisdictions in the study.[28] Imprisonment is even less well used. In many of the jurisdictions in the study the availability of an imprisonment penalty is too recent to provide any data on its imposition, but in the rest, jail sentences, even when imposed, have most often been suspended.[29]

Table 10.2 examines competition law changes in the first decade of the twenty-first century. The table illustrates two important trends. First, there is a rather remarkable trend in adopting competition law changes relating to these two remedies. During the 2000s, ten of the thirteen jurisdictions in the study enacted competition law changes affecting either the private right of action or imprisonment. Two important jurisdictions, India and China, adopted major legal revisions to their entire competition law regimes. Both included some form of private action, although neither included an imprisonment remedy.[30]

Second, at the end of the decade there was a distinct movement toward the imprisonment remedy. In 2009, Australia and South Africa added new statutory provisions providing for imprisonment,[31] Canada refocused its criminal statute on per se cartel offenses and increased the maximum term from five to fourteen years,[32] and Japan increased the maximum jail time for criminal violations of its Antimonopoly Act from three years to five, making it less likely that a jail sentence would be suspended.[33] The only imprisonment outlier in the study during this period is Chile, which repealed its criminal provision in 2003, at the same time making follow-on civil actions easier to bring.[34] But even this example is not as much of an outlier as it might otherwise seem. Prosecutors are making efforts to use other criminal

Table 10.2   Major statutory changes, 2000–2010

Year	Country	Private enforcement	Criminal enforcement
2002	India	New competition law statute; creates private right	
2003	United Kingdom		Amends 1958 statute to create first criminal offense
	Chile	Adds follow-on benefits to competition law statute	Repeals criminal provision in competition law statute
2005	Germany	Major statutory change	
	Korea	Major statutory change	
2008	China	New competition law statute; creates private right	
2009	Australia		Adds criminal penalty
	Canada		Major statutory change
	Japan		Increases imprisonment to five years
	South Africa		Adds criminal provision; not yet in force

provisions in Chilean law to prosecute cartels, and bills have been introduced in the legislature to reinstitute the criminal provision in Chile's competition law.[35]

What might explain the spread of these two remedies? One possibility is that the phenomenon would be linked to the size of the economy. Another possibility is that the adoption of these remedies is related to a jurisdiction's legal traditions or culture. Table 10.3 indicates, however, that neither size nor legal culture explains the spread of the two remedies in the studied jurisdictions.

Although there are likely individual political economy stories explaining the legal changes in each of these countries, there may also be a relatively simple explanation for the general movement toward these two remedies— the time of adoption. As Table 10.2 shows, the 2000s were a vibrant period for statutory changes in competition law. As jurisdictions considered these changes they also had the experience of other jurisdictions to draw on, particularly the United States, which has been an evangelist for incarceration while providing a cautionary tale for private remedies. This evangelism may partly explain the movement (not unanimous, of course) toward incarceration that we see in Table 10.2;[36] and the concern about perceived excesses in private actions in the United States may partly explain the unanimous rejection of treble damages in the studied jurisdictions.[37] Thus, the overall trends

Table 10.3 Enforcing jurisdictions, by GDP and legal tradition

Jurisdiction	Private right	Jail	GDP	Legal tradition	
				Civil law	Common law
European Union	No	No	N/A[1]	X	
China	Yes	No	2	X	
Japan	Yes	Yes	3	X	
Germany	Yes	Yes	4	X	
United Kingdom	Yes	Yes	6		X
Brazil	Yes	Yes	7	X	
India	Yes	No	9		X
Canada	Yes	Yes	10		X
Korea	Yes	Yes	14	X	
Australia	Yes	Yes	15		X
South Africa	Yes	Yes	28		X
Israel	Yes	Yes	41		X
Chile	Yes	No	43	X	

NOTE:
[1] European Union would have largest GDP if it were a single country.
SOURCE: World Bank Data Catalogue, Gross Domestic Product 2010, http://siteresources.worldbank.org/DATASTATISTICS/Resources/GDP.pdf.

shown in the three tables lend some support to a Brandeisian experimentalist view of institutional design, where some legal regimes act as "economic laboratories" and other legal regimes learn from their experience,[38] a phenomenon that has been described as a "last mover advantage."[39]

Although there is a general trend toward both incarceration and private actions, there are important institutional variations among the jurisdictions that can affect the effectiveness of both remedies. Tables 10.4 and 10.5 set out some of the key variations.

If a jurisdiction decides to provide for incarceration of competition law violators, one of the first questions of institutional design that must be addressed is whether the competition agency will be responsible for bringing the criminal prosecutions. In the United States, the Antitrust Division, as part of the Justice Department, has been given this responsibility, but this is more the result of historical development than a conscious design to centralize civil and criminal enforcement.

As Table 10.4 indicates, the U.S. institutional structure is replicated in only one of the jurisdictions in the study (Israel) and partially replicated in another (the U.K. competition agency has concurrent authority with a public prosecutor, the Serious Frauds Office).[40] The dominant model, found in the eight remaining jurisdictions, is to have the public prosecutor bring the case. In four of these jurisdictions the prosecutor can act only on reference from the competition authority (which has the sole responsibility for investigating the alleged illegal conduct and deciding whether to make a criminal reference); in the other four the prosecutor has independent authority.[41]

Is there any link between these institutional arrangements and the results of criminal prosecutions? Two hypotheses can be suggested. The first is a bureaucratic incentives hypothesis. Splitting responsibility for cartel prosecution between the competition agency and a public prosecutor, but allowing the competition agency to control the institution of prosecution through the referral power, might incentivize the agency to retain control of, and thereby take credit for, bringing the cartel cases they think appropriate.[42] This would mean weaker criminal enforcement. The second, a prosecutorial competence hypothesis, might be that the farming out of cartel cases to a generalized public prosecutor could result in a downplaying of these prosecutions. Public prosecutors are likely to have priorities other than competition law violations; competition law violators are less dangerous than other offenders and consequently less in need of incarceration; and public prosecutors have a weaker understanding of competition law principles than of traditional crimes of

Table 10.4 Institutional variance: imprisonment

Jurisdiction	Separate prosecutor	Leniency program	Administrative organizational fines	Scope Broad	Scope Narrow	Separate statute
Australia	Yes, on reference	Comanaged w/ prosecutor	Yes		X	Not necessary
Brazil	Yes	Comanaged w/ prosecutor	Yes		X	Yes
Canada	Yes, on reference	Comanaged w/ prosecutor	Yes		X	No
Chile	Yes	Yes (Civil)	Yes		X	Uncertain application
China	N/A	N/A	Yes	N/A	N/A	Yes
European Union	N/A	Yes (Civil)	Yes	N/A	N/A	NCA enforcement
Germany	Yes	No	Yes		X	Yes
India	N/A	Yes	Yes	N/A	N/A	No
Israel	No	Yes	No	X		No
Japan	Yes, on reference	Yes	Yes		X	Yes
Korea	Yes, on reference	Yes	Yes	X		No
South Africa[1]	Yes	To be comanaged w/prosecutor	Yes		X	Not necessary
United Kingdom	Concurrent[2]	Comanaged, where appropriate	Yes		X	No

NOTES:

[1] Criminal provision not yet in force.

[2] Concurrent in England, Wales, and Northern Ireland; prosecution only by public prosecutor in Scotland.

violence.[43] This, too, would suggest weak criminal enforcement. If both hypotheses are borne out, the solution might be to combine criminal and civil enforcement in a single agency.

The data in this study call into question the prosecutorial competence hypothesis and lend some support to the bureaucratic incentives hypothesis. With regard to prosecutorial competence, countries in the study in which the competition agency lacks the reference power, and therefore cannot stop the public prosecutor from prosecuting cartels, actually appear to have the strongest criminal cartel enforcement and the greatest chance at imposing imprisonment. Consistent with the bureaucratic incentives hypothesis, however, countries in which the competition agency has the referral power and can control the prosecutor have the weakest criminal enforcement.

Brazil is a good example. Brazil is perhaps the most active criminal enforcement regime in the study; criminal prosecutions are relatively frequent and jail terms for cartel offenses have been imposed.[44] Brazil's competition law provides for civil fines for organizations and individuals, but does not include a criminal provision. Instead, criminal cartel behavior is prosecuted under the Economic Crimes Law, which prosecutors have authority to invoke without regard to what the competition agency does (or does not do).[45] Although Brazilian competition agencies now routinely ask prosecutors to open investigations into cartel matters that the competition agency is looking at and get help from prosecutors in investigating these matters, prosecutors do frequently bring cases on their own, without working with the competition agency.[46]

Germany is in a similar institutional position. The competition agency can impose civil fines against organizations and individuals, but public prosecutors operate under a separate bid-rigging statute that only they have the authority to invoke.[47] As in Brazil, German prosecutors have obtained a relatively large number of convictions (although actual jail time remains rare).[48]

Chile presents a similar institutional structure, but a more modest outcome. Chile decriminalized its antitrust law in 2003, but in 2011 the public prosecutor brought criminal charges against executives of three pharmacy chains for fixing prices, using provisions of the criminal code dealing with fraud.[49] This is a rare prosecution, but it shows a willingness of the public prosecutor to take on price-fixing behavior.

By contrast, in Japan, where the competition agency controls the bringing of criminal cases under Japan's competition law, criminal prosecutions have been rare and imprisonment has yet to be imposed.[50] The results are similar in Korea, where the antitrust enforcement authority has exclusive referral authority—criminal prosecutions have been relatively rare and imprisonment has not been imposed in cases where convictions have been obtained.[51]

These results thus call into question the fear that public prosecutors will not be interested in bringing cartel cases or will not be successful when they do. If anything, the institutional competence appears to run in favor of the public prosecutor rather than against it. In some ways this is not surprising. After all, public prosecutors are more familiar than the competition agency with the special procedural requirements of a criminal prosecution and have more familiarity with the investigation of criminal law matters. A competition agency taking on such tasks might very well lack sufficient experience to do them well. Indeed, support for this concern can be drawn from the U.K. competition authority's trial mistakes in its first contested criminal prosecution,[52] the scarcity of criminal prosecutions in Israel (the Israel competition agency has de facto exclusive authority to bring criminal cartel cases),[53] and the mismanagement of cartel investigations by Japan's competition agency.[54]

The grant of independent authority to a public prosecutor, however, does create an institutional problem that agencies with an integrated prosecutorial function do not face. As Table 10.4 indicates, there has been widespread adoption of the U.S. practice of granting amnesty (or some degree of leniency) to firms that inform the competition agency of their participation in cartel activities—nearly every agency in the study has some form of this program. The problem is that agency amnesty programs do not legally bind the prosecutor. If the prosecutor does not (or cannot) recognize agency amnesty agreements, the effectiveness of such agreements could be undercut because disclosures made to a competition agency under an amnesty agreement will necessarily include information about culpable company employees. If those culpable employees are the ones making the decision on seeking amnesty, they might very well decide against amnesty in the first place.

It is difficult to tell whether this potential problem has in fact adversely affected the utility of amnesty agreements. In a number of the countries in the study, public prosecutors co-manage the amnesty process and are involved in the amnesty discussions.[55] In others, public prosecutors have publicly declared that they will honor the competition agency's leniency decision even though they are not technically required to do so.[56] If actual imprisonment of individuals does increase, however, the problems of split authority over amnesty may increase, particularly in jurisdictions where the public prosecutor does not recognize the concept, as is true in Germany in our sample.[57]

Table 10.5 isolates four institutional factors that might affect the private remedy's effectiveness. The first important factor parallels the referral power in criminal prosecutions: Can an injured party bring a damages action even if the competition agency has not acted (a "stand-alone right") or is the cause of action dependent on the competition agency's finding that the competition act has been violated? The latter approach, of course, gives the competition agency more control over enforcement policy and the scope of competition law, similar to the ability to control the criminal prosecution referral.

The jurisdictions in the study follow varied approaches. Most follow the U.S. model of creating a stand-alone private right of action for damages as part of the competition law itself, the exercise of which does not depend on prior action by the enforcement agency,[58] but there are significant deviations. India

Table 10.5 Institutional variance: private damages

Jurisdiction	Standalone right	Procedural benefits	Claim aggregation	Use of other statutes
Australia	Yes	Yes	Yes	Not necessary
Brazil	Yes	Uncertain	Restricted	Not used
Canada	Yes	Yes	Yes	Yes, added claims
Chile	Yes	Yes	No	Not used
China	Yes	Uncertain	Uncertain	Uncertain
European Union	N/A	N/A	N/A	Member state law
Germany	Yes	Yes	Restricted	Not used
India	No	Yes	Restricted	Not used
Israel	Yes	Yes	Yes	Not necessary
Japan	No	Yes	No	Yes
Korea	Yes	Yes	Restricted	Yes
South Africa	No	Yes	Yes	Not used
United Kingdom	No	Yes	Yes	Yes

and the United Kingdom allow private damages suits under the competition law to be brought only before their competition appellate tribunals and then only after a competition agency finding of a violation.[59] Japan and South Africa permit suits under competition law to be brought in civil court, but only after a finding of a violation of the competition law by the competition agency (in the former)[60] or by the competition tribunal (in the latter).[61]

Not permitting a stand-alone action may put a strong damper on private litigation over competition law violations, but it does not necessarily end such litigation. In a number of jurisdictions in the study, competition law violations are considered torts and can be litigated in civil court under general tort law. Both Japan and the United Kingdom, for example, permit suits under general tort law for violations of their competition laws (or for violations of the Treaty on the Functioning of the European Union, in the case of the United Kingdom), and in both countries there are procedural advantages to using general tort law.[62]

Whether stand-alone actions are permitted or not, nearly all the jurisdictions in the study provide a variety of procedural advantages to plaintiffs that bring suit under the competition law. Many jurisdictions provide some degree of preclusion once the competition agency makes a finding of a violation, whether by making the finding prima facie proof of a violation[63] or making it binding as to liability.[64] Other jurisdictions lower the burden of proof of intent in private cases brought under the competition act[65] or allow evidence from the administrative proceeding to assist in the computation of damages.[66]

Despite these procedural advantages, private litigation remains relatively infrequent, and the litigation that does occur is generally brought by business firms rather than consumers.[67] One likely reason for the lack of consumer claims is the difficulty in bringing actions that aggregate claims on behalf of large numbers of claimants, each of whom may have suffered only a small amount of damage. As Table 10.5 indicates, two of the jurisdictions in the study have no mechanism for representative actions to aggregate claims. Four of the jurisdictions have some form of restricted representative actions, generally either allowing plaintiffs to opt into a single action or allowing a specified public representative to bring an action to create a fund for claimants.[68] One of those jurisdictions, Germany, creatively allows for the transfer of damages claims to a third party that may then enforce them collectively; using this provision, a company called "Cartel Damage Claims Holding SA" has brought suit in several cases involving multiple purchasers.[69] None of these mechanisms, however, is effective at remedying an injury done to a dispersed class of plaintiffs that cannot be assembled prior to filing suit.

The lack of a full opt-out class action mechanism may not, in itself, explain the paucity of private competition law litigation. Four of the countries in the study arguably have liberal rules allowing broad representative actions, but in none of them has a significant number of class actions been reported.[70] This may indicate that factors outside the scope of this study (lack of lawyers and judges trained in competition law, lack of a damages multiplier, lack of tools for discovering evidence, or the general expense of civil litigation) may be more salient with regard to ensuring a full recovery of damages by those injured by competition law violations.

. . .

The major finding of the study presented in this chapter is that the jurisdictions in the study are moving closer to the two remedies that have been important features of U.S. antitrust enforcement: imprisonment and private damages. Actual imprisonment of antitrust offenders remains rare, but there is general consensus on making cartel violations criminal offenses and offering leniency as a device to destabilize cartels and increase enforcement. Private litigation is not yet widespread, but all of the countries in the study have private rights of action, most have stand-alone rights that can be pursued by injured parties without leave of the enforcement agency, and private parties do benefit in various ways from an enforcement agency's prior finding of a violation.

Oddly, the outlier in the study is the EU itself, where there is no Community-wide criminal provision or private right of action. Specific problems with implementing each remedy might explain the current state of affairs. The competition provisions of the treaty apply only to "undertakings," not individuals, and the Commission has no statutory power to impose imprisonment.[71] Private actions must be brought in Member State courts, whose procedures and legal traditions vary enormously. Mandating some sort of effective private action across the twenty-seven different countries that make up the EU is a daunting task and the Commission, despite its apparently positive view of a Community-wide private right, has been unable to bridge this gap.[72] Thus, the task of implementing such rights is currently being left to the Member States themselves, which, if the trends detailed in this study prevail, will likely move toward adopting and implementing both remedies.

Are these two remedies appropriate for broad adoption? The answer is yes. To the extent that a jurisdiction is serious about competition policy, the logic of both remedies is compelling. Deterrence of violations and compensation of victims are good ideas, ones that are not country specific; the remedies advance both. Until we find out that they do not, it is hard to argue against them.

Of course, in any country both remedies sit within a broader legal and institutional framework. Each country's civil and criminal procedures will affect how these remedies are carried out; as discussed above, institutional variance may affect efficacy. Indeed, the appropriate use of both remedies will depend strongly on the institutional infrastructure available to carry them out. A compensation-based private damages remedy may fail if recoveries are not distributed, in some way, to those injured by the violation.[73] The use of criminal sanctions may produce unjust results unless there are substantial due process protections for the accused, including a commitment to greater transparency than many jurisdictions currently afford.

It also may take time in individual jurisdictions to understand fully how competition law violations harm individual consumers or competitors, or to accept the view that certain competition law violations should be labeled "crime" and deserve the severe penalty of imprisonment. But, as discussed above, both ideas were not immediately popular in the United States either. There is no reason to expect immediate full-fledged acceptance elsewhere.

Brandeisian institutional experimentation continues, of course, and learning is not a one-way street. Perhaps the universal rejection of treble damages will cause the United States to look more closely at this feature and come up with a better way to incentivize private litigation, to the extent that such incentives are still necessary in the United States. Or perhaps the United States will look more closely at the terms of imprisonment we impose on antitrust violators and examine whether this costly sanction has become excessive. One thing is clear, however. Experimentation in antitrust remedies is now a global enterprise, not confined to any single jurisdiction.

11

Rethinking Competition Advocacy in Developing Countries

Allan Fels and Wendy Ng

Competition advocacy is a critical component of a competition agency's role, especially in developing countries. Developing countries are typically undergoing significant economic reforms such as developing and opening their markets and privatizing state-owned assets and enterprises. Competition advocacy can help to ensure that competition principles are incorporated into this transition process. The method of competition advocacy that is usually championed by development agencies and a number of competition agencies in developed countries, and adopted by competition agencies, revolves around general advocacy and advice to governments, with little consideration of the underlying problem and its political dimensions. This "traditional" approach to competition advocacy has significant limitations, which are exacerbated in developing countries.

In this chapter, we review the traditional model of competition advocacy and explore its relevance to and limitations in developing countries. In light of these limitations, we consider an alternative approach to competition advocacy, a "national competition policy" approach. We discuss Australia's experience with its national competition policy and its relevance for developing countries.

Traditional Advocacy Approach

The International Competition Network (ICN) defines competition advocacy as "those activities conducted by the competition authority related to the promotion of a competitive environment for economic activities by means of non-enforcement mechanisms, mainly through its relationships with other governmental entities and by increasing public awareness of the benefits of competition."[1] Competition advocacy has two main purposes. First, it aims to build a competition culture, which is an awareness by economic agents and the general public of competition rules.[2] Second, it is a way to influence other government authorities not to adopt anticompetitive laws and regulations.[3] Both dimensions of competition advocacy are important and relevant for developing countries.

Competition agencies often engage in activities to raise general awareness of the benefits of competition and competition laws, regulations, and policies. These activities are undertaken in an effort to build a strong competition culture, which helps to enhance the effectiveness of enforcement and advocacy.[4] This aspect of competition advocacy is particularly important for countries that are transitioning from a command economy to a market economy or undergoing development, as a strong competition culture is generally considered to be essential to the successful establishment of a market economy.[5] In this realm, competition advocacy is aimed at educating other government agencies, the judiciary, economic agents, and the general public about the benefits of competition to society and the role of competition law and policy in promoting societal welfare.[6] Government agencies that are more familiar with the benefits of competition may be less inclined to adopt anticompetitive laws and regulations. Judges who are more knowledgeable about competition principles, laws, and policies will be better placed to handle competition law cases that come before them. A business community and public more informed about the benefits of competition and competition laws could facilitate enforcement. They may bring more instances of anticompetitive conduct to the competition agency's attention, bring private actions to enforce the law themselves, or prevent economic agents from engaging in anticompetitive conduct in the first place.[7] Overall, competition advocacy can foster conditions that will promote a more competitive market and competitive market behavior without the direct intervention of the competition agency.[8] Activities that are typically undertaken by competition agencies to raise public awareness of the benefits of competition and competition law and policy include distributing publications such as annual reports, official gazettes, guidelines, newsletters, discussion papers, journal articles, and surveys; using mass media such as websites, press releases, radio, and television; conducting seminars and workshops; making speeches, giving public lectures, and participating in conferences; undertaking market studies; conducting public consultation exercises; and creating education and compliance programs.[9]

Government activities such as regulatory rulemaking and intervention also can have anticompetitive effects.[10] Such activities can be a particularly serious threat to competition in developing countries.[11] The traditional advocacy approach regards consultation on legislative or regulatory procedures as one of the primordial tasks of competition agencies and the most important component of competition advocacy.[12] In this capacity, competition agencies use a variety of tools to conduct competition advocacy vis-à-vis other government agencies. One of the most commonly used tools is consultation with other government bodies, which includes issuing opinions and recommendations, making submissions on draft legislation and regulations, meeting stakeholders, and conducting workshops.[13] Such consultation may be formal or informal. Executive and legislative bodies are the most common targets of advocacy efforts as they can influence the drafting of legislation and regulations that impact competition. Other mechanisms typically used to advocate include advising on market definition, entering into cooperation agreements, and drafting guidelines and codes of conduct.[14] There has also been a recent focus on conducting market studies.[15]

A number of competition agencies have reported some success with their advocacy activities. Examples include, in Russia, the Federal Antimonopoly Service's advocacy for the introduction of additional rules providing for non-discriminatory access of electricity producers and consumers to power transmission and infrastructure facilities following the reform of Russia's electric power industry;[16] in Indonesia, the Commission for the Supervision of Business Competition's advocacy for the revision of airline regulations that originally provided an exclusive right to a business association to regulate and fix tariffs among airline carriers;[17] and in Hungary, the Hungarian Competition Authority's establishment of its Competition Culture Centre, which deals with its competition culture affairs such as business and consumer education and supporting academic research.[18] These successes, and advocacy efforts more generally, tend to be pursued as individual cases or projects (which may reflect the case-oriented enforcement mind-set of competition agencies) rather than as part of a wider, systematic program of competition advocacy.

Limitations of the Traditional Advocacy Approach

The traditional advocacy approach has two principal shortcomings, which are particularly pronounced in the developing country context. First, it fails to explicitly recognize and incorporate strategies for dealing with the magnitude of the political challenge involved in overturning anticompetitive laws. Anticompetitive laws are often supported and maintained by political considerations such as competing policy objectives, the high level of government involvement in the economy, and interest group pressures. Of course, that is not to say that there are no political forces that support competition reform. For example, governments have incentives to promote and protect competition because their prospects for reelection are judged by the electorate, in part, on how well they deliver on economic growth and development, which is related to how well competition policy works, and the fact that competition law has spread around the world despite frequent opposition by businesses is a sign of political support. Second, it does not sufficiently consider the impact of institutional arrangements on the method and effectiveness of competition advocacy. Further, developing countries face a number of challenges that make it more difficult for competition agencies to engage in advocacy or for advocacy to find sufficient support or reception.

Often in developing countries, competition policy is but one of a number of tools used to pursue broader development objectives.[19] The government might not pursue competition for its own sake but as a means to promote economic development. Hence, competition law objectives might be pursued only insofar as they are consistent with other development goals or be subordinated to other government policies (such as trade or foreign investment policies) if that is believed to be more conducive to economic development.[20] The state might also adopt laws and regulations that further other public interests despite their anticompetitive effects. For example, during the recent global financial crisis, governments and parliaments adopted measures that were aimed at restoring confidence in and ensuring the stability of financial markets. These measures often had anticompetitive effects.[21]

Industrial policy, in particular, plays a much bigger role in developing countries than in developed countries and might conflict with competition policy. The state is often considered a key driver of economic growth and adopts industrial policy measures in furtherance of that role.[22] Governments of developing countries might adopt policies aimed at fostering national champions or protecting domestic enterprises from foreign competition so that these companies can better compete in the global market or with foreign companies in the domestic market.[23] They might also use industrial policy to offset the negative effects of integration into the global economy, such as job losses.[24] An example of where industrial policy considerations have been explicitly incorporated into competition policy is China's Anti-Monopoly Law, which protects the lawful business activities of state-owned enterprises in industries that are "critical to the wellbeing of the national economy and national security, as well as industries in which exclusive operation and exclusive sales are the norm of business in accordance with the law." [25]

Competition policy objectives may also be thwarted by other government agencies that prioritize the achievement of their own objectives over competition.[26] There may even be competing priorities within the competition agency itself. It is not uncommon for competition agencies in developing countries to have noncompetition responsibilities or officials who work in related areas within other government bodies.[27] In these circumstances, competition policy goals could be deferred or overlooked by the competition agency itself. Moreover, while the generally accepted objective of competition laws in developed countries is economic efficiency and consumer welfare,[28] the objectives of competition law in developing countries may include goals other than those. For example, the objectives of South Africa's Competition Act include promoting employment, ensuring the equal participation of small and medium-sized enterprises in the economy, and increasing the ownership stakes of historically disadvantaged persons.[29] These public interest objectives impact on competition law decisions in South Africa, as illustrated by the recent proposed acquisition by Walmart, the U.S. retail giant, of Massmart, a South African retailer. On its face, the proposed acquisition raised no competition concerns because Walmart did not compete with Massmart and had only a very small presence in South Africa. However, three South African government departments[30] and a number of unions[31] were concerned that the proposed acquisition would adversely affect employment and employment conditions, switch some of the postacquisition entity's procurement away from local manufacturers to imports, and lead to the closure of small and medium-sized businesses and businesses owned by historically disadvantaged individuals.[32] The proposed acquisition was conditionally approved by the Competition Tribunal with conditions that were aimed at addressing concerns about employment and local procurement.[33] However, the three government departments and the South African Commercial, Catering and Allied Workers' Union each appealed that decision on the grounds that there were serious flaws in the Competition Tribunal's process and that it had failed to give adequate consideration to the public interest, respectively.[34] They argued that more stringent conditions should have been attached to the proposed acquisition. The Competition Appeal Court rejected the appeal, although it did require that Massmart reinstate the employees that it had retrenched in 2009 and 2010 and that the parties conduct a study to explore how local suppliers could participate in Walmart's global supply chain.[35]

Another political obstacle to competition reform arises from the state's various roles in the market. Many developing countries are still in transition and the state remains significantly involved in the market either as a participant or a regulator.[36] The economies of many developing countries are characterized by state-owned monopolies in infrastructure sectors and a high degree of government involvement in other sectors.[37] The state also regulates industries at the local, regional, and/or national levels.[38] While the state's involvement in the market may further a particular public interest, it can also lead to anticompetitive outcomes.[39]

Many developing countries have traditionally based their economic policies not on competition but on direct government control. This legacy can be hard to overcome as government departments may resist the introduction of market mechanisms and the loss of rights or control.[40] The government also derives significant political and economic benefits from its state-owned enterprises and has the incentive and ability to adopt protectionist and other anticompetitive measures to protect these enterprises, which do little to foster competitiveness and instead lead to inefficiencies.[41] Further, where the state participates directly in the economy, it tends to be the monopolist or dominant market player, especially in sectors where the state has traditionally provided those goods and services. Transition processes such as the privatization of state-owned enterprises and deregulation can also lead to anticompetitive effects.[42] For example, the government has an interest to maximize its revenue from privatization sales. One way to do this would be to create a business with market power so that it will be more valuable to the potential buyer. However, this merely converts a public monopoly into a private monopoly and hinders the prospects for competition in the postprivatization period.[43]

Where the state is the regulator, it may be subject to political pressure from various interest groups both in the establishment of the regulatory regime and in the postestablishment period.[44] Regulators in developing countries are especially prone to interest group pressures and capture due to the often close nexus between government and businesses.[45] Economic and political power tend to go hand in hand, especially in developing countries where concentrated markets are more prevalent and businesses fund various political activities. Politicians may also have personal business interests to protect.[46] Further, networks of family groups, trade associations, political party alliances, labor unions, ethnic groups, and regional groups are typically more important and influential in developing countries, especially as policy making tends to be less transparent and rent-seeking behavior is often conducted through or facilitated by these networks.[47] In developing countries, these well-connected and powerful interest groups often do not face particularly strong countervailing power from interest groups that support competition. The beneficiaries of competition are usually small and medium-sized businesses and consumers, which are generally dispersed, less experienced with competition law, less organized, and harder to mobilize.[48] There also tends to be asymmetry between the expected transition costs and long-term benefits of competition—the costs are generally borne by big businesses whereas the benefits are dispersed among consumers and small and medium-sized businesses and their individual share of the benefit tends to be small.[49] Therefore, as big business interests have much more to lose (or expect less to gain) from competition policy, they will organize and seek to lobby the government.[50] In developed countries, such political influence may be counterbalanced somewhat by the existence of an active civil society, an independent media, and a stronger competition culture, but these conditions are less likely to exist in developing countries.[51]

A recent example of how strong political opposition can derail competition reform is the Indian retail sector. The Indian retail sector has traditionally been protected from foreign competition; foreign multibrand retailers (such as Walmart) are restricted to wholesale operations and foreign single-brand retailers (such as Apple) can own only 51 percent of their Indian operations. In late November 2011, the Indian government decided to liberalize the retail market by allowing 51 percent foreign ownership of multibrand retailers and 100 percent foreign ownership of single-brand retailers. This decision came after more than two years of debate and was spurred by a declining economic environment. The policy change, which was an executive decision that did not require the approval of the Indian Parliament, sparked fierce opposition from political parties (both in opposition and in the ruling coalition) and small retailers. Parliament was disrupted, key bills were stalled, and numerous trade associations staged protests. In response to this widespread political pressure, the Indian government partially reversed its policy change, retracting its decision on multibrand retailers (but not its decision on single-brand retailers, which did not attract political opposition) less than two weeks after its initial announcement,[52] although it now appears that the Indian government might be reconsidering multibrand retail reform.[53] This example illustrates that, even in a climate where competition reform would clearly help improve economic performance, a multitude of political factors—such as competing policy objectives, political incentives, and interest group pressures—prevented reform. Therefore, it is inadvisable and unrealistic to ignore the political dimension of competition advocacy.

In light of these political challenges involved in overturning anticompetitive laws, it is clear that the traditional advocacy approach is inadequate for the task in developing countries. The role of the competition agency under the traditional advocacy approach consists largely of advising and educating government departments about the public interest aspects of their laws. Mere explanation and exposition of the anticompetitive effects of laws by competition agencies, though desirable, is unlikely to have a big effect on some government departments, especially those that are controlled by ministers, have politically appointed heads, or are involved in the political process. A more fundamental analysis of the political embeddedness of anticompetitive laws and regulations and consideration of a broader policy approach to this challenge are required.

Aside from the political challenges, a weak competition culture, weak institutional foundations, and lack of resources and expertise often hinder competition advocacy in developing countries.

A strong competition culture is more often found in developed countries with mature market economies and an experienced competition agency, whereas a weak competition culture is generally associated with developing countries, especially those countries that are transitioning to a market economy and have an inexperienced competition agency.[54] In developing countries, the competition law regime is typically relatively new and the competition authority and the judiciary have not had much experience with competition law and its related economic concepts.[55] Economic actors and the general public have been less exposed to competition and might not accept or understand competition principles, especially if cooperation and collaboration, rather than competition, are characteristic of the prevailing culture.[56] The government might not embrace competition principles because it is accustomed to intervening in the market, particularly where the country is transitioning from a centrally planned economy to a market economy.[57] Moreover, it is much more difficult to convince economic actors, the government, and the public of the benefits of competition if their experience with competition has been largely negative, as the introduction of competition might have led to the closure of inefficient businesses, job losses, and increased prices as previously controlled prices rose to their market levels.[58] All these circumstances contribute to a weak competition culture and present challenges to a competition agency's efforts to develop a stronger one. The difference in the level of competition culture is considered to be one of the most important and relevant differences between developed and developing countries.[59]

The institutional foundations in developing countries tend to be much weaker than in developed countries.[60] Market institutions, transparency, accountability mechanisms, and governance arrangements tend to be inadequate, and there is a general lack of competition law expertise in the judiciary, legal profession, and academia.[61] Developing countries also are likely to have a higher incidence of corruption, in both the judicial and administrative systems.[62] These institutional weaknesses can be exacerbated by competition reforms, especially if those reforms create further opportunities for government intervention and judicial scrutiny. This might undermine and unravel the benefits that competition reforms sought to achieve in the first place. These present challenges to competition enforcement, the development of competition culture, and competition advocacy.

Competition agencies in developing countries also typically lack sufficient human, material, and financial resources, severely limiting their ability to enforce the competition law and conduct competition advocacy.[63] As noted above, the competition law regime tends to be relatively new and professional and technical staff conversant in the relevant legal and economic concepts is scarce.[64] This, along with the prospect of private practice being more lucrative, makes it difficult for the competition agency to recruit and retain skilled staff.[65] Competition agencies also often lack the technical expertise that is required to make advocacy efforts directed at regulated industries informed and effective.[66] Competition agencies might also find it difficult to secure sufficient funding due to lack of public recognition of the importance of competition or they might need to rely on political connections to gain funding, which in turn might compromise enforcement efforts.[67] These factors present serious hurdles to effective competition law enforcement and advocacy and are compounded in developing countries due to often strong political opposition to competition.[68]

In light of these challenges, it might be advisable for a competition agency in a developing country to devote relatively more resources to competition advocacy and limit its initial enforcement activities to obvious cases of infringement, leaving the pursuit of a more comprehensive enforcement program to a later stage when it has gained more experience.[69] While the primary role of most competition agencies is the enforcement of competition laws, it involves complex legal and economic concepts and issues and competition agencies and courts in developing countries are often ill-equipped to deal with them.[70] A legal proceeding may take several years to work its way through the judicial process and therefore consume valuable resources during the intervening period.[71] Enforcement also requires cooperation from its subjects, especially with respect to providing private information, which may be less than forthcoming in developing countries where the judicial system and competition culture are weak.[72] Of course, it is important to remember that advocacy might not be any easier. Advocacy still requires sufficient expertise, especially if it is directed toward influencing the regulatory framework.[73] Further, a competition agency's credibility and reputation are keys to the success of its advocacy efforts.[74] They are vital for competition agencies in developing countries, as such agencies tend to be less established and well known and need to build up that credibility and reputation. This cannot be based on advocacy alone and needs to be built upon a solid foundation of successful enforcement, particularly cases that are widely viewed to be beneficial to consumers.[75] In short, advocacy and enforcement reinforce each other.[76]

Another limitation of the traditional advocacy model is that it does not take into account the institutional locus of the competition agency and how it may impact on competition advocacy. The traditional advocacy approach assumes that the competition agency is a decentralized agency of the executive branch of government with a certain amount of independence.[77] In reality, however, there is a range of institutional arrangements in different countries (especially developing countries) that brings competition agencies to varying degrees of closeness in their interaction with government.[78] This affects how a competition agency conducts advocacy and how effective it may be.[79] For example, a competition agency that is situated within a ministerial system is the responsibility of a government minister, and the head of the competition agency reports to that minister. The competition agency is supposed to work through its sponsoring ministry, which may see itself, and not the agency, as the competition policy advocate within the government. In contrast, if the head of the competition agency is a member of the cabinet or a high-ranking member of the executive branch (which is more frequent in developing than developed countries),[80] the competition agency will be present when major decisions are made and it can bring its knowledge to enhance the quality of those decisions. For example, the head of the European Union's Competition Commission is a member of the European Commission and the chairman of the Korea Fair Trade Commission is a minister and a member of South Korea's cabinet. Another option would be to directly prohibit government agencies from misusing their administrative powers to promote, manipulate, impede, or prevent economic activities or intervene in market activities. An example of this model is China's Anti-Monopoly Law.[81]

Also, competition agencies are often located at the fringes of government that have minimal involvement in lawmaking and economic reform (for example, as attachments to departments of law or attorneys general) as opposed to being situated near the center of government (such as departments of the prime minister or treasury) where the real political power lies and economic reforms are formulated and implemented. As a result, competition agencies tend to be politically weak. They also often find it difficult to get access to ministers or political leaders, especially outside their own sponsoring department. Even if a competition agency is located within a department of treasury, which tends to be more receptive to arguments for competition reform and proactive in pursuing competitive outcomes, it may nonetheless be difficult for the competition agency to argue for competition reform. This is because treasury often pursues a number of other reforms and policies (such as tax and trade policy) that might relegate competition policy and reform to lower priorities on its agenda.

Further, the dual roles of competition agencies—enforcement and advocacy—can lead to a trade-off between independence and advocacy.[82] On the one hand, an independent competition agency, or one that maintains arm's-length relationships with other government institutions, will have relative freedom in carrying out its enforcement role. The perception of independence increases the public's confidence in competition enforcement and enhances the competition agency's credibility.[83] This is especially important for new competition agencies. On the other hand, an independent agency may lack sufficient access to ministers and political leaders and may not be consulted in decisions that affect competition, thus hindering its ability to influence government policies effectively.[84] However, if a competition agency is involved in the political process, while it may enhance its effectiveness as an advocate, it may lose its credibility with consumers, businesses, and the general public and compromise its effectiveness as an enforcement agency. Therefore a choice should be made and a balance struck between the dual roles of competition agencies and their closeness to the center of government.

Hence, competition agencies need to be more aware of their institutional environment and role in the political process to enhance their effectiveness as competition advocates. Some strategies a competition agency could adopt to improve its effectiveness within its institutional environment, and hence its advocacy efforts, may be to align itself with powerful government departments to boost its political influence, engage in general discussions about competition with government departments rather than pursue them on specific matters, be involved in advance of or at the beginning stages of any competition issue, and consider using publicity as a weapon (although this may be unwelcome and result in negative consequences such as reduced resources and loss of jurisdiction).

Beyond Traditional Advocacy: A Policy Approach

Given the pervasiveness and politically embedded nature of anticompetitive laws, there needs to be an equally comprehensive approach to reforming these laws. It is therefore necessary to rethink the concept of competition advocacy. Rather than general actions that competition agencies might take to influence competition decisions within the government, competition advocacy could instead be a comprehensive program that targets underlying anticompetitive laws. Such an approach would cover not only traditional competition laws but also policies concerning international and interstate trade, intellectual property, foreign ownership and investment, tax, small businesses, the legal system, public and private ownership, licensing, public procurement, and bidding for monopoly franchises. This task is much more complex and resource intensive than that understood pursuant to the traditional advocacy approach, and it requires activities that go well beyond the normal scope of advocacy typically undertaken by a competition agency. Australia was a pioneer in taking such a comprehensive approach to competition reform in the mid-1990s. It is considered to be one of the most successful examples of procompetitive reform and represents the "gold standard" in competition reform.[85]

During the 1970s and 1980s, Australia suffered from poor economic performance and significant inefficiencies existed across the Australian economy, fostered by high trade barriers, various regulatory and institutional restrictions on domestic competition, and a business culture that was focused on rent seeking rather than on improving efficiency and innovation or meeting customer needs.[86] In the early 1980s, in response to the worsening economic climate and growing political pressure from businesses, Australian governments undertook some economic reforms, covering trade liberalization, capital markets, infrastructure deregulation, the labor market, tax, and macroeconomic policy.[87] While these reforms achieved some success, they were variable across jurisdictions and incomplete as some sectors, such as education, public services, and intellectual property, were not covered. It was also widely acknowledged that Australia's broader competition policy framework was impeding economic performance and the creation of national markets for infrastructure and other services.[88] Therefore, an independent inquiry (the Hilmer Review) was established in October 1992 to devise a framework for competition reforms across all jurisdictions. The Hilmer Review reported its findings in August 1993 and found that "Australia, for all practical purposes, [was] a single integrated market, increasingly exposed to domestic and international competition";[89] it recommended the adoption of a national competition policy that would aim to "promote and maintain competitive forces to increase efficiency and community welfare, while recognizing other social goals."[90]

In April 1995, all Australian governments—federal, state, and territory—agreed to a series of agreements that set out a comprehensive and nationally coordinated microeconomic reform program, that is, a national competition policy based on the framework established by the Hilmer Review.[91] The guiding principle underlying Australia's National Competition Policy (NCP) was that nothing that limited competition was warranted unless it could be demonstrated at an independent public inquiry that the restriction was justified and that the public interest objectives could not be achieved in a less anticompetitive manner.[92] The components of the NCP included (1) legislation review and reform, which involved the federal, state, and territory governments each identifying, reviewing, and, where appropriate, reforming legislation that restricted competition; (2) adoption of the principle of competitive neutrality, whereby governments ensured that their publicly owned businesses would not enjoy any net competitive advantage because of being publicly owned and committed to applying the Trade Practices Act (Australia's competition statute as it was then called) to all businesses and levels of the economy; and (3) sector-specific reforms.[93]

This process placed significant political, legal, and administrative demands on Australia's national, state, and territory governments. It took ten years to review and reform the mass of anticompetitive laws and government actions that limited competition. At the end of the reform program, the governments had achieved a large majority of the planned reforms and the NCP had delivered substantial benefits to the Australian community, contributing to increased productivity growth, real per capita income, and business innovation, and reduced unemployment and prices. Overall, these benefits had greatly outweighed any transactional or adjustment costs.[94] The elements of the NCP that contributed to its success included adopting basic principles of competition policy, priority areas, and policy prescriptions; allowing flexibility in how individual jurisdictions met their commitments; establishing and resourcing an institutional machinery to identify and review all anticompetitive laws; adopting a transparent and independent process for monitoring progress and outcomes; and providing financial incentives for governments that met reform commitments.[95]

Beyond the design of the NCP itself, several overarching factors underlay its successful implementation. Most importantly, there was a strong political will and commitment to competition reform. Australia's long period of poor economic performance, increasing pressure from international competition, and the findings of the Hilmer Review were the main drivers of this political support. Bipartisan political support came from economically literate key political leaders at the federal and state levels, unions, businesses, key opinion leaders (such as newspapers and think tanks), and senior bureaucrats.[96] This political commitment to competition reform was crucial not only in initiating but in sustaining reform throughout the ten-year period.

There was also a widespread culture of community support for competition reform and an awareness of the benefits that it could bring.[97] This was fostered in part by the advocacy of a number of strong institutions. For example, the Industry Commission[98] and its predecessor, the Tariff Board, had published numerous reports about the harm to competition caused by trade restrictions and government actions. The Trade Practices Commission and the Prices Surveillance Authority (which combined to form the Australian Competition and Consumer Commission, Australia's competition regulator, in 1995) had also conducted a number of studies on competition and the harm caused by monopolies. Vigorous enforcement of the Trade Practices Act was also effective in building and enhancing this culture of support for competition policy.

Rather than adopt a "big bang" approach to economic reform in the 1980s, Australia approached its economic reforms gradually, adopting a number of reforms prior to the NCP. This helped to minimize the adjustment and distribution costs of the NCP.[99] The sequencing of reforms was also important. For example, trade liberalization not only exposed businesses in the traded sector to competition, but also exposed the inefficiencies in the nontraded sector of the economy, in particular public utility services and the labor market. The dual effects of trade liberalization helped generate political pressure for domestic market reform. The NCP was hence seen as the natural next step as it would consolidate and extend the reforms undertaken in the 1980s.

We do not argue that all countries should adopt Australia's NCP approach. Rather, we believe that, in light of Australia's NCP, the concept of competition advocacy itself, which has been dominated by the traditional advocacy approach to date, must be reframed. Under the traditional advocacy approach, the competition agency engages in advocacy, typically on a case-by-case basis. In contrast, the NCP was a comprehensive and systematic reform program that covered all industries and levels of government. The governments themselves—and not the competition agency, which had only a marginal role—implemented the NCP, with progress monitored by an independent government agency (the National Competition Council) established for that purpose.[100] The NCP reinforces the view expressed in this chapter that the task of securing comprehensive competition reform is much broader than that undertaken under the traditional advocacy approach.

As the Australian experience demonstrates, a national competition policy requires strong political will and commitment to competition reform, institutional support, and significant resources. Although these features are often lacking in developing countries, this does not mean that the national competition policy approach is irrelevant to developing countries.[101] For example, Mexico committed to a national competition policy in 2007 and currently India is seriously considering its adoption.[102] Australia's NCP was also the blueprint for the Competition Assessment Toolkit[103] (OECD Toolkit) that has been developed and promoted globally (including in developing countries) by the Organisation for Economic Cooperation and Development (OECD) as a way to help eliminate barriers to competition, although the

OECD presents competition reform as a technical rather than a political exercise. This shows that the national competition policy approach has a practical, operational relevance in developing countries.

The OECD recommends that governments conduct competition assessments of their laws and regulations to identify restrictions on competition and to avoid them where possible.[104] The OECD Toolkit provides an analytical framework to help governments identify unnecessary restraints on competition and develop less restrictive alternatives that still achieve important public interest objectives.[105] The framework can be applied to evaluate proposed and existing laws and regulations and used by government departments to assist with the development and review of policies.[106] It consists of two main components. First, there is a "competition checklist" that poses a series of questions to identify laws and regulations that have the potential to unnecessarily restrain competition. These are laws and regulations that (1) place limits on the number or range of suppliers, the ability of suppliers to compete, and the choices and information available to customers; and (2) reduce the incentives for suppliers to compete.[107] The checklist acts as a screen so that government resources can be focused on those areas where competition assessment is most needed.[108] Where the checklist suggests that there may be a potentially excessive restraint on market activity, a more comprehensive competition assessment is conducted.[109]

An example of where the OECD Toolkit is being implemented is Mexico. In 2007, the Mexican government and the OECD signed an agreement to implement the OECD Toolkit and Mexico began to embark on reforms to improve the competitiveness of the Mexican economy by using the framework provided by the OECD Toolkit.[110] The reforms centered on increasing competition in product markets and regulatory improvement. To date, pro-competitive banking reforms (based on OECD Toolkit studies on credit cards and deposit accounts) have been implemented; reports on the airline, pharmaceutical, and telecommunications sectors have been completed; and reports on intercity bus transportation, retail competition/supermarkets, and government standard setting are forthcoming.[111] Although some progress is being made, Mexico's current institutional arrangements and political structures are not conducive to reform and create conditions that enable interest groups to block reforms.[112] These circumstances present some clear challenges to the continued implementation of the OECD Toolkit in Mexico and it will require a strong political consensus and political will and commitment to competition reform to overcome these challenges. While some resistance to reform is natural in many countries, Mexico's experience with the OECD Toolkit exposes one of its main flaws: it presents competition reform as a purely technical exercise and does not address the political nature of the task. As we have emphasized in this chapter, this political dimension simply cannot be ignored, especially in developing countries where the issue is exacerbated by the lack of supporting institutions.

.   .   .

The concept of competition advocacy requires reformulation, especially in the context of developing countries. The traditional approach to competition advocacy, which tends to focus on advocacy and advice to governments on a case-by-case basis, is deficient because it does not take into account the political challenges, institutional and resource limitations, and weak competition culture typically faced by competition agencies in developing countries. In contrast, the national competition policy approach conceptualizes competition advocacy directed toward government as a comprehensive program that targets anticompetitive laws and allows for explicit consideration of the obstacles to competition advocacy that exist in developing countries.

The aim of this chapter is not to argue that a national competition policy should be adopted for all countries. We recognize that it is an ambitious undertaking that places greater political, institutional, and resource demands than under traditional advocacy and therefore may not necessarily be realistic or feasible for adoption in many developing countries. However, we do believe that the national competition policy approach clearly shows that competition advocacy is a much broader and more complex, resource intensive, institutionally dependent, and politically driven endeavor than put forward under the traditional advocacy approach. It is therefore necessary to rethink the concept of competition advocacy.

What such a new concept of competition advocacy might entail, however, requires further research and consideration. There remain a wide range of activities that lie on the spectrum between traditional advocacy at one end and national competition policy at the other. For example, an incremental approach to competition advocacy that aims at setting the scene for competition reform; engaging with policy makers, interest groups, and other stakeholders; and fostering the establishment of supporting institutions may be appropriate. We do believe, however, that any new concept of competition advocacy needs to take into account its political, institutional, and other relevant contexts.

12

Domestic and Cross-Border Transfer of Wealth

Ariel Ezrachi

Protection of consumer welfare is a central pillar of competition law enforcement. Although not the sole goal pursued by competition law, such protection—preventing unjustified transfer of wealth from consumers to producers—is a common feature of modern competition regimes.

In the domestic sphere, "transfer of wealth" is a consistent and clear benchmark in competition law enforcement. However, this is not necessarily the case in an international setting. As will be illustrated, the assessment of transfer of wealth in a cross-border setting may distort competition law enforcement. While extraterritoriality and cooperation between national competition authorities can, at times, remedy suboptimal enforcement, this may not always be the case.

This chapter will review the negative welfare implications of transfer of wealth for small and developing economies. The discussion begins with a short introduction to the concept of consumer welfare and transfer of wealth in competition law. The focus then shifts to the review of this concept in a cross-border setting and the welfare externalities it triggers. The chapter then considers the implications of these distributive effects for developing and small economies.

Consumer Welfare: Transfer of Wealth
in a Domestic Setting

Competition laws are often concerned with the effects that certain activities may have on consumer welfare and on the possible transfer of wealth from consumers to corporate entities engaged in anticompetitive activity.

The focus on consumer welfare is not always immediately apparent.[1] Furthermore, even among those who share the core value of protecting consumer welfare, differences emerge as to the exact meaning of the term and the best ways of achieving it.[2] Similarly, the measurement of welfare in competition law has also been the subject of varying approaches, from the protection of total welfare[3] to a focus on consumer surplus.[4] While the latter has dominated the antitrust landscape in recent years in both the United States[5] and the European Union (EU),[6] it has been viewed by some as an imperfect proxy of consumer welfare.[7]

Despite the inconsistencies and variations regarding the exact scope and measurement of consumer welfare, the notion that competition law protects (among other things) consumers' welfare is common to all regimes.

The focus on consumer harm naturally draws attention to the transfer of wealth from consumers to conspirators. If one accepts that competition law strives to enhance consumer welfare, the subsequent quest of competition enforcement is to prevent negative, unjustifiable transfer of wealth from consumers to corporate entities engaged in anticompetitive activity.[8]

Interestingly, when applied in an international context, the way in which welfare is measured may distort competition law enforcement and, at times, fail to protect consumers as a class.

Distributive Effects of Competition Law Enforcement
in a Global Environment

The globalization of markets has led to a marked increase in cross-border trade and competition. Inevitably, anticompetitive practices and their effects now span borders too. These processes necessitated convergence and cooperation between competition agencies concerned with enhancing the effectiveness of competition enforcement. With the aid of bilateral, regional, and multinational cooperation, competition regimes all over the world now speak a similar lingo. Indeed, they are on a path of assimilation. These trends have resulted in increased coordination of enforcement, an assimilation of remedies and a corresponding reduction in conflicts.

Nonetheless, these global trends by no means override the inherent domestic perspective in competition law enforcement. By their very nature, domestic competition regimes are empowered to protect competitiveness and consumer welfare in their national markets.[9] As such they represent discrete islands of enforcement operating in an international landscape. Thus, while competition and the restraints on it become increasingly transnational, enforcement remains domestic in nature.

Interestingly, the domestic focus of competition law enforcement has distributive effects globally. To illustrate, consider first a purely domestic setting in which national competition law is applied to a domestic anticompetitive activity. In such a case, the competition analysis takes into account the totality of effects and actions. Crucially, whichever goal one advances as part of the national regime, whether it be efficiency or distribution driven, the analysis is carried out in a "confined economy" where both violators and injured parties are present. By contrast, in cases with a cross-border dimension, domestic competition regimes use domestic laws and values to appraise international activities while predominantly focusing on competition in the domestic market.[10] Not surprisingly, the imperfect overlap between the effects of the conduct and the reviewing jurisdictions may trigger inconsistencies and friction. Each jurisdiction, under its own mandate, strives to protect competition in its territory and hence will focus on domestic effects.[11] When the effects of particular conduct span across jurisdictions, a national competition authority will not consider all the actions and effects, but only the effects in its jurisdiction. While such approach is a natural by-product of the domestic-driven competition policies around the world, it does have distributive welfare consequences as decision making differs from that under a purely domestic setting.

In many cases, despite the imperfect overlap, the enforcement result overall may still reflect a desirable competition outcome, as one or more jurisdictions may curtail the anticompetitive activity. This is especially so when consumer surplus serves as the leading benchmark in competition law analyses. Yet, at times, this imperfect overlap may deviate from optimal enforcement and result in over- or underdeterrence. This would be the case in particular when the positive and negative impacts of an activity are not spread equally across jurisdictions.

Take, for example, the competitive effects of export cartels. These anticompetitive agreements target foreign markets without generating domestic anticompetitive effects. Consequently, the "home jurisdiction" may refrain from challenging activities of an export cartel, despite adverse effects on consumers elsewhere. Negative, yet external, anticompetitive effects remain unchallenged.[12]

As these practices are not designed to generate anticompetitive effects in the domestic markets where the companies operate, some jurisdictions have adopted formal procedures that exempt these arrangements from domestic competition law.[13] Common justifications for exempting export cartels have focused on cost reduction, risk sharing, and the target jurisdiction's better position to confront and deter such activities.[14] In addition, it has been argued at times that some export cartels are procompetitive when the colluding companies are small firms with no market power that combine forces to form effective export entities and at times in order to compete with powerful cartels elsewhere.[15]

With the growing consensus on the need to battle cartel activity worldwide, the explicit exemption of export cartels has been criticized.[16] Increased international cooperation[17] and the introduction of tougher and more determined policies in relation to cartel activities[18] have led to a reduction in the number of such provisions.[19] Still, recall that even absent formal exemptions, competition regimes are geared, by design, to protect and appraise effects on the local markets. Subsequently, the decline in formal exemptions of export cartels does not eliminate the implicit domestic bias in competition law enforcement.

As nations lack the incentive or authority to intervene, export cartels may remain unchallenged. This suboptimal enforcement results in welfare externalities and transfer of wealth from foreign consumers to local businesses.

Cross-Border Transfer of Wealth

So far, the discussion has assumed a consistent enforcement equation that leads to a suboptimal result due to the focus on domestic effects. A further distortion at an international level may stem from *changes* to that enforcement equation.

Due to the domestic focal point, the enforcement equation may shift from the prevention of negative transfer of wealth from consumers to conspirators, to the prevention of transfer of wealth from the domestic jurisdiction to elsewhere. In other words, in an international setting, a new variant that may be described as *cross-border transfer of wealth* may be added, and override variants previously adopted in the domestic analysis.

To clarify, the cross-border transfer of wealth consideration is substantially different from the notion of domestic transfer of wealth described earlier. When influenced by cross-border transfer of wealth considerations, a competition authority is not solely concerned with transfer of wealth from consumers to producers. Rather, it focuses on transfer of wealth from the domestic market to the foreign market and vice versa. In other words, its focal point is calibrated by a desire to enhance positive transfer of wealth into the domestic market and discourage negative transfer of wealth to external markets.

To illustrate, when the anticompetitive activity concerns limited local sales and significant exports, the exporting jurisdiction may shift from consumer welfare back to the total welfare benchmark. This is because it internalizes benefits at a corporate level and externalizes consumer welfare losses. On the other hand, when the activity harms local consumers and originates abroad (cartels or mergers), the enforcement equation is likely to emphasize consumer welfare.[20] Furthermore, the focus on "cross-border transfer of wealth" may result in the collapse of competition analysis and the use of distorted analysis in which the outcome is determined by industrial or social considerations.[21] Needless to say, this is an inconsistent equation that is not likely to be manifested publicly. In fact, it is predominantly dependent on a lack of transparency in competition appraisal.

Coming back to the example of export cartels, a cross-border transfer of wealth equation provides a more pressing reason for the exporting jurisdiction not to intervene. In such a scenario, the exporting state experiences an increase in producer welfare (as well as an increase in employment and revenue from taxation), with no reduction in consumer welfare. On the other hand, the importing state suffers a loss in consumer welfare that is not offset by welfare gains upstream.[22] The added distortion is noticeable when an export cartel generates *negative spillover* in the exporting state. In a regime driven by consumer welfare, such effects would have been likely to trigger the application of the domestic competition rules. Yet, under a cross-border transfer of wealth equation, the exporting state may ignore the spillover because there is a net total welfare gain.

A more subtle example concerns the tension that sometimes surrounds cross-border merger transactions. When a merger spans jurisdictions, it may permit a jurisdiction to advance local considerations and internalize many of the merger's benefits, while ignoring the external costs laid on corporations and consumers outside its borders. A given jurisdiction may try to shield its local markets from a negative transfer of wealth, while the jurisdiction that receives the positive transfer of wealth caused by the anticompetitive behavior of its local corporations may be reluctant to act against such behavior. Each authority, concentrating on its own domestic economic realities, may justify the differences in their decisions. Such distortions in appraisal may be amplified by social, industrial, and political considerations.[23]

These distortions can be best dealt with by ensuring the presence of clear legal and economic benchmarks for assessment and transparent competition appraisal. Dialogue between enforcers and case-by-case cooperation can play a significant role in preventing and exposing political and industrial considerations that transform the legitimate transfer of wealth benchmark into its distorted version of cross-border transfer of wealth.

Extraterritoriality and Cooperation

As illustrated, in an international setting the domestic perspective and the focus on cross-border transfer of wealth may distance competition law analysis from its core values and result in a tendency toward both Type I errors (false positive) [24] and Type II errors (false negative).[25] Two powerful tools, however, may bring the equation closer to its origins. These are extraterritoriality and cooperation.

Extraterritoriality

The extraterritorial application of competition laws is an essential tool used by competition agencies to address infringements that take place outside the jurisdiction. When such infringements or transactions have consequences within the local market, the competition agency is often empowered to scrutinize the activity.[26]

As such, extraterritoriality can remedy under-enforcement and curtail negative transfer of wealth by blocking anticompetitive transactions and activities that were not challenged elsewhere.

Long-arm jurisdiction permits more than the termination of anticompetitive actions. It also allows the domestic authority to penalize the violating corporations and provide deterrence. This function is of value even if the anticompetitive activity was brought to an end by other jurisdictions. The penalty or remedy imposed by each jurisdiction aims to reflect or correct the harm to the local market and is therefore valuable, irrespective of enforcement elsewhere.

Linked to this is the role extraterritoriality plays at enhancing the power of the state when faced with multinational corporations. Absent extraterritorial powers, the ability to enforce and deter international actors is significantly hampered.[27] The ability to apply competition provisions to foreign undertakings makes it harder for those corporations to ignore that jurisdiction. When backed by adequate enforcement capacity and cooperation frameworks, extraterritoriality serves as a valuable tool to curtail corporate power.

Two qualifying comments are in order. First, extraterritoriality may have a detrimental impact when it leads to over-enforcement. This may be the case when a jurisdiction blocks a remote transaction or activity that is overall beneficial yet has an adverse effect within the jurisdiction. Second, while effective in dealing with under-enforcement, extraterritoriality cannot remedy over-enforcement by one jurisdiction that undermines welfare gains in another. Accordingly, in an international setting, when domestic perspective results in over-enforcement, welfare loss cannot be salvaged through extraterritoriality.

On this point it is worth noting that domestic-oriented enforcement will rarely account for the totality of anti- and procompetitive effects.[28] Assuming all affected competition regimes can apply their laws to the anticompetitive activity, the amalgamation of enforcement efforts will result in a similar outcome as under a "confined economy." Interestingly, when one or more of the competition enforcers take into account cross-border transfer of wealth, the aggregated result is likely to reflect over-enforcement, as the most restrictive decision prevails. On the other hand, under-enforcement in a global setting is likely to occur when one or more of the affected jurisdictions fail to apply their competition provisions to the anticompetitive activity. This may be the case, for example, when a small or developing economy lacks the resources, capacity, and political will to enforce competition law against anticompetitive activity that affects the local market but does not affect other jurisdictions.[29]

Cooperation

Cooperation, assimilation, and harmonization also play a significant role in limiting the influence of the domestic perspective. Cooperation can support unilateral cross-border assertion of jurisdiction. It facilitates extraterritoriality, information gathering, investigation, and sanctioning. In addition, cooperation provides a valuable tool to relax the focus on cross-border transfer of wealth and to take into account comity principles.[30] More generally, harmonization and assimilation, fostered through cooperation, provide valuable and transparent benchmarks for assessment and deepen the trust between competition enforcers. As hinted above, the more transparent and assimilated the analytical process is, the harder it is for noncompetitive variants to find their way into the analysis.

Three main limitations of cooperation are noteworthy in the context of transfer of wealth. First, cooperation links distinct regimes. As such, cooperation will only relax the domestic perspective, but the domestic perspective will still pervade. Second, the ability to foster positive transfer of wealth from one market to another may create disincentives for entering into cooperative agreements. As long as a jurisdiction is capable of protecting its own market from foreign anticompetitive activity, it may object to binding or voluntary frameworks aimed at curtailing its ability to foster positive, incoming transfer of wealth.[31] Third, cooperating jurisdictions may exert similar externalities as a group on non-members. This would be the case when transfer of wealth affects the position of one group relative to another. As a result, externalities may emerge between cooperation blocks that aim to protect their own members, sometimes at the expense of non-members.

Implications for Small and Developing Economies

The discussion above highlights how, in a global setting, domestic regimes provide the engine for aggregated competition law enforcement. While the domestic focus may alter the transfer of wealth equation and at times lead to an alternative cross-border transfer of wealth equation, the effect can be limited through extraterritoriality, cooperation, and assimilation.

This regained equilibrium is, however, harder to achieve in the case of small and developing economies. In other words, they may remain exposed, more than others, to externalities and negative transfer of wealth. This exposure stems, predominantly, from shortcomings linked to enforcement capacity, extraterritorial powers, and cooperation. The significance of each of these variants is explored below.

Effective competition law enforcement serves as the first building block that ensures the welfare of domestic consumers and prevention of negative transfer of wealth. One should distinguish, in this context, between the mere adoption of competition provisions, possibly due to international pressure, and genuine implementation and enforcement efforts.[32] Evidently, some small and developing economies may wish to focus their efforts in developing local industry and economy and may have reservations as to the merit of introducing a competition regime at an early stage. However, transfer of wealth across borders ought to make the adoption of a domestic competition regime a priority, irrespective of whether the jurisdiction has fully transitioned into a liberalized market economy concerned with consumer protection.

Due to the domestic nature of competition law enforcement, a decision not to adopt an effective competition regime may result in exposure to negative externalities generated by other jurisdictions. In some instances, this exposure will be limited, since enforcement efforts elsewhere serve the interests of the small or developing economies. In those cases, when the affected markets tend to be global, the interests of several jurisdictions align and one may be able to *free ride* on enforcement efforts elsewhere. However, note that the benefits in these instances are incidental in nature. Free riding will fail to provide relief in cases of under-enforcement elsewhere. As markets and economic effects differ widely between jurisdictions, a free riding policy is a perilous one.[33]

In addition, lack of effective domestic competition enforcement may encourage sophisticated undertakings to target the small or developing domestic jurisdictions, while avoiding scrutiny by effective competition regimes elsewhere. For example, it has been reported that due to the risk of harsh financial penalties and custodial sentences, international cartels choose at times not to extend their cartel activity to the United States.[34] At the same time, the characteristics of small and developing economies, such as the limited level of competition enforcement in the domestic market and the likely absence of buyer power, may attract anticompetitive activity as it is easier for foreign players to obtain market power and engage in transfer of wealth.

Linked to this is the ability to curtail the anticompetitive activity. While multinational corporations are willing to abide by the enforcement powers of powerful jurisdictions, they may refuse to acknowledge the legitimate interests of small economies. Their economic power and the income they channel into the local economy give them a strong bargaining position and can enable them to curtail enforcement attempts or negotiate favorable remedies. Without a credible threat of enforcement and effective leniency programs, the local jurisdiction remains largely exposed to anticompetitive activities. For example, some firms have been reported to set aside funds for the payment of damages and fines in large jurisdictions while perceiving the need to allocate sums to small economies to be negligible.[35] Similarly, the lack of effective enforcement may result in merger transactions being completed with no domestic scrutiny or remedies. These transactions may be subject to restrictions in other jurisdictions but may go unchallenged in developing ones.[36]

Accordingly, beyond the domestic perspective, institutional growth and capacity building—which lead to an effective, independent competition enforcement regime—should be viewed as paramount goals for competition regimes at an early stage. They provide essential shielding of the domestic market from both corporate and state power, which may foster negative transfer of wealth from that jurisdiction to corporate actors abroad

Unfortunately, the limited enforcement capacity of developing economies with infant competition regimes undermines their ability to utilize extraterritorial enforcement. These jurisdictions often find it hard to grapple with domestic activities and the need to foster competition culture. An attempt to curtail sophisticated international anticompetitive activity and impose effective remedies on the international violators may be beyond their reach.[37] Until they develop such capacity, they remain exposed to negative transfer of wealth as long as the cross-border activity is not challenged by other, more powerful jurisdictions.

Beyond extraterritoriality, cooperation—whether bilateral, subregional, regional, or multinational—supports capacity building, facilitates domestic and extraterritorial enforcement, and may provide a valuable tool for rebalancing the transfer of wealth equation. Cooperation may serve as both a shield and a sword. As a shield, cooperation fosters communication, assimilation, and trust between enforcers, all of which support transparent and effective competition enforcement in which a policy based on cross-border transfer of wealth is less likely to materialize. As a sword, cooperation helps support domestic enforcement capacity as well as extraterritorial enforcement. With respect to the latter, it may prove crucial in exchange of information, coordination of enforcement, and remedies.

Yet small and developing jurisdictions will not always find it easy to establish effective cooperation in competition law.[38] That may be particularly so at a bilateral level where they may find it hard to secure meaningful agreements with strong, developed jurisdictions. The limited level of trade between jurisdictions, the limited enforcement capacity, and the cost of maintaining cooperative links may render such agreements unattractive. Other variables that may affect the desirability and success of such frameworks include political and industrial parameters, interest groups, domestic politics, economic considerations, employment opportunities, and political stability.

One would expect to see, and does see, stronger bilateral links between jurisdictions that share similarities in relation to these variables.

Evidently, the decision whether to establish bilateral cooperation in competition law results from a wide range of political and economic considerations and may be contrary to the interests of both developed and developing economies. In the confined context of transfer of wealth, powerful jurisdictions may lack the incentive to establish meaningful bilateral cooperation with small and developing regimes, when such cooperation undermines externalities and ongoing positive transfer of wealth. On the other hand, they may support capacity building and cooperation with other jurisdictions when wider externalities are absorbed in the developed countries.

At the multinational level, cooperation efforts can be distinguished based on whether they form a binding or voluntary agreement. Failed attempts to establish a meaningful, binding wide multinational (as opposed to focused multinational) agreement on competition law showcased their practical inferiority. The disparity of interest and the heterogeneous nature of membership crippled attempts at the World Trade Organization and earlier binding initiatives.[39] With the exception of the unique example of the EU, binding wide-multinational frameworks failed to provide a viable channel for cooperation in competition law.[40] Accordingly, they are unlikely to be used by small and developing economies to rebalance the transfer of wealth equation.

By contrast, voluntary multinational agreements have proven valuable in providing a channel for communication, assimilation, and a source of support and capacity building. Three forums are particularly influential in the multilateral scene, advancing nonbinding frameworks and promoting cooperation in competition law.[41] These are the United Nations Conference on Trade and Development (UNCTAD), the Organisation for Economic Cooperation and Development (OECD), and the International Competition Network (ICN). In contrast with previous unsuccessful attempts to advance binding multinational frameworks in competition law, these forums provide soft convergence and voluntary frameworks. As such, they serve as a valuable tool for small and developing economies since they foster slow processes of assimilation and enable valuable interaction between jurisdictions. Participation in initiatives advanced by these forums provides a voice for small and developing economies, which form part of an evolving international consensus on competition law enforcement. In the context of transfer of wealth, processes that stem from this dialogue serve to relax externalities through cooperation and the strengthening of the domestic enforcement regimes.

Another level of cooperation that is noteworthy in the context of small and developing economies is that of regional, subregional, or focused multinational agreements.[42] In principle, the move from wide multilateral, to focused multinational, or regional, facilitates the finding of common ground. Where political, trade, and economic interests are aligned, there is a more concrete framework for cooperation. In the context of competition law enforcement and transfer of wealth, such initiatives may play a particular role in enhancing the international standing of members and facilitate the enforcement of competition law.[43] By being part of a wider homogeneous group, each jurisdiction is empowered by the regional framework in its interaction with foreign private and state actors. Entities may find it harder to ignore the enforcement efforts of a jurisdiction where such a move would have consequences within other members of the regional alliance. Similarly, the aggregation of power may tilt the transfer of wealth equation between jurisdictions. The regional group may be able not only to block the negative transfer of wealth but, at times, to inflict it. The ability of the group to externalize costs onto other jurisdictions increases the incentive of others to cooperate with the group. As such it not only serves to shield members from external transfer of wealth, but also facilitates cooperation that may further reduce the likelihood for unchallenged externalities.

Noteworthy in this respect are ongoing efforts by UNCTAD to support the use of existing and new regional frameworks to enhance collaboration in competition law enforcement.[44] Another interesting initiative, also promoted by UNCTAD, concerns the development of nonconfidential information exchange platform. The initiative, first proposed at the 12th Session of the Intergovernmental Group of Experts on Competition Law and Policy,[45] will see the creation of a collaborative information platform for competition agencies. The platform will enable developing and young competition regimes to pool their resources, support case-by-case investigations, and enhance agencies' effectiveness in dealing with cross-border anticompetitive activities.

Concluding Remarks

Global enforcement of competition law relies, primarily, on the efforts of disparate domestic enforcement regimes and cooperative frameworks between them. This is borne out of reality, rather than from any belief in the superiority of such an approach. Past attempts to advance a truly global antitrust enforcement regime have been blocked by the harsh truth of jurisdiction, politics, and sovereignty.[46]

The unilateral approach has been supplemented by cooperation at bilateral, regional, and multinational levels. These frameworks, whether binding or voluntary, have provided a valuable channel for increased convergence, assimilation, coordination, and facilitation of competition enforcement activities.[47] Cooperation has also proven crucial in limiting friction between jurisdictions in their domestic and extraterritorial application of their competition regimes.

Cooperation, however, cannot override the domestic nature of competition enforcement. In a global setting, when faced with cross-border activity, the domestic focal point may sometimes fail to account for the totality of effects and as such divert the analysis from an optimal level of enforcement.

Exploring these processes through the viewpoint of transfer of wealth provides valuable insights. First, the consideration of transfer of wealth yields different results when faced with cross-border activity. While the enforcement equation remains the same, the imperfect overlap between the effect and the jurisdiction may lead to suboptimal enforcement. Second, the domestic perspective may result in a transition in a competition authority's focus from transfer of wealth between consumers and producers to transfer of wealth between jurisdictions. Third, since each competition regime is not likely to take account of the totality of effects, the global enforcement landscape is based on the premise that each jurisdiction will protect its domestic market, at times through extraterritorial application of its competition laws.

As illustrated, in a global economy, domestic competition law serves a vital role in protecting the local market from harmful externalities. Effective competition enforcement, backed by long-arm jurisdiction, can serve to remedy under-enforcement elsewhere. It increases bargaining power when dealing with multinational corporations and foreign states. Cooperation at bilateral or wider multinational levels enables capacity building and facilitates unilateral enforcement. It also serves a crucial role in communication and assimilation, all central to reducing the likelihood of overregulation and externalities.

From a small or developing economy's perspective, the need to promote effective competition enforcement should therefore not only be viewed from a domestic perspective or stem from external international pressure to foster market mechanisms. Rather, it should stem from the realization that irrespective of domestic challenges, the global competition landscape necessitates it.

13

The Patent-Antitrust Interface in Developing Countries

Thomas K. Cheng

Despite the push for convergence in recent years, there seems to be a growing awareness that developed and developing countries may require different approaches to competition law. Not only may enforcement priorities need to be set differently—as developed and developing countries may be beset by dissimilar competition problems—but there are also reasons to believe that more fundamental adjustments must be made before antitrust doctrines and analytical approaches fashioned in industrialized economies can be successfully implemented by developing countries. The disparate states of economic development and sociopolitical environment of developed and developing countries often mean that their markets function differently, which may necessitate adjustments to prevailing analytical approaches in antitrust.

An area of antitrust law for which adjustments may be needed is the patent-antitrust interface, which is one of the most complex areas of antitrust law. This complexity stems from the need to balance the patent law focus on innovation incentives and the overriding antitrust concern with consumer welfare. The patent system generates innovation incentives by granting an inventor a period of exclusivity of exploitation and commercialization, which allows the inventor to charge a higher price than otherwise possible for the invention. This supracompetitive price produces an abnormal profit for the inventor, which presumably allows him to recoup his research and development (R&D) outlay. Consumers are made to bear welfare loss in the short term to attract innovations. The general belief is that without patent exclusivity, society would suffer from insufficient innovation. In the short term at least, there is an ostensible conflict between patent and antitrust policies.

There is a wide range of views on the patent-antitrust interface. Some note that the conflict between the two areas of law is more apparent than real[1] while some believe that patent policy should be given primacy and have proposed a framework in which innovation is the common denominator between patent and antitrust policies.[2] In one of the seminal articles on the patent-antitrust interface, Professor Louis Kaplow argues that a proper resolution of the interface requires delicate balancing and propounds his famous ratio test.[3] Whatever view one holds of the patent-antitrust interface in developed countries, a different approach to it is called for in developing economies. One cannot facilely assume that the sacrifice of short-run consumer welfare to generate innovation incentives will necessarily be socially beneficial; there may be no potential inventors to take advantage of the incentives generated by the patent system. Developing countries also lack the institutional infrastructure, such as venture capital financing and capability in scientific research, to generate genuine innovations. The loss of consumer welfare may be incurred in vain.

Moreover, developing countries may pursue more goals than economic efficiency and consumer welfare in their antitrust laws. They may need to incorporate developmental concerns: the satisfaction of basic human needs such as food, medicine, and basic education; the alleviation of poverty through the promotion of small and medium-sized enterprises; and the development of technological capacity through both domestic innovation and imitation of foreign technology. To the extent that these considerations can be meaningfully incorporated, they should be accorded due weight in antitrust analysis. One may legitimately wonder how this can be done, especially in light of the inherent complexity of the patent-antitrust interface. The exercise is doubtless going to be fraught with difficulty. Yet it does not mean that it should not be attempted. For developing countries, developmental concerns are simply too important to be ignored if antitrust does not want to risk being implemented in a vacuum. There is perhaps nothing more important to a developing country than the pursuit of economic development. For many developing countries, given their distance from the global technological frontier, economic development may not derive much benefit from the encouragement of innovation. Excessively generous intellectual property protection, however, may create significant obstacles to the attainment of other development objectives.

The central thesis of this chapter is that developing countries need to take different approaches to the patent–antitrust interface. This is particularly true in light of the stringent intellectual property protections mandated by the Agreement on Trade-Related Aspects of Intellectual Property Rights (hereinafter known as the TRIPS Agreement), which has been observed to have resulted in a significant wealth transfer from developing country consumers to multinational corporations. Not only should the approaches be different from that of the industrialized economies, but developing countries should also not be treated as a monolith as far as the patent–antitrust interface is concerned. In light of their differences in terms of stages of economic development, per capita income, and technological capacity, there is no single approach to the interface that suits all of them. Developing countries must be distinguished on one basis or another to reflect these differences. In fact, a country-specific approach may still be too crude. A developing country may possess fairly advanced technological capacity in one industry but be a laggard in another. Moreover, there is a wealth of empirical evidence indicating that the extent to which patent protection helps to spur innovation varies across industries. A more discriminating approach to the patent–antitrust interface in developing countries may need to be industry specific.[4]

Why Developing Countries Need a Different Approach to the Patent-Antitrust Interface

The first issue that needs to be addressed is whether and why developing countries need to adopt a different approach from that of the industrialized economies to the patent-antitrust interface. Although it is probably a simplification to say that developed countries have a singular approach to the interface, the prevailing view is one of deference to patent policy. This is evident from both the scholarship and the case law. Leading commentators on both sides of the Atlantic have all emphasized the need to protect innovation incentives in patent-antitrust cases.[5] Courts from the leading jurisdictions have expressed a similar sentiment. A review of the Microsoft cases decided by the United States Court of Appeals for the District of Columbia and the then European Court of First Instance reveals considerable deference, albeit it to varying degrees, to innovation.[6] Beyond the Atlantic, the Japan Fair Trade Commission's guidelines on intellectual property and antitrust affirm the importance of innovation for consumer welfare.[7] In sum, developed countries have tended to place significant emphasis on patent policy in their approach to patent–antitrust cases.

The basic argument for deference to innovation in patent–antitrust cases is a familiar one that probably does not warrant repetition. While patent protection results in higher prices for consumers, it is generally believed that the short-term loss in consumer welfare will be more than made up for by the dynamic efficiency gains over the long run. There is ample evidence that innovation is responsible for vastly more of the productivity gains and improvement in standards of living over the last decades than short-run allocative efficiency.[8] The tacit trade-off is that present consumers will bear some loss in exchange for much greater gains later on, when new products are brought to the market.

The veracity of this argument is not entirely beyond challenge. There is considerable empirical evidence that shows that the incentive effects of patent protection have been overstated.[9] If new inventions will still be created in a sufficient number despite weaker patent protection or more restrictive antitrust rules on patent exploitation, the tacit trade-off spoken of earlier may no longer be worth making. It is beyond the ambit of this chapter to attempt to resolve this debate.[10] What is clear is that whatever merit this argument has for developed countries, the argument has even less validity for developing ones. There are two reasons for this.

First, the extent to which patent protection will produce dynamic efficiency gains in the domestic economy crucially depends on the existence of potential inventors to take advantage of the innovation incentives. It is perhaps too obvious to point out that if a developing country possesses no innovative capacity, the innovation incentives generated by its domestic patent system will create few benefits. It has been noted that even after the TRIPS Agreement came into force and required a host of developing countries such as Argentina and India to provide patent protection for pharmaceutical products, the pharmaceutical firms in these countries were unlikely to become important sources of innovation globally.[11] One can easily imagine other examples in which innovation incentives will not create meaningful dynamic efficiency gains in a developing country. With the exception of South Africa, the sub-Saharan African countries are unlikely to be significant contributors of innovation in most industries.

A lack of present innovative capacity does not negate the possibility of dynamic efficiency gains in the future. Domestic firms may respond to the innovation incentives and develop innovative capacity in the future. There is some validity to this argument. The development of technological capacity is probably one of the most important means by which developing countries achieve and sustain meaningful economic growth. To the extent that innovation incentives generated by the domestic patent system have a realistic prospect of attracting future innovative capacity, antitrust laws in these countries should take care not to undermine them. The pivotal assumption in this admonition is realistic prospect. If there is no realistic prospect for innovative capacity to emerge, the admonition loses its force. While it is true that the future is difficult to predict and that what seems improbable at the moment may turn out to be the reality, it is possible to identify sectors in a developing country that have no realistic prospect of innovation in the near future.

To further advance this argument, it is important to introduce the concepts of production, imitative, and innovative capacity. Development economists have distinguished a country's state of technological prowess by way of these concepts.[12] Production and innovative capacities are intuitively obvious. Production capacity refers to the ability to produce a product with no corresponding domestic capability to innovate. Innovative capacity is the ability to produce innovation. Imitative capacity is the one that requires the most explanation and describes the ability to imitate technologies that have originated elsewhere, be it another domestic firm or foreign firms. Economists have noted that even imitation itself can be technologically intensive and requires substantial technical know-how.[13] Imitation can take an even longer time and cost more than innovation itself.[14] This is because the imitating firm must possess the capability to comprehend whatever information is incorporated in the patent application, which is publicly available, or to reverse-engineer the technology from the product. Replicating a technology also requires tacit know-how, which is often not easily transferable or decipherable from the product.[15] Contrary to popular belief, imitation is not accessible to any firm that has the financial and human capital to enter an industry. Imitation itself is a technologically intensive endeavor that requires substantial technical expertise.

If a developing country does not even currently possess imitative capacity in an industry, it is unlikely that it will acquire innovative capacity in the near future. This is especially true if the industry at issue is highly complex technologically or if the country does not possess much technological capacity in related industries.[16] Given the lack of current imitative capacity, a developing country may conclude that there is little realistic prospect for innovative capacity to emerge. Few dynamic efficiency gains will redound to that industry because of innovation incentives generated by the domestic patent system.

The second reason that the aforementioned argument has less validity for developing countries has to do with foreign inventors. The innovation incentives generated by a domestic patent system are not only reaped by domestic firms; they also benefit foreign inventors. Innovation incentives spill over national borders. All that is required of a foreign inventor to take advantage of the innovation incentives generated by the domestic patent system is to patent its invention in that country. This spillover effect may be referred to as "innovation incentive externality." Therefore, when deciding whether the consumer welfare loss inflicted by the domestic patent system is justified, attention must be paid to both domestic and foreign inventors. There are, however, two important qualifications to this assertion.[17]

First, there is no reason to assume that a multinational corporation inventor takes into account the innovation incentives provided by every single patent system in the world. In fact, that is highly unlikely to be the case. This is confirmed by the fact that inventions are usually patented only in the major jurisdictions.[18] A firm does not obtain patent protection for its invention in every conceivable jurisdiction. Patent protection is obtained only if the benefits from patenting exceed its costs. If firms do not bother to apply for a patent in a particular country, the innovation incentives provided by that country's patent system are unlikely to have featured prominently in their technology investment decisions. And if firms do not pay much heed to the innovation incentives provided by a particular country, there is little reason for that country to consider dynamic efficiency benefits when approaching the patent–antitrust interface.

The obvious challenge to this argument is that there is only one reliable way for a country to know whether a foreign inventor considers the innovation incentives provided by its patent system: whether the inventor chooses to patent its invention in that country. If the firm does not apply for a patent, the invention does not enjoy patent protection in that country. There will be no patent–antitrust issues to begin with. But if the firm does apply for patent protection in that country, it means that it takes into account the innovation incentives provided by that country, which then should consider innovation incentive externality when resolving patent–antitrust cases. In short, the scenario in which a developing country should ignore the incentive effects on

foreign inventors rarely exists. If foreign inventors do not consider the innovation incentives provided by that country, there will be no patent–antitrust
issues to deal with. And if patent–antitrust cases do arise, they do so only in
situations where the innovation incentives provided by the country were
considered by foreign inventors.

While this challenge seems logical at first blush, it assumes that firms patent in order to take advantage of innovation incentives. This assumption has
been proven wrong by a number of empirical studies, which have suggested
that firms patent for a variety of motivations, some of which are entirely strategic in nature and have nothing to do with a desire to reap patentee reward.[19] It has been shown that firms patent in order to preempt future infringement suits, to harass rivals with infringement suits on their own, and to
gain bargaining chips in future cross-licensing negotiations, among other
reasons.[20] The fact that firms have chosen to patent in a particular jurisdiction does not indicate that they considered the innovation incentives provided by that country. Moreover, it is not true that patent–antitrust issues
will not arise unless a firm has patented its invention in a jurisdiction. If the
firm is confident that there are no potential imitators or competitors and
does not seek to license its technology to any firm in a country, it may have
few reasons to patent its invention. Patent protection is not necessary for a
firm that merely seeks to sells its product in a country where there is little
threat of imitation.

One is still left with the question of how a country is supposed to tell
whether foreign inventors consider the innovation incentives provided by its
patent system. One proxy indicator for the importance of the innovation
incentives provided by a country is the size of its domestic market. Large
developing countries such as China, India, and Brazil are likely to feature
prominently in the investment decisions of multinational technology developers. Small developing countries such as Laos, Nepal, and many of the sub-
Saharan countries are unlikely to matter much to these developers. If these
developers did not consider the innovation incentives provided by these
small developing countries initially, allowing them to reap patentee reward
in them now amounts to a windfall. It provides no dynamic efficiency gains
but inflicts substantial consumer welfare loss on the consumers in these
countries. Ultimately, this is an empirical question that can be answered only
with a survey of multinational technology developers. Without the benefit of
such empirical evidence, the best one can do is to provide some rough classifications of developing countries based on market size. The largest ones

clearly do create innovation incentive externalities, and the smallest and poorest ones do not. In the middle lie a number of countries for which definitive conclusions are difficult to draw.

The second important qualification to the aforementioned assertion is whether developing countries should sacrifice domestic consumer welfare to create innovation incentives for multinational technology developers, especially if the consumers at issue come from the lower income groups in their societies. This is a particularly relevant consideration for the middle group of countries for which definitive conclusions about the significance of the innovation incentives generated by their patent systems cannot be drawn. Developing countries may rightfully wonder whether a wealth transfer from the lower income groups in their countries to multinational corporations is at all justified. It may be argued that such a wealth transfer would be justified if the invention would not be created without the innovation incentives from these countries. However, as F. M. Scherer has noted, if an invention will not be created absent such marginal patentee reward, its benefits barely exceed their costs and society will not be much worse off without such an invention.[21]

One major difference between developed and developing countries is that a much larger proportion of the population in the latter is likely to be poor, inadequately educated, malnourished, and of poor health. Even in one of the most successful developing countries, China, it is estimated that over 10 percent of the population lives below the poverty line.[22] In fact, until the recent revision, it has been argued that the official definition of poverty in China may have understated the extent of poverty in the country.[23] Without access to basic health care, education, and food, much of the population in developing countries stands little chance to fulfill their full potential and become productive members of their economies. These individuals will be condemned to a lifetime of dependency and poverty. The welfare loss sustained by consumers in markets involving these basic necessities goes beyond the short term and carries dire long-term consequences. If patent protection results in higher prices for foodstuffs, medicine, and educational tools, not only are these low-income consumers priced out of the market, they are also denied the opportunity to achieve their full potential. The result is a significant loss in productivity and development potential for developing countries. Therefore, in markets involving basic necessities, weighing against dynamic efficiency gains is not only static welfare loss, but also loss in development potential and long-term productivity. All else equal, the balance in the patent–antitrust interface hence should be more tilted toward antitrust policy in developing countries than in developed economies.

The only way for developing countries to catch up with developed economies is by acquiring technological capacity and improving their productivity. The importance of the acquisition of technological capacity to development has been highlighted by a number of prominent development economists.[24] The overriding question is, how can technological capacity be acquired? The experiences of the developed economies are that imitation is often the most effective way for the technological laggard nations to narrow their distance from the global technological frontier.

History is full of examples of laggard nations lowering intellectual property protection or withholding it from foreigners altogether to allow domestic industries to grow and catch up with their foreign counterparts. The United States was a major culprit of intellectual property infringements in the nineteenth century, copying technologies from the United Kingdom and denying foreign authors copyright protection in order to give its low-cost domestic printing industry a boost.[25] The United States developed its early industrial capacity by free riding on the innovations developed by the leading European nations. Examples include the United Kingdom for textiles, steam engines, and machinery, and France for gunpowder.[26]

Other developed nations adopted similar strategies of free riding or cheap riding in their early stages of development.[27] Japan's patent system initially was designed to facilitate technology transfer. Similar to the United States, foreigners were initially barred from applying for patents in Japan.[28] This discriminatory policy ended only in 1899, when Japan acceded to the Paris Convention.[29] Even after the Second World War, the patent system and intellectual property generally were only seen as "one component of a broader complex of policies for trade, industry and technology that focused on reconstruction and 'catch-up' with the West, especially the United States."[30]

Despite repeated attempts to introduce a patent system, Switzerland adopted one only after the domestic watch industry had become threatened by foreign imitation and technologically sophisticated enough to benefit from it.[31] Even then, the original patent law provided protection only to mechanical inventions and not chemical inventions. This was a deliberate policy choice, as the domestic watch industry produced only mechanical inventions. Meanwhile, the emerging Swiss chemical industry wanted to catch up with its more advanced German counterpart by way of imitation.[32] The domestic chemical industry, alongside the textile industry, which also relied heavily on foreign technology, strongly opposed the introduction of a patent system.[33] Switzerland did not extend patent protection to chemicals until Germany threatened trade sanctions.[34]

The strategic use of intellectual property protection was an integral part of the development policy of many developed nations in the past. The TRIPS Agreement has closed the door on such a strategy. The fact, however, remains that imitation is a very important means for the technological laggard nations to catch up with the leaders. Economist Elhanan Helpman notes that "in less developed countries, imitation is a major effort that involves the development of absorptive capacity for advanced technologies on the one hand and particular efforts to assimilate and adopt foreign technologies on the other."[35] It has also been noted that the definition of innovation needs to be flexibly applied to developing countries and that for some of them, imitation is tantamount to innovation for developed nations.[36]

While the TRIPS Agreement sets a minimum standard for intellectual property protection, it also permits exceptions to such protection if an anti-competitive use of intellectual property can be established. While the precise contours of the exceptions have not been definitively delineated—although there have been some cases tackling the scope of Article 40 of the TRIPS Agreement—there is considerable leeway for developing countries to apply these exceptions and override patent protection. To the extent consistent with the TRIPS Agreement, developing countries should attach significant weight in the patent-antitrust interface to the acquisition of domestic technological capacity, through imitation or otherwise.

An Appropriate Approach to the Patent-Antitrust Interface

The discussion thus far has focused on the distinctions between developed and developing countries. This treatment is justified in that, as far as the patent-antitrust interface is concerned, the gap between developed and developing countries is greater than that among developing countries themselves. This, however, does not imply that developing countries should be treated as a monolith. As alluded to earlier, developing countries vary along a number of dimensions that bear on the patent-antitrust interface. In attempting to fashion an appropriate approach for the patent-antitrust interface for developing countries, it is important to consider these cross-country differences.

One of the most important dimensions along which developing countries may differ is their technological capacity, which determines the importance of dynamic efficiency considerations in the patent-antitrust interface. Ideally, there would be empirical studies that directly measure and compare the technological capacity of the various developing countries. In the absence of such studies, one must resort to research that uses proxy indicators to ascertain the state of technological capacity in these countries.

As it turns out, economists have established an empirical relationship between income per capita and the state of intellectual property protection in a country. As Keith Maskus notes, "the strength of IPRs [intellectual property rights] appears to be a nonlinear function of economic development, at first falling as income rises and then increasing after that."[37] He found that the strength of patent protection increases with per capita income, with the most significant increase happening between mid-income and high-income countries.[38] In a separate study, Maskus and Penubarti found that there is in fact a U-shaped relationship between income per capita and the level of patent protection.[39] Countries tend to lower the level of their patent protection as income rises and then begin to strengthen it after a certain point. That point was found to be approximately $2,000 per capita in 1985 international dollars.[40]

The level of patent protection of course does not necessarily reflect technological capacity. The two may differ for a variety of reasons. For example, a country may have been pressured by free-trade agreements and other international treaty obligations to raise the level of patent protection beyond that which is justified by its existing state of technological capacity. Or it may have kept its level of patent protection artificially low due to powerful consumer lobbying. As such, the results from Maskus and Penubarti do not directly address the central question in this discussion. Fortunately, a number of other empirical studies lend support to a correlation between level of income per capita and technological capacity, which drives the domestic demand for intellectual property protection.

One of them is Chen and Puttitanun. Their study confirmed the U-shaped relationship established by Maskus and Penubarti, and the minimum point of the curve was shown to be 854.06 USD in per capita gross domestic product (GDP) in 1995 prices.[41] They attributed the U-shaped relationship to the fact that for a country with a low level of economic development, "an initial increase in [the] country's technological ability has a greater impact on the efficiency of imitating northern [developed countries'] technologies than on the efficiency of domestic innovations, which makes it desirable for the country to lower IPRs."[42] However, at some point in economic development, "imitation effect is dominated by the innovation effect and the optimal protection of IPRs increases with the level of development."[43] The results from Ginarte and Park's study also suggests that patent protection is in part driven by domestic demand for it, which is in turn dependent on domestic R&D intensities.[44] Using regression analysis, they demonstrated that the correlation between per capita income and patent protection is better explained by domestic R&D intensities and human capital inputs. In other words, what drives higher patent protection may not be higher income as such, but the desire of domestic inventors to protect their inventions. The amount of domestic inventions is in turn reflected in R&D intensities and human capital inputs.

Even though the real driver behind demand for domestic intellectual property protection is the amount of domestic invention, income per capita can still be used as a proxy indicator for that if direct measurements are unavailable. Maskus and Penubarti as well as Chen and Puttitanun established a U-shaped relationship between per capita income and intellectual property protection. The implication is that for low-income countries, domestic innovation is minimal, which means that dynamic efficiency considerations play a relatively insignificant role in the resolution of the patent–antitrust interface. These considerations will become more relevant as a developing country becomes wealthier, which often also means that it is moving up the global technology ladder.

Basheer and Primi have proposed a classification of developing countries based on their technological capacity. In particular, based on (1) the share of medium- or high-technology products in total manufacturing value added and (2) R&D expenditure as a percentage of GDP, they classify developing countries into three categories: (1) technologically proficient developing countries, which include the BRIC countries (Brazil, Russia, India, China), Argentina, Taiwan, South Africa, Ukraine, Belarus, Chile, Turkey, and Mexico; (2) potentially innovative developing countries, such as Morocco, Tunisia, Malaysia, Thailand, Egypt, Indonesia, the Philippines, Armenia, Macedonia, Venezuela and Pakistan and (3) all other developing countries.[45]

Consistent with Ginarte and Park's and Chen and Puttitanun's findings, there seems to be a rough correlation between income per capita and technological capacity. Most of the countries classified as technologically proficient by Basheer and Primi have relatively high income per capita. Meanwhile, with the exception of South Africa, the sub-Saharan countries, which are some of the poorest countries in the world, are absent from the technologically proficient and potentially innovative categories. Technologically proficient developing countries will need to accord sufficient weight to dynamic efficiency considerations in resolving the patent–antitrust interface. Countries that are neither technologically proficient nor potentially innovative should instead focus on consumer welfare and developmental concerns.

Apart from income per capita and technological capacity, the domestic market size is another factor to be considered in determining the importance of dynamic efficiency considerations in the patent–antitrust interface. Helpman notes that there is an inherent link between market size and the incentive to innovate.[46] He explains that "[s]ince the incentive to innovate is larger the more plentiful are the monopoly profits from new products—be they horizontally or vertically differentiated—and since the monopoly profits from new products are higher the larger the market in which the products are sold, it follows that larger markets encourage more R&D."[47] This is consistent with Basheer and Primi's classifications. Many of the technologically proficient countries, such as the BRIC countries, Turkey, and Mexico, have large populations. The large domestic markets can provide a somewhat captive group of consumers for domestic innovations.[48] All else being equal, developing countries with a large domestic population will have an advantage over other developing countries in expanding domestic technological capacity. This in turn means that dynamic efficiency considerations should be accorded greater weight in their approach to patent–antitrust cases.

A country-specific approach to the patent–antitrust interface is certainly an improvement from an indiscriminate approach whereby developing countries are treated as one and the same. Developing countries may be distinguished based on their income per capita, technological capacity (however it is measured), and domestic market size. All three criteria seem to produce the same group of developing countries for which dynamic efficiency considerations are likely to be important: China, India, Brazil, Russia, Mexico, Turkey, South Africa, and so on. These are developing countries that have performed well economically over the last decade. Based on the same criteria, there is a sizable group of developing countries that have low prospects for domestic innovation.

A country-specific approach, however, is likely to remain unsatisfactory. It assumes that the technologically proficient developing countries possess the same level of technological capacity in all industries. This is unlikely to be the case. For many of these countries, one can single out industries in which they have particularly strong capabilities: India in IT and pharmaceuticals, China in aerospace and telecommunications, and Brazil in agricultural technology. But these countries are not uniformly strong in all industries. The same can be said of countries outside of the technologically proficient group. While they may not have strong technological capacity overall, they may excel in one or two industries in particular. A country-specific approach to the patent-antitrust interface is hence too crude; the extent to which dynamic efficiency considerations are taken into account needs to be decided on an industry-by-industry basis.

An industry-specific approach to the patent-antitrust interface is further supported by empirical findings that show that the extent to which patent protection spurs innovation varies across industries. Economists have found in a number of empirical studies that while some industries are heavily reliant on patent protection, others place greater emphasis on first-mover advantages, learning curve advantages, and sales and marketing as appropriation mechanisms, which refer to the means by which firms recover their R&D outlay. In a 1986 paper, economist Edwin Mansfield reported that patent protection was only deemed to be important for the development and commercialization of over 30 percent of the innovations in the pharmaceutical and chemical industries and for 10 percent to 20 percent of the innovations in petroleum, machinery, and fabricated metal products.[49] Patent protection was only of limited importance in electrical equipment, office equipment, motor vehicles, instruments, primary metals, rubber, and textiles.[50] In a larger-scale survey of industry R&D executives published in 1987, Richard Levin and his coauthors reported that only pharmaceuticals, organic chemicals, plastic materials, and steel mill products industries rated patent protection as a highly effective appropriation mechanism.[51] Firms in most other industries relied on lead time, learning curve advantages, and sales and promotion efforts over patent protection to recoup their R&D investment.[52] For process innovations, patent protection was found to be the least effective appropriation mechanism.[53] These results were largely confirmed by a survey done by Wesley Cohen and his coauthors more than a decade later.[54]

A variety of factors affect the importance of patent protection as an appropriation mechanism. These factors include industry structure, the nature of the innovation—process or product, and the characteristics of the technology—and its codifiability and ease of imitation. If an industry relies heavily on patent protection as an appropriation mechanism, the dynamic efficiency benefits of patent protection could be significant, and the patent-antitrust interface must take such benefits into account. If, however, other appropriation mechanisms such as first-mover advantage dominate the industry, or innovations are hard to decipher or reverse-engineer, patent protection will play a much less significant role in inducing innovations, and the patent-antitrust interface can focus less attention on dynamic efficiency considerations.

Recall the earlier discussion about imitation as an important means for developing countries to improve their technological capacity. When one adopts an industry-specific approach to the patent-antitrust interface in developing countries, not only must one ascertain the existence of technological capacity in an industry, one must examine the nature of that capacity, i.e., whether it is imitative or innovative, or both. Therefore, even if it has been found that patent protection is an important appropriation mechanism for the industry at issue, attention must then be paid to determine the nature of the technological capacity. If a developing country possesses only imitative capacity in an industry, a pro-patent approach to patent-antitrust cases will bring few dynamic efficiency benefits to the domestic firms, which can only imitate foreign technology. In fact, such an approach may hamper domestic imitation. If a developing country possesses both imitative and innovative firms in an industry, the situation becomes more complicated. An approach to the patent-antitrust interface that facilitates imitation will benefit the imitators but may harm the domestic innovators. A satisfactory resolution of patent-antitrust cases will require a careful balancing of dynamic efficiency benefits to the domestic innovators, and possible harm to consumers and domestic imitators, all within the context of the developmental considerations discussed earlier.

.   .   .

The resolution of the patent-antitrust interface in the developing country context is highly complex. It requires consideration of an even broader range of factors than those customarily considered in developed countries. This chapter argues that an industry-specific approach that takes into account the importance of patent protection as an appropriation mechanism and the nature of domestic technological capacity in that industry is needed. While developed countries may be able to afford a generally pro-patent approach, which results in unjustified consumer welfare loss in some instances, developing countries must make every effort to protect their domestic consumers and scrutinize dynamic efficiency claims much more closely. In a way, a less pro-patent approach to the patent-antitrust interface for developing countries is a corollary of the widely recognized notion that developing countries stand to benefit less from a high level of patent protection. Now that the TRIPS Agreement has set a minimum standard for intellectual property protection across the globe, developing countries should be particularly vigilant in applying their antitrust laws to protect their domestic consumers.

14

Embedding a Competition Culture

Holy Grail or Attainable Objective?

David Lewis

In recent years, among the most remarked upon phenomena in competition law and policy is, first, the widespread growth in acceptance of the centrality of markets as the principal mechanism for allocating resources and driving innovation (and thus economic dynamism). Second, and related to this first phenomenon, is the burgeoning of national competition authorities.

The dominance of market mechanisms has not been the outcome of a smooth or "natural" process. On the contrary, it has frequently been a disruptive and difficult process. It has usually followed root and branch political change, followed by seismic shifts in economic policy, generally captured under the rubric of "liberalization." It has also been marked by major social disruption often underpinned by rising inequality within and between national economies. But the introduction of market reforms has also lifted millions out of abject poverty and opened up new areas of economic activity for individuals and countries previously at, or beyond, the margins of international trade and investment.

The economic policies most closely associated with this era of liberalization are reduced cross-border barriers to trade and investment, as well as the lowering of regulatory barriers in national markets—often expressly directed at easing business entry—and widespread privatization. In those national markets where policy makers, often strongly influenced by powerful state-owned enterprises, have been reluctant to deregulate their domestic markets, new technologies and innovative business methods have frequently swept aside outmoded practices and the firms that benefited from them. The upheavals in telecommunications and air travel markets are simply two outstanding examples among them. They are examples, moreover, in which consumers have been the principal beneficiaries.

Thus the triumph of markets has given rise to mixed outcomes: widening inequality, the lifting of many millions of people off the lowest rungs of the economic ladder, and, in many markets, clear consumer benefits. But even with the tumult of recent years, there can be no gainsaying the widespread acceptance of the central role of markets. Expressed otherwise, competition policy—in fact, a diverse portfolio of measures designed to create, promote, and protect market processes—has been at the front and center of national economic policies.

In these circumstances the rise of national competition laws is to be expected. Indeed, what is remarkable is how frequently liberal market policies were implemented without first introducing the competition rules necessary to underpin the effective functioning of the newly "liberated" markets. This latter omission has opened the door to monopolization and concomitant abuses, which have caused a great deal of the misery and inequality that often accompanied liberalization. This is contrary to the common misconception that it is the fact of liberalization itself, rather than the lack of competition regulation, that has led to such misery and inequality. But be that as it may, it is clear that this nettle has now been grasped, as reflected in the proliferation of national competition laws and authorities. The great number of these new authorities are to be found either in emerging market economies that were until relatively recently characterized by central planning or in developing economies that were characterized by statist and protectionist policies. These policies were the hallmark of postcolonial development economics scholarship and policy.

These competition laws and the institutions charged with their implementation were thus planted in inhospitable terrain. These were societies in which the state, for a long time, had played the central, and in many cases the only, role in organizing economic activity, including the setting of key prices. In these societies, markets did not merely have to be defended; they frequently had to be created. Because many of these institutions were introduced in an environment characterized by increases in the prices of basic commodities, rising levels of unemployment, and inequality—indeed the massive enrichment of politically connected individuals and the removal of any semblance of a social safety net—the introduction of competition laws was often popularly expected to introduce an element of "fairness" into this new economic order. It was frequently expected—and, in many cases, still is—that the competition authorities would assume responsibility for controlling prices (indeed in many instances the former price-setting body formed the core of the new competition authority) and would protect struggling domestic firms from better-resourced and more innovative foreign competitors.

The Creation of Competition Culture

In brief, the "culture" of the societies in which many of these new statutes and agencies were being set up was distinctly inimical to even the least orthodox versions of competition law. Arguably, the "culture" of many developed European and Asian societies, with their strong history of active industrial policies, was not particularly competition friendly either. But, for the most part, these were countries in which markets were long established and in which the application of competition rules was an accepted, albeit frequently compromised, aspect of the business environment.

This "cultural deficit" confronting the new competition agencies partly accounted for a firmly held view that the first task of these fledgling agencies was advocacy in order to establish a culture that supported competition law enforcement and policy. Having created a competition-friendly culture, the standard recipe prescribed that law enforcement activities, notably against cartel conduct, would follow and eventually merger review mechanisms would be put in place.

This formulaic sequencing that prioritized advocacy over enforcement and merger review is misplaced. While I recognize the importance of creating a supportive social and policy environment for the introduction and enforcement of competition law, I firmly believe that even though the underlying national circumstances for the enactment of competition law differ, as do the expectations and sophistication of the lawmakers and the general public, a principal imperative for the introduction of competition law is an often inchoate notion that competition law will serve to restrain the conduct of powerful business entities. This may take many forms, but the usual stuff of advocacy—publicity campaigns, op-ed articles, speeches, stakeholder engagements—will not suffice to overcome these powerful opponents or the popularly held notion that the state is the most effective and reliable instrument for meeting the economic needs of the citizenry. In the face of these powerful opponents and popular perceptions, traditional forms of advocacy are insufficient. What is required is a demonstrated capacity on the part of the competition authority to go head-to-head with powerful business interests and to win!

In the South African case, merger review has, quite apart from its substantive competition significance (particularly in an economy undergoing deep structural adjustment), played a critical advocacy role. That is, in South Africa it was merger review that established the competition authorities as professional, robust institutions capable of standing up to the most powerful private interests. In the process, merger review also educated competition practitioners in the intricacies of competition law and economics and, aided by carefully nurtured relationships with some particularly able journalists and a highly transparent decision-making process, taught the public—and particularly the business community—the fundamental principles and practices underpinning the aims, objectives, and methodologies of competition law. Merger review in South Africa certainly is the function that was rightly prioritized not least because of the advocacy role that it inadvertently performed and the contribution that it thereby made to establish a competition culture. The benefit of hindsight has undoubtedly informed this view. Indeed, for a time the South African authorities were criticized by no less than the Organisation for Economic Co-operation and Development for their focus on merger review. But there can be little doubt that it was this task that established the reputation of the competition authorities. Merger review constituted the most effective form of advocacy and, by extension, the building of a culture of respect for competition law enforcement.

Having gained invaluable experience in competition analysis and established a solid reputation for robust independence, the competition authorities in South Africa then moved aggressively and with notable success into the area of cartel investigation and prosecution. This was immeasurably aided by a corporate leniency program, which in turn was underpinned by the growing reputation of the authorities, a reputation largely established in the merger review arena. It is interesting but predictable and perfectly consistent with the view advanced here that the leniency program only proved effective once the competition authorities had established something of a reputation for robust intervention, notably in the merger field. After the authorities had proved their mettle by stopping some large mergers, it occurred to businesses that the competition authorities were a force to be reckoned with and they began to take advantage of the corporate leniency program in order to avoid or, at least, mitigate the attention of these aggressive enforcement agencies.

Cartel convictions, particularly of cartels that involved basic commodities such as bread, significantly raised the profile of the competition authorities. Convictions effectively moved the authorities beyond the business pages into the general news pages, from the broadsheets to the tabloids and the radio.

This enhanced profile was undoubtedly abetted by purposeful awareness-raising measures. Hence when prominent firms had admitted to participating in cartels and had agreed to enter into consent decrees, the order was confirmed at open hearings of the Competition Tribunal. In such settings, the Competition Commission—the investigative and prosecutorial authority—was given the opportunity to outline in the full glare of television cameras what it had discovered. Groups representing low-income consumers who were particularly harmed were given the opportunity to vent their opinions in these open hearings. Major figures in South African business life were made, possibly for the first time in their working lives, to publicly account for their activities, to accept the imposition of relatively massive fines, and to apologize to the community of customers whom they had so poorly and deceitfully served. These public lynchings were not particularly pleasant to witness but they were extraordinarily effective tools of advocacy and major factors in the building of a competition culture.

And so, in the first phase of the South African Competition Commission's life, let us call it the merger review phase, the business community was, with considerable reluctance, obliged to accept that competition considerations had to be factored into its decision making. Competition law had become part of the culture of business. In the second phase, let us call it the enforcement phase, the broader public came to understand, in no uncertain terms, that it was the victim of anticompetitive conduct. Thus, the culture of competition spread, like the proverbial wildfire, into the broader realms of public life in South Africa. For both the business community and the general public, competition had, or so it appeared, come to be viewed as a public good secured by an independent public authority.

It appeared then that in the space of a mere eight years, the South African competition authorities had established a vibrant competition culture, an achievement that had eluded many of the longer established authorities in the developed world, let alone the fledgling "new" authorities of the developing world and the emerging market economies. And its principal weapon did not, for the most part, belong to the traditional arsenal of advocacy but was honed by the competition authorities pursuing their principal functions of merger review and enforcement. These efforts undoubtedly embedded a culture of competition and enabled the commission to become an effective advocate using the more traditional instruments of advocacy. Traditional advocacy led to widespread media coverage, drew attention to the commission's op-ed articles and media releases, and got competition officials invited to address business conferences and union meetings. Indeed, anyone attending cartel consent order hearings or observing the intensity of the media coverage could be forgiven for thinking that competition had taken on the semblance of a social movement in South Africa. It had become, in the expression used by David Gerber to describe the depth of respect for competition in the United States and Germany, a "fundamental social value."[1]

The development of a powerful competition culture in South Africa could not have been easily predicted. The party that took the reins of government with the advent of democracy in South Africa, the African National Congress (ANC), while a broad church liberation movement, would certainly have placed itself at the left of center and was in an explicit alliance with the South African Communist Party and with the avowedly left-wing and powerful Congress of South African Trade Unions. For a long time, the competition policy orientation most closely identified with the ANC was its support for nationalization of the "commanding heights," notably the banks and mines. But the ANC's manifestos and pamphlets also inveighed against the "monopolies" and promised vigorous antitrust action designed to break up these concentrations.

It was never clear whether antitrust enforcement was viewed as an adjunct to nationalization or as a second-best substitute. The deep chasm between these policies—the former designed to substitute the state for the market, the latter designed to strengthen market mechanisms—was lost on those who thought about the nature of a post-apartheid economy. What nationalization and robust antitrust did have in common was that both were perceived as instruments for weakening and disciplining a powerful and racially concentrated social force—big business—that was, not unjustifiably, widely thought to have benefited from apartheid and to be, at best, a reluctant supporter of democratization. These were going to be the mechanisms whereby the economic kingdom would be conquered by the post-apartheid rulers. They were mechanisms whereby, at the very least, concentrated markets and centralized ownership structures, and the powerful interest groups that they supported, were going to be fragmented.

It was the elimination of the nationalization instrument that brought antitrust enforcement to the fore in South Africa. The presence of a powerful and hostile force—namely, powerful business concentrations—at the heart of the South African economy was going to be confronted by an industrial policy that would seek to direct private investment decisions and accorded a central role to state-owned enterprises; by black economic empowerment policies that were intended to deracialize and, in the intentions of some at least, democratize ownership; and by antitrust policies that would assume the role of fragmenting the powerful economic and social force of big business and would punish those who resisted this trajectory. Industrial policy and black economic empowerment, whatever their other merits, did not have the promotion of competition at their center. Indeed, many of the measures associated with industrial policy and black economic empowerment were distinctly inimical to increased competition.

In the South African story, robust competition law was never part of the economic liberalization narrative. It was rather part of the democratization narrative. As soon as the competition authorities proved themselves able and willing to pursue their core mandate of disciplining business, they received widespread support and media coverage. The most mundane merger decisions were regularly reported in the press; more complex and controversial cases were reported in detail and were frequently analyzed in the opinion pages. Although the media reportage of competition law decisions is unusually sophisticated, their major popular appeal lay in their ability to take on, in a manner that was considered fair but robust, the anticompetitive conduct of powerful business interests.

This focus against powerful business interests could of course have given rise to a highly populist version of competition law. Indeed, in the statute—which emerged from a statutory tri-partite (organized business, organized labor, and the government) process of negotiation—noncompetition criteria such as employment impact are enshrined in the merger review process. The statute also uses reverse onuses as well as some controversial presumptions, for example the market share–based presumption to determine dominance. However, for all that, the enforcement of competition law in South Africa has remained within broad orthodox parameters. A number of factors account for this, among which are the strong insertion of the South African authorities into the international community of antitrust enforcers and an act that specifically enjoins South Africa's competition decision makers to note comparative competition jurisprudence.

By 2009, at the end of the first decade of the new competition regime, the South African authorities had every reason to feel pleased with themselves. Their record on merger review was solid; cartels were falling like proverbial skittles. The competition authorities had engaged with the difficulties of prosecuting abuse of dominance cases to an extent sufficient to ensure that dominant firms factored competition considerations into their decision making. These authorities had a prominent presence in the global community of antitrust enforcement. Above all they had acquired a reputation for robust independence and for procedural and substantive fairness. Their decisions managed to engage simultaneously with both the specificities of South Africa and with international experience and current debates. It seemed that a culture of respect for competition was firmly in place.

But there was trouble brewing in paradise. It would soon become apparent that a competition culture was not, in fact, well established. With hindsight the likely sources of opposition to a competition culture were reasonably clear, these being the government in the shape of the department notionally responsible for competition policy and, as such, responsible for competition legislation. Second, there were the courts. In the context of this chapter, both are of particular interest because both reflected, in their different ways, serious deficiencies in the strength of the competition culture in which the competition authorities were hubristically basking. I will briefly refer to the courts, but my remarks will concentrate on the relationship between the government and the competition authorities.

Government, Industrial Policy, and the Environment for Competition Law

I will not attempt a comprehensive history of the marked deterioration in these critical relationships. I will simply note, by way of background, that for about the first eight years of the life of the new competition regime, the relationship between the competition authorities and the Department of Trade and Industry is best described as one of relatively benign mutual neglect.

The South African government's support for robust competition law enforcement on the one hand, and an active industrial policy on the other hand, may suggest an early adherence to the "new industrial policy," one that provided both for a state that was active in countering market failures and for market-based incentives that were the principal drivers of dynamic growth and allocators of economic resources. However, this would not be an accurate conclusion to draw.

The truth is that South African policy makers talk an Asian-style industrial policy but do not much walk it. Above all, South Africa's adherence to industrial policy is expressed in a fervent and largely misguided belief that

South Africa's rich natural resource endowment, and particularly its minerals, should give it privileged access to upstream and intermediate products for the purposes of downstream fabrication. This privileged access, known as "beneficiation" in South African parlance, is at the front and center of South African industrial policy. Again, these efforts have either run into the sand—as with the long-running attempt to convert its iron ore bounty into a discounted steel price and into a price advantage for metal fabricators—or they have reverberated to the considerable disadvantage of the natural resource producers, as with the attempt to develop a jewelry manufacturing cluster on the back of the country's diamond riches.

Competition law enforcement and competition policy never featured directly in these industrial policies. One exception to this is the endless and unsuccessful attempt by the government to persuade the steel monopoly to discount its steel price, matched by a privately initiated effort to persuade the competition authorities to use the excessive-pricing provisions of the Competition Act against the steel monopoly, an attempt that met with success in the Competition Tribunal but whose finding of excessive pricing was overturned by the Competition Appeal Court.[2]

The truth then is, as already intimated, that competition law and industrial policy have not had much to do with each other, despite the fact that competition *policy*—at least insofar as it consisted of policy responsibility for the Competition Act—was the responsibility of the Department of Trade and Industry (DTI), the department of state responsible for industrial policy. The DTI bumbled along, pursuing a rather inept industrial policy, while the competition authorities vigorously pursued their mandate to review mergers and to police private anticompetitive conduct. In the process, the DTI was viewed with general skepticism by industrialists and the public, while the competition authorities attracted positive and numerous media reviews, earning the grudging respect of business and considerable public support.

However, the point at issue here is that the competition authorities barely attempted to extend their interventions beyond the realm of law enforcement and merger review. On one occasion when the government attempted, ultimately unsuccessfully, to introduce manifestly anticompetitive legislation governing beer distribution, the commission opposed the DTI at an appearance before a parliamentary committee hearing, in the process incurring the extreme displeasure of the department. But it never took on some of the blatantly anticompetitive aspects of the DTI's industrial policy. Nor did it confront some of the anticompetitive omissions of the DTI—for example, the barriers to new entry consequent upon the truly extraordinary incompetence of the Companies and Intellectual Property Registration Office, which is also a responsibility of the DTI. And the DTI for its part hardly ever exercised its right to make submissions to the commission's investigators or before the tribunal. Interestingly, while other departments of state increasingly began to consult with the competition authorities about the competition implications of policies and intended legislation, there was little interaction between the DTI and the competition authorities over the content of industrial policy.

The Competition Commission, for its part, did give explicit recognition to government policy and to key national policy objectives. For example the commission has publicly articulated a prosecutorial strategy aligned with the government's pro-poor emphasis. In particular, the commission focused investigatory resources on the food value chain. In the process it successfully apprehended a cartel in baking and milling. It also discovered a milk cartel, although the investigation was effectively halted—after admissions had been made by key participants—on technical grounds by the Supreme Court of Appeal.[3]

The commission has also focused on bid rigging. This work has been similarly aimed at supporting the pro-poor strategy, culminating in the investigation and successful apprehension of a major cartel in the provision of medical equipment to public hospitals.[4] The bid rigging investigations have also focused on the government's key infrastructure build program and have recorded major successes in apprehending cartels in construction and in cement and cement products. The commission also responded to concerns expressed by the government and the public regarding the alleged anticompetitive conduct of the country's banking oligopoly by undertaking a major public market enquiry of the retail banking market. Effectively, any initiative to interface competition law with the government's broader social and economic objectives has come from the competition authorities rather than from the government.

A notable exception to the otherwise marked absence of interface between the competition authorities and industrial policy is contained in the inclusion in the preamble to the Competition Act, in its general purposes clause and, of most practical significance, in the criteria for merger review, of noncompetition or "public interest" objectives. These objectives include employment, the promotion of black economic empowerment, and the promotion of international competitiveness. These objectives fall squarely within the stated objectives of industrial policy. Yet where they related to matters that fall within the purview of the competition authorities, most notably the prospect of employment loss consequent upon a merger, they fall within the jurisdiction of the Competition Act.

International experts cautioned the drafters of the Competition Act against the inclusion of these noncompetition objectives. However, the latter took the pragmatic view that all major economic legislation in post-apartheid South Africa was, wisely or not, bound to include key social objectives, notably centered on employment and race-based domination of economic activity. Moreover, in its implementation of the act and particularly the merger review provisions, the competition authorities approached its public interest mandate by arguing that, while it was bound to take seriously this part of its mandate, each of the public interest objectives were supported by their own legislative framework and enforcement mechanisms and that the Competition Act would seek to complement these mechanisms rather than substitute for them.[5] Interestingly, even when the competition authorities considered their public interest mandate, the DTI rarely, if ever, elected to participate in making submissions at the various stages of the proceedings.

At the conference marking the tenth anniversary of the passing of the Competition Act immediately following the end of my second and final term as chairperson of the Competition Tribunal, I observed that while the first ten years of the authorities' life had been devoted to pursuing private restraints of trade, the next ten years should see a more active engagement with public restraints of trade.[6] Put differently, I argued that the competition authorities were now well placed to use their standing and the respect that they had earned to tackle public restraints. Following a similar program that had been initiated in Mexico, the South African competition authorities should propose to deal with the problem of rapidly escalating administered prices combined with evidence of deep-seated problems in the quality of public provision.

In making this proposal I did not envisage an aggressive clash with the government. I rather naively assumed that the standing of the competition authorities had engendered a culture of respect for competition within the government. And so while I absolutely accepted that particular market failures and the imperative to meet particular social objectives would necessitate selective anticompetitive interventions on the government's part, my implicit assumption was that competition and ease of business entry would be the default positions of the government. I could not have been more wrong.

This proposal was made in the presence of the minister of economic de-velopment, a recently created ministry that had been given responsibility for the major institutions of the DTI with direct influence over industrial policy, including the formidably well-resourced, state-owned industrial develop-ment bank as well as, surprisingly, the competition authorities. This was surprising because this was a ministry—and a minister—in search of a pur-pose and, more to the point, in search of power and resources. The Competi-tion Act seemed to offer neither resources nor a direct instrument of policy leverage and power. However, this conclusion rested on a number of presup-positions: first, respect for the rule of law; second, respect for the indepen-dence of quasi-judicial administrative authorities; third, respect for the com-petitive process. Absent these principles, competition law not only could become a direct instrument of economic policy but, by utilizing the public interest provisions, it could, as we had been warned some ten years previ-ously, become a direct instrument of an industrial policy explicitly hostile to the fundamental premises underpinning competition law and policy.

The Walmart Saga

There are a number of staging posts at which this shift in the position of the government became increasingly apparent. There was the direct interven-tion of the minister in the imposition of a remedy in respect of participation in a bread cartel. There was the ministerial intervention in the acquisition of a dominant South African coatings (paint) firm by a large Japanese multina-tional firm. There is also the *Walmart* case, not yet concluded at the time of writing but a remarkable example of a clash between an incoherent, piece-meal industrial policy and an established, highly regarded competition law enforcement agency.

It is difficult to capture the whole Walmart saga in the space of a few paragraphs. However, to cut an extremely long—and still continuing—story as short as possible, Walmart, the iconic and notorious U.S. retailer, acquired Massmart, a large South African retailer although by no means the largest among South Africa's formidable and intensely competitive grocery and gen-eral retailers.

It is common ground that there are no competition issues at stake in the merger. Walmart is a new entrant and, as already noted, the South African grocery and general retail market is, for the most part, intensely competi-tive. But Walmart carries some unpalatable baggage, not least a notorious

reputation for generally poor employment practices and a particularly aggressive antiunion stance. It was thus to be expected that the South African
unions, abetted by a U.S. union-based anti-Walmart coalition, would take a
jaundiced view of Walmart's entry into the country. And so they did. They
attempted to argue that Walmart's entry would result in job loss in Massmart,
a public interest criterion that the competition authorities were obliged to
consider. However, the merging parties effectively dispelled this. Although
the unions have not conceded this, the evidence clearly suggests that the direct employment consequences of the merger are, if anything, likely to be
positive. The unions also argued that Walmart would engage in practices
contrary to South African labor relations legislation. This consideration is
not part of the mandated public interest criteria but, given Walmart's reputation, it was bound to be raised.

However, it is the minister of economic development's intervention in
this matter that is, for present purposes, of most interest. His stated concern
was not merely with the direct employment consequences of the merger, but
rather with the prospect that Walmart would substitute imported—read
"Chinese" —goods for South African products in their newly acquired
stores. And so the minister wanted a commitment that the merged entity
would maintain local procurement at the same level as Massmart, the South
African target entity. In short, what was demanded was a wholly protectionist condition, effectively the imposition of a local procurement quota.
Walmart made it clear that it would not willingly submit to this condition.

Moreover, not only did the minister intervene extremely late in the investigatory process but he chose to intervene, not by making submissions to the
commission's investigators—as he is entitled to—but rather by entering into
private negotiations with the merging firms, clearly holding out the promise
that were the firms to reach agreement with him, he would ensure that the
agreement would be rubber-stamped by the competition authorities. In other
words, he promised that the commission would recommend approval of the
merger to the tribunal and the tribunal would accept the recommendation.

While these negotiations were under way, the commission's time period
for conducting a merger investigation expired. It recommended to the tribunal that it approve the merger unconditionally but advised that the merging
parties and the minister of economic development were in negotiations regarding the public interest implications of the transaction. The commission
effectively reserved its position on the public interest pending the conclusion
of the discussion between the minister and the merging parties.

However, because of the procedural requirements of the adjudicative process, this meant that the minister of economic development, with the ministers of trade and industry and agriculture in tow, was then effectively com-
pelled to emerge from his smoke-filled room and to have his officials argue
his case in front of the tribunal. He could no longer hide behind the skirts of
the Competition Commission. The first of the ministers' contributions was
to petition for a delay in the entire proceedings. When the hearing finally
got under way, the ministers' legal counsel argued for the procurement-
related condition, or, failing that, outright prohibition. The unions asked for
the merger to be prohibited on employment grounds. In the alternative, they
proposed certain employment-related conditions.

The tribunal ultimately approved the transaction but imposed a number
of conditions upon the merged entity, all of which related to employment
and industrial relations issues and all of which were uncontested by the
merging parties. However, the tribunal refused to impose a procurement-
related condition.[7] A variety of reasons were given by the tribunal for its re-
fusal to accept such a condition. It was found to be unworkable, unenforceable, and asymmetric. Although the tribunal did not finally have to decide
this point, it also appeared to accept that the imposition of a procurement-
related condition of the kind sought would be contrary to South Africa's international trade obligations.

These reasons aside, the tribunal rested its rejection on the consumer impact of a protectionist condition:

> The problem is that the concern raised in relation to local procurement/
> imports is also associated with important benefits for consumers. A possible
> loss of jobs in manufacturing of an uncertain extent must be weighed up
> against a consumer interest in lower prices and job creation at Massmart.
> Since the evidence is that the likely consumers who will benefit most from
> the lower prices associated with the merger are low income consumers and
> those consumers without any means of support of their own, thus the poorest
> of South Africans, the public interest in lower prices is no less compelling.[8]

And again:

> Further the conditions will contradict the major objective of competition
> regulation—to secure lower prices. The procurement conditions would
> likely affect the merged entity's ability to provide customers with the lowest
> possible prices. Competition authorities do not lightly impose conditions that

contradict their primary mandate, unless there is overwhelming justification for doing so. If we are not for competition then who is?[9]

Remarkably, it is left to the tribunal to point out to senior government representatives, supposedly wedded to a contemporary version of industrial policy, the availability of competition-friendly conditions that would simultaneously meet industrial policy objectives:

> What period should the condition operate for? SACTWU suggests 5 years, the SMMEs' suggested three years. If this were part of an industrial policy program the period of the restraint might be linked to some other measures designed to make the domestic firms more competitive whilst they benefit from the period of protection. No such other policy is contemplated here. This raises the question of the rationale for the time period chosen. This links to the further issue that the proposed procurement conditions are not linked to any industry in particular, but suppliers in general. Surely not all manufacturing requires protection and some because of other government policy may be more deserving than others.[10]

Accordingly, it is the tribunal that unearths a procompetitive "investment remedy" previously proposed by the merging parties, as opposed to the protectionist "procurement remedy" favored by government representatives. This investment remedy obliges the merged entity to set up a R100 million fund to assist in developing the competitiveness of its domestic suppliers. In deciding on disbursements of this fund the tribunal said:

> The investment undertaking is a more positive response to the domestic procurement concern. Instead of insulating local industry from international competition for a period, it seeks to make local industry more competitive to meet international competition. Whilst at a macroeconomic level the remedy is modest, at the level of a single firm commitment it is not. Expenditure of R 100 million over a three year period is significant. Further the remedy seeks to engage those very critics of Walmart in the decision making process over the disbursement of the funds, including representatives of SMMEs. It also obliges the merged party to account for the expenditure to the Commission annually on the anniversary of the effective date about its progress.[11]

The unions have filed an appeal against the decision of the tribunal to permit the merger to proceed. Unlike the unions, the ministers do not have a right of appeal against the substantive decision of the tribunal. However, as with any litigant, they do have the right to review the proceedings. Remarkably, the ministers have chosen to do so on the extremely flimsy and transparently contrived grounds that the tribunal had limited the extent of discovery that they had asked for and that the tribunal had imposed limits on the number of witnesses it would hear. They have accordingly petitioned the Competition Appeal Court to remit the matter to the tribunal for another hearing that will be untainted by the procedural defects that they allege. The tribunal had set these rules for the hearing largely to expedite an already delayed process. The review is clearly designed to achieve the opposite. It is designed to prolong the decision-making process, with a view to extort a larger industrial development fund from the merged entity. It appears that the ministers would settle for a bounty of R500 million rather than the R100 million imposed by the tribunal.

The message that the minister of economic development is sending is clear. He is effectively saying that merger decisions—and this need not refer only to cross-border mergers—will be used to exercise leverage to attain industrial policy goals. This will be done by politicizing the decision-making process, by effectively compromising the ability of the competition authority to make independent, evidence-based decisions.

The ministers have also made it clear that neither competition nor consumer interests will be considered when making these decisions. The senior official of the Department of Trade and Industry has explicitly stated that it is the government's intention to expand—apparently by their ad hoc, opportunistic interventions rather than by a legislative amendment—the definition of public interest. In short, the government has decided to elevate the place of public interest over competition in the decision-making process and to take upon itself a primary role in determining public interest remedies. These "remedies" will be imposed even where there is little evidence that the public interest, as defined in the act, has been compromised. The government will simply use the existence of a public interest test as leverage, either by the simple expedient of imposing costly delays on merger approvals or by the threat of an adversarial future relationship with the government, a prospect that few businesses lightly entertain.

Nor are the ministers who engaged in the Walmart saga constrained by the consumer interests defended by the tribunal. Quite the contrary; interviewed by one journalist, the Minister of Trade and Industry "acknowledged that Walmart's arrival might help consumers" but said "we have taken the decision [to intervene] in favour of the production sector at the expense of other sectors such as the consumer sector."[12]

Life after *Walmart*

While *Walmart* certainly does not sound the death knell for the independent decision-making power of the competition authorities or for their ability to defend and promote competition, its significance should not be underestimated. As already noted, it is not the only instance of ministerial usurpation of the jurisdiction of the competition authorities. Nor is the lack of regard for competition confined to the government. The courts have also clearly indicated that when competition—and its associated relationship with consumer interests and rights—is weighed against more generally accepted rights of procedural fairness, competition and consumers will come off second best, even when the violation of procedural rights is, at most, relatively slight, the evidence of contravention of the Competition Act is strong, and the interests of the very poorest consumers is compromised.[13]

Opposition—albeit coincidental rather than concerted—from opponents as powerful as the government and the courts cannot be discounted. In *Walmart*, both the commission and the tribunal have refused to buckle in the face of the government's most anticompetitive demands. However if, as in the *Walmart* case, the government manages to attract powerful interest groups, such as the unions, to its side, it is difficult to believe that the ability of an administrative authority to independently promote competition will ultimately prevail, if only because the government retains the power to periodically appoint the commissioner as well as the chairperson and members of the tribunal.

Moreover, the lack of regard for competition and for the independence of administrative bodies is firmly inscribed in government policy. This is particularly reflected in the loudly proclaimed assertion of the "elected representatives"—the executive—to prevail over other centers of decision making, including the courts; the rhetoric of the "developmental state"; and the strong support for an active industrial policy.

There is not much that the competition authorities can, on their own, do to defend their independence. The best that they can do is to demonstrate that, notwithstanding their independence, they have consciously sought alignment between their objectives and actions on the one hand, and the government's pro-poor strategies on the other. This should be complemented by advocacy campaigns that seek to demonstrate the positive outcomes of their actions. It is notoriously difficult to put a figure on the positive impact of competition enforcement. However, there are authorities—the U.K. Office of Fair Trading is probably the leading example—that have developed methodologies that seek to do just this, and the commission similarly needs to focus its advocacy efforts on demonstrating the positive consequences of its actions.

Where, as in the *Walmart* case, the competition authorities arrive at conclusions diametrically opposed to the government, they need to aggressively publicize the basis for their decisions. For example, the government's (and the unions') assertion that Walmart's acquisition of Massmart would lead to both direct and indirect employment loss was clearly not borne out by the evidence. This needs to be put on the public record, not simply by way of a paragraph in the tribunal's decision but by concerted publicity.

The attack on their independence is unlikely to come by way of a legislative amendment that would subordinate their decision-making power to that of the executive. In *Walmart* it was clear that the ministers preferred to have the commission act as their proxy in recommending a domestic procurement quota; they did not want to appear opposed to foreign investors. However, neither did they want to oppose union demands, much less their own protectionist instincts. The imposition of the procurement quota is at one with an essentially protectionist and ad hoc industrial policy. An amendment that placed responsibility for the public interest decision directly in the government's hands may present similarly difficult choices and, in any event, it would be an amendment that would attract significant opposition.

Hence the government's intervention will more likely come in the form that it has in *Walmart*, by government signalling that it is open to cut deals with merging parties as a condition for not opposing their mergers. And then, in those instances in which it is not convenient to take responsibility for the eventual outcome, it will have the commission represent its position and, if possible, have the tribunal rubber-stamp an agreement apparently struck between the commission and the merging parties.

In the face of this approach, the best strategy for the commission would appear to be similar to that followed—whether by accident or design—in the *Walmart* case, and that is by having as little as possible to do with government-sponsored negotiations, thus obliging the government to make its case in the public hearings of the tribunal. Not only does this subject the government's arguments to public scrutiny (in this instance ultimately obliging a minister to publicly concede the subordination of consumer interests to producer interests), it also inadvertently compels the government to give public recognition to the independence, and the decision-making authority that this implies, of the competition authorities. There will of course be many occasions on which the government and the commission arrive at similar or identical conclusions. But this should come following the government's formal submissions in the commission's investigatory processes, rather than by way of the commission participating in closed-door government-sponsored negotiations.

The government has made clear its intention to use the public interest test in the merger review process as a mechanism for using competition law as a lever of industrial policy. This not only makes for bad merger review, it also makes for a particularly random, haphazard industrial policy. The government has no control over mergers that will be filed for competition review. It then effectively has the makers of the so-called industrial policy loitering around the commission's registry, in a manner akin to the proverbial highwayman waiting at the narrowest point in the pass for the passing stagecoach, although of course at least the highwayman has advance notice of when the coach will pass and, often, the riches that it will contain. The industrial policy makers do not know this—one day it may be a cross-border merger in the retail or paints business; the next day it may be a domestic merger in the platinum market.

In the face of the government's apparent determination to intervene in merger review, I would favor a strategic retreat on the part of the competition authorities. Many countries have a review mechanism dedicated to assessing cross-border mergers whereby a domestic firm is acquired by a foreign entity. Preferable to the current uncertainty created by the formal commission investigatory process and the thoroughly unspecified and unaccountable informal government process would be an arrangement whereby the government assumed a formal, specified, and accountable role in the assessment of cross-border mergers. Given international precedent, this would be a relatively uncontroversial intervention both from the perspective of cross-border merger regulation and from the narrower perspective of competition law.

There are reasons, however, to fear this approach. If the government chose simply to insert itself into the process, to impose, in other words an additional step in the evaluation of cross-border mergers, this would not necessarily require a legislative amendment. If, however, it chose to remove public interest jurisdiction from the unions in cross-border mergers, then there are no reasons to believe that it will stop there.

The ministers of economic development and trade and industry have loudly insisted that their intervention in *Walmart*, and in the earlier case of a

Japanese multinational paint producer's acquisition of the dominant South African participant in this market, should not be interpreted as suspicion about or hostility toward foreign acquisitions. I think they protest too loudly. I discern that their action does indeed reflect suspicion of foreign acquisition of domestic firms. It also reflects a calculation that foreign firms are vulnerable to jingoism and are, for this reason, more likely to want to gain the approval of domestic governments. Thus, foreign firms are more vulnerable to the opportunistic imposition of conditions that the ministers have attempted to impose on both Kansai and Walmart.

Unacceptable though this jingoism and opportunism may be, if the government's intervention is, indeed, not intended to discriminate against foreign acquirers of domestic assets, but rather reflects a calculation that by playing a gatekeeper role in relation to mergers in general, it will be able to extract concessions from firms in the midst of a delicate and time-sensitive corporate decision. If so, then the logic would be to remove public interest jurisdiction from the competition authorities altogether and to hand it over to a review mechanism firmly under the thumb of the government.

While competition law purists may welcome this because it leaves the competition review process unsullied by noncompetition criteria, it would not be a welcome development in an economy in which the government has so little regard for competition issues or consumer interests. It would significantly diminish the weight and significance of the competition evaluation in merger control as the government sought to make public interest the dominant criteria. This approach—that is, removing jurisdiction over public interest from the competition authorities and placing it in the hands of the government—would naturally require a significant amendment to the Competition Act. Although South African business organization is politically and technically weak, one cannot but believe that an amendment of this sort would be strongly resisted.

·   ·   ·

Ministers come and go. The South African competition authorities are currently having to contend with a ministerial regime that, in marked contrast with its predecessors, is unusually interventionist and opportunistic, determined to use the powers of the competition authorities as an instrument for attaining ad hoc industrial policy goals, aggressively opposed to administrative independence and manifestly intent upon promoting producer interests above consumer interests.

While this could easily change under a changed ministerial regime, it would only do so to the extent that the situation returned to the previous mode that I have characterized as benign neglect. It is clear that as successful as the competition authorities have been in their regulation of private conduct both in the merger review and enforcement actions, as much as they have established a reputation for professionalism and competence, as much as they have become part of the business culture and decision-making process, they have not succeeded in elevating respect for competition and consumers in the ranks of policy makers.

In the space of a few short years it has become clear that competition law enforcement will struggle to thrive in a policy environment hostile to competition. And so I am confirmed in my opinion that if the first decade of the South African competition authorities was focused on tackling private anticompetitive conduct, then the second decade must focus on confronting public anticompetitive conduct. However, recent events have established that this is far from the case. It is clear now that the competition authorities are going to have to aggressively assert their jurisdictional exclusivity in the private sphere as well.

But this does not necessarily portend an aggressive confrontation with the government. There are public spheres in which competition problems abound. In 2009, I argued for a leading role for the competition authorities in investigating modalities for establishing competitive outcomes in critical markets dominated by state-owned enterprises and public regulation. Energy, telecommunications, transport, and banking were given as examples.[14] Health care has recently emerged as another critical area in which a creatively constructed combination of market forces and public institutions and policy has a critical role to play in securing quality provision at affordable prices. Moreover, recent amendments to the Competition Act offer the competition authorities a powerful weapon—formally constituted and empowered market enquiries—that will enable them to play an important and constructive role in advocating for the role of competition in securing positive public outcomes.

These opportunities must be seized if competition is to firmly establish itself as a key instrument of economic growth and development.

15

India's Tryst with "the Clayton Act Moment" and Emerging Merger Control Jurisprudence

Intersection of Law, Economics, and Politics

Rahul Singh

Although the fundamental issue surrounding the Indian merger control regime is one of legal transplant, the hiatus between the enforcement of conduct-related provisions and merger control is not very different from the dominant antitrust paradigms of the United States or the European Union (EU). India has had its own version of competition law (including merger control) since 1969. The catalogue of events in India indicates that in spite of available international and domestic antitrust experience, the implementation of Indian merger control seems haphazard, thereby ensuring that India undergoes its sui generis Clayton Act moment.

This chapter will argue that the emerging merger control jurisprudence of the Competition Commission of India (CCI) may be elucidated from the vantage point of the intersection between law, economics, and politics. While the political aspect of this intersection is exemplified by the business lobbying of corporate interests, the economics of merger control regulations is a bundle of contradictions, with on the one hand relatively high jurisdictional monetary thresholds required for the applicability of merger control and on the other hand the nascent government proposal to subject all pharmaceutical merger cases (irrespective of the jurisdictional monetary thresholds) to the CCI notification and approval process. This case study of implementation of merger control in India illustrates the type of problems that many young competition regimes have in implementation of not only merger control but competition law more broadly.

In the face of such political and economic complexities, the CCI has taken refuge under the letter (as opposed to the spirit) of the law and has adopted a literal interpretation of merger control law, leading to some absurd interpretational outcomes. Contrary to the intent behind the hectic corporate lobbying, the CCI's attitude portends high transaction costs for the businesses.

Structurally, this chapter has been divided into several parts. The first part explores the historical evolution of the merger control regime under Indian competition law. This part analyzes the repealed competition law and various expert committee reports leading to the new competition law regime. The next part closely examines the politics of corporate lobbying and its impact upon the Indian merger control regime. It also deals with the economics of the Indian merger control regime and the inherent contradictions that the politics of corporate lobbying has infused under Indian merger control. The last part analyzes the available merger precedents at the CCI and interprets the underlying philosophy, or lack thereof, of the precedents. The chapter concludes that India's new merger control implementation is a mess and it will take some time to work out its poor design.

Historical Introduction to India's Competition System

The enactment governing Indian competition law is christened the Competition Act, 2002 (Competition Act). The year of the legislation is a misnomer. Though the act was passed by the Indian Parliament in 2002, it received presidential assent only on January 13, 2003. In India, the mere passage of an enactment does not automatically guarantee enforcement. The executive arm of the government retains exclusive control over the date of enforcement of the enactment.[1] In spite of its notoriety for hyperactivism[2], the Indian judiciary is loath to issue a mandamus against the executive's prerogative to determine the date of enforcement of an enactment.[3]

Though the CCI was established on October 14, 2003, it was not functional because the constitutionality of the Competition Act was challenged at the Supreme Court of India in the case of *Brahm Dutt v. Union of India* (*Brahm Dutt*).[4] Interestingly, the petitioner, Brahm Dutt, was an attorney.[5] His ground for the writ petition was that the CCI, the institutional authority being set up through the Competition Act, was envisaged as being headed by a bureaucrat and not a judge.[6] Indeed, the Monopolies and Restrictive Trade Practices Commission (MRTP Commission), the institutional authority set up back in 1969 and being replaced through the CCI, was headed by a retired Supreme Court judge or a retired chief justice of a high court.[7]

Brahm Dutt's case settled this political tussle between the executive and the judiciary through a simple truce: the government undertook to amend the Competition Act and set up an appellate authority that, à la the MRTP Commission, would be headed by a retired Supreme Court judge or a chief justice of a high court.[8]

The above tacit bargain in *Brahm Dutt* between the judiciary and the executive to create sinecures for the executive and the judiciary at the incipient stage of the CCI prepared the background for later political tussles surrounding the Competition Act. Business interests were the central players in this political tussle. Indeed, hectic business lobbying ensured that the Competition Act, despite the amendments undertaken in 2007 pursuant to the *Brahm Dutt* case, remained unenforceable until May 20, 2009.[9]

The CCI finally saw the light of day on February 28, 2009, with the first chairperson taking office.[10] The Competition Act was partially enforced on May 20, 2009, with the notification of the provisions related to the anticompetitive agreements and abuse of dominance. The merger control provisions were notified on June 1, 2011.

Interestingly, this sequence of events, with a hiatus between the enforcement of the conduct-related provisions and the merger provisions of competition law, is not unique to India. Indeed, in the United States, though the Sherman Act is of an 1890 vintage, it was the Clayton Act of 1914 that initiated the merger control provisions.[11] Similarly, in the EU, though the Treaty of Rome in 1957 laid down conduct-related provisions of competition law, it was not until 1989 that the EU had its own "Clayton Act moment" with the adoption of merger regulations.[12]

From the MRTP Act to the 2007 Amendment to the Competition Act

The international competition literature recurrently refers to two dominant paradigms—the U.S. antitrust model and the EU competition law model. Many assume that these were the only two competition law models available until 1975.[13] Scholars acknowledge a spurt in the adoption of competition law around the world post-1975. Contrary to this belief, India had a sui generis model of competition law as early as 1969 in the form of the Monopolies and Restrictive Trade Practices Act (MRTP Act).[14] This section traces the transformation of the merger control regime from the MRTP Act to the merger control regime made effective on June 1, 2011.

India wrested her independence from the British on August 15, 1947. The government, dominated by freedom fighters, made a conscious decision to follow neither the capitalist nor the communist model of development, but to adopt a mixed economy where the private and state-owned enterprises would coexist. The concern for redistribution was quite perceptible in the actions of the nascent nation. Owing to the concern for uneven impact of growth upon poor people, the government adopted a broader pan-India five-year economic planning method. The first plan period (1950–1955), with its focus upon agriculture, was very successful.[15] The government then turned its attention toward industrialization of the Indian economy during the second plan period (1956–1960). Unlike the first five-year plan, the second five-year plan turned out to be insipid. The government, perhaps, looked for an opportunity to pin the blame for the disastrous performance on private enterprise.

Indeed, on August 22, 1960, while moving the draft outline of the third five-year plan, Prime Minister Jawaharlal Nehru commented, "an advance in our per capita income has taken place and, I think, it is desirable that we should enquire more deeply as to where this has gone."[16] Consequently, an expert committee under the stewardship of noted economist P. C. Mahalanobis was established (Mahalanobis Committee).[17] The mandate of the Mahalanobis Committee was to study distributional inequity.[18] In spite of the then dominant role played by the state in economic planning, the Mahalanobis Committee was quick to blame private enterprise.[19]

Interestingly, the conclusions of the Mahalanobis Committee have been relied upon and cited by none other than George Akerlof in his work on the theory of markets with asymmetric information, which earned him the Nobel Prize in 2001. In his famous "lemons market" article published in the *Quarterly Journal of Economics* in 1970, Akerlof, while dealing with credit markets in underdeveloped countries, noted that "in India a major fraction of industrial enterprise is controlled by 'managing agencies' (according to a recent survey, these 'managing agencies' controlled 65.7 per cent of the net worth of public limited companies and 66 per cent of total assets)."[20] The concept of "managing agents" was a British legacy under which companies in India were owned by shareholders in London but operated in India through the managing agents.

Notwithstanding Akerlof's unalloyed reliance on the Mahalanobis Committee report, the unarticulated major premise of the committee was that state-owned enterprises were per se in the interest of the people and economic power acquired by private enterprise was illegitimate. Based upon the advice of the Mahalanobis Committee that "the sooner the government sets up the necessary machinery for collection, examination and analysis of all relevant data on the subject, the easier it would be for it eventually to formulate the necessary policy that will combine industrialization with social justice and economic development with dispersal of economic power,"[21] on April 16, 1964, the government appointed the Monopolies Inquiry Commission under the chairmanship of Justice K. C. Das Gupta (Das Gupta Committee). The mandate of the Das Gupta Committee was to conduct specific inquiry into the extent and effect of the concentration of economic power in private hands.[22] Like its predecessor Mahalanobis Committee, the Das Gupta Committee, too, conveniently blamed private enterprise and observed that the existing powers of the government have not been able to check the growth of concentration of private economic power.[23] The committee recommended an independent regulatory authority with a mandate to regulate the concentration of economic wealth.

Accordingly, the MRTP Commission was established with a broad antimonopoly purpose embedded in the preamble of the MRTP Act. The influence of the Constitution of India on this broad purpose of the MRTP Act is conspicuous. The Directive Principles of State Policy contained in Part IV of the Indian Constitution seek to ensure that the ownership and control of material resources of the community are so distributed as best to serve the common good[24] and also that the operation of the economic system does not result in the concentration of wealth and means of production to the common detriment.[25]

Although the mandate of the Indian Constitution refers broadly to the "economic system" and is not merely confined to the private sector, in tune with the recommendations of the Mahalanobis Committee and the Das Gupta Committee, the MRTP Act exempted the state-owned enterprises from its purview and applied only to private entities.[26]

Curiously, at this stage of development of Indian competition law, the MRTP Act took its cue from the antitrust experience in the United States and contained merger review provisions that obviated the need for any Clayton Act–type moment.[27] The MRTP Act, however, had a checkered history of enforcement. While on the one hand it has been discredited for transforming into an albatross around the neck of businesses planning expansion of capacity,[28] on the other hand it has been decried for partisan enforcement.[29]

Amid such widely oscillating opinions, coinciding with the inception of economic reforms, the merger review provisions of the MRTP Act were repealed in 1991, as it had been the experience of the government that pre-entry restriction under the MRTP Act on the investment decision of the corporate sector had outlived its utility and had become a hindrance to the speedy implementation of industrial projects.[30]

Therefore, it appears that the repeal was pursuant to the government's philosophy of promoting national champions and encouraging the emergence of Indian multinationals.[31] For a newly independent country facing scarcity of resources and capital and following a socialist model of development, perhaps premerger notification and an approval process for expansion of capacity made a modicum of sense. However, for an economy liberalized and opened to global competition in 1991, followed by infusion of the capitalist model of development, it was logical to amend the MRTP Act.[32] The amendment to the MRTP Act, repealing premerger notification and approval for expansion of capacity, was effected on September 27, 1991.[33]

The 1991 amendment to the MRTP Act, effecting a reverse Clayton Act moment for (the then effective) Indian competition law, came into sharp focus in the case of *Hindustan Lever Employees' Union v. Hindustan Lever*. *Hindustan Lever* was decided on October 24, 1994, by a three-judge bench of the Supreme Court of India, after several rounds of litigation in the high court acting as the company court. *Hindustan Lever* involved an interesting horizontal merger between the Hindustan Lever Limited (HLL) and the Tata Oil Mills Company Limited (TOMCO).

TOMCO, owned by the Tata group, was the first Indian company. It was founded in 1917[34] and manufactured soaps, detergents, toiletries, and animal feeds.[35] It was a beneficiary of socialist India's friendship with the erstwhile Soviet Union, but upon the collapse of the Soviet Union in August–December 1991, TOMCO's financial health failed.[36] HLL was an Indian subsidiary of global, fast-moving consumer goods behemoth Unilever, with its headquarters in London.[37]

Although Unilever had entered the Indian market in 1888 during British rule, HLL was renamed Hindustan Unilever in 2007.[38] TOMCO's minority shareholders, employees' union (of HLL and TOMCO), and consumer action groups challenged the Tata group's decision to sell TOMCO's assets to HLL under the Indian Companies Act, 1956 as well as the MRTP Act (since both enactments envisaged concurrent jurisdictions).[39]

Remnant of a time when India had just changed its economic philosophy from socialism to capitalism, the foreign origin of the multinational corporation, Unilever, was one of the significant arguments advanced by the minority shareholders challenging the merger.[40] This argument, couched as a violation of "public policy" (relevant under the Companies Act but not under the MRTP Act), seemed attractive due to the alleged undervaluation of TOMCO's assets.[41] The Supreme Court conceded that the touchstone of public policy may involve analysis of the foreign origin of the acquirer.[42] In light of the foreign identity of the acquirer, the court seemed to take a sympathetic note of a wider framework for analysis based on strategic trade theory rather than the benchmark for merger review provided under the [Indian] Companies Act.[43] However, invoking its fidelity to the purpose of the statute and deference to the new economic reforms initiating capitalism, the Supreme Court rejected the xenophobic arguments of the minority shareholders.[44]

Invoking the reverse Clayton Act moment under the MRTP Act, the counsel representing a consumer association argued that even though merger control provisions had been repealed, because of the existence of the power of divestiture relating to conduct cases (§§ 27 and 27A of the MRTP Act), the MRTP Commission would continue to have jurisdiction over the merger of HLL and TOMCO. Accordingly, the consumer representative argued that unless the companies received prior approval under the MRTP Act, the courts ought to keep their approvals in abeyance.[45] While the 1991 amendment repealed §§ 20 through 26 of the MRTP Act, *Hindustan Lever* was specifically concerned with § 23, which governed mergers, amalgamation, and takeovers.[46]

The Supreme Court was not persuaded by this argument. The Court noted the rationale behind the 1991 amendment of the MRTP Act, repealing the requirement of premerger notification and approval for expansion of capacity, as the reduction of transaction costs for businesses.[47] Indeed, the Supreme Court found the argument to be "unnatural and artificial."[48] Curiously, the Supreme Court reasoned that if the argument were to be accepted, it would mean that the requirement for premerger notification under the MRTP Act was unnecessary.[49] Nevertheless, in a back-handed compliment to the reverse Clayton Act moment, the Supreme Court conceded that though there was no requirement for premerger notification, the MRTP Commission, if the situation arises, would be free to decide under an applicable conduct case.[50]

In spite of the 1991 amendment, with the passage of time the government found the MRTP Act to be unsuited to the requirements of a globalized economy and in 1999 decided to set up a high-level committee under the leadership of S. V. S. Raghavan (Raghavan Committee) to analyze the need for a modern competition law.[51] The Raghavan Committee faced similar tribulations about the premerger notification regime suitable for the Indian context.

Starting from where the Supreme Court of India had left off in *Hindustan Lever*, the Raghavan Committee launched its work on the premise that usually there is no need for ex ante merger review, as anticompetitive conduct could be caught by the remainder of competition law.[52] The Raghavan Committee, therefore, felt that merger review provisions ought to be carefully calibrated.[53] Accordingly, the committee hoped that merger review would be utilized sparingly.[54] Continuing with the sentiment of establishing national champions, the Raghavan Committee hoped that Indian competition law would aid domestic enterprises in their growth.[55]

The Raghavan Committee, therefore, had a cautious approach toward merger review provisions under competition law. Akin to the governmental concerns expressed in 1991, the committee was wary of the potential adverse impact that delays in merger review may have on the growth of Indian companies. Interestingly, though the Raghavan Committee was aware of the absence of merger review under the amended MRTP Act, it did ultimately find it worthwhile to have the provisions. The committee merely hoped that the government and the competition authority would be extra careful in their approach to mergers. It felt that an intrusive merger review would harm the process of competition itself.[56]

However, the Raghavan Committee envisaged a full Clayton Act moment for Indian competition law and recommended a merger review regime with mandatory prenotification above a certain threshold.[57] Yet the Raghavan Committee categorically stipulated that the mandatory prenotification ought to have a concomitant strict timeliness requirement.[58]

The Raghavan Committee's recommendation for a mandatory merger control regime was in tune with the international best practices; only a handful had opted for voluntary merger control regimes. In spite of the Raghavan Committee's recommendation for a full Clayton Act moment, the business lobbies ensured that the recommended mandatory regime was altered to a voluntary regime, thus making it a half Clayton Act moment.[59] Indeed, the voluntary, optional merger control regime was in sync with the

U.K. merger control regime.[60] Though the government departed from the Raghavan Committee's recommendation and changed the nature of obligation for premerger notification, it stood by the suggested strict timeline of 90 days. Due to the voluntary nature of the premerger notification requirement, there was no penalty provided for failure to notify the CCI.

While the merger control provisions, introduced in 2002, were akin to those of the United Kingdom, the 2007 amendment to the Competition Act sought to align Indian competition law with the U.S. and the EU models through the requirement of mandatory premerger notification.[61] As noted above, in accordance with the concerns expressed by the Raghavan Committee, the 2002 version of the Competition Act had a strict timeline of 90 days.[62] Ironically, though the 2007 amendment of the Competition Act made the premerger notification mandatory, it unjustifiably stretched the timeline to 210 days.[63] The Statement of Objects and Reasons accompanying the 2007 amendment of the Competition Act, without any compelling justification behind the extension of the timeline, merely cursorily mentioned the change as "consequential" in nature.[64] Additionally, with a mandatory premerger notification requirement, a penalty for failure to notify was also added.[65]

The stretched timeline of 210 days is contrary to the spirit of the Raghavan Committee's suggestions. While aware of the problem of unscrambling the egg and avoidable social costs, the Raghavan Committee had suggested mandatory premerger notification. However, bearing in mind the bureaucratic delays and consequent adverse impact upon the growth of enterprise, the Raghavan Committee had settled for a ninety-day timeline.[66] Additionally, the Raghavan Committee's insistence upon ninety days as a strict timeline was due to the concurrent involvement of other regulatory authorities during the merger review process that increases the transaction costs for enterprises.[67]

The Raghavan Committee's concerns about enhanced transaction costs were also perhaps justified in light of the lack of professional expertise at the CCI.[68] This lack is exacerbated by the funneling process that merger review usually entails. It is well known that most mergers create no competitive concerns; very few may create potential anticompetitive harm that may run afoul of the competition law. Nonetheless, crystal ball gazing for ex ante merger review would occupy a disproportionately great amount of time of the CCI staff.[69] Accordingly, in order to mitigate the potential transaction costs for enterprises, the Competition Act, in 2002, prior to the 2007 amendment, did envisage the strict timeline of 90 working days. For the enterprises, however, the 2007 amendment of the Competition Act appears to be a double whammy with a mandatory premerger notification and an extended timeline of 210 days.

The timeline of 210 days is clearly out of sync with international best practices. With the high transaction costs entailed by a 210-day review staring in their faces, businesses were evidently concerned about the enforcement of the merger control provisions of the Competition Act. Therefore, though the 2007 amendment introduced the idea of a mandatory premerger notification, the merger control provisions were not enforced by the government until June 1, 2011.

Post-2007 Amendment of the Competition Act to the Current Merger Control Regime

This section provides analysis of a number of provisions of the realities of Indian merger control to show the motivations for the internal contradictions in the system. This analysis does not exhaust all sections of India's merger control but it provides representative examples of the complexity of Indian merger control that will take quite some time to fix.

The 2007 amendment to the Competition Act engendered businesses' concerns related to the abnormal timeline. The sponsoring ministry of the CCI, the Ministry of Corporate Affairs (MCA), was successful in piloting the 2007 amendment in the Parliament. The 2007 amendment of the Competition Act was not challenged in the Supreme Court, indicating that the amendment was broadly acceptable to the petitioner in *Brahm Dutt*. The MCA, however, did not immediately staff the CCI. While hectic corporate lobbying was partially responsible for the delay, the MCA also seemed keen to pack the CCI with cherry-picked, pliable chairperson and members.

Upon the president's assent granted to the Competition Act on January 13, 2003, the CCI was to be established through the appointment of a member and chairperson.[70] Though the sole member who had initially been appointed immediately took office, the person offered the position of chairperson cited the pending Supreme Court decision in *Brahm Dutt* and refused to take office.[71] The single member continued to hold office during the 2007 amendment to the Competition Act and resigned prematurely in June 2008 even though his term was not to expire until February 2009.[72] The CCI officially came into existence on February 28, 2009, with the first chairperson taking office.[73]

Pursuant to the central government's undertaking in *Brahm Dutt*, the 2007 amendment of the Competition Act provided for the establishment of an appellate authority, the Competition Appellate Tribunal, to be headed by a retired Supreme Court judge or a chief justice of a high court.[74] The appellate tribunal was established on May 15, 2009.[75] The establishment of the appellate tribunal paved the way for the enforcement of anticompetitive agreements and abuse of dominance provisions of the Competition Act on May 20, 2009.[76] Indicating its interest in the enforcement of the merger control provisions of the Competition Act, the CCI issued several draft versions, and the finalized Merger Regulations were issued on May 11, 2011.

The CCI's several versions of Draft Merger Regulations indicate as if the CCI took the legislative mandate of the autonomy for delegated legislation seriously.[77] However, in spite of the autonomy guaranteed by the legislative mandate, the CCI in its zeal to keep the MCA on good terms had sent a draft of the Merger Regulations to the MCA.[78] The MCA did not return the courtesy and unbeknownst to the CCI issued four notifications on March 4, 2011 (MCA Notifications) that drastically altered the milieu of merger control under the Indian competition law.[79] The MCA Notifications relate to (1) the date of enforcement of merger control provisions being fixed for June 1, 2011;[80] (2) the enhancement of jurisdictional monetary threshold under the Competition Act;[81] (3) exemption based upon the size of the acquired enterprise;[82] and (4) effective amendment to the definition of "group" under the Competition Act.[83]

Since the February 2011 Draft Merger Regulations had recently been issued for public comments, the MCA Notification of March 4, 2011, fixing the date of enforcement of the merger control provisions for June 1, 2011, created a sense of urgency at the CCI to finalize the Merger Regulations. The entire set of MCA Notifications, however, were far from innocuous and had tremendous bearing upon the jurisprudence of merger control. In accordance with the recommendation of the Raghavan Committee, the Competition Act continues with the jurisdictional monetary threshold requirements for finding whether acquisition, acquisition of control among horizontal entities, or merger/amalgamation are a "combination"[84] triggering premerger notification.[85] Under the Competition Act, a transaction would attract the merger control provisions only if the combined size of acquirer and the acquired enterprise, upon completion of the transaction, would meet jurisdictional monetary thresholds (which were higher than the thresholds in the United States or the EU). However, through the MCA Notifications,[86] the

Table 15.1 Jurisdictional monetary thresholds under Indian merger control regime

	Basis for computation of thresholds	Assets			Turnover	
Purely domestic transactions	Enterprise-wise basis	INR 1,500 Crores (USD 272.7 million)		Or	INR 4,500 Crores (USD 818.18 million)	
		Or			Or	
	Group-wise basis	INR 6,000 Crores (USD 1.09 billion)		Or	INR 18,000 Crores (USD 3.27 billion)	
Parties with cross-border presence		Assets			Turnover	
		Global	Indian		Global	Indian
	Enterprise-wise basis	USD 750 million	INR 750 Crores (USD 136.36 million)	Or	USD 2.25 billion	INR 2,250 Crores (USD 409 million)
		Or			Or	
	Group-wise basis	USD 3 billion	INR 750 Crores (USD 136.36 million)	Or	USD 9 billion	INR 2,250 Crores (USD 409 million)

NOTE: Conversion ratio of 1 USD = INR 55 approx. used.

jurisdictional monetary thresholds were further enhanced, as illustrated in Table 15.1.

Such high thresholds were evidently a result of pressure from the business lobbies to aid the growth of national champions. However, there are two significant problems with the arbitrary enhancement of the jurisdictional monetary thresholds.

First, the 50 percent enhancement of the jurisdictional monetary threshold through the MCA Notification is ultra vires and illegal under the Competition Act. Presumably, the enhancement has been carried under § 20(3) of the Competition Act, which is similar to the revision of jurisdictional thresholds under § 7A of the Clayton Act.[87] Section 20(3) authorizes the central government to adjust the jurisdictional monetary thresholds based on the variables of inflation and fluctuations in exchange rate.[88] This power of the central government is to be exercised in consultation with the CCI. While it is unclear whether the CCI was consulted prior to the enhancement of the jurisdictional monetary threshold by 1.5 times, § 20(3) mandates that enhancement can be done only two years after the commencement of the Competition Act.

As discussed above, the anticompetitive agreements and abuse of dominance related provisions of the Competition Act commenced on May 20,

2009. Hence, the central government may have assumed that on June 1, 2011, the date fixed for the commencement of merger control provisions, the precondition of two years under § 20(3) will be satisfied. Interestingly, neither the CCI nor the central government noticed the proviso to § 1(3) of the Competition Act, which states that the reference to the commencement of the Competition Act in any provision shall be interpreted to mean enforcement of a particular provision and not the enforcement of other, unrelated provisions.[89] Accordingly, the central government's notification related to the enhancement of jurisdictional monetary thresholds by 1.5 times violates § 1(3) of the Competition Act and is illegal.

Second, besides the illegality, the government's recent actions themselves indicate that it is ambivalent about the rationality of this enhancement. The central government has recently decided that all pharmaceutical mergers (irrespective of the jurisdictional monetary thresholds) will be subject to the premerger notification requirement at the CCI.[90] The CCI has been given six months to build capacity for reviewing pharmaceutical mergers.[91] The government's decision to do away with the jurisdictional monetary threshold indicates that even the government now perhaps understands that it may have notified an irrationally high threshold through the MCA Notifications.

Although of doubtful legal validity, the extension of the CCI's jurisdiction to all pharmaceutical mergers may be construed as a vote of confidence in the CCI's nascent merger review abilities. However, what government gave with one hand it took away with the other. The government has, simultaneously, decided to exempt some bank mergers from the premerger notification requirements to the CCI.[92] Interestingly, both the inclusion of all pharmaceutical mergers and exclusion of some banks' mergers have been justified on the ground of consumer welfare. The justification appears contradictory and unclear. If the concern for consumer welfare in pharmaceutical mergers mandate CCI merger review, why is the same yardstick not applicable to bank mergers?

Under Indian competition law, the jurisdictional monetary thresholds are used to signal that a legal fiction of "combination" will be created through the process of acquisition or merger or amalgamation, and this triggers premerger notification.[93] As indicated in Table 15.1, the jurisdictional monetary thresholds under the Competition Act depend upon the combined size of the acquirer and the acquired enterprise and are computed on the basis of assets in terms of value and turnover (assessed on enterprise-wise or group-wise basis). In essence, the touchstone for premerger notification in India adopts the size of person test, i.e., size of acquirer and acquired enterprise test. Unlike the United States, Indian competition law does not have the size of transaction test. Further, in the interest of certainty and predictability, unlike the U.K. competition law, the jurisdictional monetary thresholds requirement under Indian competition law does not follow the market share test.

The MCA Notifications, however, effectively amend the definition of "combination"; besides the combined size of the acquirer and the acquired enterprise, it introduces an additional step related to the size of the acquired enterprise. In accordance with the amendment, under the relevant MCA Notification, a transaction does not attract the merger control provisions of the Competition Act unless the size of the acquired enterprise is at least INR 2.5 billion in terms of assets in India[94] and INR 7.5 billion in terms of turnover in India. In other words, transactions will be exempt where the size of the acquired enterprise is either[95] less than INR 2.5 billion in terms of value of assets in India or less than INR 7.5 billion in terms of turnover in India.

Ideally, such a change in the definition of "combination" ought to have been carried through an amendment of the parent legislation. Presumably, due to the tortuous time process of undertaking an amendment to the Competition Act, the government settled for a delegated legislation of exemption notification. The exemption based on the size of the acquired enterprise is legally valid and has been made in the light of the "public interest" clause under the legislative authority of § 54 of the Competition Act.[96] The exemption, nevertheless, since it has been carried through a delegated legislation and not an amendment of the parent legislation, is temporary—available only for five years.

An unintended consequence of the effective amendment to the definition of "combination" has been the exemption of all new joint ventures from the merger control regime. Since a new joint venture will always have negligible turnover (even if one assumes infusion of assets by joint venture partners), it will be able to seek the benefit of the exemption based on the size of acquired enterprise. This may mean that in order to escape the merger control regime, businesses may have an incentive to create a new joint venture instead of investing in an existing corporate entity. This was perhaps not the intent of the introduction of the exemption based upon the size of the acquired enterprise. Interestingly, through amendments of the Merger Regulations on February 23, 2012, the CCI has sought to partially address this concern by indicating that if assets are transferred to an entity (including a newly incorporated entity), then for the purposes of merger review the assets and the turnover of the transferor will be imputed to the transferee.[97]

Some commentators have, however, erroneously interpreted the definition of enterprise under the Competition Act to argue that joint ventures are exempt, irrespective of the exemption based upon the size of the acquired enterprise. Based on the EU competition law distinction between "full-function joint ventures" and "non-full function joint ventures," it has been argued that a newly incorporated company is not engaged in any activity and hence is not an enterprise within the meaning of the Competition Act. Since the definition of "combination" also relies upon the definition of enterprise, the argument is that a new joint venture company will not qualify as a combination.[98] Such an argument relies too heavily upon the qualifier "has been" which precedes the phrase "any [economic] activity" in the definition of enterprise.[99]

The argument stems from a disingenuous reading of the definition of enterprise under the Indian Competition Act where the kernel of the definition is "any [economic] activity." Indeed, the definition is so broadly worded as to mention not only what is covered but also what is not covered. Accordingly, any economic activity undertaken by a person (including state-owned enterprises[100]) is covered under the definition of enterprise. The narrow exception relates to the economic activity of the government, which may be interpreted as sovereign functions of the government such as atomic energy, currency, defense, and space. The word "activity" has been elaborated upon as an example to relate, inter alia, to "acquisition or control of articles or goods" or "the provision of services." Significantly, the words "article" and "service" have been explained to include "a new article" and "a new service" respectively.[101]

Therefore, it is erroneous to pin the blame on the language of "enterprise" under the Competition Act. However, due to the MCA Notification related to the exemption based on the size of acquired enterprise, new joint venture companies will be exempt from the merger control regime (unless the transaction involves transfer of assets). Clearly, the real culprit behind the exemption of new joint ventures is the MCA Notification and not the Competition Act. Ironically, there is a government proposal, nevertheless, to amend the Competition Act in order to ensure that new joint venture companies do not remain exempt from the purview of the merger control regime. In an added ironic twist, the governmental panel that suggested the amendment of the Competition Act to include joint ventures under the merger control regime includes a former chairperson of the CCI, secretary of the MCA, and a legal expert who was a member of the Raghavan Committee!

Besides the enhancement of jurisdictional monetary threshold and exemption based on the size of acquired enterprise, the MCA Notifications effected another amendment—that of the definition of "group" under the Competition Act. The definition of "group" has been drafted quite inelegantly under the Competition Act.[102] Notwithstanding the convoluted phrasing of the definition, the intent appears to be to define "group" to include all entities—controlled, controlling, and those under common control.[103] Accordingly, the definition incorporates elements of de jure control (through exercise of 26 percent or more of the voting rights, which is in conformity with veto rights under general corporate law, or power to appoint more than 50 percent of the board of directors) and de facto control (management control).

The benchmark of 26 percent in the definition of "group," as mentioned in the Competition Act, is significant because the jurisdictional monetary threshold is calculated on an enterprise-wise as well as group-wise basis. A benchmark of 26 percent, while analyzing a group, was intended to be expansive while determining the boundaries of entities to be covered in terms of its affiliates. The purpose was to ensure that while calculating the jurisdictional monetary thresholds, based on the value of assets and turnover, all entities including the affiliates within a group will be taken into account.

The 26 percent cap was evidently seen by the businesses as too low. The MCA buckled and issued a clarification through the MCA Notifications and effectively amended the definition of "group" to ensure that the barometer of 26 percent became 50 percent and a "group" exercising less than 50 percent of voting rights was exempt from the calculation of jurisdictional monetary thresholds under competition law.[104] If the purpose of defining a group at the barometer of 26 percent was expansive, the hike in the benchmark to 50 percent is definitely regressive.

Of course, the foolhardy lobbying that went into effecting the change in barometer came back to haunt the businesses. The raising of the bar to 50 percent also increased the threshold for claiming the safe harbor for groups under the Merger Regulations.[105] Under the safe harbor conceded by the CCI in the Merger Regulations, intragroup acquisitions are unlikely to cause anticompetitive effects and hence "need not normally" be notified to the CCI.[106] If the barometer for claiming the safe harbor is 50 percent instead of

26 percent, fewer transactions will be able to claim the safe harbor under the Merger Regulations. Businesses, through their hectic lobbying, appear to have hurt rather than helped themselves.

The Clayton Act Moment and Merger Precedents: The Emerging Jurisprudence

The merger precedents are evidence of the emerging jurisprudence of merger control. As a response to trenchant criticisms by the businesses, the CCI has, through the Merger Regulations, initiated some prudent provisions in the Indian merger control regime. The Merger Regulations, for instance, impose a deadline of 30 calendar days on the CCI for the formulation of a prima facie opinion, effectively introducing the idea of a "waiting period" under Indian competition law with enterprises free to consummate their transactions after the 30 calendar days' waiting period. Also, the Merger Regulations clarified that the merger control regime will be applicable prospectively (where the binding documents are executed on or after June 1, 2011) and the CCI will endeavor to pass a final order within 180 calendar days rather than 210 days referred to in the parent legislation.

Besides the infusion of pragmatism in the Merger Regulations, there is simultaneously an interesting merger control jurisprudence that is emerging in India. The emerging jurisprudence indicates the CCI's continuing penchant for engendering credibility among stakeholders on the one hand, and an unexpected, spirited push-back against the business lobbies on the other. The CCI's push-back, as discussed below, is not devoid of transaction cost as for the stakeholders.

In the sixty-six cases decided up to August 17, 2012, the CCI has managed to decide cases within the deadline of 30 calendar days. This is intended to engender credibility for its abilities within the stakeholders. Further, many (thirty-two out of sixty-six) merger orders up to August 17, 2012, have involved foreign acquirers, and this has had little impact on the CCI's competition analysis. In all fairness, however, the CCI has yet to grapple with a complex merger situation, and the real test of the CCI's abilities in keeping the deadline and even-handedness against foreign acquirers will probably need to await a complex merger case.

CCI, through the Merger Regulations, has ushered some pragmatism into the merger control regime. Simultaneously, perhaps owing to the end game of lobbying in the drafting of finalized Merger Regulations, the CCI is also seemingly pushing back against the encroaching corporate lobbies. In its spirited fight against the corporate lobbies, the CCI has taken refuge under the letter (as opposed to the spirit) of laws and has adopted a literal (rather than purposive) interpretation of competition law. This contradictory approach of the CCI has created an artificial dichotomy and led to some absurd interpretational outcomes. Contrary to the intent behind the hectic corporate lobbying, this portends high transaction costs for the businesses.

In transactions involving acquisition of a division of business rather than the entire corporate entity, an obvious question arose about the interpretation of the exemption—will the exemption be computed based upon the size of the corporate entity or based upon the size of the unit being acquired? For instance, in the case involving G&K Baby Care Private Limited's acquisition of the nutrition business of Workhardt Limited and contract manufacturing business of Carol Info Services Limited and Danone Asia Pacific Holdings Pte Limited's acquisition of intellectual property rights of Wockhardt EU Operations Swiss AG, (the Danone case), the CCI had informally confirmed that the assets and turnover thresholds for the exemption based on the size of acquired enterprise was calculated on an enterprise-wise[107] basis and not on the basis of business unit, business division, or subsidiaries.[108] The case of AICA Japan[109] was similar when it was acquiring the sunmica division of the acquired enterprise, Bombay Burmah Trading Company Limited (BBTCL). Presumably, the assets in terms of value and turnover of the sunmica division of BBTCL were less than INR 2.5 billion and INR 7.5 billion, respectively. However, the assets in terms of value and turnover of the corporate entity, BBTCL, exceeded INR 2.5 billion and INR 7.5 billion, respectively. The CCI rejected the claim for exemption made by the acquirer, AICA Japan.

In the case of NHK Automotive,[110] the acquirer, NHK Japan, was acquiring the springs division of the acquired enterprise, BBTCL. The assets in terms of value and turnover computed for springs division did not exceed INR 2.5 billion and INR 7.5 billion, respectively. The CCI rejected the claim for exemption made by the acquirer, NHK Automotive.

In Danone, AICA Japan, and NHK Automotive, the CCI has interpreted the word "enterprise" used in the MCA Notification literally to be inclusive of unit, division, and subsidiaries. Such a literal interpretation has ensured that transactions such as Danone, AICA Japan, and NHK Automotive were subject to premerger notification requirements. Interestingly, though the new CCI chairperson has, on record, spoken of Indian competition law's affinity to the EU competition law,[111] such an interpretation of the exemption based upon the size of acquired enterprise is at variance with similar inter-pretation for exemption of de minimis transactions in the EU.

Further, the CCI has interpreted the word "acquisition" literally to sug-gest that the exemption based on the size of the acquired enterprise is avail-able only for acquisitions and not for mergers/amalgamations. This has created an artificial dichotomy between acquisitions on the one hand, and mergers/amalgamations on the other. From the perspective of the impact on the market, there appears to be little qualitative difference between, say, 100 percent acquisition of shares/voting rights and merger/amalgamation be-tween two entities. The CCI's creation of the artificial dichotomy between the two has led to a bizarre outcome; while 100 percent acquisition of shares/voting rights will benefit from the exemption based on the size of acquired enterprise, merger/amalgamation between the same entities will be subject to premerger notification. Since the MCA Notification mandating the ex-emption based on the size of acquired enterprise has been enforced by the government in the "public interest," it is absurd to say that acquisitions are in the "public interest," while mergers/amalgamations are not![112] Through the Merger Regulations amendments of February 23, 2012, the CCI has slightly changed this by introducing a new category of exemptions related to intra-group mergers and amalgamations, but that is limited only to wholly owned subsidiaries.[113]

Similar to the literal interpretation of the exemption based on the size of the acquired enterprise, the CCI has also adopted a literal interpretation of the safe harbor it conceded for intragroup transactions under the Merger Regulations. Since the safe harbor uses the word "acquisition," rather than "mergers/amalgamations," the CCI has interpreted the safe harbor to be available only for intragroup acquisitions but not to intragroup mergers/amalgamations.[114]

Indeed, in the case relating to internal group restructuring of entities within the Alstom Group (Alstom),[115] the CCI, in its analysis of anticompeti-tive effects of the merger noted that the amalgamated entity will remain with the same ultimate parent entity.[116] Similar reliance upon the absence of change in the ultimate parent entity was also noted by the CCI in the case relating to intragroup restructuring of Siemens (Siemens).[117]

Some commentators have criticized the CCI's irrational fascination with intragroup restructurings on the ground that the CCI's actions militate against the purpose of the statute.[118] The rationale behind the criticism may not be sound, as the term "group" under the Competition Act was defined widely to incorporate all affiliates for the purpose of the computation of jurisdictional monetary thresholds.

Indeed, continuing to hide behind the letter of the law, the CCI has attempted to put the mutual contradictions of the regulations under the carpet. For instance, besides the safe harbor for intragroup transactions, there was another safe harbor that the CCI had conceded under the Merger Regulations. An acquisition of shares or voting rights, where the acquirer already has 50 percent or more of shares or voting rights in the acquired entity, will not be subject to premerger notification. The only exception to this will be cases that entail change in quality of control from "joint control" to "sole control."[119] This safe harbor, based on a preexisting 50 percent of shares or voting rights sans change in quality of control, contradicts the safe harbor envisaged for intragroup transactions. It is unclear why enterprises that have prior control of 50 percent of an enterprise would not claim the safe harbor for intragroup transactions and instead fall within the exception of change in quality of control mandating premerger notification.

Faced with a situation where the safe harbor for intragroup transaction was applicable, but the safe harbor for preexisting 50 percent of shares or voting rights sans change in quality of control was not, the CCI has taken a literal interpretation, leading to another absurd outcome, that unless all safe harbors are applicable instead of merely one of them, the transaction will be subject to premerger notification. Accordingly, in Disney group's acquisition of an additional stake in the target, UTV Software Communications Limited,[120] even though Disney had a preexisting 50.44 percent of shares in the target (making the target its subsidiary), the transaction was considered subject to the premerger notification requirement because of the change in quality of control.[121] This was in spite of the applicability of the safe harbor for intragroup transactions because UTV, as a subsidiary entity, would have been classified as part of Disney's group.

If the CCI is aware of the history of the MRTP Act, it should know that its illogical and absurd interpretation of the safe harbors for intragroup transactions may boomerang. The MRTP Commission, constituted under the MRTP Act, had harbored an irrational fascination for dealing with "unfair trade practices" of standards of service rather than anticompetitive "monopolistic trade practices" and "restrictive trade practices."[122] Such an illogical affinity for contractual disputes related to deficient services had boomeranged on the MRTP Commission by crowding out other genuine, competition-related cases, eventually leading to a monumental failure and the winding up of the MRTP Commission. Through the absurd interpretation of the intra-group safe harbor, the CCI runs the risk of crowding out genuine merger cases that it ought to review. The prioritization for hard-core merger cases is a fortiori significant because of the scarcity of skilled human resources at the CCI.[123]

Unfortunately, though the CCI cites its fidelity to the law behind its adoption of literal interpretation of the MCA Notifications (for the defini-tion of "enterprise" and interpretation of "acquisition" in the exemption based upon the size of the acquired enterprise) and the Merger Regulations (for safe harbor relating to intragroup transactions), the merger precedents do not contain any detailed legal analysis. The stakeholders are left to fend for themselves to gather the jurisprudence, if any. The merger precedents, far from being stare decisis, seem nontransparent and of little use for the parties planning to rely upon them to arrange their affairs for future transactions.

Unlike the EU law, the CCI's merger precedents, in the public domain, do not analyze the applicability of the jurisdictional monetary thresholds available either under the Competition Act or the MCA Notification's ex-emption based on the size of the acquired enterprise. This leads to uncer-tainty in business planning.

The Competition Act contains several provisions related to delineation of the relevant market.[124] In spite of such a statutory mandate, the CCI has ex-hibited little inclination to adopt literal interpretation or any modicum of fidelity to legislative provisions for defining the relevant market. The Compe-tition Act, in addition, contains a list of factors, such as cost benefit analysis, barriers to entry, and level of competition, that the CCI is supposed to utilize for its review process.[125] The merger precedents, however, do not necessarily reflect any comprehensive analysis these factors. Indeed, even in horizontal merger cases, the CCI has not analyzed the change in the Herfindahl–Hirschman Index (HHI) in order to elucidate market concentration. At this stage of development of the CCI, it is perhaps too much to expect it to utilize critical loss analysis or upward pricing pressure in appropriate cases.

Moreover, in most merger cases, the CCI has not substantively analyzed the concept of relevant market. In a case such as that of NHK Automotive, the CCI has broadly applied a deferential standard of review to delineate the relevant market and has agreed with the submission of the parties.

Such an absence of rigorous legal or economic analysis in merger prece-dents indicates that the CCI's refuge under a literal interpretation of the MCA Notifications and Merger Regulations is a mistake. The narrow, literal interpretations adopted by the CCI are likely to lead to crowding out of genuine competition cases and increase Type II errors. Any inconsistencies and errors by the CCI are bound to further increase transaction costs for businesses.

.   .   .

On one level, the fundamental issue in India's merger control system seems to be of legal transplant. Though Indian merger control has been influenced by the international experience, its implementation seems haphazard. On another level, India has had its own competition law in a wholly different form since 1969 and a brand new one since 2002 with the merger control provisions of the new competition law implemented since June 1, 2011. The emerging merger control jurisprudence seems to be messy, patchy, and at times inchoate. Perhaps this is because the CCI remains hobbled by its inadequate appreciation of the law and economics of the Competition Act (including the delegated legislations) on the one hand, and continuing, mindless corporate lobbying on the other. This case study of implementation of merger control offers a warning to relatively new competition agencies as they consider implementation of merger control regimes.

Notes

Introduction

1. World Bank, Global Economic Prospects and the Developing Countries 97–125 (2002).

2. Mark A. Dutz & Maria Vagliasindi, *Competition Policy Implementation in Transition Economies: An Empirical Assessment*, 44 Eur. Econ. Rev. 762, 771 (2000).

3. Eleanor M. Fox & D. Daniel Sokol, Competition Law and Policy in Latin America (2009) (discussing the Latin American experience); William E. Kovacic & Carl Shapiro, *Antitrust Policy: A Century of Economic and Legal Thinking*, 14 J. Econ. Perspectives 43, 58 (2000) (discussing the U.S. experience).

4. Agence France Presse, *BRIC Nations Stronger, But Not in Unison*, Econ. Times, Jan. 4, 2012.

5. *China Overtakes Japan as World's Second Biggest Economy*, BBC News, Feb. 14, 2011.

6. Brett Arends, *IMF Bombshell: Age of America Nears End*, Wall St. J., April 25, 2011.

7. D. Daniel Sokol, *Competition Policy and Comparative Corporate Governance of State-Owned Enterprises*, 2009 B.Y.U. L. Rev. 1713; David E. M. Sappington & J. Gregory Sidak, *Competition Law for State-Owned Enterprises*, 71 Antitrust L.J. 479 (2003).

8. *See generally*, Ha-Joon Chang, The East Asian Development Experience: The Miracle, the Crisis and the Future (2006); Dani Rodrik, One Economics, Many Recipes: Globalization, Institutions, and Economic Growth (2007); Alice Amsden, The Rise of "the Rest": Challenges to the West from Late-Industrializing Countries (2001).

9. Amartya Sen, Development as Freedom 1–5 (1999).

Chapter 1

1. For further discussion of global convergence issues in competition law, see David J. Gerber, Global Competition: Law, Markets and Globalization 273–92 (2010).

2. Herbert Hovenkamp, The Antitrust Enterprise: Principle and Execution (2005).

3. The term "competition law" ("antitrust law" in the United States) refers to a system of legal norms and procedures whose stated objective is to deter restraints on competition. For discussion, see David J. Gerber, *Competition Law*, in Oxford Handbook of Legal Studies 510 (2003).

4. *See, e.g.*, Thomas K. Cheng, Convergence and Its Discontents: A Reconsideration of the Merits of Convergence of Global Competition Law, 12 Ch. J. Intl L.433 (2012).

5. *See, e.g.*, Philippe Aghion & Rachel Griffith, Competition and Growth: Reconciling Theory and Evidence (2005).

6. *See, e.g.*, Amartya Sen, Development as Freedom (1999).

7. *See* Gerber, *supra* note 1, at 281–92.

8. A convergence process in this sense does not require that participating decision makers specifically seek to emulate the convergence point model. The process consists of decisions to alter characteristics of the legal regime that reduce the differences between a given competition law system and the model, regardless of the reasons for those decisions.

9. David J. Gerber, *System Dynamics: Toward a Language of Comparative Law*, 46 Am. J. Comp. L. 719 (1998).

10. David J. Gerber, *Beyond Balancing: International Law Restraints on the Reach of National Laws*, 10 Yale J. Int'l L. 192 (1985). Until recently, the main concern was armed conflict among states.

11. Other forms of international jurisdiction refer to the right of a state to adjudicate claims ("judicial jurisdiction") and to enforce judgments resulting from such adjudication ("enforcement jurisdiction").

12. Gerber, *supra* note 1, at 273–81.

13. For further discussion, see Kevin C. Kennedy, Competition Law and the World Trade Organization: The Limits of Multilateralism (2001).

14. See Aditya Bhattacharjea, *The Case for a Multilateral Agreement on Competition Policy: A Developing Country Perspective*, 9 J. Int'l Econ. L. 293 (2006).

15. The United States did not officially "oppose" the plan, but its failure to support it was widely interpreted as opposition and the comments of U.S. officials confirmed this interpretation.

16. Paul Lugard, The International Competition Network at Ten (2011).

17. Gerber, *supra* note 1, at 111–16.

18. David J. Gerber, *Competition Law and the Institutional Embeddedness of Economics, in* Economic Theory and Competition Law 20–44 (Josef Drexl et al. eds., 2008).

19. The classic presentation of this model is Robert Bork, The Antitrust Paradox (1978).

20. Such intermingling may have rhetorical benefits for those advocating particular positions, but it is unacceptable from an analytical perspective, particularly where, as here, the distinction may have significant policy consequences.

21. For discussion, see, e.g., Thomas J. Biersteker, *The "Triumph" of Neoclassical Economics in the Developing World: Policy Convergence and Bases of Governance in the International Economic Order, in* Governance Without Government: Order and Change in World Politics (James N. Rosenau & Ernst Otto Czempiel eds, 1992).

22. *See supra* text accompanying notes 4–5.

23. Earlier views of development tended to emphasize particular "stages of maturation" that were presented as "natural" and even necessary. All economies could be expected to move through them. More recent discussions of economic development tend to emphasize the heterogeneity of the process. For discussion, see H. W. Arndt, Economic Development: The History of an Idea (1989); Colin Leys, The Rise and Fall of Development Theory (1996).

24. Several aspects of this relationship are discussed in A. E. Rodriguez & Ashok Menon, The Limits of Competition Policy: The Shortcomings of Antitrust in Developing and Reforming Economies 117–33 (2010).

25. *See, e.g.*, Howard J. Wiarda, Non-Western Theories of Economic Development (1999).

26. *See* Competition Law and Regionalization in Developing Countries (Josef Drexl et al. eds., 2012).

27. *See* Bhattacharjea, *supra* note 14.

28. *See, e.g.*, Florian Coulmans, Sociolinguistics (2005); Laurel Smith-Doerr & Walter W. Powell, *Networks and Economic Life, in* Handbook of Economic Sociology 279–402 (Neil J. Smelser & Richard Swedberg eds., 2005); Robert Wuthnow, Communities of Discourse (1989).

29. *See* Gerber, *supra* note 1, at 248–58.

30. *See* Massimo Motta, Competition Policy: Theory and Practice 8–22 (2004).

31. *See, e.g.*, Rodriguez & Menon, *supra* note 24.

32. For further details, see Gerber, *supra* note 1, at 134–51, 187–202.

33. *See, e.g.*, George K. Lipimile, *Competition Policy as a Stimulus for Enterprise Development, in* UNCTAD, Competition, Competitiveness and Development: Lessons from Developing Countries (UNCTAD/DITC/CLP/2004/1/, Geneva 2004), at 176, available at http://www.unctad.org/en/docs/ditcclp20041ch3_en.pdf.

34. Gerber, *supra* note 18.

35. Authorities in developed countries are also likely to achieve significant economies of scale and repetition in performing such analyses.

36. For discussion and examples, see Drexl et al., *supra* note 18.

Chapter 2

1. Albert O. Hirschman, *The Rise and Decline of Development Economics, in* Albert O. Hirschman, Essays in Tresspassing: Economics to Politics and Beyond 4 (1981).

2. Albert O. Hirschman, The Strategy of Economic Development (1958).

3. Alexander Gerschenkron, Economic Backwardness in Historical Perspective, A Book of Essays (1962).

4. Eleanor M. Fox, *Economic Development, Poverty and Antitrust: The Other Path*, 13 Sw. J.L. & Trade in Americas 211 (2007).

5. *See* Abel Mateus, *Competition and Development*, 33 World Competition 275 (2010).

6. Heinz Wolfgang Arndt, *Economic Development: A Semantic History*, 29 Econ. Dev. & Cultural Change 457, 458 (1981).

7. Gerald Meier, Biography of a Subject: An Evolution of Development Economics 38 (2005).

8. *See* Robert Solow, *A Contribution to the Theory of Economic Growth*, 70 Q. J. Econ. 64 (1956).

9. Joseph Schumpeter, The Theory of Economic Development (Transaction Publishers 2005) (1934). As Schumpeter observes, "[d]evelopment . . . is a distinct phenomenon, entirely foreign to what may be observed in the circular flow or in the tendency towards equilibrium." *Id*. at 64.

10. Kenneth J. Arrow, *An Extension of the Basic Theorems of Classical Welfare Economics, in* J. Neyman, Proceedings of the Second Berkeley Symposium on Mathematical Statistics and Probability 507 (1951); Kenneth J. Arrow & Gérard Debreu, *Existence of an Equilibrium for a Competitive Economy*, 22 Econometrica 265 (1954).

11. Ronald H. Coase, *The Nature of the Firm*, 4 Economica 386 (1937).

12. Deepal Lal, The Poverty of Development Economics (2000).

13. *Id*. at 9.

14. Roy F. Harod, *An Essay in Dynamic Theory*, 49 Econ. J. 14 (1939); Evsey D. Domar, *Capital Expansion, Rate of Growth and Employment*, 14 Econometrica 137 (1946).

15. *See* David Vines, *Comments, in* Frontiers of Development Economics 135, 136 (Gerald M. Meier & Joseph E. Stiglitz eds., 2001).

16. Meier, *supra* note 7, at 54.

17. *Id*. at 56.

18. Arthur Lewis, *Economic Development with Unlimited Supplies of Labor*, 22 Manchester Sch. 139 (1954).

19. Walt Whitman Rostow, The Stages of Economic Growth: A Non-Communist Manifesto (1960).

20. Paul N. Rosenstein-Rodan, *Problems of Industrialization of Eastern and Southeastern Europe*, 53 Econ. J. 202, 210–11 (1943).

21. Paul N. Rosenstein-Rodan, *The International Development of Economically Backward Areas*, International Affairs, Royal Inst. Int'l Aff., Apr. 1944, 157.

22. Ragnar Nurske, Problems of Capital Formation in Underdeveloped Countries (1953).

23. *Id*. at 6.

24. *Id*. at Chapter VII.

25. Gilbert Rist, The History of Development: From Western Origins to Global Faith 124 (3d ed. 2009).

26. James M. Cypher & James L. Dietz, The Process of Economic Development 168 (3d ed. 2009).

27. U.N. Dept. of Econ. Affairs, Econ. Comm'n for Latin America, The Economic Development of Latin America and Its Principal Problems (1950)(by Raúl Prebisch); Hal Singer, *Comments to the Terms of Trade and Economic Development*, 40 Rev. Econ. & Stat. 84 (1950).

28. *See* Rist, *supra* note 25, at 125.

29. Paul Baran & Paul Sweezy, The Monopoly Capital: An Essay on the American Economic and Social Order (1968).

30. *See* Jerzy Makarczyk, Principles of a New International Economic Order: A Study of International Law in the Making (1988); Robin C. A. White, *A New International Economic Order*, 24 Int'l & Comp. L.Q. 542 (1975).

31. See, e.g., the adoption by UNCTAD of The Set of Multilaterally Agreed Equitable Principles and Rules for the Control of Restrictive Business Practices, Conference on Restrictive Bus. Practices, U.N. Doc. TD/RBP/Conf/10/Rev.2 (Apr. 22, 1980). *See* Ioannis Lianos, *The Contribution of the United Nations to Global Antitrust*, 15 Tul. J. Int'l & Comp. L. 415 (2007).

32. Cypher & Dietz, *supra* note 26, at 16.

33. Paul Strassman, *Development Economics from a Chicago Perspective*, 19 J. Econ. Issues 63 (1976).

34. Anne Krueger, *The Political Economy of the Rent-Seeking Society*, 64 Am. Econ. Rev. 291 (1974).

35. Kaushik Basu, Prelude to Political Economy: A Study of the Social and Political 195–96 (2000).

36. *Id.* at 217. Further empirical research of the ISI policies showed the detrimental impact of the costs of rent seeking resulting from them: Anne Krueger, The Benefits and Costs of Import Substitution in India: A Microeconomic Study (1975).

37. *See* Peter. T. Bauer, Dissent on Development: Studies and Debates in Development Economics (2008).

38. Milton Friedman, Capitalism and Freedom 7–17 (1962).

39. Peter Preston, Development Theory: An Introduction 255 (1996).

40. John Williamson coined the term in 1990 in order to refer to "the lowest common denominator of policy advice being addressed by the Washington-based institutions to Latin American countries as of 1989." John Williamson, A Short History of the Washington Consensus (Sept. 24–25, 2004) (unpublished manuscript), available at http://www.iie.com/publications/papers/williamson0904-2.pdf.

41. These policy reforms could be summarized in the following propositions: (1) fiscal discipline; (2) redirection of public expenditure priorities toward fields offering both high economic returns and the potential to improve income distribution, such as primary health care, primary education, and infrastructure; (3) tax reform (to lower marginal rates and broaden the tax base); (4) interest rate liberalization; (5) competitive exchange rate; (6) trade liberalization, liberalization of inflows of foreign direct investment; (7) privatization; (8) deregulation (to abolish barriers to entry and exit); and (9) secure property rights.

42. Joseph Stiglitz, *More Instruments and Broader Goals: Moving Toward the Post–Washington Consensus*, Wider Annual Lecture (Jan. 7, 1998), available at http://www.wider.unu.edu/publications/annual-lectures/en_GB/AL2/.

43. *See* Ha-Joon Chang, Bad Samaritans: Rich Nations, Poor Policies and the Threat to the Developing World (2007). The dominant view is that "good institutions" are those of the developed countries, especially in the Anglo-American world. Ha-Joon Chang, *Kicking Away the Ladder: "Good Policies" and "Good Institutions,"* *in* K. Gallagher, Putting Development First: The Importance of Policy Space in the WTO and IFIs (2005). Good governance has attributes common to the Rostovian monoeconomics view for development.

44. Helen Shapiro, *Industrial Policy and Growth* 14 (DESA Working Paper No. 53, 2007).

45. Comm'n on Growth & Dev., The Growth Report Strategies for Sustained Growth and Inclusive Development 30–31 (2008).

46. Karla Hoff & Joseph Stiglitz, *Modern Economic Theory and Development*, *in* Frontiers of Development Economics 389 (Gerald M. Meier & Joseph E. Stiglitz eds., 2001).

47. *Id.*

48. *Id.*

49. Edmund Phelps, *Perspectives on the Performance of the Continent's Economies, Introductory Remarks*, Conference of CESifo and Center on Capitalism and Society (July 21, 2006), available at http://capitalism.columbia.edu/files/ccs/3Opening.pdf.

50. Mancur Olson, The Rise and Decline of Nations: Economic Growth, Stagflation and Social Rigidities (1982).

51. Mancur Olson, The Logic of Collective Action, Public Goods and the Theory of Groups (1965).

52. Per Krusell & José-Víctor Ríos-Rull, *Vested Interests in a Positive Theory of Stagnation and Growth*, 63 Rev. Econ. Stud. 301 (1996); Stephen L. Parente & Edward C. Prescott, *Monopoly Rights: A Barrier to Riches*, 89 Am. Econ. Rev. 1216 (1999).

53. Gene M. Grossman & Elhanan Helpman, *Protection for Sale*, 84 Am. Econ. Rev. 833 (1994).

54. Devashish Mitra, *Endogenous Lobbying Formation and Endogenous Protection: A Long-Run Model of Policy Determination*, 89 Am. Econ. Rev. 1116 (1999).

55. Kishore Gawande & Usree Bandyopadhyay, *Is Protection for Sale? Evidence on the Grossman-Helpman Theory of Endogenous Protection*, 82 Rev. Econ. & Stat. 139 (2000).

56. Alberto Andes & Rafael Di Tella, *Rents, Competition and Corruption*, 89 Am. Econ. Rev. 982 (1999).

57. Gary S. Becker & George J. Stigler, *Law Enforcement, Malfeasance and Compensation of Enforcers*, 3 J. Legal Stud. 1 (1974).

58. Daron Acemoglu et al., *Distance to Frontier, Selection and Economic Growth* (NBER Working Paper 9066, 2002); Stephen L. Parente & Edward C. Prescott, *Monopoly Rights: A Barrier to Riches*, 89 Am. Econ. Rev. 1216 (1999).

59. Hoff & Stiglitz, *supra* note 46, at 393.

60. Mark A. Dutz & Shyam Khemani, *The Instruments of Competition Policy and Their Relevance for Economic Development, in* Regulatory Policies and Reform: A Comparative Analysis (Claudio Frischtak ed., 1995); Ajit Singh, *Competition Policy, Development and Developing Countries* (Indian Council for Research on Int'l Econ. Relations, Working Paper No. 50, 2000); Ajit Singh, *Competition and Competition Policy in Emerging Markets: International and Developmental Dimensions* (G-24 Discussion Paper Series, Paper No. 18, 2002).

61. *See* Jean Tirole, *The Institutional Infrastructure of Competition Policy, in* Proceedings of the Annual Bank Conference on Development Economics in Europe 113–18 (2000); Carlos M. Correa, *Competition Law and Development Policies, in* Towards WTO Competition Rules 361 (1999); Frédéric Jenny, *Cartels and Collusion in Developing Countries: Lessons from Empirical Evidence*, 29 World Comp. L. Rev. 109 (2006); William E. Kovacic, *Institutional Foundation for Economic Legal Reform in Transitional Economics: The Case of Competition Policy and Antitrust Enforcement*, 77 Chi.-Kent L. Rev. 265 (2001); Simon Evenett, *What Is the Relationship Between Competition Law and Policy and Economic Development, in* Competition Policy and Development in Asia (Douglas H. Brooks & Simon J. Evenett eds., 2005); Paolo Buccirossi et al., *Competition Policy and Productivity Growth: An Empirical Assessment* (WZB Working Paper No. SP II, 2009); UNCTAD, *The Role of Competition Policy in Promoting Economic Development: The Appropriate Design and Effectiveness of Competition Law and Policy* (2010); UNCTAD, *The Relationship Between Competition, Competitiveness and Development* (2002).

62. Michael Spence, *Cost Reduction, Competition and Industry Performance*, 52 Econometrica 101 (1984); Mark Dutz & Aydin Hayri, *Does More Intense Competition Lead to Higher Growth?* (World Bank Working Paper No. 2320, 2000).

63. Philippe Aghion, Mathias Dewatripont & Patrick Rey, *Competition, Financial Discipline and Growth*, 66 Rev. Econ. Stud. 825 (1999).

64. Philippe Aghion et al., *Competition, Imitation and Growth with Step-by-Step Innovation*, 68 Rev. Econ. Stud. 467 (2001).

65. Edward P. Lazear & Sherwin Rosen, *Rank-Order Tournaments as Optimum Labor Contracts*, 89 J. Pol. Econ. 841 (1981); Barry J. Nalebuff & Joseph E. Stiglitz, *Prizes and Incentives: Towards a General Theory of Compensation and Competition*, 14 Bell J. Econ. 21 (1983).

66. Philippe Aghion & Peter Howitt, Endogenous Growth Theory (1998).

67. Jonathan Haskel, *Imperfect Competition, Work Practices and Productivity Growth*, 53 Oxford Bull. Econ & Stat. 265 (1991).

68. There are a lot of variants of this doctrine from the narrower (that we need big firms to generate innovation) to the broader (that industrial policies should take precedence to competition polices or that too much competition is bad for development).

69. Philippe Aghion & Peter Howitt, *A Model of Growth Through Creative Destruction*, 60 Econometrica 323 (1992).

70. Gene Grossman & Elhanan Helpman, *Innovation and Growth in the Global Economy* (1991).

71. Aghion et al., *supra* note 64.

72. Michael Porter, *The Competitive Advantage of Nations* (2000).

73. Philippe Aghion & Rachel Griffith, Competition and Growth: Reconciling Theory and Evidence (2005).

74. Kenneth Arrow, *Economic Welfare and the Allocation of Resources for Inventions, in* The Rate and Direction of Inventive Activity: Economic and Social Factors (R. Nelson ed., 1962).

75. Robert E. Lucas, *On the Mechanics of Economic Development*, 22 J. Monetary Econ. 3 (1988).

76. Philippe Aghion et al., *Entry and Productivity Growth: Evidence from Micro-Level Panel Data*, 2 J. Eur. Econ. Ass'n. 265 (2003).

77. These empirical models immediately narrow the problem by relating some measure of market concentration to the number of patents, citations, or any other related measure related with R&D. The empirical work has been carried out for the United Kingdom, a developed country.

78. Richard Disney et al., *Restructuring and Productivity Growth in UK Manufacturing*, 113 Econ. J. 666 (2003).

79. Nicholas Bloom & John van Reenen, *Measuring and Explaining Management Practices Across Firms and Across Countries*, 120 Q. J. Econ. 1351 (2007).

80. Stephen J. Nickell, *Competition and Corporate Performance*, 104 J. Pol. Econ. 724 (1996); Silke Januszewski et al., *Product Market Competition, Corporate Governance and Firm Performance: An Empirical Analysis for Germany*, 56 Research Econ. 299 (2002); Richard Blundell et al., *Market Share, Market Value and Innovation in a Panel of British Manufacturing Sector*, 66 Rev. Econ. Stud. 529 (1999); Aghion & Griffith, *supra* note 73.

81. Dutz & Hayri, *supra* note 62.

82. James Tybout, *Manufacturing Firms in Developing Countries: How Well Do They Do and Why?*, 38 J. Econ. Lit. 11 (2000).

83. John Haltiwanger et al., *Effects of Tariffs and Real Exchange Rates on Job Reallocation: Evidence from Latin America*, 7 Pol'y Reform 191 (2004).

84. Marcela Eslava et al., *The Effects of Structural Reforms on Productivity and Profitability Enhancing Reallocation: Evidence from Colombia*, 75 J. Dev. Econ. 333 (2004).

85. Nina Pacvnick, *Trade Liberalization, Exit and Productivity Improvements: Evidence from Chilean Firms*, 69 Rev. Econ. Stud. 245 (2002).

86. Philippe Aghion et al., *The Unequal Effects of Liberalization: Evidence from Dismantling the License Raj in India*, 94 Am. Econ. Rev. 1397 (2008).

87. Philippe Aghion et al., *Competition and Productivity Growth in South Africa*, 16 Econ. Transition 741 (2008).

88. Wendy Carlin et al., *A Minimum of Rivalry: Evidence from Transition Economies on the Importance of Competition for Innovation and Growth* (William Davidson Institute Working Paper No. 670, 2004).

89. *See* UNCTAD, Competition, Competitiveness and Development: Lessons from Developing Countries (2004).

90. *See* Eleanor M. Fox, *In Search of a Competition Law Fit for Developing Countries* (NYU Law & Econ. Research Paper Series, Working Paper No. 11-04, 2011); Economic Development: The Critical Role of Competition Law and Policy (Eleanor M. Fox & Abel M. Mateus eds., 2011); Tay-Cheng Ma, *The Effect of Competition Law Enforcement on Economic Growth*, 7 J. Competition L. & Econ. 301 (2011); Abel Mateus, *supra* note 5.

91. OECD, Promoting Pro-Poor Growth: Private Sector Development 43 (2006).

92. Michal S. Gal, *The Ecology of Antitrust: Preconditions for Competition Law Enforcement in Developing Countries*, *in* Competition, Competitiveness and Development: Lessons from Developing Countries 20 (P. Brusick et al. eds., 2004).

93. Michal S. Gal, *The "Cut and Paste" of Article 82 of the EC Treaty in Israel: Conditions for a Successful Transplant* (NYU Law and Econ. Research Paper No. 08-03, 2008).

94. Fox, *supra* note 90.

95. Singh, Competition Policy, Development and Developing Countries, *supra* note 60.

96. Singh, *supra* note 60.

97. Ma, *supra* note 90; Abel Mateus, *Competition and Development: What Competition Law Regime?*, Chapter 7 in this volume.

98. Fox & Mateus, *supra* note 90.

99. Abhijit Banerjee & Esther Duflo, *Poor Economics: A Radical Rethinking of the Way to Fight Global Poverty* (BBS Publications, 2011).

Chapter 3

I would like to thank Danny Sokol for his meticulous editing and helpful comments on an earlier draft of this chapter. The usual disclaimer applies.

1. Michael Trebilcock et al., The Law and Economics of Canadian Competition Policy 10 (2002).

2. *Id.* at 12–14

3. Thomas Ross, *Canadian Competition Policy: Progress and Prospects*, 37 Canadian J. Econ. 243, 252 (2004).

4. Trebilcock et al., *supra* note 1, at 16–17.

5. Richard A. Posner, Antitrust Law 34 (2d ed, 2001).

6. Michael Whinston, Lectures on Antitrust Economics 6 (2006). As an eminent antitrust economist facetiously suggested while commenting on my presentation at the New Delhi conference that gave rise to this volume, had the Sherman Act been passed today, legislators would have tried to show that it would further world peace and reduce global warming.

7. Keith N. Hylton, Antitrust Law: Economic Theory and Common Law Evolution 38 (2003) (citing other scholars who have expressed this view).

8. *Id.* at 39.

9. 166 U.S. 290 (1897).

10. Appalachian Coals, Inc. v. United States, 288 U.S. 344 (1933).

11. Jason E. Taylor, *The Output Effects of Government Sponsored Cartels During the New Deal*, 50 J. Indust. Econ. 1 (2002).

12. D. Daniel Sokol, *Limiting Anticompetitive Interventions That Benefit Special Interests*, 17 Geo. Mason L. Rev. 119, 128 (2009).

13. Posner, *supra* note 5, at 27–28.

14. Posner, *id.* at 126; Hylton *supra* note 7, at 320.

15. Posner, *supra* note 5, at 35.

16. Paolo Buccirossi, *Introduction*, *in* Handbook of Antitrust Economics xi (2008).

17. F. M. Scherer, Competition Policies for an Integrated World Economy 23–27 (1994); Ha-Joon Chang, Kicking Away the Ladder: Development Strategy in Historical Perspective 91–92 (2002).

18. Tim Frazer, Monopoly, Competition and the Law ch. 5 (1992).

19. Stephen Wilks, In the Public Interest: Competition Policy and the Monopolies and Mergers Commission (1999).

20. *Id.* at 25.

21. *Id.* at 335.

22. *Id.* at 340.

23. *Id.* at 346.

24. Ioannis Kokkoris, *Should Crisis Cartels Exist Amid Crises?* 55 Antitrust Bull. 727, 732 (2010).

25. Alison Jones, *The Journey Toward an Effects-Based Approach Under Article 101 TFEU—The Case of Hardcore Restraints*, 55 Antitrust Bull. 783, 812 (2010) (also indicating that more recently the Commission no longer entertains such arguments); Kokkoris, *supra* note 24, *passim*.

26. Kokkoris, *supra* note 24, at 757.

27. This account draws on Sadao Nagaoka, *International Trade Aspects of Competition Policy* (National Bureau of Economic Research Working Paper 6720, Sept. 1998); Lawrence S. Liu, *In Fairness We Trust?—Why Fostering Competition Law and Policy Ain't Easy in Asia* (SSRN Working Paper, Oct. 2004, accessible at SSRN: http://ssrn.com/abstract=610822 or http://dx.doi.org/10.2139/ssrn .610822), at 19–22; Michael E. Porter & Mariko Sakakibara, *Competition in Japan*, 18 J. Econ. Persp. 27 (2004). The last-cited paper argues that many Japanese industries do nonetheless display vigorous competition, as measured by concentration ratios, profit margins, and entry and that the most dynamic and internationally competitive sectors were those that did not receive official protection and guidance. This may well be a persuasive critique of interventionist industrial policy, but the relevant point for the present discussion is that competition flourished in many sectors despite the weak enforcement of competition law.

28. Eleanor Fox has forcefully made this argument with respect to the current state of U.S. antitrust law, as constrained by recent Supreme Court decisions in monopolization cases. *See* Eleanor M. Fox, *Competition, Development and Regional Integration: In Search of a Competition Law Fit for Developing Countries* (Law & Economics Research Paper Series Working Paper No. 11-04, NYU Center for Law, Economics and Organization, Oct. 2012), at 9–10.

29. Liu, *supra* note 27, at 9–19.

30. Aditya Bhattacharjea, *India's New Competition Law: A Comparative Assessment*, 4 J. Competition L. & Econ. 609 (2008); Aditya Bhattacharjea, *India's New Competition Regime: The First Two Years of Enforcement*, 57 Antitrust Bull. 449 (2012).

31. Pradeep Mehta, Manish Agarwal & V. V. Singh, *Politics Trumps Economics—Lessons and Experiences on Competition and Regulatory Regimes from Developing Countries* (2007), available at www.circ.in.

32. Tay-Cheng Ma, *The Effect of Competition Law Enforcement on Economic Growth*, 7 J. Competition L. & Econ. 301 (2011).

33. James R. Tybout, *Manufacturing Firms in Developing Countries: How Well Do They Do and Why?*, 38 J. Econ. Lit. 11, 26–28 (2000); Jack Glen, Kevin Lee & Ajit Singh, *Corporate Profitability and the Dynamics of Competition in Emerging Markets: A Time Series Analysis*, 113 Econ. J. 465 (2003). See also Porter & Sakakibara, *supra* note 27, on Japan.

34. Consider the sixty years (1890–1950) from the Sherman Act to the Celler-Kefauver Act in the United States and the thirty-three years (1957–1990) from the Treaty of Rome to the enforcement of the European Commission's Regulation 4064 in Europe. There were, of course, episodic attempts at merger regulation in the intervening periods, based on section 7 of the Clayton Act in the United States and the endorsement by the European Court of Justice of application of first Article 86 and then Article 85—as they were then numbered—of the treaty. See Frazer, *supra* note 18, at 85–89.

35. Nicholas Economides, *Public Policy in Network Industries*, *in* Buccirossi, *supra* note 16, at 511. Similar skepticism about regulatory intervention is expressed by Jean-Charles Rochet & Jean Tirole, *Competition Policy in Two-sided Markets, with a Special Emphasis on Credit Cards* in the same volume.

36. See *supra* note 15 and related text.

37. Although growing inequality and brazen examples of crony capitalism in many countries may yet provoke a populist backlash.

38. Eleanor M. Fox & Abel M. Mateus, Economic Development: The Critical Role of Competition Law and Policy, vol. II (2011), especially the chapters by Fox, Brusick & Evenett, and Jenny.

39. See my articles cited *supra* note 30. More recently, however, the Competition Commission of India has taken decisive action in several cases involving cartels and abuse of dominance.

40. A good introduction for the general reader is Amartya Sen, Development as Freedom (1999).

41. The two best known are the Human Development Index and its various offshoots, developed in successive issues of the Human Development Report of the United Nations Development Program, and the Millennium Development Goals of the United Nations.

42. See my discussion of this issue and references to other literature in Aditya Bhattacharjea, *The Case for a Multilateral Agreement on Competition Policy: A Developing-Country Perspective*, 9 J. Int'l Econ. L. 293 (2006), at 301–03. See also Thomas Cheng, *Striking a Balance Between Competition Law Enforcement and Patent Policy: A Developing Country's Perspective*, *in* The Effects of Anti-Competitive Business Practices on Developing Countries and Their Development Prospects 633–59 (Hassan Qaqaya & George Lipimile eds., 2008).

43. For a critical review of the WTO debate, see Bhattacharjea, *supra* note 42. That article also discussed the fallout of the *Empagran* judgment and other options for developing countries to confront foreign anticompetitive conduct if developed-country cooperation along these lines is not forthcoming. For some earlier (pre-*Empagran*) suggestions, see also Margaret Levenstein & Valerie Y. Suslow, *Contemporary International Cartels and Developing Countries: Economic Effects and Implications for Competition Policy*, 71 Antitrust L.J. 801 (2004).

44. See the articles reproduced in Fox & Mateus, *supra* note 38.

45. Levenstein & Suslow, *supra* note 43.

46. Fox, *supra* note 28, at 19–23.

Chapter 4

Portions of this chapter appeared in Thomas C. Arthur, *The Unsatisfactory Application of the Antitrust Statutes of the United States by the Federal Courts*, *in* Modernisation of European Competition Law: The Commission's Proposal for a New Regulation Implementing Articles 81 and 82 EC 61–77 (J. Stuyck & H. Gilliams eds., 2002).

1. *See* D. Daniel Sokol, *Anticompetitive Government Regulation*, *in* The Global Limits of Competition Law 93–94 (Ioannis Lianos & D. Daniel Sokol eds., 2012).

2. Although full political and civil rights were limited, at least in practice, to white males in most states, the United States was the most democratic country in the world by nineteenth-century standards. *See generally* Alexis de Tocqueville, Democracy in America (J. P. Mayer ed., 1969, original eds. 1835 (vol. 1), 1840 (vol.2)); James Bryce, The American Commonwealth (2d ed. 1889).

3. Tocqueville, *supra* note 2, at xiv (The new American republic "has preserved all rights. Private Property is better guaranteed there than in any other land on earth. Anarchy is as unknown as despotism."). *See also* Bryce, *supra* note 2, at 259–61, 265–66 (independence and integrity of federal judiciary).

4. J. Willard Hurst, Law and the Conditions of Freedom in the Nineteenth-Century United States 92–93 (1956); Thomas K. McCraw, Prophets of Regulation 17–20, 57–65 (1984); Loren Beth, The Development of the American Constitution, 1877–1917, at 3 (1971); Bryce, *supra* note 2, at 15.

5. Alfred Chandler Jr., Size and Scope: The Dynamics of Industrial Capitalism 47 (1990) ("From the 1890s on, the United States was the world's leading industrial nation").

6. *See generally* George Rogers Taylor, The Transportation Revolution, 1815–1860 (1951); Daniel Walker Howe, What Hath God Wrought: The Transformation of America, 1815–48, at 211–21 (2007).

7. Howe, *supra* note 6, at 222–35, 690–98.

8. Taylor, *supra* note 6, at 207–49; Glenn Porter, The Rise of Big Business, 1860–1890, at 27–31 (1973).

9. *Compare* Charles Sellers, The Market Revolution, Jacksonian America, 1815–1846 (1991) *and* John Larson, The Market Revolution in America: Liberty, Ambition and the Eclipse of the Common Good (market revolution after American Revolution) *with* Howe, *supra* note 6, at 5; Louis Hartz, The Liberal Tradition in America (1955) (Americans were liberal, entrepreneurial, and capitalistic from the beginning). *See also* Gordon Wood, *Inventing American Capitalism*, N.Y. Rev. Books, July 1, 2011 (summarizing recent research, especially that indicating emergence of market economy in New England in 1780s).

10. *Compare* Larson, *supra* note 9, at 98–140 (coercion) *with* Howe, *supra* note 6 (voluntary).

11. For the role of the post office in American economic development in the nineteenth century, see Howe, *supra* note 6, at 225–27; Larson, *supra* note 9, at 80–81. For the creation of the patent system, see Kenneth Dobyns, The Patent Pony: A History of the Patent Office 21–29, 35–36, 41–47, 95–103 (1994). The postal and patent systems were specifically authorized in the U.S. Constitution. U.S. Const, art. 1, § 8.

12. For a detailed study of these "internal improvements" in the nineteenth century, see generally John Larson, Internal Improvement: National Public Works and the Promise of Popular Government in the Early United States (2001). *See also* Taylor, *supra* note 6, at 24–26, 32–36, 42–52, 67–69, 86–96, 128–31 (state and federal involvement with roads, canals, steamships, railroad, and merchant marine).

13. McCraw, *supra* note 4, at 17–21 ("the first modern regulatory agency"). Prior efforts at railroad regulation had been by statute, such as statutes limiting rates. *Id.* at 34. Legislatures had previously regulated tolls for roads, inns, and bridges.

14. As Bryce put it at the time of the framing of the Sherman Act, "that which Europeans call the machinery of government is in America conspicuous chiefly by its absence." Bryce, *supra* note 2, at 15.

15. Larson, *supra* note 9, at 25–29, 59–60; Hurst, *supra* note 4, at 55–58, 79–80.

16. James McPherson, Battle Cry of Freedom: The Civil War Era 29–30 (1998) (support for public schools); Frederick Rudolph, The American College and University: A History 184–89 (states), 247–63 (land grant colleges and universities) (1962).

17. McPherson, *supra* note 16, at 450–51.

18. The protective tariff was especially unpopular in South Carolina, which even threatened to "nullify" the Tariff Acts of 1828 and 1832, provoking a constitutional crisis. *See* William W. Freehling, The Road to Disunion: Secessionists at Bay, 1776–1854, at 255–57 (1990).

19. John Milton Cooper Jr., Woodrow Wilson: A Biography 216–19 (2009).

20. Alfred Chandler Jr., The Visible Hand: The Managerial Revolution in American Business 498–99 (1977).

21. Cooper, *supra* note 19, at 174 (Eugene V. Debs's 6 percent of presidential vote in 1912 is "the best showing a Socialist or any left-wing party candidate would make at any time in American history") (footnote omitted).

22. Larson, *supra* note 12, at 149–93; McPherson, *supra* note 16, at 27, 192–95.

23. Hurst, *supra* note 4, at 44–50.

24. Beth, *supra* note 4, at 166–90.

25. 5 U.S.C. §§ 12–27.

26. 5 U.S.C. §§ 41–58.

27. *See generally* Richard Hofstadter, The Age of Reform 227–56 (1955); William Letwin, Law and Economic Policy in America: The Evolution of the Sherman Antitrust Act 54–70 (1966); Hans Thorelli, The Federal Antitrust Policy: Origination of an American Tradition 108–63 (1954).

28. Combinations came in two forms, popularly known as "loose" (cartels) and "tight" (monopolistic mergers). Hans Thorelli, *supra* note 27, at 72–85. These combinations were perceived as using predation to maintain the dominance obtained from combining. *See* Phillip Areeda, Louis Kaplow & Aaron Edlin, Antitrust Analysis: Problems, Text and Cases 34–35 (6th ed. 2004) (perceived predation).

29. Thomas Arthur, *Farewell to the Sea of Doubt: Jettisoning the Constitutional Sherman Act*, 74 Calif. L. Rev. 263, 283–84 (1986).

30. Thomas Arthur, *The Core of Antitrust and the Slow Death of Dr. Miles*, 62 SMU L. Rev. 437, 441–44 (2009).

31. *Id.* at 444–46; Arthur, *supra* note 29, at 285–91.

32. Hurst, *supra* note 4, at 92–93.

33. Arthur, *supra* note 29, at 279–84.

34. *Id.* at 293–302; Thomas Arthur, *A Workable Rule of Reason: A Less Ambitious Antitrust Role for the Federal Courts*, 68 Antitrust L.J. 337, 341–45 (2000).

35. Arthur, *supra* note 29, at 298–302.

36. Arthur, *supra* note 34, at 345–46; Thomas Arthur, *Workable Antitrust Law: The Statutory Approach to Antitrust*, 62 Tulane L. Rev. 1163, 1173–75 (1988).

37. Letwin, *supra* note 27, at 253–78.

38. *Id.* at 216–34.

39. E. Thomas Sullivan, Herbert Hovenkamp & Howard Shelanski, Antitrust Law, Policy and Procedure: Cases, Materials, Problems 802–03 (6th ed. 2009).

40. See Brown Shoe Co. v. United States, 370 U.S. 294, 310–23 (1962) (legislative history of amendments).

41. See text accompanying notes 70–79 *infra*.

42. For a detailed description of the Antitrust Division and its operations, see I ABA Section of Antitrust Law, Antitrust Developments 691–722 (6th ed. 2007) [hereinafter cited as "Antitrust Developments"]. Shorter descriptions can be found in L. Sullivan & W. Grimes, The Law of Antitrust: An Integrated Handbook 888–95, 898–902 (2000); H. Hovenkamp, Federal Antitrust Policy: The Law of Competition and Its Practice 642–45 (4th ed. 2011).

43. Antitrust Developments, *supra* note 42, at 718–19, 721–22.

44. Courts are not required to defer to an agency interpretation unless it is issued in either a formal agency adjudication or a rulemaking proceeding (if the agency's governing statute has authorized it to issue binding regulations). Where the agency only brings enforcement proceedings, its "guidance, " e.g., guidelines, policy statements, opinion letters, and the like are not binding on the courts. Instead, they "are 'entitled to respect' . . . but only to the extent that those interpretations have the 'power to persuade.'" Christensen v. Harris Cnty, 529 U.S. 576, 587 (2000), quoting Skidmore v. Swift & Co., 323 U.S. 134, 140 (1944).

45. For a detailed discussion of the FTC, see Antitrust Developments, *supra* note 42, at 643–90.

46. Federal Trade Commission Act § 5, 15 U.S.C. § 45.

47. Arthur, *supra* note 34, at 350, 384; FTC v. Sperry & Hutchinson Co., 405 U.S. 233, 239 (1972) (language quoted in text).

48. With the decisions of these regulatory agencies, the role of judicial review is to ensure that the policy decisions are not inconsistent with the agency's governing statute and are promulgated

via appropriate procedures. *See generally* Alfred Aman & William Mayton, Administrative Law 238–413 (2d ed. 2001).

49. Two prominent examples in which reviewing courts declined to defer to the Commission's view of the scope of FTC Act § 5 are E. I. du Pont De Nemours & Co. v. FTC, 729 F.2d 128 (2d Cir. 1984) and Boise Cascade Corp. v. FTC, 637 F.2d 573 (9th Cir. 1980). Both are discussed in Hovenkamp, *supra* note 42, at 646.

50. This has been especially true with regard to the agencies' joint guidelines on horizontal mergers. *See generally* Hillary Greene, *Guideline Institutionalization: The Role of Merger Guidelines in Antitrust Discourse*, 48 Wm. & Mary L. Rev. 771 (2006).

51. To name an important instance, the Supreme Court's decision to apply the per se price-fixing rule in Arizona v. Maricopa Med. Soc'y, 457 U.S. 332 (1982), despite the fact that the practice there was functionally indistinguishable from the one held not to be subject to the rule in Broadcast Music, Inc. v. CBS, 441 U.S. 1 (1978), see Arthur, *supra* note 29, at 357, may be explained by the fact that the Justice Department as amicus curiae supported that result. But there are many examples to the contrary, and the Supreme Court often declines to follow the agencies' views. For prominent examples, see Eastman Kodak Co. v. Image Technical Servs., 504 U.S. 451 (1992); Monsanto Co. v. Spray-Rite Serv. Corp., 465 U.S. 752, 761 (1984) (declining Justice Department request to reconsider per se rule against resale price maintenance).

52. For a prominent example, see California Dental Ass'n v. FTC, 526 U.S. 756 (1999) (reversing FTC's interpretation of § 1 of the Sherman Act).

53. Aman & Mayton, *supra* note 48, at 307–37, 444–536.

54. See Martin Shapiro, Law and Politics in the Supreme Court: New Approaches to Political Jurisprudence 327 (1964) (antitrust decisions "are not basically judicial decisions, in the sense of individual applications of existing statutes, but law-making decisions based immediately and ultimately on the Court's vision of what the economy ought to be."). For an extended discussion of Supreme Court policy making in antitrust, see *id.*, at 262–327.

55. The Sherman Act, by far the most important, has only two substantive sections. The first, roughly comparable to Article 101 of the EC Treaty, states merely that "[e]very contract, combination in the form of trust or otherwise, or conspiracy, in restraint of trade . . . is declared to be illegal," and then proceeds to establish penalties for its violation. Similarly, section 2 declares baldly that "[e]very person who shall monopolize, or attempt to monopolize, or combine or conspire . . . to monopolize any part" of interstate or foreign commerce "shall be deemed guilty of a felony," and then states the penalties for violation. The key terms "restraint of trade" and "monopolize" are not defined. The substantive provisions of the Clayton and Federal Trade Commission Acts are equally vague. *See* 15 U.S.C. §§ 13–14, 18 (Clayton Act §§ 2–3, 7, prohibiting specific practices, but only where their effect "may be substantially to lessen competition or tend to create a monopoly"), 45 (FTC Act § 5, prohibiting "unfair methods of competition").

56. See Arthur, *supra* note 29, at 272–291.

57. *Id.* at 292–309.

58. Appalachian Coals, Inc. v. United States, 288 U.S. 344, 359–60 (1933). The Supreme Court often cites this language. *See, e.g.*, United States v. United States Gypsum Co., 438 U.S. 661, 672 (1982).

59. In the words of one prominent scholar and federal judge who subscribes to the standardless delegation interpretation, the Sherman Act "told the courts to make up a law on the subject of restraint of trade." Frank Easterbrook, *Vertical Arrangements and the Rule of Reason*, 53 Antitrust L.J. 135, 136 (1984). *See also* Easterbrook, *Is There a Ratchet in Antitrust Law?*, 60 Tex. L. Rev. 705, 706 (1982) ("Sherman and Clayton Acts authorized the Supreme Court to invent and enforce a law of restraint of trade") (footnotes omitted); Easterbrook, *Workable Antitrust Policy*, 84 Mich. L. Rev. 1696, 1703 (1986) (Sherman Act is "a blank check" to federal courts).

60. William Baxter, *Separation of Powers, Prosecution Discretion and the "Common Law" Nature of Antitrust Law*, 60 Tex. L. Rev. 661, 672 (1982) (emphasis added).

61. Shapiro, *supra* note 54, at 327.

62. In the 123 years since its passage, Congress had not amended the substantive prohibitions of the Sherman Act, the basic competition law statute. It has amended the substantive provisions of the 1914 Clayton Act, a far less important statute, only twice, the last time in 1950. Even the 1950

amendments, which form the statutory basis for U.S. merger law, are so generally worded that the Court has been left as the real lawmaker. *See* 15 U.S.C. § 18 (prohibiting mergers whose effect "may be substantially to lessen competition, or to tend to create a monopoly").

63. See text accompanying notes 94–104 *infra*.

64. There are twelve appellate circuits, each hearing appeals from trial courts within a defined geographical area, and a thirteenth court with special appellate jurisdiction over certain intellectual property issues.

65. Antitrust Developments, *supra* note 42, at 276–81.

66. Thomas Arthur, *The Costly Quest for Perfect Competition: Kodak and Nonstructural Market Power*, 69 N.Y.U. L. Rev. 1, 23–26 (1994) (federal courts on market power).

67. On the inability of jurors to comprehend complex antitrust issues, see Arthur Austin, *The Jury System at Risk from Complexity, the New Media and Deviancy*, 73 Denver U. L. Rev. 51, 52–59 (1995).

68. The Supreme Court has held that this is a requirement of the judiciary article of the federal constitution.

69. The Supreme Court may choose the cases it will hear, but the other courts must hear every case properly brought to them.

70. Hovenkamp, *supra* note 42, at 645–47.

71. Clayton Act §§ 4 (damage suits), 16 (injunctions), 15 U.S.C. §§ 15, 26.

72. 5 U.S.C. §§ 15c–h (authorizing *parens patriae* injunction suits). On the role of state-initiated antitrust suits, see generally Antitrust Developments, *supra* note 42, at 723–32.

73. For example, the FTC investigated the original allegations against Microsoft and decided not to proceed, whereupon the Justice Department brought its first *Microsoft* case. Phillip Areeda & Herbert Hovenkamp, Antitrust Law: An Analysis of Antitrust Principles and Their Application II § 302c at 12–14 (2d ed. 2000).

74. 1995 Vertical Restraints Guidelines of the National Association of Attorneys General, reprinted at 4 Trade Reg. Rep. (CCH) ¶13,400.

75. 1993 Horizontal Merger Guidelines of the National Association of Attorneys General, reprinted at 4 Trade Reg. Rep. (CCH) ¶13,406.

76. Willaim H. Page & John E. Lopatka, The Microsoft Case: Antitrust, High Technology and Consumer Welfare 246 (2007).

77. For a good example of the Supreme Court disregarding the Justice Department's views to uphold a private plaintiff's claims, see Eastman Kodak Co. v. Image Technical Servs, Inc., 504 U.S. 451 (1992). For a detailed explanation and critique of *Kodak*, see Arthur, *supra* note 66.

78. Frank Easterbrook, *Monopolization, Past, Present, Future*, 61Antitrust L.J. 99, 109 (1992) ("our complex system of two federal agencies, fifty states, bevies of private prosecutors and courts beyond number, produces cost, confusion and a least common-denominator approach. No other nation does things this way.").

79. 5 U.S.C. § 18a.

80. *See, e.g.*, Thomas Sullivan, *The Antitrust Division as a Regulatory Agency: An Enforcement Policy in Transition*, 64 Wash. U. L.Q. 197 (1986).

81. U.S. Dept. of Justice & Federal Trade Commission, Horizontal Merger Guidelines (2010).

82. Hovenkamp, *supra* note 42, at 543. There are two reasons for this. First, a competitor cannot maintain an action unless it can show that the merger will cause it "antitrust injury," that is, an injury that antitrust is meant to prevent. This is very hard for a competitor to show, inasmuch as the most likely source of injury is that the new firm will be more efficient and thus a stronger competitor of the plaintiff. Yet the plaintiff's best theory of liability in most horizontal merger cases is that the transaction will lead to actual or tacit collusion among competitors, which would benefit the plaintiff, not harm it. *Id.* at 654–56. Second, while a consumer could easily pass the "antitrust injury" test while posing a collusion theory, it is also necessary for a private plaintiff to show that it has or will suffer actual injury, a more rigorous burden than U.S. merger law poses for the agencies, which only have to show that the merger *may* substantially lessen competition, not that it will. *Id.* at 657.

83. See Antitrust Developments, *supra* note 42, at 81–90, 100–04.

84. *Id.* at 734–35.

85. There is an even more important area where the law is so clear that violations simply do not occur. The original "trusts" that give American competition law its peculiar name were monopolistic mergers aimed at creating dominant firms. No such merger has even been attempted since the turn of the last century.

86. For the uncertainty that existed as of 1986 in the application of the most important antitrust provision, section 1 of the Sherman Act, see Arthur, *supra* note 29, at 354–57, 359–362, 364–69, 370–73. This analysis is updated in the areas of greatest activity in Arthur, *supra* note 34, at 357–67. For the uncertainty that has traditionally existed in the entire body of federal antitrust law, see Arthur, *supra* note 36, at 1191–1201.

87. For dissents from the current consensus, see Robert Pitofsky, How the Chicago School Overshot the Mark: The Effect of Conservative Economic Analysis on U.S. Antitrust (2008).

88. Richard Posner, The Federal Courts: Crisis and Reform 251 (2d ed. 1996).

89. The literature on the antitrust goals issue is vast. *See e.g.*, Arthur, *supra* note 29, at 318–19 & n.305; Arthur, *supra* note 36, at 1167–68, 1201–03, 1205–11; Arthur, *supra* note 34, at 368 & nn.203–06.

90. Each of the contending factions can find support for its position in the legislative histories of the antitrust statutes. See Areeda & Hovenkamp, *supra* note 73, at I § 103, 40–61.

91. In American competition law, these economic issues arise in the application of the rule of reason (the U.S. equivalent of Article 101(3) analysis) and in the assessment of monopolists' conduct (the American analogue to Article 102 analysis).

92. See generally Arthur, *supra* note 29, at 321 & n.313; Arthur, *supra* note 36, at 1203–05, 1209–12; Arthur, *supra* note 34, at 368–70.

93. See Arthur, *supra* note 34, at 369–70.

94. See Easterbrook, *supra* note 59, at 1703–04.

95. See *supra* text accompanying notes 68–69.

96. The Supreme Court conceded as much in the famous *Sylvania* case. Continental T.V., Inc. v. GTE Sylvania, 433 U.S. 36, 48–49 & n.14 (1977).

97. Two famous examples make the point. In *Jefferson Parish Hosp. Dist. No. 2 v. Hyde*, 466 U.S. 2 (1984), the Court by a 5-4 majority retained the per se rule against tying arrangements, despite the fact that the underlying rationale for the rule, that all tie-ins were naked restraints with no redeeming efficiency justifications, had long been discredited. *Id.* at 9–18. Just recently, four justices argued strenuously to retain the per se prohibition on resale price maintenance in the face of overwhelming economic opinion, cited to the Court in amicus briefs by both the Justice Department and the FTC, that resale price maintenance is often procompetitive. Leegin Leather Prods., Inc. v. PSKS, Inc., 127 S. Ct. 2705, 2725 (2007) (Breyer, J., dissenting). See Arthur, *supra* note 30, at 486–90 (discussing dissenting opinion).

98. See Arthur, *supra* note 29, at 309–14. The Court's struggle with resale price maintenance provides a case study of the judicial inability to provide clear antitrust policy. See generally Arthur, *supra* note 30.

99. See Arthur, *supra* note 34, at 371–72; Easterbrook, *supra* note 78, at 100, 109.

100. Easterbrook, *supra* note 78, at 99, 109. This is a matter of necessity, inasmuch as, with minor exceptions, American courts are not specialized, even as to criminal and civil cases. This is especially true of the federal (national) court system. Federal trial and appellate courts decide a wide array of civil and criminal cases.

101. Loren Beth, Politics, the Constitution and the Supreme Court: An Introduction to the Study of Constitutional Law 96–102 (1962); Walter F. Murphy & C. Herman Pritchett, Courts, Judges and Politics: An Introduction to the Judicial Process 122–30 (3d ed. 1979).

102. Beth, *supra* note 101, at 102 (an American judge "will almost always have been active in politics").

103. Murphy & Pritchett, *supra* note 101, at 123 (in making Supreme Court nominations, "the President's principal concern tends to be the general ideology of the nominee and the way the nominee can be expected to vote on the Court").

104. Easterbrook, *supra* note 78, at 109.

105. Robert Pitofsky, Harvey Goldschmid & Diane Wood, Trade Regulation: Cases and Materials 165 (6th ed. 2010).

106. See Arthur, *supra* note 66, at 23–26. Making things worse, the Court has held that the degree of market power necessary in a monopolization case is greater than in other cases. For example, the Court has suggested that the degree of market power in a tying case is not as great as in a monopolization case. For another, even more important example, the market shares necessary to defeat a merger are far lower than to establish monopoly power.

Chapter 5

1. *See, e.g.*, Dani Rodrik, *Goodbye Washington Consensus, Hello Washington Confusion? A Review of the World Bank's Economic Growth in the 1990s: Learning from a Decade of Reform*, 44 J. Econ. Lit. 973 (2006).

2. Eleanor M. Fox, *In Search of a Competition Law Fit for Developing Countries*, (NYU Law & Economics Research Paper Series, Working Paper No. 11-04, at 5–10, 2011).

3. OECD, Promoting Pro-Poor Growth, Private Sector Development 43 (2006).

4. Ajit Singh & Rahul Dhumale, *Competition Policy, Development and Developing Countries in Trade-Related Agenda*, Development and Equity (T.R.A.D.E.) (1999).

5. *See* Calixto Salomao Filho, Antitrust, Regulatory Perspectives and Development: A Neo-Structural Perspective (2009).

6. Fox, *supra* note 2.

7. *Id.* at 14, citing Taimoon Stewart, Regional Integration in the Caribbean: The Role of Competition Policy (2011).

8. For an excellent discussion of this point see William E. Kovacic, *Institutional Foundations for Economic Legal Reform in Transition Economies: The Case of Competition Policy and Antitrust Enforcement*, 77 Chi-Kent L. Rev. 265 (2001).

9. *Id.*

10. Parker v. Brown, 317 U.S. 341 (1943). For a more recent iteration, see City of Columbia v. Omni Outdoor Adver., Inc., 499 U.S. 365 (1991).

Chapter 6

I am grateful to Danny Sokol and Thomas Cheng for numerous helpful suggestions and careful editing of the previous versions of this chapter.

1. Some of the papers that cover the spectrum of issues on competition policy and law enforcement in developing and transition economies include, for example: Aditya Bhattacharjea, *Who Needs Antitrust in* Competition Law and Development ch. 3 (D. Daniel Sokol, Thomas Cheng, & Ioanis Lianos eds., 2013); Mark A. Dutz & Maria Vagliasindi, *Competition Policy Implementation in Transition Economies: An Empirical Assessment*, 44 Eur. Econ. Rev. 762 (2000); Louis Kaplow, *Transition Policy: A Conceptual Framework*, 13 J. Contemp. Legal Issues 161 (2003), William E. Kovacic, *Institutional Foundations for Economic Legal Reform in Transition Economies: The Case of Competition Policy and Antitrust Enforcement*, 77 Chi.-Kent L. Rev. 265 (2001). In a more general context, see Timothy J. Muris, *Principles for a Successful Competition Agency*, 72 U. Chi. L. Rev. 165 (2005).

2. D. Daniel Sokol, *Antitrust, Institutions and Merger Control*, 17 Geo. Mason L. Rev. 1055, 112829 (2010).

3. D. Daniel Sokol & Kyle W. Stiegert, *Exporting Knowledge Through Technical Assistance and Capacity Building*, 6 J. Competition L. & Econ. 233 (2009); D. Daniel Sokol, *The Future of International Antitrust and Improving Antitrust Agency Capacity*, 103 Nw. U. L. Rev. 1081 (2009).

4. Vivek Ghosal, *Regime Shift in Antitrust Laws, Economics and Enforcement*, 7 J. Competition L. & Econ. 733 (2011); Vivek Ghosal, *The Genesis of Cartel Investigations: Some Insights from Examining the Dynamic Interrelationships Between U.S. Civil and Criminal Antitrust Investigations*, 4 J. Competition L. & Econ. 61 (2008).

5. Elizabeth Bailey & Anne Friedlaender, *Market Structure and Multiproduct Industries*, 20 J. Econ. Lit. 1024 (1982); John C. Panzar & Robert D. Willig, *Economies of Scope*, 71 Am. Econ. Rev. 268 (1981).

6. Sam Peltzman, *Toward a More General Theory of Regulation*, 19 J.L. & Econ. 211 (1976).

7. Antoine Faure-Grimaud & David Martimort, *Regulatory Inertia*, 34 RAND J. Econ. 413 (2003).

8. Vivek Ghosal, *Economics, Politics and Merger Control, in* Recent Developments in Antitrust: Theory and Evidence (Jay Pil Choi ed., 2007); Vivek Ghosal & Joseph Gallo, *The Cyclical Behavior of the Department of Justice's Antitrust Enforcement Activity,* 19 Int'l J. Indus. Org. 27 (2001).

9. Vivek Ghosal & Siddhartha Mitra, *Adoption and Reform of Competition Laws and Their Enforcement: A Cross-Country Perspective, in* Evolution of Competition Laws and Their Enforcement: A Political Economy Perspective (Pradeep S. Mehta ed., 2011) (presenting descriptive details on these issues for some of the countries in the sample).

10. Along with the OFT, the United Kingdom also has a companion agency, the Competition Commission (CC). Unfortunately, I was not able to obtain detailed data for the CC's activities. Since details about the respective roles played by OFT and CC are well documented, I do not repeat them here. These agencies have recently been combined into a single new agency, the Competition and Markets Authority.

11. One possible explanation relates to a note in the U.K. document that "the OFT embarked on a program of radical change inside our organisation." It may well be that this "restructuring" contributed to the patterns in Table 6.1.

12. While Ireland's per capita income is high, it is bit of an anomaly. Ireland's growth, to a large extent, was based on a boom in real estate and financial services with easy credit and very low corporate taxes and other incentives, which resulted in numerous multinationals setting up operations and shell companies to benefit from tax incentives. Ireland did not turn into an economy like South Korea, which developed a broad and sophisticated base. In this sense, Ireland is not as good an example of a developed country, at par with the likes of the other countries in the sample like Finland, Australia, or the United Kingdom.

13. My correspondence with the Turkish Agency did not resolve the issue of obtaining the more standardized and basic statistics. They were unable to provide the more standardized core statistics.

14. Apart from the above considerations, Poland had a different structure with a large number of local offices to oversee the privatization and deregulation process. Since this was bundled into the Agency's functions, its staff numbers are large. Turkey's ratio is also high, but admittedly not related to the Eastern European bloc issues noted above.

Chapter 7

1. Abel Mateus, *Competition and Development,* 33 World Competition 275 (2010).

2. Edward L. Glaeser & Andrei Shleifer, *The Rise of the Regulatory State,* 41 J. Econ. Literature 401 (2003).

3. Michael Spence, *Cost Reduction, Competition and Industry Performance,* 52 Econometrica 101 (1984).

4. Richard Disney et al., *Restructuring and Productivity Growth in UK Manufacturing,* 113 Econ. J. 666 (2003).

5. Nick Bloom & John van Reenen, *Measuring and Explaining Management Practices Across Firms and Across Countries,* 122 Q. J. Econ. 1321 (2007).

6. Stehphen Nickel et al., *What Makes Firms Perform Well?,* 41 Eur. Econ. Rev. 783 (1997).

7. Richard Blundell, *Market Share, Market Value and Innovation in a Panel of British Manufacturing Sector,* 66 Rev. Econ. Stud. 529 (1999).

8. Philippe Aghion, et al., *Entry Liberalization and Inequality in Industrial Performance,* 3 J. Euro. Econ. Ass'n 291 (2005).

9. OECD, Sources of Economic Growth (2003).

10. Mark A. Dutz & Aydin Hayri, *Does More Intense Competition Lead to Higher Growth?* 1 (World Bank Policy Research, Working Paper No. 2320, 1999).

11. James Tybout, *Manufacturing Firms in Developing Countries: How Well They Do and Why?,* 38 J. Econ. Literature 11 (2000).

12. John Haltiwanger, *Effects of Tariffs and Real Exchange Rates on Job Reallocation: Evidence from Latin America,* 7 J. Pol'y Reform 191 (2004).

13. Marcela Eslava, *The Effects of Structural Reforms on Productivity and Profitability Enhancing Reallocation: Evidence from Colombia,* 75 J. Dev. Econ. 333 (2004).

14. Pedro Ferreira & Jose Luis Rossi, *New Evidence from Brazil on Trade Liberalization and Productivity Growth,* 44 Int'l Econ. Rev. 1383 (2003).

15. Nina Pacvnik, *Trade Liberalization, Exit and Productivity Improvements: Evidence from Chilean Plants*, 69 Rev. Econ. Stud. 245 (2002).

16. Philippe Aghion, et al., *Entry Liberalization and Inequality in Industrial Performance*, 3 J. Euro. Econ. Ass'n 291 (2005).

17. Philippe Aghion, et al., *Competition and Productivity Growth in South Africa*, mimeo, 2007.

18. Philippe Aghion & Mark Schankerman, *On the Welfare Effects and Political Economy of Competition-Enhancing Policies*, 114 Econ. J. 800 (2004).

19. *See* Mateus, *supra* note 1.

20. By extortion we mean, like Glaeser and Shleifer, the costs of legal fees to lawyers and waiting time for decisions (normal in developed countries), along with (in less developed countries) costs of bribes and other types of side payments. In a more general sense it may mean also the payments required under the "protection for sale" theories.

21. We intend to assemble these indicators in future research.

22. In fact, if an Authority approves all the mergers proposed, it may be because undertakings have already fully internalized competition law and do not present to the Authority problematic mergers; or because the criteria used by the Authority are too permissive. The first hypothesis is not consistent with an environment where competition law is violated, which happens even in the institutionally most advanced countries. Another possibility is that undertakings carry out unlawful mergers and do not submit them to the Authority, which in our measure will weight in terms of no prohibitions.

23. Number of cases is a surrogate for the number of violations, but data on the latter is very hard to collect. There have been some surveys of lawyers trying to measure it, but we do not have data covering enough countries to introduce it in our database.

24. Daniel Kaufmann, *Corruption, Governance and Security: Challenges for the Rich Countries and the World*, Global Competitiveness Report 2004/2005 (Sept. 2004), available at www.worldbank .org/wbi/governance/pubs/gcr2004.html.

25. There might be some economies of scale for countries above, e.g., 30 to 40 million persons. These might translate to four to five professionals per 1 million population and even fewer, about three to four professionals, above 100 million. Another factor to take into consideration is the fact that some sector regulatory agencies may also enforce competition law in their own sector, which decreases the number of personnel required at the NCA.

26. Belgium has the lowest score, perhaps because it considers itself a very open economy that does not need closer scrutiny in competition matters.

27. We have no data regarding the qualifications of the personnel of NCAs.

28. This position should be contrasted with one of the most important regulators around the world, central banks.

29. Data for 2005 based on World Bank Atlas.

30. As we see, well above the 3,000 USD considered by the World Bank.

31. Except Hong Kong in our sample, which does not have a competition law regime.

32. Above 9,200 USD.

33. It is worrisome that in institutionally weak countries courts strike down a large percentage of NCA decisions or reduce sanctions substantially. In most of the developing countries, decisions are annulled based on procedural issues. It would be better for courts to assume a more justice-oriented outcome by trying to remedy some of those perceived errors during the course of the trial.

34. If the dominant economic ideology of the government is socialist or corporatist, it is not even possible to discuss the introduction of a competition policy.

35. L. Kekic, "The Economist Intelligence Unit's Index of Democracy," available at http://www .economist.com/media/pdf/DEMOCRACY_INDEX_2007_v3.pdf.

36. In a number of countries with a lower level of institutional development, very few persons are in jail for corruption, except for individuals who commit crimes of petty corruption or opponents of the political regime.

37. However, we do not agree with Glaeser and Shleifer that laissez faire reduces extortion.

38. It is easy to show, using game theory, that leniency programs will not work within the other regimes, since the benefit that firms obtain largely surpasses the probability of detection times the probable fines.

39. All prices refer to 2005.

Chapter 8

The support of the Economic and Social Research Council (United Kingdom) is gratefully acknowledged.

1. Frederic Jenny, *Cartels and Collusion in Developing Countries: Lessons from Empirical Evidence*, 29 World Competition L. Rev. 109 (2006).

2. Margaret Levenstein & Valerie Y. Suslow, *Contemporary International Cartels and Developing Countries: Economic Effects and Implications for Competition Policy*, 71 Antitrust L.J. 801, 813–16 (2004).

3. Michal Gal, *Free Movement of Judgments: Increasing Deterrence of International Cartels Through Jurisdictional Reliance*, 51 Va. J. Int'l L. 57 (2010).

4. *See* Simon J. Evennett, Can Developing Economies Benefit from WTO Negotiations on Binding Disciplines for Hard Core Cartels? (UNCTAD discussion document, 2003).

5. John M. Connor & Robert H. Lande, *The Size of Cartel Overcharges: Implications for U.S. and EU Fining Policies*, 51 Antitrust Bull. 983, 987 n.16 (2006); Emmanuel Combe & Constance Monnier, *Fines Against Hard Core Cartels in Europe: The Myth of Over Enforcement* (Cahiers de Recherche PRISM–Sorbonne Working Paper, June 2009). *See also* opposing findings in: Marie-Laure Allain, Marcel Boyer, Rachidi Kotchoni & Jean-Pierre Ponssard, *The Determination of Optimal Fines in Cartel Cases: The Myth of Underdeterrence* (CIRANO Working Paper, 2011).

6. F. Hoffman-LaRoche Ltd. v. Empagran, S.A., 542 U.S. 155 (2004).

7. Robert H. Lande, *Are Antitrust "Treble" Damages Really Single Damages?*, 54 Ohio St. L.J. 115, 161–68 (1993).

8. Michal Gal, *Antitrust in a Globalized Economy: The Unique Enforcement Challenges Faced by Small and Developing Jurisdictions*, 33 Fordham Int'l L.J. 1 (2009).

9. *See, e.g.*, Hugh M. Hollman & William E. Kovacic, *The International Competition Network: Its Past, Current and Future Role*, 20 Minn. J. Int'l L. 274 (2011); D. Daniel Sokol, *Monopolists Without Borders: The Institutional Challenge of International Antitrust in a Global Gilded Age*, 4 Berkeley Bus. L.J. 37 (2007).

10. *See* Gal, *supra* note 8, at 55.

11. The European Competition Network has formulated a "'Model Leniency Programme" aimed at alleviating the burden associated with multiple filings, but this simply promotes harmonization rather than setting up a coordinated system of leniency. *See* Céline Gauer & Maria Jaspers, *ECN Model Leniency Programme—A First Step Towards Harmonised Leniency Policy in the EU*, Competition Pol'y Newsl., no. 1, Spring 2007.

12. Richard M. Locke & Monica Romis, *The Promise & Perils of Private Voluntary Regulation: Labor Standards and Work Organizations in Two Mexican Factories*, 17 Rev. Int'l Pol. Econ. 45 (2010).

13. Marjo Siltaoja & Meri Vehkaperä, *Constructing Illegitimacy? Cartels and Cartel Agreements in Finnish Business Media from Critical Discursive Perspective*, 93 J. Bus. Ethics 493 (2010).

14. Rafael La Porta et al., *Corporate Ownership Around the World*, 54 J. Fin. 471 (1999).

15. D. Daniel Sokol, *Cartels, Corporate Compliance and What Practitioners Really Think About Enforcement*, 78 Antitrust L.J. 201 (2012).

16. OFT, Competition Law Compliance Survey, June 2011; Christine Parker & Vibeke Lehmann Nielsen, *How Much Does It Hurt? How Australian Businesses Think About the Cost and Gains of Compliance and Noncompliance with the Trade Practices Act*, 32 Melbourne L. Rev. 554 (2008).

17. Andreas Stephan, *Survey of Public Attitudes to Price-Fixing and Cartel Enforcement in Britain*, 5 Competition L. Rev. 123 (2008); Caron Beaton-Wells et al., *The Cartel Project: Report on a Survey of the Australian Public Regarding Anti-Cartel Law and Enforcement* (University of Melbourne Legal Studies Research Paper No. 519, 2011).

18. Marc C. Suchman, *Managing Legitimacy: Strategic and Institutional Approaches*, 20 Acad. Manag. Rev. 571 (1995); Charles J. Fombrun, Reputation: Realizing Value from the Corporate Image (1996); Andreas Stephan, *Cartel Criminalisation: The Role of the Media in the Battle for Hearts and Minds*, *in* Criminalising Cartels: Unexplored Dimensions and Unforeseeable Consequences (Caron Beaton-Wells & Ariel Ezrachi eds., 2011).

19. OFT, *Evaluation of the Impact of the OFT's Investigation into Bid Rigging in the Construction Industry: A Report by Europe Economics* (OFT 1240, June 2010).

20. Johan J. Graafland, *Collusion, Reputation Damage and Interest in Codes of Conduct: The Case of a Dutch Construction Company*, 13 Bus. Ethics: A Euro. Rev. 127 (2004).

21. Tarun Khanna & Yishay Yafeh, *Business Groups in Emerging Markets: Paragons or Parasites?*, 45 J. Econ. Lit. 331 (2007).

22. D. Daniel Sokol, *The Development of Human Capital in Latin American Competition Policy*, in Competition Law and Policy in Latin America (Eleanor Fox & D. Daniel Sokol eds., 2009).

23. Joseph E. Harrington, *Optimal Corporate Leniency Programs*, 41 J. Indust. Econ. 215 (2008).

24. Andreas Stephan, *Cartel Laws Undermined: Corruption, Social Norms and Collectivist Business Cultures*, 37 J.L. & Soc'y 345, 359 (2010).

25. *See, e.g.*, Taimoon Stewart, *An Empirical Examination of Competition Issues in Elected CARICOM Countries: Towards Policy Formulation* (2004), available at http://web.idrc.ca/uploads/user-S /11682895281CARICOM-Final_Report.pdf; See also examples discussed in Michal S. Gal, *The Ecology of Antitrust: Preconditions for Antitrust Enforcement in Developing Countries*, in Competition, Competitiveness and Development: Lessons from Developing Countries (Philippe Brusick et al. eds., 2004).

26. D. Daniel Sokol, *Limiting Anticompetitive Government Interventions That Benefit Special Interests*, 17 Geo. Mason L. Rev. 119 (2009).

27. Stephan, *supra* note 24, at 349.

28. Bianca Clausen et al., *Corruption and Confidence in Public Institutions: Evidence from a Global Survey*, 25 World Bank Econ. Rev. 212 (2011).

29. Gal, *supra* note 25.

30. Stephan, *Cartel Laws Undermined*, *supra* note 24.

31. Christopher R. Leslie, *Cartels, Agency Costs and Finding Virtue in Faithless Agents*, 49 Wm. & Mary L. Rev. 1621 (2008).

32. Alexander Dyck et al., *Who Blows the Whistle on Corporate Fraud?*, 65 J. Fin. 2213 (2010).

33. Robert M. Bowen et al., *Whistle-Blowing: Target Firm Characteristics and Economic Consequences*, 85 Accounting Rev. 1239 (2010) (correlating whistle-blowing to situations where (1) firms tend to be large companies with significant goodwill but have poor governance, (2) firms tend to have blurry lines of communication within the firm, in part because of personnel changes, and (3) firms tend to be concentrated in industries in which there are significant government purchases).

34. Janet P. Near et al., *Explaining the Whistle-Blowing Process: Suggestions from Power Theory and Justice Theory*, 4 Org. Sci. 393 (1993).

35. Dianne Vaughan, *Rational Choice, Situated Action and the Social Control of Organizations*, 32 L. & Soc'y Rev. 23, 29–30 (1998); Lauren B. Edelman & Mark C. Suchman, *The Legal Environments of Organizations*, 23 Ann. Rev. Soc. 479, 505 (1997).

36. Charles O'Reilly III & Jennifer Chatman, *Organizational Commitment and Psychological Attachment: The Effects of Compliance, Identification and Internalization on Prosocial Behavior*, 71 J. Applied Psychol. 492 (1986); Donald Lange, *A Multidimensional Conceptualization of Organizational Corruption Control*, 33 Acad. Mgmt. Rev. 710, 720–21 (2008).

37. Cécile Aubert et al., *The Impact of Leniency and Whistleblowing Programs on Cartels*, 24 Int'l J. Indust. Org. 1241 (2006); William E. Kovacic, *Private Monitoring and Antitrust Enforcement: Paying Informants to Reveal Cartels*, 69 Geo. Wash. L. Rev. 766, 768–72 (2001).

38. Byungbae Kim (Director General, Korea Fair Trade Commission), *Measures to Improve Cartel Detection (Other than Leniency)*. Speech given to ICN Cartel Workshop (November 8, 2005). The United Kingdom offers a £100,000 bounty, which seems too low an incentive to produce additional information of cartel violations. To date no individual has been given the bounty in the United Kingdom.

39. *See* Marc Ivalidi et al., *The Economics of Tacit Collusion*, Final Report for DG Competition, European Commission (2003).

40. *See* Felix Mezzanotte, *Using Abuse of Collective Dominance in Article 102 TFEU to Fight Tacit Collusion: The Problem of Proof and Inferential Error*, 33 World Competition L. & Econ. Rev. 77–102 (2010). The principles underpinning collective dominance were set out in the mergers case: Airtours plc v. Commission (case T-342/99) [2002] 5 C.M.L.R. 7.

41. Elina Cruz & Sebastian Zarate, *Building Trust in Antitrust: The Chilean Case*, in Competition Law and Policy in Latin America (Eleanor M. Fox & D. Daniel Sokol eds., 2009).

42. Andreea Cosnita-Langlais & Jean-Philippe Tropeano, *Fight Cartels or Control Mergers? On the Optimal Allocation of Enforcement Efforts Within Competition Policy* (Université de Paris Ouest Nanterre La Défense Working Paper, May 20, 2011).

43. *See e.g.*, Bjarke Fog, *How Are Cartel Prices Determined?*, 5 J. Indus. Econ. 16, 19–21 (1956).

44. Robert D. Anderson et al., *Ensuring Integrity and Competition in Public Procurement Markets: A Dual Challenge for Good Governance, in* The WTO Regime on Government Procurement: Challenge and Reform (Sue Arrowsmith & Robert D. Anderson eds., 2011).

45. OECD, Public Procurement: The Role of Competition Authorities in Promoting Competition (2007).

46. Luke M. Froeb et al., *What Is the Effect of Bid-Rigging on Prices?*, 42 Econ. Letters 419 (1993).

47. FNE, Tackling Bid Rigging in Public Procurement, OECD Latin American Competition Forum (2009).

48. OECD, Global Forum on Competition, Collusion and Corruption in Public Procurement, Contribution from Brazil (2010).

Chapter 9

1. *See, e.g.*, William E. Kovacic, *Getting Started: Creating New Competition Policy Institutions in Transition Economies*, 23 Brook. J. Int'l L. 403 (1997); Clive S. Gray & Anthony A. Davis, *Competition Policy in Developing Counties Undergoing Structural Adjustment*, 38 Antitrust Bull. 425 (1993). International agencies have similarly encouraged the development of competition laws in transition economies; *see, e.g.*, UNCTAD, Report by the UNCTAD Secretariat, Empirical Evidence on the Benefits from Applying Competition Law and Policy Principles to Economic Development in Order to Attain Greater Efficiency in International Trade and Development (1998).

2. Douglass C. North, Institutions, Institutional Change and Economic Performance 54 (1990).

3. *See, e.g.*, Thomas Carothers, *The Rule of Law Revival*, 77 Foreign Aff. 95, 95 (1998).

4. Michael Trebilcock & Jing Leng, *The Role of Formal Contract Law and Enforcement in Economic Development*, 92 Virginia L. Rev. 1517 (2006). See also Michael Trebilcock & Mariana Mota Prado, What Makes Poor Countries Poor? (2011).

5. Trebilcock & Leng, *supra* note 4, at 1523–24.

6. Kevin E. Davis & Michael Trebilcock, *The Relationship Between Law and Development: Optimists Versus Skeptics*, 61 Amer. J. Comp. L. 895 (2008).

7. *Id.* at 933–34.

8. Elinor Ostrom, Governing the Commons: The Evolution of Institutions for Collective Action (1990).

9. Avinash Dixit, Lawlessness and Economics: Alternative Modes of Governance (2004).

10. Avner Greif, Institutions and the Path to the Modern Economy: Lessons from the Medieval Trade (2006); Avner Greif et al., *Coordination, Commitment and Enforcement: The Case of the Merchant Guild*, 102 J. Pol. Econ. 744 (1994).

11. Marcel Fafchamps, *Market Institutions in Sub-Saharan Africa: Theory and Evidence* (2004)

12. Janet T. Landa, *A Theory of the Ethnically Homogeneous Middleman Group: An Institutional Alternative to Contract Law*, 10 J. Legal Stud. 349 (1981).

13. Marc Galanter, *Why the "Haves" Come Out Ahead: Speculations on the Limits of Legal Change*, 9 Law & Soc'y Rev. 95 (1974).

14. Robert Ellickson, Order Without Law (1990); Barak Richman, *How Communities Create Economic Advantage: Jewish Diamond Merchants in New York*, 31 Law & Soc. Inquiry 383 (2006).

15. Lisa Bernstein, *Opting Out of the Legal System: Extralegal Contractual Relations in the Diamond Industry*, 21 J. Legal Stud. 115 (1992); Lisa Bernstein, *Private Commercial Law in the Cotton Industry: Creating Cooperation Through Rules, Norms and Institutions*, 99 Mich. L. Rev. 1724 (2001); Barak D. Richman, *Firms, Courts and Reputation Mechanisms: Towards a Positive Theory of Private Ordering*, 104 Colum. L. Rev. 2328 (2004).

16. Bernstein, *supra* note 15.

17. Richman, *supra* note 14; Barak D. Richman, *The Antitrust of Reputation Mechanisms: Institutional Economics and Concerted Refusals to Deal*, 95 Va. L. Rev. 325 (2009).

18. Interview, March 13, 2008, Diamond District, Mumbai, India.

19. Paul Milgrom, Douglas North, and Barry Weingast, *The Role of Institutions in the Revival of Trade: The Law Merchant, Private Judges, and the Champaign Fairs*, 2 Econ. & Politics 1 (1990).

20. Richman, *Antitrust*, *supra* note 17.

21. *See, e.g.*, Fashion Originators' Guild of America v. FTC, 312 U.S. 457 (1941) (applying the per se rule to horizontal refusals to deal even if the restraints enjoy procompetitive justifications or are designed to vindicate legal rights).

22. *See, e.g.*, Associated Press v. United States, 326 U.S. 1 (1945).

23. *See, e.g.*, United States v. Container Corp., 393 U.S. 333 (1969).

24. *See, e.g.*, Broad. Music, Inc. v. CBS, Inc., 441 U.S. 1 (1979); Cal. Dental Ass'n v. FTC, 526 U.S. 756, 786 (1999).

25. In addition to having a rich history in India—from the world's first discovery of diamonds in 800 BCE until diamond finds in Brazil in 1844, the Indian subcontinent was the world's only source of diamonds—the diamond industry is now part of India's economic resurgence. Over 700,000 Indians work as diamond cutters, and diamond exports are among India's leading foreign exchange earners.

Chapter 10

I thank Kojiro Fujii, Jorge Grunberg, Aris Gulapa, and Maria Jose Henriquez, NYU LL.M.'s, for their excellent research assistance. A research grant from the Filomen D'Agostino and Max E. Greenberg Research Fund at New York University School of Law provided financial assistance for this chapter.

1. As of 2011, the membership of the International Competition Network consisted of competition authorities from 106 jurisdictions. This does not include China, which is not an ICN member.

2. *See, e.g.*, Richard A. Posner, Antitrust Law 267 (2d ed. 2001) (criterion for punishment is efficiency, "an especially appropriate one to use in designing remedies for antitrust violations").

3. *See* Scott D. Hammond, Asst. Att'y Gen., U.S. Dep't of Justice, *Charting New Waters in International Cartel Prosecutions* 13 (Mar. 2, 2006).

4. This consensus on criminalization is limited to price-fixing, bid rigging, and territorial allocations among competitors. *See, e.g.*, Gregory J. Werden & Marilyn J. Simon, *Why Price Fixers Should Go to Prison*, 32 Antitrust Bull. 917 (1987).

5. The earliest criminal case involving a manufactured product appears to be Moore v. United States, prosecuted in 1894. *See* Albert H. Walker, History of the Sherman Law of the United States of America 108 (1910). One earlier criminal case, United States v. Cassidy, was a Section 1 criminal prosecution for taking part in the Debs railroad strike; the defendant was discharged after the jurors split. *See id.* at 103.

6. The first case of imprisonment appears to be United States v. American Naval Stores, 172 F. 455 (S.D. Ga. 1909) (two of five convicted individual defendants sentenced to jail for three months; each of the five defendants fined $17,500). Their convictions are subsequently vacated in United States v. Nash, 229 U.S. 273 (1913) (error in the charge). *See* Walker, *supra* note 5, at 272. On the early unwillingness to impose imprisonment, see In Re Charge to the Grand Jury, 151 F. 834, 846 (E.D. Ga. 1907) (no jail sentence on guilty plea; judge accepted their assurance "that they would not again violate the laws against combinations in restraint of trade").

7. Criminal prosecutions, whether of individuals or corporations, were generally low in the first half century of the Sherman Act. *See* Richard A. Posner, *A Statistical Study of Antitrust Enforcement*, 13 J. Law & Econ. 365, 385 (1970) (Table 15) (173 criminal prosecutions, less than 3.5 criminal cases per year).

8. The prosecution is discussed in, e.g., J. Herling, The Great Price Conspiracy: The Story of the Antitrust Violations in the Electrical Industry (1962). For sentences, see Posner, *supra* note 7, at 389.

9. See Antitrust Division Workload Statistics, 58 Antitrust & Trade Reg. Rep. (BNA) 112 (1990) (compiled by Antitrust Division).

10. *See* Charles R. Rule, *Criminal Enforcement of the Antitrust Laws: Targeting Naked Cartel Restraints*, 57 Antitrust L.J. 257, 260 (1988) (contemporaneous listing of cases).

11. *See* U.S. Sentencing Comm'n, Sentencing Guidelines and Policy Statements (April 13, 1987) (noting "inappropriately high percentage" of probationary sentences for economic crimes, including antitrust, rendering such sentences "ineffective").

12. *See* Scott D. Hammond, Deputy Ass't Att'y Gen. for Criminal Enforcement, U.S. Dep't of Justice, Antitrust Div., *The Evolution of Criminal Antitrust Enforcement Over the Last Two Decades* at 9

(average sentence length of 31, 25, and 24 months for 2007, 2008, and 2009). Since 2005 judges have not been required to follow the Sentencing Guidelines, *see* United States v. Booker, 543 U.S. 220 (2005), although they generally still do so.

13. *See* Daniel A. Crane, *Optimizing Private Antitrust Enforcement*, 63 Vand. L.J. 675, 677 (2010) (arguing that private litigation has "rarely advanced the two assumed goals of private enforcement: deterrence and compensation").

14. *See* Atlanta v. Chattanooga Foundry & Pipeworks, 203 U.S. 390, 399 (1906) (construing state statute of limitations so as to be sure to give redress "to the sufferer").

15. *See* Homer Clark, *The Treble Damage Bonanza: New Doctrines of Damages in Private Antitrust Suits*, 52 Mich. L. Rev. 363 (1954) (contemporaneous review of the cases).

16. *See, e.g.*, Perma Life Mufflers v. International Parts Corp, 392 U.S. 134 (1968) (rejecting *in pari delicto* defense in franchise exclusive dealing case); Fortner Enterprises v. United States Steel Corp., 394 U.S. 495 (1969) (tying agreement); Zenith Radio Corp. v. Hazeltine Research, 395 U.S. 100 (1969) (patent pool exclusion).

17. Reiter v. Sonotone Corp., 442 U.S. 330, 344 (1979).

18. *See* 1980 Annual Rep. of Dir. Admin. Off. of U.S. Cts. at 63.

19. *See* B. Zorina Kahn, *Symposium on Antitrust*, 9 Cornell J. Law & Pub. Pol. 133, 137 (1999) (Figure 1).

20. *See, e.g.*, Bell Atlantic v. Twombly, 550 U.S. 544 (2007) (heightened pleading requirements); Credit Suisse Securities LLC v. Billing, 551 U.S. 264 (2007) (denying recovery where anticompetitive practices were within the "heartland" of agency regulation). For an earlier discussion of this trend, see Stephen Calkins, *Summary Judgment, Motions to Dismiss and Other Examples of Equilibrating Tendencies in the Antitrust System*, 74 Geo. L.J. 1065 (1986).

21. *See, e.g.*, Daniel Crane, *supra* note 13, at 677 (urging reorientation of private action from deterrence and compensation "toward policing market problems from a problem-solving perspective"). For an earlier critical view, see William H. Page, *Antitrust Damages and Economic Efficiency: An Approach to Antitrust Injury*, 47 U. Chi. L. Rev. 467 (1979).

22. The term "enforcing jurisdictions" is used rather than "countries" because the EU fits into the former category but not the latter.

23. Some jurisdictions outside the study provide damages multipliers that are discretionary with the court. *See, e.g.*, Taiwan: Fair Trade Act, Art. 32 (up to treble damages for intentional violations); Turkey: Act No. 4054, Art. 58 (discretionary treble damages for concerted practices).

24. Germany: Act Against Restraints of Competition, Art. 33(3) (intentional or negligent violations); United Kingdom: Competition Act of 1998, as amended by the Enterprise Act of 2002, sec. 47A.

25. In China prosecutions for bid rigging are possible under the criminal code, Article 233, promulgated originally in 1997, but it is unclear whether this provision is being enforced since the adoption of the Antimonopoly Law. *See* Jessica Su & Xiaoye Wang, *China: The Competition Law System and the Country's Norms, in* The Design of Competition Law Institutions: Global Norms, Local Choices 196 (Eleanor M. Fox & Michael J. Trebilcock eds., 2013) (hereinafter Design of Competition Law Institutions) (criminal law statute applies if circumstances are serious; conviction could lead to fines, detention, and up to three years imprisonment).

26. For discussion, see *infra* notes 44–49 and accompanying text.

27. Australia: *See* Brooke Dellavedova, Vince Morabito & Brian Sweeny, *Australia, in* The International Handbook on Private Enforcement of Competition Law 501 (Albert A. Foer & Jonathan W. Cuneo eds. 2010) (hereinafter International Handbook) (class actions have changed the focus of litigation to damages actions in recent years). Canada: *See* Edward Iacobucci & Michael J. Trebilcock, *Canada: The Competition Law System and the Country's Norms, in* The Design of Competition Law Institutions, *supra* note 25, at 115 (between 2004 and 2010, twenty-four class actions filed for cartel violations, an increase attributed to more liberal Provincial class action procedures); Charles M. Wright, *Canada, in* International Handbook, *supra*, at 449–51 (discussing cases). Israel: *See* Eytan Epstein, Tamar Dolev-Green & Shiran Shabtai, *Israel, in* The Private Competition Enforcement Review 125–26 (Ilene Knable Gotts ed., 3d ed., 2010) (hereinafter Private Enforcement) (discussing changes after class action law adopted in 2006). United Kingdom: *See* Peter Scott & Mark Simpson, *England and Wales, in* Private Enforcement, *supra*, at 41 (noting seven significant

cartel cases filed in 2009); Renato Nazzini, *Private Litigation in England and Wales*, CPI Antitrust J., May 2010 (2) at 2–3 (although England and Wales are "well placed" to be an effective forum, significant obstacles include lack of a clearly established procedure for collective claims).

28. China: *See* China Competition Bull. 3–4 (Sept. 2010) (ten cases accepted by the courts from inception of statute in 2008 until 2010). Japan: *See, e.g.*, Harry First & Tadashi Shiraishi, *Concentrated Power: The Paradox of Antitrust in Japan*, *in* Law in Japan: A Turning Point 529 nn. 47–48 (Daniel H. Foote ed. 2007) (listing examples of relatively recent private litigation); Kozo Kawai & Madoka Shimada, *Japan*, *in* Private Enforcement, *supra* note 27, at 157 (listing two large settlements of bid rigging in 2008 and 2009). Korea: *See* Hwang Lee & Byung Geon Lee, *Korea*, *in* International Handbook, *supra* note 27, at 542 (gradual increase in private litigation, with twelve to sixteen cases pending at the end of 2008).

29. Brazil: *See* OECD, Competition Law and Policy in Brazil: A Peer Review 18 (2010) (of thirty-four recent convictions, ten defendants sentenced to jail but none has served the sentence). Germany: *See* Florian Wagner-Von Papp, *What if All Bid Riggers Went to Prison and Nobody Noticed? Criminal Antitrust Enforcement in Germany*, *in* Criminalising Cartels: Critical Studies of an International Regulatory Movement 169, 182 (Caron Beaton-Wells & Ariel Ezrachi eds., 2011) (reporting 184 criminal convictions for bid rigging from 1998 to 2008, but with jail terms suspended in all but one case) (hereinafter Criminalising Cartels). Japan: *See* Harry First & Tadashi Shiraishi, *Japan: The Competition Law System and the Country's Norms*, *in* Design of Competition Law Institutions, *supra* note 25, at 234 (no individual has ever served a jail sentence). Korea: *See* Joseph Seon Hur & Paul S. Rhee, *Recent Enforcement of Cartel Regulations in Korea* at 6 (September 2008) (individuals have only been given suspended sentences).

30. China: *See* Wu Peng, Michael ZP Gu & Xue Yi, *China*, *in* The Public Competition Enforcement Review 94 (Shaun Goodman ed., 2d ed., 2010) (no criminal liability). India: The Competition Act 2002, No. 12 of 2003 §§ 42, 53Q (imprisonment only for acting in contravention of orders of competition commission or appellate tribunal).

31. Australia: *See* Caron Beaton-Wells, *Cartel Criminalisation and the Australian Competition and Consumer Commission: Opportunities and Challenges*, *in* Criminalising Cartels, *supra* note 29, at 183–99 (discussing new statute). South Africa: The Competition Amendment Act, 1 of 2009, §§ 12, 13 (up to ten years in prison for violation).

32. *See* The Competition Act § 45; Davies Ward Phillips & Vineberg LLP, *Amendments to the Competition Act: What Do They Mean for You?* (2009) (explaining changes in law).

33. *See* First & Shiraishi, *Japan*, *supra* note 29, at 235; Kozo Kawai, Futaba Hirano & Kojiro Fujii, *Japan*, *in* Public Competition Enforcement Review, *supra* note 30, at 243.

34. *See* Francisco Agüero & Santiago Montt, *Chile: The Competition Law System and the Country's Norms*, *in* Design of Competition Law Institutions, *supra* note 25, at 151–59 (discussing history and scope of the legal changes).

35. *See id.* at 5. *See also* Ron Knox, *Chile Charges Pharma Executives with Cartel Crimes*, Global Competition Review, Mar. 18, 2011.

36. *See* Caron Beaton-Wells, *Criminalising Cartels: Australia's Slow Conversion*, 31 World Competition 205, 205–06 (2008) (decision to criminalize cartels in Australia follows worldwide trend "led by the United States").

37. *See, e.g.*, Neelie Kroes, European Commissioner for Competition Policy, *Collective Redress – Delivering Justice for Victims* at 4, Address at ALDE Conference (Mar. 4, 2009), available at http://europa.eu/rapid/pressReleasesAction.do?reference=SPEECH/09/88&format=HTML&aged=0&language=EN&guiLanguage=en ("I would like to assure you we are not proposing anything like the US system. Not at all. We are striking a European model that protects against excesses and unmeritorious litigation. . . . Clearly, we do not want an excessive litigation culture.")

38. See New State Ice v. Liebmann, 285 U.S. 262, 386–87 (1932) ("It is one of the happy incidents of the federal system that a single courageous state may, if its citizens choose, serve as a laboratory; and try novel social and economic experiments without risk to the rest of the country.") (Brandeis, J. dissenting). For discussion of the theory that developments in competition law require continuous learning, see Wolfgang Kerber & Oliver Budzinski, *Competition of Competition Laws: Mission Impossible?*, *in* Competition Laws in Conflict: Antitrust Jurisdiction in the Global Economy 31, 37–39 (Richard A. Epstein & Michael S. Greve eds. 2004).

39. *See* William E. Kovacic, *Criminal Enforcement Norms in Competition Policy: Insights from US Experience, in* Criminalising Cartels, *supra* note 29, at 73 (attributing phrase to Khalid Mirza, former head of Pakistan's Competition Authority).

40. For the allocation of authority between the two, see Memorandum of Understanding Between the Office of Fair Trading and the Director of the Serious Fraud Office, October 2003, OFT 547.

41. The investigation/reference model is complicated in two of the jurisdictions in the study. Chile has no criminal provision in its competition law, but the prosecutor has attempted to exercise its authority under general criminal fraud law to bring a criminal cartel case. *See supra* notes 34–35 and accompanying text. Japan's Antimonopoly Act requires a reference from the Japan Fair Trade Commission to the public prosecutor for any criminal prosecution under the act, see Antimonopoly Act Arts. 74, 96, but the public prosecutor has independent authority to enforce other criminal statutes that can be applied to bid rigging of government contracts. For a rare example of the exercise of this authority, see Harry First, *Antitrust Enforcement in Japan*, 64 Antitrust L.J. 137, 168 (1995) (Public Prosecutor's successful criminal prosecution of bid rigging).

42. I thank Professor Maarten Schinkel, of the University of Amsterdam, for suggesting this bureaucratic incentive effect, advanced as an explanation for the unwillingness of the Dutch Competition Authority to refer important cartel cases to the Dutch prosecutor for criminal prosecution.

43. *See* Von-Papp, *supra* note 29, at 175 (Germany).

44. *See* OECD Peer Review Report, *supra* note 29, at 18–19 (in a "few short years" Brazil developed "one of the most active" programs in the area of criminal competition law enforcement) (activity between 2002 and 2009). Nevertheless, no defendant has yet served a sentence of imprisonment. *See supra* note 29.

45. *See id.* at 19.

46. *See id.* at 18–19.

47. *See* Von-Papp, *supra* note 29, at 165.

48. *See id.* at 169 (jail terms suspended in all but one case).

49. *See* Agüero & Montt, *Chile, supra* note 34, at 154.

50. *See* note 29, *supra*. The JFTC recently revised its investigative procedures so that it can prosecute cartels more effectively, which may lead to an increase in criminal prosecutions. Interview with Tetsuya Nagasawa, Partner, Attorney-at-Law, Oh-Ebashi LPC & Partners, Tokyo, Japan, Aug. 9, 2011.

51. *See* Monopoly Regulation and Fair Trade Act ("MRFTA"), Art. 71; KFTC Annual Report 2011 (English version) at 22 n.7 *supra*. For data on prosecutions, *see* KFTC Annual Report 2011 at 245 (four referrals in 2010); KFTC Annual Report 2010 at 99 (English version) (five referrals in 2009). *See also* Hur & Rhee, *supra* note 29, at 6 ("individuals have only been given suspended prison sentences or probation").

52. *See* Julian Joshua, *DOA: Can the UK Cartel Offense Be Resuscitated?, in* Criminalising Cartels, *supra* note 29, at 129, 140–41 (describing prosecution of four British Airways executives).

53. Email to the author from Professor Michal Gal, University of Haifa School of Law, Nov. 27, 2011. *See also* Restrictive Trade Practices Law § 46 (investigative authority); Annual Report on Competition Policy Developments in Israel, January 2008–April 2009 (discussing one indictment and one conviction during the period).

54. *See* Kazuyuki Funahashi, Deputy Dir.-Gen., Investigation Bur. Japan Fair Trade Comm'n, International Cooperation to Crack International Cartels—Japanese Successes and Failures at 4–6 (Nov. 24, 2004) (attributing failure in vitamins and graphite electrodes cases to lack of leniency policy).

55. Australia: *See* Memorandum of Understanding Between the CDPP and ACCC Regarding Serious Cartel Conduct, § 7.2 (July 2009) (prosecutor decides on immunity based on prosecutorial policy, after recommendation from competition authority); Beaton-Wells, *supra* note 31, at 190–91 (describing prosecutor's "far more conservative approach" to negotiations with cooperating parties). Brazil: *See* Antitrust Law, Art. 35-C (leniency agreement prevents criminal case from being brought to court), OECD Peer Review, *supra* note 29, at 18 (antitrust agency asks prosecutors to sign leniency agreements so that leniency applicant will not be subject to parallel criminal prosecu-

tion). Canada: D. Martin Low & Casey W. Hallady, *Redesigning a Criminal Cartel Regime: The Canadian Conversion*, in Criminalising Cartels, *supra* note 29, at 100–101 (describing relationship between competition authority and prosecutor; grant of immunity ultimately decided by prosecutor).

56. *See* First & Shiraishi, *Japan*, *supra* note 29, at 243 (statement made during Diet session).

57. *See* Von-Papp, *supra* note 29, at 176 ("immunity provisions for criminal offenses are not unknown, but they are regarded with deep suspicion").

58. Korea changed its statute in 2005 to create a stand-alone action, in the hopes of increasing the number of private suits. *See* Hwang Lee & Byung Geon Lee, *supra* note 28, at 543.

59. India: *See* The Competition Act § 53N. United Kingdom: Competition Act of 1998, as amended by the Enterprise Act of 2002, sec. 47A.

60. *See* Japan Antimonopoly Act, Arts. 25, 26.

61. *See* Competition Act, § 65.

62. *See* First & Shiraishi, *Japan*, *supra* note 29, at 235–37; Scott & Simpson, *England and Wales*, *supra* note 27, at 42–43 (courts willing to exercise broad territorial jurisdiction and provide injunctive relief in addition to damages).

63. *See, e.g.,* Australia: Trade Practices Act § 83 (prima facie effect of findings in competition agency proceedings). Israel: Restrictive Trade Practices Law § 43(e) ("The General Director's Determination shall constitute *prima facie* proof of its subject matter in any legal procedure.").

64. *See, e.g.,* Chile: Competition Act, Art. 30 (civil court "shall base its ruling" on the conduct established by the Competition Tribunal). Germany: Act Against Restraints of Competition, § 33(4) (court bound by final decision by competition authority in Germany, other EU countries, or the European Commission finding infringement). South Africa: Competition Act, § 65(2) (prior determination of issues by Competition Tribunal or Competition Appeal Court binding on civil court). United Kingdom: Competition Act § 58A(3) (courts bound by Office of Fair Trade or Competition Appeal Tribunal infringement decision).

65. *See, e.g.,* Japan: Antimonopoly Act Art. 25(2) (making violation strict liability; suit can be brought only after JFTC finding of violation). Korea: MRFTA Art. 56 (shifting burden of proof on intent to defendant).

66. *See, e.g.,* Korea: MRFTA Arts. 56(2), 57 (court shall decide damages "based on the result of [the KFTC's] evidentiary investigation").

67. *See, e.g.,* Dellavedova et al., *supra* note 27, at 501 (private actions "regular part" of Australian competition law landscape, but generally limited to competitor v. competitor or commercial buyer v. commercial seller); Niv Zecker, Michal Gal & Yariv Han, *Israel*, in International Handbook, *supra* note 27, at 515 (in Israel, most private antitrust claims center around contract disputes).

68. Brazil: Bruno L Peixoto, *Brazil*, in Private Enforcement, *supra* note 27, at 24–25 (public collective actions for damages brought by, e.g., government agencies, to create fund under which injured parties may collect). Germany: Act Against Restraints of Competition, §33 (2) (representative actions by certain associations available for injunction only). India: Competition Act § 53N(4) (opt-in form of class action). Korea: Lee & Lee, *supra* note 28, at 545–46 (opt-in mechanism allowing multiple parties to bring damages action jointly).

69. *See* Michael Dietrich & Marco Hartmann-Ruppel, *Germany*, in Private Enforcement, *supra* note 27, at 95. For a description of the company's efforts to obtain recovery from the German cement cartel, see http://www.carteldamageclaims.com/German%20Cement (suit on behalf of thirty-six purchasers of cement, claiming damages of €176 million).

70. Canada: *See* Iacobucci & Trebilcock, *supra* note 27, at 115 (class actions for criminal violations allowable under provincial laws; twenty-four brought between 2004 and 2010). South Africa: Kasturi Moodaliyar, *South Africa*, *in* International Handbook, *supra* note 27, at 558–59 (no class action suit for damages under Competition Law reported as of 2010). United Kingdom: *See* Vincent Smith, Anthony Maton & Scott Campbell, *England and Wales*, in International Handbook, *supra* note 27, at 303 (narrow construction given to opt-out class actions, which have been "relatively infrequent").

71. *See* Wouter P. J. Wils, Efficiency and Justice in European Antitrust Enforcement 164 (2008) (discussing meaning of "undertaking").

72. For a review of those efforts and a discussion of possible reasons for the lack of success so far, see Robert O'Donoghue, *Europe's Long March Towards Antitrust Damages Actions*, CPI Antitrust Chronicle, April 2011 (describing the commission as taking "a rather languid course with no clear end-point in sight." *Id.* at 2).

73. Daniel Crane forcefully argues that compensation is an impossible goal to achieve even in the United States. *See* Crane, *supra* note 13, at 678–90.

Chapter 11

1. International Competition Network (ICN), Advocacy and Competition Policy 25 (2002).

2. *Id.* at 31–32.

3. *Id.* at 25.

4. *Id.* at 32, 77, 89; A Framework for the Design and Implementation of Competition Law and Policy, 99 (R. Shyam Khemani ed. 1998); William E. Kovacic, *Getting Started: Creating New Competition Policy Institutions in Transition Economies*, 23 Brooklyn J. Int'l L. 439, 448 (1997).

5. Khemani, *supra* note 4, at 94; John Clark, *Competition Advocacy: Challenges for Developing Countries*, 6(4) OECD J. Competition L. & Pol'y 69, 77–79 (2005).

6. ICN, *supra* note 1, at 25.

7. *Id.* at 31–32.

8. Khemani, *supra* note 4, at 93.

9. ICN, *supra* note 1, at 31, 81–84; ICN, Advocacy Toolkit: Part I: Advocacy Process and Tools 13–14 (2011).

10. ICN, *supra* note 1, at 30.

11. Kovacic, *supra* note 4, at 441.

12. *Id.* at 58, 93; ICN, Report on Assessment of ICN Members' Requirements and Recommendations on Further ICN Work on Competition Advocacy 20 (2009).

13. ICN, *supra* note 12, at 20–22, 42.

14. ICN, *supra* note 1, at 72; ICN, *supra* note 12, at 58–59.

15. *See, e.g.*, ICN Market Studies Project Report (2009).

16. ICN, *supra* note 12, at 39.

17. *Contribution by Indonesia: Questionnaire on the Challenges Facing Young Competition Authorities.* Paper, OECD Global Forum on Competition: Session III, DAF/COMP/GF/WD(2009) 5 (2009).

18. *Contribution by Hungary: Questionnaire on the Challenges Facing Young Competition Authorities.* Paper, OECD Global Forum on Competition: Session III, DAF/COMP/GF/WD(2009) 47 (2009).

19. William E. Kovacic, *Designing and Implementing Competition and Consumer Protection Reforms in Transitional Economies: Perspectives from Mongolia, Nepal, Ukraine and Zimbabwe*, 44 DePaul L. Rev. 1197, 1213 (1995).

20. Ajit Singh, *Competition and Competition Policy in Emerging Markets: International and Developmental Dimensions* 15–16 (UNCTAD, G-24 Discussion Paper No. 18, 2002) available at http://unctad.org/en/Docs/gdsmdpbg2418_en.pdf; Pradeep S. Mehta & S. Chakravarthy, *Dimensions of Competition Policy and Law in Emerging Economies* 19–22 (Discussion paper, CUTS Centre for Competition, Investment & Economic Regulation, Jaipur, 2010); Khemani, *supra* note 4, at 7–8.

21. Frédéric Jenny, *Competition Authorities: Independence and Advocacy* (IDRC Pre-ICN Forum on Competition & Development: Alliance Building for a Culture of Compliance 2011).

22. *See, e.g.*, Mehta & Chakravarthy, *supra* note 20, at 20–22; Khemani, *supra* note 4, at 7–8.

23. Pradeep S. Mehta, Manish Agarwal, & V. V. Singh, *Politics Trumps Economics—Lessons and Experiences on Competition and Regulatory Regimes from Developing Countries* 21–22 (2007); Mehta & Chakravarthy, *supra* note 20, at 20–21.

24. Clark, *supra* note 5, at 74; Taimoon Stewart et al., *Competition Law in Action: Experiences from Developing Countries* 38 (International Development and Research Centre, 2007).

25. Fan long duan fa [Anti-Monopoly Law (P.R.C.)] (promulgated by the Nat'l People's Cong., Aug. 30, 2007, effective Aug. 1, 2008), art 7 (hereinafter AML).

26. ICN, *supra* note 1, at 72.

27. Maher M. Dabbah, *Competition Law and Policy in Developing Countries: A Critical Assessment of the Challenges to Establishing an Effective Competition Law Regime*, 33 World Competition 457, 467 (2010).

28. *See generally, Report on Antitrust Policy Objectives* (American Bar Association Antitrust Section, Feb. 2003).

29. Competition Act 1998 (South Africa) § 2(c), (e), (f).

30. The Departments of Economic Development, of Trade and Industry, and of Agriculture, Forestry, and Fisheries.

31. The South African Commercial, Catering and Allied Workers' Union, the South African Clothing & Textile Workers' Union, and other unions organizing workers in industries that sell products into the retail sector, and their federation, the Congress of South African Trade Unions.

32. Competition Tribunal of South Africa, Tribunal Statement on the Conditional Approval of the Merger Between Wal-mart Stores Inc. and Massmart Holdings Limited (May 31, 2011); Economic Development Department, the Department of Trade and Industry and the Department of Agriculture, Forestry and Fisheries, Joint Press Statement by the Economic Development Department, the Department of Trade and Industry and the Department of Agriculture, Forestry and Fisheries on the Walmart/Massmart Merger (Aug. 2, 2011), available at http://www.info.gov.za /speech/DynamicAction?pageid=461&sid=20417&tid=38551; Mike Cohen, *Wal-Mart's Massmart Purchase Faces South Africa Court Appeal*, Bloomberg Business Week, Oct. 20, 2011, available at http://www.businessweek.com/news/2011-10-20/wal-mart-s-massmart-purchase-faces-south-af-rica-court-appeal.html; Annaleigh Vallie & SAPA, *Massmart Court Battle Enters Second Day*, Business Day, Oct. 21, 2011, available at http://www.bdlive.co.za/articles/2011/10/21/massmart-court -battle-enters-second-day.

33. Competition Tribunal of South Africa, In the Matter Between Wal-Mart Stores Inc and Massmart Holdings Inc., Case No. 73/LM/Nov10, May 31, 2011.

34. Economic Development Department et al., *supra* note 32; Cohen, *supra* note 32; Vallie & SAPA, *supra* note 32.

35. Devon Maylie, *Wal-Mart Gets Nod in Africa*, Wall St. J., June 1, 2011; Richard Wachman, *South Africa Resists March of Walmart*, Guardian, Oct. 10, 2011.

36. Mehta et al., *supra* note 23, at 25.

37. ICN, *supra* note 1, at 67–69; Clark, *supra* note 5, at 75.

38. Mehta et al., *supra* note 23, at 25; Kovacic, *supra* note 4, at 422.

39. Dabbah, *supra* note 27, at 463–64.

40. Mehta et al., *supra* note 23, at 21; A. E. Rodriguez & Ashok Menon, *What Is Different in Developing and Transition Economies?, in* The Limits of Competition Policy: The Shortcomings of Antitrust in Developing and Reforming Economies 122 (2010).

41. Kovacic, *supra* note 4, at 422–23; Rodriguez & Menon, *supra* note 40, at 125.

42. ICN, *supra* note 1, at 38; Clark, *supra* note 5, at 72, 75; Khemani, *supra* note 4, at 98.

43. Clark, *supra* note 5, at 72–73, 75–76; Khemani, *supra* note 4, at 98; Kovacic, *supra* note 4 at 443.

44. ICN, *supra* note 1, at 28–29; Khemani, *supra* note 4, at 93; Mehta et al., *supra* note 23, at 35.

45. Khemani, *supra* note 4, at 93; Clark *supra* note 5, at 76; Stewart et al., *supra* note 24, at 27.

46. Mehta et al., *supra* note 23, at 24.

47. *Id.* at 23; Rodriguez & Menon, *supra* note 40, at 121, 127; A. E. Rodriguez & Mark D. Williams, *The Effectiveness of Proposed Antitrust Programs for Developing Countries*, 19 N.C.J. Int'l L. & Com. Reg. 209, 220–22 (1994).

48. ICN, *supra* note 1, at 33; Mehta et al., *supra* note 23, at 21; Deborah Platt Majoras, Promoting a Culture of Competition (Remarks, Chinese Academy of Social Sciences, Beijing, April 2006).

49. Rodriguez & Menon, *supra* note 40, at 132.

50. Rodriguez & Williams, *supra* note 47, at 220; Secretariat, *Challenges/Obstacles Faced by Competition Authorities in Achieving Greater Economic Development Through the Promotion of Competition* 2 (Background note, CCNM/GF/COMP(2003)6, OECD Global Forum on Competition, Feb. 12–13, 2004).

51. Mehta & Chakravarthy, *supra* note at 20; Mark Dutz & R. Shyam Khemani, Competition Law and Policy: Challenges in South Asia 11 (2007).

52. Ashok Malik, *India's Unwillingness to Open Doors to Investment*, Epoch Times, Dec. 25, 2011, available at http://www.theepochtimes.com/n2/opinion/indias-unwillingness-to-open-doors-to -investment-164250.html; *India MPs in Uproar Over Retail Reform Plans*, BBC News, Nov. 25, 2011,

http://www.bbc.co.uk/news/world-asia-india-15885004; Manoj Kumar, *India Retail Reform Un-ravels After Backlash*, Reuters, Dec. 7, 2011, available at http://www.reuters.com/article/2011/12/07/us-india-politics-idUSTRE7B60FW20111207.

53. Ross Colvin & Rajesh Kumar Singh, *Analysis: India Poised to Revive Retail Reform Plan*, Reuters, June 24, 2012, available at http://www.reuters.com/article/2012/06/24/us-india-econ omy-retail-idUSBRE85N0PP20120624.

54. ICN, *supra* note 1, at x, 78.

55. *Id.* at x.

56. Mehta et al., *supra* note 23, at 21–22; Dabbah, *supra* note 27, at 469–70.

57. ICN, *supra* note 1, at 78.

58. Khemani, *supra* note 4, at 94.

59. ICN, *supra* note 1, at xiv.

60. Kovacic, *supra* note 4, at 408; Dutz & Khemani, *supra* note 51, at 9.

61. ICN, *supra* note 1, at 37–38. For a deeper discussion of the weaknesses in the institutional foundations of developing countries, see Kovacic, *supra* note 4, at 417–29.

62. Mehta & Chakravarthy, *supra* note 20, at 24; Kovacic, *supra* note 4, at 420–21.

63. ICN, *supra* note 1, at xii; Kovacic, *supra* note 4, at 418.

64. Mehta et al, *supra* note 23, at 41.

65. *Id.*

66. *Id.* at 72–73.

67. *Id.* at 73.

68. *Id.* at 42.

69. *Id.* at 34–35.

70. *Id.* at 35.

71. *Id.* at 36.

72. *Id.* at 35.

73. *Id.* at 36.

74. Clark, *supra* note 5, at 78–79.

75. *Id.* at 79.

76. ICN, *supra* note 1, at 36.

77. *Id.* at 40, 93.

78. *Id.* at 44–52.

79. Jenny, *supra* note 21.

80. ICN, *supra* note 1, at 49.

81. AML arts. 32–37.

82. Clark, *supra* note 5, at 70–71.

83. *Id.* at 78–79.

84. *See, e.g.*, ICN, *supra* note 1, at 54–55.

85. OECD, Competition Assessment Toolkit: Volume 1: Principles 3 (2011); Mehta & Chakravarthy, *supra* note 20, at 19–20.

86. Australian Government Productivity Commission, Review of National Competition Pol-icy Reforms, xiii (Inquiry report, Commonwealth of Australia, February 2005).

87. Gary Banks, An Economy-wide View: Speeches on Structural Reform 6–7 (Productivity Commission, 2010).

88. Australian Government Productivity Commission, *supra* note 86, at xiv.

89. Australian Committee of Inquiry, National Competition Policy Review xvii (1993).

90. *Id* at v.

91. National Competition Council, National Competition Policy: Overview, available at http://ncp.ncc.gov.au/pages/overview.

92. Competition Principles Agreement between The Commonwealth of Australia, The State of New South Wales, The State of Victoria, The State of Queensland, The State of Western Aus-tralia, The State of South Australia, The State of Tasmania, The Australian Capital Territory and The Northern Territory of Australia (11 April 1995) § 5(1) (Competition Principles Agreement). *See also* Australian Government Productivity Commission, *supra* note 86, at xiv; John Feil, *Up a Down Escalator: National Competition Policy—A Little History and a Glance Forward*, 35 Network 1, 1 (2010).

93. National Competition Council, National Competition Policy: About the NCP, available at http://ncp.ncc.gov.au/pages/about; Australian Government Productivity Commission, *supra* note 86, at xv.

94. Australian Government Productivity Commission, *supra* note 86, at xvi–xxiii.

95. Competition Principles Agreement, supra note 92; Australian Government Productivity Commission, supra note 86, at xxiii; Feil, *supra* note 92, at 5–6.

96. Simon Corden, *Australia's National Competition Policy: Possible Implications for Mexico* 6 (2009).

97. Committee of Inquiry, *supra* note 89, at iii.

98. Now known as the Productivity Commission.

99. Governments provided adjustment assistance measures to those groups that were affected adversely by the NCP: Australian Government Productivity Commission, *supra* note 86, at 148.

100. Simon Corden, *supra* note 96, at 40.

101. Mehta & Chakravarthy, *supra* note 20, at 19–20.

102. OECD, Strengthening the Competition and Regulation Framework, available at http://www.oecd.org/document/34/0,3746,en_2649_37463_44948578_1_1_1_37463,00.html; Committee for Framing the National Competition Policy and Related Matters, National Competition Policy Statement of the Government of India—Draft for Discussion (July 28, 2011).

103. OECD, *supra* note 85,.

104. Council of the Organisation for Economic Cooperation and Development, Recommendation of the Council on Competition Assessment (Oct. 22, 2009).

105. OECD, *supra* note 85, at 3.

106. *Id.*

107. *Id.* at 7–17.

108. *Id.* at 3.

109. *Id.*

110. OECD, *supra* note 102; Eduardo Pérez Motta, *The OECD's Competition Assessment Toolkit in Mexico* (Presentation, Session IV of the Global Forum on Competition, Paris, France, Feb. 20, 2009).

111. OECD, *supra* note 102.

112. Roberto Newell, Political Economy of Reform in Mexico (Richard Snape Lecture, Productivity Commission, Melbourne, Oct. 11, 2011).

Chapter 12

1. For a review of the wide range of goals advanced by antitrust law, see Maurice E. Stucke, *Reconsidering Antitrust Goals*, 53 B.C. L. Rev. 551 (2012).

2. *See, e.g.*, ICN, Competition Enforcement and Consumer Welfare (2011).

3. The approach involves an aggregate economic welfare standard, which takes the possible effects on consumers, producers, and competitors into account. Accordingly, a transaction or activity is permitted when the total welfare gain outweighs the total loss, regardless of distributional considerations and effects on consumers. Aggregate economic welfare is also referred to as an "efficiency" or "total surplus" standard. Steven C. Salop, *Question: What Is the Real and Proper Antitrust Welfare Standard? Answer: The True Consumer Welfare Standard*, 22 Loy. Consumer L. Rev. 336 (2010); Douglas Ginsburg, *Judge Bork, Consumer Welfare and Antitrust Law*, 31 Harv. J.L. & Pub. Pol'y. 449 (2008).

4. The welfare gain to consumers provides the focal point for assessment. The consumer surplus benchmark condemns conduct that reduces the welfare of consumers irrespective of any impact on sellers and competitors. Also referred to as "true" consumer welfare standard or "pure consumer welfare." See Salop, *supra* note 3.

5. Many courts and the federal enforcement agencies today appear to have opted for the true consumer welfare standard. *Id. See also* Robert H. Lande, *Chicago's False Foundation: Wealth Transfers (Not Just Efficiency) Should Guide Antitrust*, 58 Antitrust L.J. 631 (1989).

6. In the EU, it is evident, among others, in Article 101(3) TFEU, the Commission report on competition policy, the Commission's Art 102 TFEU Guidance, Article 101(3) Guidelines, Horizontal merger guidelines. *See, e.g.*, The Competition Auth. v. Beef Indus. Dev. Soc'y & Barry Bros.

(Carrigmore) Meats 2008 (101 TFEU); Microsoft v. Comm'n 2008 (102 TFEU); Synetairismos Farmakopoion Aitolias & Akarnanias (Syfait) v. GlaxoSmithKline 2004 (102 TFEU).

7. See ICN, *supra* note 2.

8. Robert H. Lande, *Wealth Transfers as the Original and Primary Concern of Antitrust: The Efficiency Interpretation Challenged*, 34 Hastings L.J. 65 (1982–1983).

9. On the narrow assumption of jurisdiction, see F. Hoffman-La Roche Ltd. v. Empagran S.A., 524 U.S. 155 (2004).

10. The scope of analysis depends to a large extent on the definition of the relevant geographic market-domestic, regional, or global.

11. An illustrative example may be an international transaction leading to different effects in different, distinct, regional markets. Each reviewing jurisdiction will focus on its local market reality. See, for example: COMP/M.1630 Air Liquide/BOC [18/01/2000]. The European Commission cleared the transaction, subject to conditions, noting that the decision did not prejudge a separate decision in the United States. In the United States, the FTC raised concerns as to the effect the transaction will have on the regional market. The parties abandoned the transaction.

12. For a critical review see D. Daniel Sokol, *What Do We Really Know About Export Cartels and What Is the Appropriate Solution?*, 4 J. Competition L. & Econ. 967 (2008); Florian Becker, *The Case of Export Cartel Exemptions: Between Competition and Protectionism*, 3 J. Competition L. & Econ. 97 (2007).

13. Justifications for exemptions also include the size of the firms and the low likelihood of anticompetitive effects. Some regimes require notification and authorization of the export cartel, others do not. *See generally,* Aditya Bhattacharjea, *Export Cartels—A Developing Country Perspective*, 38 J. World Trade 331 (2004); *Exceptions, Exemptions and Exclusions Contained in Members' National Competition Legislation*, Note by Secretariat, WTO Doc WT/WGTCP/M/172 (2001).

14. For a review of the academic debate on export cartels see Bhattacharjea, *supra* note 13. The decision not to confront export cartels has been referred to as a "sensible allocation of enforcement authority." *See* Einer Elhauge & Damien Geradin, Global Competition Law and Economics 1012 (2010).

15. *See* U.S. submissions to the WTO *Report by Secretariat*, WTO Doc WT/WGTCP/M/21 (2003), cited in Brendan Sweeney, *Export Cartels: Is There a Need for Global Rules?*, 10 J Int'l Econ. L. 87 (2007).

16. Margaret C. Levenstein & Valerie Y. Suslow, *The Changing International Status of Export Cartels*, 20 Am. U. Int'l L. Rev. 785 (2005).

17. Terry Calvani, *Conflict, Cooperation and Convergence in International Competition*, 72 Antitrust L.J. 1127 (2005).

18. Christopher Harding, *Business Collusion as a Criminological Phenomenon: Exploring the Global Criminalisation of Business Cartels*, 14 Critical Criminology 181 (2006).

19. Levenstein & Suslow, *supra* note 16.

20. It may be worth clarifying that in cases involving purely welfare-reducing behavior one would expect the total welfare and consumer surplus analysis to lead to the same result. This is because there are no offsetting efficiencies at the upstream market to outweigh the detrimental effect on consumer surplus. Lande, *supra* note 5.

21. I.e., it is not governed by the desire to protect consumer surplus (or total welfare) but rather by industrial policies aimed at protecting the domestic market and preventing any form of negative transfer of wealth.

22. Alan O. Sykes, *Externalities in Open Economy Antitrust and Their Implications for International Competition Policy*, 23 Harv. J.L. & Pub. Pol'y 89 (1999).

23. Ariel Ezrachi, *Globalisation of Merger Control—A Look at Bilateral Cooperation Through the GE-Honeywell Case*, 14 Fla. J. Int'l L. 397 (2002).

24. Over-enforcement: for example, a jurisdiction challenging and blocking an overall welfare-enhancing international merger transaction because of negative effects within the domestic territory.

25. Under-enforcement: where a jurisdiction should condemn the conduct but refrains from doing so because the consumer harm mainly lies abroad. (See above discussion of export cartels.)

26. See, for example, the approach in the EU (implementation doctrine) and the United States (effects doctrine), which serve as the basis for the extraterritorial application of the competition

laws: United States v. Aluminum Co. of America (Alcoa), 148 F.2d 416 (2d Cir. 1945); Timberland Lumber Co. v, Bank of America, 549 F.2d 596 (9th Cir. 1976); Hartford Fire Ins. Co. v. California, 113 S. Ct. 2891 (1993); Joined Cases C-89/95, C-104/85, C-114/85, C116-117/85, C 125-129/85 Re Wood Pulp Cartel: A Ahlstrom Oy v. Commission [1988] E.C.R. 5193 [1988] 4 C.M.L.R. 901; Case T-102/96 Gencor Limited v. E.C. Commission [1999] 4 C.M.L.R. 971.

27. For an account on the effect of jurisdictional limitations on the enforcement of competition law in Mexico, see Michael Wise, *Review of Competition Law and Policy in Mexico*, 1 OECD J. Comp. L. & Pol'y (1999).

28. John M. Connor, *Extraterritoriality of the Sherman Act and Deterrence of Private International Cartels* 9–10 (Purdue Univ. Dep't of Agric. Econ., Staff Paper No. 04-08, 2004), where the author shows (on the basis of facts concerning operation and prosecution of the global Vitamins Cartel) that "even under ideal prosecutorial outcomes, in the absence of full extraterritoriality, the global reach of modern cartels insures that the monetary payouts of guilty international cartelists cannot succeed in disgorging all the illegal cartel profits" at 18; On the point that one "need a global fine to deter global harm," see also Maurice E. Stucke, *Am I a Price-Fixer? A Behavioral Economics Analysis of Cartels*, *in* Criminalising Cartels: A Critical Interdisciplinary Study of an International Regulatory Movement (Caron Beaton-Wells & Ariel Ezrachi eds., 2011).

29. Eleanor M. Fox, *Can We Solve the Antitrust Problems of Globalization by Extraterritoriality and Cooperation? Sufficiency and Legitimacy*, 48 Antitrust Bulletin 355, 359–60 (2003).

30. Note that comity, reciprocal deference, is a concept founded on process, not outcome. *See* Testimony of Eleanor M. Fox, Walter J. Derenberg Professor of Trade Regulation, New York University School of Law, Before the Antitrust Modernization Commission Hearing on International Issues, Washington, D.C., Feb. 15, 2006.

31. For proposals to confront export cartels at the international level see Bhattacharjea, *supra* note 13; Sokol, *supra* note 12; Becker, *supra* note 12.

32. Maher Dabbah, *Competition Law and Policy in Developing Countries: A Critical Assessment of the Challenges to Establishing an Effective Competition Law Regime*, 33 World Competition 457, 459 (2010).

33. Domestic considerations may also make the reliance on foreign jurisdictions for enforcement politically unpalatable. *See generally* John Fingleton, *Competition Agencies and Global Markets: The Challenges Ahead* (June 5, 2009), www.oft.gov.uk/shared_oft/speeches/2009/spe0909paper.pdf.

34. Scott D. Hammond, *Cornerstones of an Effective Leniency Program*, ICN Workshop on Leniency Programs (Sydney, Nov. 22–23, 2004) 8–9, or *Optimal Sanctions, Optimal Deterrence*, ICN Annual Conference (Bonn, June 6, 2005) 9.

35. Michal S. Gal, *Antitrust in a Globalized Economy: The Unique Enforcement Challenges Faced by Small and Developing Jurisdictions*, 33 Fordham Int'l L.J. 1, 28 (2009).

36. Terry Winslow, *OECD Competition Law Recommendations, Developing Countries and Possible WTO Competition Rules*, 3 OECD J. Competition L. & Pol'y. 115, 130 (2001).

37. On the limits of extraterritoriality and the experience of developing and young competition regimes, see note by the UNCTAD Secretariat: *Cross-Border Anticompetitive Practices: The Challenges for Developing Countries and Economies in Transition* (April 19, 2012).

38. To be distinguished from a decision to sign a bilateral agreement in competition as part of a political move with no prospect of meaningful implementation.

39. Barbara Ingham, From ITO to WTO: Trade and Protection in a Changing World (1998); Lynden Moore, The Growth and Structure of International Trade Since the Second World War 42–50 (1985); Clair Wilcox, A Charter for World Trade 103–13, 153–60 (1949); The Munich Draft International Antitrust Code; reprinted in (1993) Antitrust & Trade Regulation Report 65, No. 1628; Robert Anderson & Frédéric Jenny, *Competition Policy, Economic Development and the Role of a Possible Multilateral Framework on Competition Policy: Insights from the WTO Working Group on Trade and Competition Policy*, available at www.ifc.org; WTO Doha Ministerial Declaration, WT/MIN(01)/DEC/1.

40. For a review of these frameworks see, e.g., Ariel Ezrachi, *Merger Control and Cross Border Transactions—A Pragmatic View on Cooperation, Convergence and What's in Between*, *in* Handbook on Trans-Atlantic Antitrust 622–41 (Philip Marsden ed. 2007).

41. Ariel Ezrachi, *The Role of Voluntary Frameworks in Multinational Cooperation over Merger Control*, 36 Geo. Wash. Int'l L. Rev. 433 (2004).

42. For example, Southern Common Market (MERCOSUR), Caribbean Community (CARICOM), Common Market for Eastern and Southern Africa (COMSA), and the West African Economic and Monetary Union (UEMOA).

43. On the benefit of regional competition agreements see Michal S. Gal, *Regional Competition Law Agreements: An Important Step for Antitrust Enforcement*, 60 U. Toronto L.J. 239 (2010).

44. Note for example UNCTAD's COMPAL program, which provides for technical assistance on competition and consumer protection policies for Latin America and is supported by the Swiss State Secretariat for Economic Affairs (SECO).

45. Ariel Ezrachi & Hassan Qaqaya, *UNCTAD's Collaborative Information Platform*, Concurrences Journal No. 4-2012 (2012) .

46. See *supra* note 39.

47. Ezrachi, *supra* note 40, at 622–41.

Chapter 13

1. Susan Scotchmer, Innovation and Incentives 161 (2004).

2. *See* Michael A. Carrier, *Unraveling the Patent-Antitrust Paradox*, 150 U. Pa. L. Rev. 761 (2002).

3. Louis Kaplow, *The Patent-Antitrust Intersection: A Reappraisal*, 97 Harv. L. Rev. 1813, 1833–34 (1984).

4. Professors Dan Burk and Mark Lemley have argued for the same under U.S. patent law. *See* Dan L. Burk & Mark A. Lemley, *Policy Levers in Patent Law*, 89 Va. L. Rev. 1575 (2003).

5. Carrier, *supra* note 2, at 761–62; Pierre Régibeau & Katharine Rockett, *The Relationship Between Intellectual Property Law and Competition Law: An Economic Approach*, *in* The Interface Between Intellectual Property Rights and Competition Policy 505 (Steven D. Anderman ed., 2007).

6. United States v. Microsoft Corp., 253 F.3d 34 (D.C. Cir. 2001); Microsoft Corp. v. Commission: T-201/02 [2007] E.C.R. II-000, [2007] 5 C.M.L.R. 846.

7. Japan Fair Trade Commission, Guidelines on the Use of Intellectual Property Under the Antimonopoly Act, 3 (2007), available at http://www.jftc.go.jp/en/legislation_guidelines/antimonopoly_guidelines.html.

8. Herbert Hovenkamp et al., IP and Antitrust: An Analysis of Antitrust Principles Applied to Intellectual Property Law 1–13 (2011).

9. Edwin Mansfield, *Patents and Innovation: An Empirical Study*, 32 Mgmt. Sci. 173 (1986); Richard C. Levin et al., *Appropriating the Returns from Industrial Research and Development*, 1988 Brookings Papers on Econ. Activity 783; Wesley M. Cohen et al., *Protecting Their Intellectual Assets: Appropriability Conditions and Why U.S. Manufacturing Firms Patent (Or Not)* 2 (Nat'l. Bureau of Econ. Research Working Paper No. 7552, 2000).

10. This author has argued elsewhere that the assumption that patent protection is necessary for inducing innovations is true only for some industries and not others. This assumption is certainly not sufficient to justify a general deference to patent policy in the patent-antitrust interface, certainly not in the context of developing countries.

11. Keith Maskus, *Intellectual Property Rights in the Global Economy* 165 (2000); Carsten Fink, *Patent Protection, Transnational Corporations and Market Structure: A Simulation Study of the Indian Pharmaceutical Industry*, *in* Intellectual Property and Development: Lessons from Recent Economic Research 251 (Carsten Fink & Keith E. Maskus eds., 2005).

12. Prima Braga and Fink of the World Bank distinguish between production capabilities and innovative capacity. *See* Carlos A. Prima Braga & Carsten Fink, *The Relationship Between Intellectual Property Rights and Foreign Direct Investment*, 9 Duke J. Comp. & Int'l L. 163, 167 (1998). Some development economists have further distinguished between imitative and innovative capacities. *See, e.g.*, Carmelo Pierpaolo Parello, *A North-South Model of Intellectual Property Rights Protection and Skill Accumulation*, 85 J. Dev. Econ. 253 (2008); Yongmin Chen & Thitima Puttitanun, *Intellectual Property Rights and Innovation in Developing Countries*, 78 J. Dev. Econ. 474 (2005); Edwin Lai, *International Intellectual Property Rights Protection and the Rate of Product Innovation*, 55 J. Dev. Econ. 133 (1998); Yong Yang, *Why Do Southern Countries Have Little Incentive to Protect Northern Intellectual Property Rights?*, 31 Canadian J. Econ. 800 (1998).

13. Edwin Mansfield et al., *Imitation Costs and Patents: An Empirical Study*, 91 Econ. J. 907 (1981); Elhanan Helpman, *Innovation, Imitation and Intellectual Property Rights*, 61 Econometrica 1247, 1276 (1993).

14. Mansfield, *supra* note 13, at 901.

15. Helpman, *supra* note 13, at 1276.

16. If there is some technological capacity in related industries, it is possible for a firm to transfer its technical experience and know-how from one industry to another.

17. The issue of innovation incentive externality of course is not confined to developing countries. Developed countries face the same issue. Given its focus on the patent-antitrust interface in developing countries, this chapter makes no attempt to address the issue in the developed country context. Suffice it to note that there are two reasons that may call for different treatment of the issue in developing countries. First, most developing countries have much smaller domestic markets. The innovation incentives generated by their domestic patent systems are less likely to be taken into account by foreign inventors. Second, while developed country consumers may be well able to bear the welfare loss needed to generate innovation incentives, the same cannot be said about consumers in developing countries. Developing country antitrust authorities need to be more cautious about sacrificing domestic consumer welfare to generate innovation incentives for foreign inventors.

18. Jeffrey Atik & Hans H. Lidgard, *Embracing Price Discrimination: TRIPS and the Suppression of Parallel Trade in Pharmaceuticals*, 27 U. Pa. J. Int'l Econ. L. 1043 (2006). Bessen and Meurer also note that "[f]irms do not patent a majority of their inventions and about 15 percent of all R&D is performed by firms that obtain no patents at all." James Bessen & Michael J. Meurer, Patent Failure: How Judges, Bureaucrats and Lawyers Put Innovators at Risk 98 (2008).

19. Cohen et al., *supra* note 9, at 16–24.

20. *Id.*

21. F. M. Scherer, *The Economics of the Patent System, in* Industrial Market Structure and Economic Performance, 439, 448 (F. M. Scherer ed., 1980).

22. According to *China Daily*, over 150 million Chinese lived below the poverty line at the end of 2009. Jin Zhu, *China to Raise Its Poverty Line*, China Daily, Oct. 28, 2010, available at http://www.chinadaily.com.cn/china/2010-10/28/content_11467561.htm.

23. Dan He, *China Takes a Tough Line on Poverty*, China Daily, Nov. 30, 2011, available at http://www.chinadaily.com.cn/china/2011-11/30/content_14184665.htm.

24. Elhanan Helpman, The Mystery of Economic Growth 34 (2004); Richard J. Gilbert, *Looking for Mr. Schumpeter: Where Are We in the Competition-Innovation Debate?, in* Innovation Policy and the Economy, vol. 6, at 159 (Adam B. Jaffe et al. eds., 2006).

25. Ove Granstrand, *Innovation and Intellectual Property Rights, in* The Oxford Handbook of Innovation 266, 284 (Jan Fagerberg et al. eds., 2005); F. M. Scherer, *A Note on Global Welfare in Pharmaceutical Patenting*, 27 World Econ. 1127 (2004).

26. Scherer, *supra* note 25, at 1140.

27. Eric Schiff, Industrialization Without National Patents 65–92 (1971).

28. Granstrand, *supra* note 25, at 272.

29. *Id.*

30. *Id.*

31. *Id.* at 270–71; Martin Khor, *Rethinking Intellectual Property Rights and TRIPS, in* Global Intellectual Property Rights: Knowledge, Access and Development, 205 (Peter Drahos & Ruth Mayne eds., 2002).

32. Erich Kaufer, The Economics of the Patent System 10 (1989).

33. Petra Moser, *How Do Patent Laws Influence Innovation? Evidence from Nineteenth-Century World Fairs*, 34–35 (Nat'l. Bureau of Econ. Research, Working Paper No. 9909, 2003).

34. Granstrand, *supra* note 25, at 271.

35. Helpman, *supra* note 13, at 1276.

36. Keith E. Maskus et al., *Intellectual Property Rights and Economic Development in China, in* Intellectual Property and Development: Lessons from Recent Economic Research 325 (Carsten Fink & Keith M. Maskus eds., 2005).

37. Maskus, *supra* note 11, at 144.

38. *Id.* at 95.

39. *Id.* at 103–04.

40. *Id.* at 108.

41. Chen & Puttitanun, *supra* note 12, at 487.

42. *Id.* at 476.

43. *Id.*

44. Maskus, *supra* note 11, at 105.

45. Shamnad Basheer & Annalisa Primi, *The WIPO Development Agenda: Factoring in the Technologically Proficient Developing Countries, in* Implementing the World Intellectual Property Organization's Development Agenda 106 (Jeremy de Beer ed., 2009).

46. Helpman, *supra* note 24, at 50.

47. *Id.*

48. Export markets help to lessen this effect, especially for small economies. However, when a developing country first develops a new technology, it may not yet be competitive in the international market. The domestic market, however, will be to some extent captive and therefore provides a space for domestic firms to refine their technology before they become globally competitive.

49. Mansfield, *supra* note 9, at 174.

50. *Id.*

51. Levin et al., *supra* note 9, at 796–97.

52. *Id.* at 795.

53. *Id.* at 794.

54. Cohen, *supra* note 9, at 1.

Chapter 14

1. David Gerber, *Global Competition: Law, Markets and Globalisation* (2010).

2. Mittal Steel South Africa Limited & others v. Harmony Gold Mining Company Limited (70/CAC/Apr07).

3. Woodlands Dairy (Pty) Ltd and another v. Competition Commission (105/2010).

4. Wal-Mart Stores, Inc./Massmart Holdings Limited (73/LM/Nov10).

5. Shell South Africa (Pty) Limited/Tepco Petroleum (Pty) Ltd (66/LM/Oct01).

6. David Lewis, Competition Law, Policy and Economic Development over the Past Decade: From Competition Law to Competition Policy (Remarks, Third Annual Competition Conference, Sept. 2009).

7. Wal-Mart Stores, Inc., *supra* note 4.

8. *Id.* at para 99.

9. *Id.* at para 115.

10. *Id.* at para 108.

11. *Id.* at para 120.

12. Business Report, Aug. 10, 2011.

13. Woodlands Dairy (Pty) Ltd and another v. Competition Commission (105/2010).

14. Lewis, *supra* note 6.

Chapter 15

I am grateful to the participants of Global Competition Law conference held in New Delhi on November 18–19, 2010, for their comments. I am thankful to Professors D. Daniel Sokol and Thomas Cheng for their inputs on an earlier version of the chapter. The usual disclaimer applies.

1. *See* § 1(3) of the Competition Act, 2002.

2. Nick Robinson, *Expanding Judiciaries: India and the Rise of the Good Governance Court*, 8 Wash. U. Global Stud. L. Rev. 1 (2009).

3. *See* A. K. Roy v. Union of India, (1982) 1 S.C.C. 271.

4. Brahm Dutt v. Union of India, (2005) 2 S.C.C. 431 [hereinafter Brahm Dutt].

5. *Id.* at 434.

6. *Id.*

7. *See* § 5(2) of the MRTP Act, 1969.

8. *See* § 53D(1) of the Competition Act, 2002, introduced through the Competition (Amendment) Act, 2007. The MRTP Commission did not have a special appellate authority, and appeals from the MRTP Commission used to directly lie with the Supreme Court of India.

9. *See generally*, Rahul Singh, *Cementing Law and Policy*, Mint, Feb. 13, 2008, available at http://www.livemint.com/2008/02/13235813/Cementing-law-and-policy.html, noting that "Companies, of course are loath towards [the Competition Act, 2002]. They wish to carry on business as usual. This is perhaps the strongest reason why business lobbies have successfully stalled implementation of the competition law so far."

10. CCI Annual Report, 2009–2010, at 33.

11. Einer Elhauge & Damien Geradin, Global Antitrust Law and Economics (2010).

12. Massimo Motta, Competition Policy: Theory and Practice 14 (2004).

13. Rahul Singh, *Shifting Paradigms, Changing Contexts: Need for a New Competition Law in India*, 8J. Corp. L. Stud. 143, 144 (2008).

14. The Monopolies and Restrictive Trade Practices Act, No. 54 of 1969, available at http://indiacode.nic.in/.

15. Ruddra Dutta & K. P. M. Sundaram, Indian Economy 283 (2006).

16. Report of the Committee on Distribution of Income and Levels of Living, Part I, at.1.

17. Committee on the Distribution of Income and Levels of Living, appointed on October 13, 1960.

18. The terms of reference of the committee were: "(i) to review the changes in levels of living during the First and Second Five Year Plans; (ii) to study relevant trends in the distribution of income and wealth; and in particular; (iii) to ascertain the extent to which the operation of the economic system has resulted in concentration of wealth and means of production." *See generally*, Report of the Committee on Distribution of Income and Levels of Living, Part I, at 1.

19. *Id.* paras. 42, 43–44.

20. George A. Akerlof, *The Market for "Lemons": Quality Uncertainty and the Market Mechanism*, 84 Q. J. Econ. 488, 497 (1970).

21. Report, *supra* note 18, para. 73, at 55.

22. The terms of reference of the Monopolies Inquiry Commission were: "(a) to inquire into the extent and effect of concentration of economic power in *private hands* and the prevalence of monopolistic and restrictive practices in important sectors of economic activity other than agriculture" (emphasis added).

23. S. M. Dugar, Law of Restrictive Trade Practices iv (1976).

24. *See* Article 39(b) of the Constitution of India.

25. Article 39(c) of the Constitution of India states, "The State shall, in particular, direct its policy towards securing . . . (c) that the operation of the economic system does not result in the concentration of wealth and means of production to the common detriment".

26. *See* § 3 of the MRTP Act.

27. *See id.* §§ 20–26.

28. Gurcharan Das, India Unbound 169 (2002), noting that "The MRTP Act turned out to be one of the most damaging in modern Indian history. Any group with combined assets above INR 20 crore was declared a monopoly and effectively debarred from expanding its business after 1969. A single company, with assets above INR 1 crore, puny by world standards, was placed under anti-monopolistic supervision and control. Freddie Mehta, a director of Tatas, told me in 1989 that the Tatas made over a hundred proposals for new business projects or to expand existing ones over the twenty years since the MRTP law. All of them were rejected. In the mid-1980s, Rajiv Gandhi's government raised the MRTP asset limit fivefold to INR 100 crore. Finally, in September 1991, the Narasimha Rao government scrapped this ridiculous law."

29. Hamish McDonald, Ambani & Sons 130–31 (2010), noting that "Thanks to the help of the Ministry of Finance, Reliance looked like having 100 per cent of India's PTA [purified terephthalic acid] production and 34 per cent of the country's combined DMT [dimethyl terephthalate] and PTA output. Its control of other feedstocks, by-products and end-products in the polyester chain ranged from 38.6 per cent up to 62.5 per cent, according to Gurumurthy. India's anti-monopoly law defined a dominant undertaking as one with more than 24 per cent of national installed capacity, but none of Reliance's applications had been referred to the Monopolies and Restrictive Trade Practices Commission."

30. Hindustan Lever Employees' Union v. Hindustan Lever Ltd., 1995 Supp (1) S.C.C. 499, at 510 (para 9).

31. Manish Agrawal, *Mergers and Acquisitions in India: Implications for Competition*, *in* A Functional Competition Policy for India 71–80 (Pradeep Mehta ed. 2006).

32. Rahul Singh, *The Teeter Totter of Regulation and Competition: Balancing the Indian Competition Commission with Sectoral Regulators*, 8 Wash U. Global Stud. L. Rev. 71, 80 (2009).

33. Hindustan Lever, 1995 Supp (1) S.C.C. 499, at 523 (para 65).

34. *Id*. at 504 (para 1).

35. *Id*. at 513 (para 21).

36. *Id*. at 518–19 (para 43).

37. *Id*. at 504 (para 1).

38. Our History, http://www.hul.co.in/aboutus/ourhistory/.

39. Hindustan Lever, at 512 (para 18).

40. *Id*. at 520 (para 49).

41. *Id*. at 508 (para 7).

42. *Id*. at 508 (para 5).

43. *Id*. at 508 (para 6).

44. *Id*. at 525–26 (paras 73, 74).

45. *Id*. at 522 (para 61).

46. Prior to the amendment, § 23 of the MRTP Act, 1969 stated, "Notwithstanding anything contained elsewhere in this Act or in any other law for the time being in force, (a) no scheme of merger or amalgamation of two or more undertakings, to which this Part applies with any other undertaking, (b) no scheme of merger or amalgamation of two or more undertakings which would have the effect of bringing into existence an undertaking to which clause (a) or clause (b) of §20 would apply; shall be sanctioned by any Court or be recognized for any purpose or be given effect to unless the scheme for such merger or amalgamation has been approved by the Central Government under this section."

47. Hindustan Lever, 526 (para 76).

48. *Id*. at 524 (para 67).

49. *Id*. at 524 (para 68).

50. *Id*. at 525 (para 71).

51. Dep't of Company Affairs, Gov't of India Report of the High Level Committee on Competition Policy and Law (2000) [hereinafter Raghavan Committee].

52. *Id*. at para 4.6.2.

53. *Id*. at para 4.6.3.

54. *Id*. at para 4.7.7.

55. *Id*. at para 4.7.7.

56. *Id*. at para 4.7.8.

57. *Id*. at para 4.7.5.

58. *Id*. at para 4.7.6.

59. Agrawal, *supra* note 31, at 77.

60. Section 6(2) of Competition Act, 2002 prior to the amendment stated: "Subject to the provisions contained in sub-section (1), any person or enterprise, who or which proposes to enter into a combination, *may, at his or its option*, give notice to the Commission, in the form as may be specified and the fee which may be determined, by regulations" (emphasis added).

61. Section 6(2) of the Competition Act, 2002 after 2007 amendment states: "Subject to the provisions contained in sub-section (1), any person or enterprise, who or which proposes to enter into a combination, *shall* give notice to the Commission, in the form as may be specified and the fee which may be determined, by regulations" (emphasis added).

62. Section 31(11) of the Competition Act, 2002 prior to the amendment.

63. Section 31(11) of the Competition Act, 2002 after the amendment.

64. Clause 24 of the Statement of Objects and Reasons accompanying the 2007 amendment to the Competition Act.

65. Section 43A of 2007 amendment to the Competition Act.

66. Raghavan Committee, para 4.7.5.

67. *Id*. at para 4.7.8.

68. *Id*. at para 4.7.9.

69. *Id.* at para 4.7.9.

70. The Statement of Object and Reasons accompanying the 2007 amendment of the Competition Act, in para 2, states, "The Competition Commission of India was established on the 14th October, 2003 but could not be made functional due to the filing of a writ petition before the Hon'ble Supreme Court."

71. Brahm Dutt v. Union of India, (2005) 2 S.C.C. 431, 434 (para 2).

72. *See* Economy Bureau, *Acting CCI Chairman Vinod Dhall Quits*, Financial Express, June 19, 2008, available at http://www.financialexpress.com/news/acting-cci-chairman-vinod-dhall-quits /325038/0. Years later in 2011, Vinod Dhall's self-description as the first chairman of the CCI was questioned. *See generally*, http://www.business-standard.com/india/news/competitive-pro test/455376/.

73. CCI Annual Report, 2009-2010, at 33.

74. The Statement of Object and Reasons accompanying the 2007 amendment of the Competition Act, in para 2, states, "While disposing of the writ petition [in *Brahm Dutt*] on the 20th January, 2005, the Hon'ble Supreme Court held that if an expert body is to be created by the Union Government, it might be appropriate for the Government to consider the creation of two separate bodies, one with expertise for advisory and regulatory functions and the other for adjudicatory functions based on the doctrine of separation of powers recognized by the Constitution."

75. *See generally*, Introduction, available at http://compat.nic.in/Introduction.html.

76. *See generally*, Notifications, available at http://cci.gov.in/index.php?option=com_content& task=view&id=21.

77. *See* § 64 of the Competition Act.

78. CCI Annual Report, 2009–2010, at 19.

79. For the opposition by the CCI of the four MCA Notifications, see Sangeeta Singh, *Antitrust Body Seeks Tighter M&A Norms*, Mint, Oct. 5, 2011, available at http://www.livemint.com /2011/10/05003136/Antitrust-body-seeks-tighter-M.html.

80. G.S.R. No. S.O. 479(E) of March 4, 2011, available at http://www.mca.gov.in/Ministry /Comp_act.html.

81. G.S.R. No. S.O. 480(E) of March 4, 2011, available at http://www.mca.gov.in/Ministry /Comp_act.html.

82. G.S.R. No. S.O. 482(E) of March 4, 2011, available at http://www.mca.gov.in/Ministry /Comp_act.html.

83. G.S.R. No. S.O. 481(E) of March 4, 2011, available at http://www.mca.gov.in/Ministry /Comp_act.html.

84. Similar to "undertaking" under the EU competition law.

85. Section 5(a) of the Competition Act deals with "any acquisition," section 5(b) of the Competition Act deals with "acquiring of control" among horizontally situated entities, and section 5(c) of the Competition Act deals with any "merger or amalgamation."

86. *See supra*, note 82.

87. *See generally*, http://www.ftc.gov/os/fedreg/2011/01/110121clayton7afrn.pdf.

88. Section 20(3) of the Competition Act states, "Notwithstanding anything contained in §5, the Central Government shall, on the expiry of period of two years from the date of commencement of this Act and thereafter every two years, in consultation with the commission, by notification, enhance or reduce, on the basis of the wholesale price index or fluctuations in exchange rate of rupee or foreign currencies, the value of assets or the value of turnover, for the purposes of that section."

89. The proviso to § 1(3) of the Competition Act, states, "Provided that different dates may be appointed for different provisions of this Act and any reference in any such provision to the commencement of this Act shall be construed as a reference to the coming into force of that provision." I am grateful to Mr. P. K. Singh, Adviser, Competition Commission of India for the argument based on § 1(3) of the Competition Act.

90. *See generally*, Shruti Shrivastava, *CCI Gets Mandate to Approve All Pharma M&As*, Indian Express, Oct. 11, 2011, available at http://www.indianexpress.com/news/cci-gets-mandate-to-ap prove-all-pharma-m&as/858266/0.

91. *Id.*

92. *See generally*, amendment to the Banking Regulation Act.

93. *See* § 5 of the Competition Act.

94. The "Indian" assets and "Indian" turnover (i.e., locus nexus) requirements of assets and turnover being in India were introduced through the Ministry of Corporate Affairs corrigendum of May 27, 2011.

95. The word "either" was introduced through the Ministry of Corporate Affairs corrigendum of May 27, 2011.

96. *See* § 54 of the Competition Act.

97. *See* Saint Gobain Produits pour la Constructions S.A.S, Combination Registration No. C-2012/01/19 decided on Feb. 16, 2012; *See also* Navyug Special Steel, Combination Registration No. C-2011/12/14 decided on Jan. 31, 2012.

98. Pallavi Shroff & Harman Singh Sandhu, *JVs and Competition Law: Uncertain Times Ahead*, India Bus. L.J., July/August 2010, at 69.

99. *See* Kiran S. Desai, Manas Kumar Chaudhuri & Manu Mohan, *Joint Ventures Under India's Competition Act*, at 4, available at http://www.mayerbrown.com/publications/article.asp?id=10438 (Feb. 14, 2011).

100. This is unlike the MRTP Act.

101. Explanation (b) to § 2(h) that defines "enterprise" states that "article" includes a new article and "service" includes a new service.

102. Explanation (b) to § 5 defines "group" to mean "two or more enterprises which, directly or indirectly are in a position to – (i) exercise 26% or more of the voting rights in the other enterprise; or (ii) appoint more than 50% of the members of the board of director in the other enterprise; or (iii) control the management or affairs of the other enterprise."

103. Rahul Singh, *A Competition Conundrum Brews*, Mint, May 27, 2011, available at http://www.livemint.com/2011/05/26224745/A-competition-conundrum-brews.html.

104. *Id.*

105. *See* Item No. 8, Schedule I of the Competition Commission of India Regulations, 2011 (procedure in regard to the transaction of business relating to combinations).

106. Regulation 4 of the Competition Commission of India Regulations, 2011 (procedure in regard to the transaction of business relating to combinations) states, "In view of the duty cast upon the Commission under §18 and powers conferred under §36 of the Act and having regard to the mandate given to the Commission to, inter alia, regulate combinations which have caused or are likely to cause appreciable adverse effect on competition in terms of sub-section (1) of §6 of the [Competition]Act, it is clarified that since the categories of combinations mentioned in Schedule I are ordinarily not likely to cause an appreciable adverse effect on competition in India, notice under sub-section (2) of §6 of the Act need not normally be filed."

107. "Enterprise" includes business units, business division, and subsidiaries.

108. Combination Registration No. C-2011/08/03 decided on Sept. 15, 2011.

109. Combination Registration No. C-2011/09/04 decided on Sept. 30, 2011.

110. Combination Registration No. C-2011/10/05 decided on Nov. 4, 2011.

111. *See generally*, *CCI Seeks More Powers*, Telegraph, Nov. 8, 2011, available at http://www.telegraphindia.com/1111108/jsp/business/story_14721311.jsp.

112. The CCI has represented to the government to delete the exemption based upon the size of acquired enterprise. *See generally*, Singh, *supra* note 79.

113. *See* Item No. 8A, Schedule I of the the Competition Commission of India Regulations, 2011 (procedure in regard to the transaction of business relating to combinations).

114. Combination Registration No. C-2011/12/12 decided on Dec. 28, 2011.

115. Combination Registration No. C-2011/10/06 decided on Oct. 19, 2011.

116. *Id.*, para 8, noting that "It is observed that AHIL [Alstom Holdings (India) Limited] and APIL [Alstom Projects India Limited] are engaged in different business activities. It is also observed that both AHIL and APIL are part of the Alstom Group of companies, the ultimate holding of which is with Alstom Holdings. Further, the amalgamated company APIL would continue to be under the same management subsequent to the implementation of the scheme of amalgamation approved by the Board of Directors of both AHIL and APIL. Given the foregoing, the proposed combination is not likely to have an adverse effect on competition in India."

117. Combination Registration No. C-2011/11/09 decided on Dec. 13, 2011. *See* para 10, noting that "The ultimate control over the business activities carried by SL [Siemens Limited], SVAI [Siemens VAI Metals Technologies Private Limited] and Morgan [Morgan Construction Company India Private Limited] before and after the proposed combination, remains with Siemens AG. Therefore, the proposed combination does not give rise to any adverse competition concern."

118. Avaantika Kakkar, *Why Would the CCI Interest Itself in Group Restructurings?*, Econ. Times, Dec. 2, 2011.

119. See Item No. 2, Schedule I of the Competition Commission of India Regulations, 2011 (procedure in regard to the transaction of business relating to combinations).

120. Combination Registration No. C-2011/08/02 decided on Aug. 25, 2011. The CCI's order can be accessed at http://cci.gov.in/May2011/OrderOfCommission/CombinationOrders /WaltCombOrder250811.pdf.

121. *See generally*, Bar and Bench News Network, *JSA's Senior Advisor Amitabh Kumar Speaks on CCI Merger Approval Process*, , Sept. 2, 2011, available at http://barandbench.com/brief/2/1700/jsas -senior-advisor-amitabh-kumar-speaks-on-cci-merger-approval-process.

122. Aditya Bhattacharjea, *India's New Antitrust Regime*, CPI Antitrust J., Nov. 2010, at 2.

123. John Samuel Raja D & Rohit Deb, *Can Understaffed Competition Commission of India Deliver Prudent Judgements,*" Econ. Times, Aug. 15, 2011.

124. *See* §§ 2(r), 2(s), 2(t), 19(5), 19(6), 19(7) of the Competition Act, 2002.

125. Section 20(4) of the Competition Act, 2002.

Index

Note: Page numbers followed by f and t indicate figures and tables.

Absolutist view, market-based principles of competition law and, 35–36, 37, 50, 79–89; differential competition law arguments, 81–85; optimal competition policy and enhanced societal welfare, 84–85, 89; optimal competition policy implementation, 87–89; optimal competition policy principles, 85–87

"Acquisition," merger control and India's definition of, 267, 269, 307n112

Affiliated-regulator setting, in competition agency structure, 99–101

African National Congress (ANC), 233

Aghion, Phillipe, 47–48, 49, 118

AICA Japan, 266

Akerlof, George, 252

Alstom Group, 267, 307n116

Appropriability effect, competition and, 47

Argentina, 215

Arrow, Kenneth J., 38

Arthur, Thomas C.: essay by, 66–78; references to, 7

Asia. See specific countries

Australia: antitrust remedies, 171, 171t, 172, 172t, 173t, 175t, 178t; competition agency statistics, 102, 104–105, 105t, 106t, 107, 109–110, 110t, 111t; enforcement in, 124, 128; National Competition Policy in, 193–198

Austria, 123, 128

Balanced growth theory, of Nurske, 40–41

Bank mergers, in India, 261

Basheer, Shamnad, 223, 224

Belgium: diamond bourse in, 161; enforcement in, 123, 128, 286n26

Bernstein, Lisa, 158

Bhattacharjea, Aditya: essay by, 52–65; references to, 6–7

Bid rigging, domestic anticartel enforcement and, 150–151, 153; in South Africa, 237

Big push theory, development economics and, 40, 41

Bloom, Nick, 48

Bolivia, 86

Bombay Burmah Trading Company Limited (BBTCL), 266

Botswana, 128

Brahm Dutt v. Union of India, 250–251, 258–259, 304n9

Brazil, 64, 118, 151; antitrust remedies, 171, 171t, 173t, 175–176, 175t, 178t; economic growth in, 2–3; enforcement in, 128; optimal competition law and, 86; patent-antitrust interface and, 224

Brown Shoe Co. v. United States, 55

Canada: antitrust remedies, 171, 171t, 172, 172t, 173t, 175t, 178t; competition law history, 53–54

Capital accumulation, development economics and, 39–40

Carlin, Wendy, 49

Carol Info Services Limited, 266

Cartels: convergence strategy and, 18, 28–29; export cartels, 201–202, 203

Cartels, contractual rights and, 155–166; development and, 156–157; diamond industry and, 158–166, 290n25

Cartels, prioritizing of enforcement and, 137–154; bid rigging, domestic, 150–151, 153; leniency programs, domestic, 143–145; leniency programs, international, 140–141, 287n11;

Cartels (*continued*)
limited benefits of international enforcement, 138–141, 139*f*; media and domestic enforcement, 141–143; merger activity, domestic, 148, 153; optimal enforcement mix, 152–154; tacit collusion, domestic, 148–150, 153; whistleblowers and bounties, domestic, 145–148, 288nn33, 38

Chen, Youngmin, 222–223

Cheng, Thomas K.: essay by, 212–227; references to, 10

Chicago School of economics, market efficiency and, 42–43, 47

Chile, 49, 86, 118; antitrust remedies, 171, 171*t*, 172–173, 172*t*, 173*t*, 175*t*, 176, 178*t*, 293n41; bid rigging in, 150–151

China: antitrust remedies, 171, 172, 172*t*, 173*t*, 175*t*, 178*t*, 291n25; competition advocacy and, 186; competition law history, 58–59; development economics and, 42; economic growth in, 2–3; effects of patent protection on poverty in, 219–220; optimal competition law and, 86; patent-antitrust interface and, 224

Clayton Act (United States), 54–55, 69–70, 71, 73–74, 87, 251, 281n62

Coase theorem, 38

Cohen, Wesley, 225

Collective action theory, of Olson, 45

Colombia, 49, 118

Commission on Growth and Development report, 44

Competition advocacy, 182–198; comprehensive national policy, as modeled in Australia, 193–198; traditional approach, 183–185; traditional approach, limitations of, 185–193

Competition Assessment Toolkit, of OECD, 196–198

Competition Commission of India (CCI), 3, 249–250; Competition Act amended in 2007, 257, 305nn60,61; Competition Act enactment and enforcement, 250–251; economics of merger control and corporate lobbying, 258–265, 260*t*; establishment of, 258, 306nn70,72; merger precedents and, 265–270

Competition culture. *See* South Africa, embedding of competition culture in

Competition economics. *See* Development economics, tension with competition economics

Competition law and policy: freedom-based and growth-focused views of, 4–5;

importance of, 1–2; problems of transplanting from developed to developing world, 2–4

Congress of South African Trade Unions, 233

Content-based claims, for convergence strategy, 19–20, 23–24

"Contract-formalist approach," to economic development, 156–157

"Contract-informalist approach," to economic development, 157

Contract rights. *See* Cartels, contractual rights and

Convergence strategy, 13–34; benefits of, 24–29, 32–33; concepts and assumptions, 14–15, 271n8; content-based incentives, 23–24; convergence point and, 15, 17–19, 23, 24–26, 31, 271n8; costs of, 23, 30–33; impact of, 29–30; as policy, 15–18; as policy, process-, and content-based justifications, 18–20, 272n20; process-based incentives, 20–23; tension between economic development and, 33–34

Cooperation, cross-border enforcement and, 205–206, 208–210, 211

Corruption/rent seeking, development economics and, 45–46

Cost factors, of convergence strategy, 23, 30–33

Country-specific approach, to patent-antitrust interface, 224–225

Coverage, of competition law regimes, 120

Cross-border cooperation, 205–206, 208–210, 211

Cuba, 86

Czech Republic, competition agency statistics, 102, 105*t*, 106*t*, 107, 109–110, 110*t*, 111*t*

Danone Asia Pacific Holdings Pte Limited, 266

Darwin, Charles, 80

Das, Gurcharan, 304n28

Davis, Kevin, 157

Debreu, Gérard, 38

Democracy, enforcement limitations and efficiencies and, 115–136

Denmark, 124, 128

Department of Justice, Antitrust Division (U.S.), 70–74

Department of Trade and Industry (DTI), in South Africa, 235–239, 243

Dependency theory, development economics and, 42

Developing countries, use of term, 14

Development, use of term, 4

Development economics, tension with competition economics, 35–51; competition and growth, 47–50; competition and institutions for growth, 45–47; historical and theoretical tensions, 37–42; phases of development economics, 39; post–Washington Consensus, 42–45

Diamond industry, 158–166, 290n25

Disney, Richard, 48

Disney group, 268

Distributional coalition concept, of Olson, 45–46

Dixit, Avinash, 158

Domestic market size, patent-antitrust interface and, 224

Dual sector model, of Lewis, 39–40

Dutt, Brahm, 250–251

Dutz, Mark A., 48

Dyck, Alexander, 145–146

Easterbrook, Frank, 73

Economic growth, use of term, 4

Economic harm, convergence strategy and, 18, 27–28

Economics-based model of competition law (EBM). See Convergence strategy

Ecuador, 86

Effects principle, jurisdiction and, 16

Efficiency wage theory, 46

Empagran. See F. Hoffman-LaRoche Ltd. v. Empagran, S.A.

Employment-related conditions, South African competition and, 239–243

Enforcement, limitations and efficiencies of, 115–136; characteristics of regimes, 120–122; costs of convergence strategy, 30–31; econometric analysis of successful regimes, 128–134, 130–131t; economics model of, 117–119; models of levels of, 132–134, 133t; policy implications, 134–136; regimes defined, 119–120; regimes' global spread, 123–128, 124t, 125t, 126t, 127t

Enforcement agencies, 90–114; challenges of new, 91–92, 112–114; cross-country benchmarking and optimal size, 107–112, 110t, 111t; economies of scale and scope, 95–97; enforcement statistics, 102–107, 105t, 106t; independence in light of political and interest group effects, 98–101; need for, 90–91; scope of enforcement and output issues, 93–95

"Enterprise," merger control and India's definition of, 269

Equilibrium theories, development economics and, 37–38

Eslava, Marcela, 49, 118

Europe, competition law history, 55–57

European Commission, competition agency independence, 100–101

European Union: antitrust remedies, 171, 171t, 173t, 175t, 178t, 180; cartel deterrence and, 139; competition advocacy and, 192; competition agency independence, 100–101; Treaty of Rome, 251

Expertise, convergence strategy and costs of, 30

Export cartels: exempted from domestic competition law, 201–202; negative spillover generation and, 203

Export trade, development economics and, 41, 43

Extraterritoriality, competition law application and, 204–205

Ezrachi, Ariel: essay by, 199–211; references to, 9–10

Fafchamps, Marcel, 158

Fannie Mae, in the United States, 88

Faure-Grimaud, Antoine, 99–101

Feasibility, of convergence strategy, 19

Federal Trade Commission (FTC) (U.S.), 69–74

Fels, Allan: essay by, 182–198; references to, 9

F. Hoffman-LaRoche Ltd. v. Empagran, S.A., 64, 139

Finland, competition agency statistics, 102, 104–105, 105t, 106t, 107, 109–110, 110t, 111t

First, Harry: essay by, 167–181; references to, 9

Foreign aid, development economics and, 39, 42

Foreign direct investment (FDI), 22; competition agency statistics and, 107; convergence strategy and, 30

Foreign inventors, patent-antitrust interface and, 217–219

Fox, Eleanor M., 49, 50, 62, 64–65, 81, 83–84

France, 55–56, 128

Freddie Mac, in the United States, 88

Free riding, cross-border enforcement and, 207

G&K Baby Care Private Limited, 266

Gal, Michal S., 49

Gandhi, Rajiv, 304n28

GDP (gross domestic product): enforcement
    effectiveness and, 117–120, 136; law
    enforcement regimes and, 123–127, 124*t*,
    125*t*, 126*t*, 127*t*
Gerber, David J.: essay by, 13–34; references
    to, 6, 233
Germany: antitrust remedies, 171, 171*t*, 172*t*,
    173*t*, 175*t*, 176, 177, 178*t*, 179; competition
    law history, 55–56; enforcement in, 123;
    patent-antitrust interface and, 220–221
Ghosal, Vivek: essay by, 90–114; references to,
    7–8
Ginarte, J. C., 223
Glaeser, Edward, 116, 119
Gould, Stephen Jay, 80
Government intervention. *See* Development
    economics, tension with competition
    economics
Greece, 128
Greif, Avner, 158
Grossman, Gene, 48
Group boycotts. *See* Cartels, contractual rights
    and
"Group," merger control and India's definition
    of, 264, 267–268, 307n102

Haltiwanger, John, 48–49, 118
Handbook of Antitrust Economics, 55
Harod-Domar growth models, 39
Hart-Scott-Rodino Act (United States),
    73–74
Hayri, Aydin, 48
Helpman, Elhanan, 48, 221
Herfindahl–Hirschman Index (HHI), 269
Hilmer Report, in Australia, 194, 195
*Hindustan Lever Employees' Union v. Hindustan
    Lever*, 254–256
Hindustan Lever Limited (HLL), 254–255
Historical analysis, of competition law, 52–65;
    application and effects, 57–60; in Asia, 87,
    277n27; in Canada, 53–54; in Europe,
    55–57; information sharing and, 64–65;
    principles for developing countries,
    60–64; in the United States, 54–55, 64,
    67–70, 278n34
Hoff, Karla, 44
Hong Kong, 112, 128
Howitt, Peter, 47–48
Hungary: competition advocacy and, 184;
    competition agency statistics, 102, 105*t*,
    106*t*, 107, 109–110, 110*t*, 111*t*; GDP and
    enforcement in, 128

Imitative capacity, patent-antitrust interface
    and, 216–217, 226

Import-substitution policies, development
    economics and, 39, 41, 43
Incarceration. *See* United States, export of
    antitrust remedies
Independent-regulator setting, in competition
    agency structure, 99–101
India, 118, 215; antitrust remedies, 171, 171*t*,
    172, 172*t*, 173*t*, 175*t*, 177–178, 178*t*;
    competition advocacy and, 188–189;
    competition law history, 59; Constitution
    and, 253, 304n25; development
    economics and, 42, 49; diamond
    exchanges in, 159, 161, 290n25; economic
    growth in, 2–3; optimal competition law
    and, 86; patent-antitrust interface and,
    224–225
India, merger control in, 249–270; economics
    of, and corporate lobbying, 258–265,
    260*t*; historical evolution of regime,
    251–258; merger precedents and
    philosophy, 265–270
Indonesia, 58, 184
Industry-specific approach, to patent-antitrust
    interface, 225–227
Innovation: development economics and,
    46–48; incentives and, 217–219, 302n17;
    innovative capacity as issue in patent-
    antitrust interface, 215–217
Intellectual property. *See* Patent-antitrust
    interface
International Competition Network (ICN),
    16–17, 139–140, 183, 209
International Monetary Fund, Washington
    Consensus and, 43, 81
Internet usage, competition agency statistics
    and, 107
Ireland, competition agency statistics, 102,
    104–105, 105*t*, 106*t*, 109–110, 110*t*, 111*t*,
    285n12
Israel: antitrust remedies, 171, 171*t*, 173*t*, 174,
    175*t*, 176–177, 178*t*; dispute resolution
    and, 161

Japan: antitrust remedies, 171*t*, 172, 172*t*,
    173*t*, 175*t*, 176, 178, 178*t*, 293n41;
    competition law history, 57, 277n27;
    economic growth in, 4; patent-antitrust
    interface and, 220
Joint ventures, India and, 262–263
Jones, Alison, 57
Judicial systems, enforcement limitations and
    efficiencies and, 115–136
Jurisdictional monetary thresholds,
    India's merger control and, 260–265,
    260*t*

Kaplow, Louis, 213
Keynes, John Maynard, 38–39

Landa, Janet, 158
Latin American Competition Network, 65
Leniency programs: antitrust remedies and, 177, 179–180; domestic anticartel enforcement, 143–145; international anticartel enforcement, 140–141, 287n11; South Africa and, 231–232
Levenstein, Margaret, 138
Levin, Richard, 225
Lewis, Arthur, 39–40
Lewis, David: essay by, 228–248; references to, 10
Lianos, Ioannis: essay by, 35–51; references to, 6
Little, Ian M. D., 43
Lyell, Charles, 80

Ma, Tay-Cheng, 50, 59–60
Mahalanobis, P. C., 252
Mahalanobis Committee, in India, 252–253, 304n18
Malaysia, 59, 128
Mansfield, Edwin, 225
Marshall, Alfred, 38
Martimort, David, 99–101
Maskus, Keith, 222, 223
Massmart. See Walmart and Massmart, in South Africa
Mateus, Abel: essays by, 35–51, 115–136; references to, 6, 8, 50, 62
Mauritius, 128
McDonald, Hamish, 304n29
Media, domestic anticartel enforcement and, 141–143
Mehta, Freddie, 304n28
Mergers: cross-border transfer of wealth and, 203–204; in developing countries, 148, 153; U.S. antitrust enforcement issues and, 73–74, 282n82. See also India, merger control in
Mexico: competition advocacy and, 196, 197–198; patent-antitrust interface and, 224
Microsoft litigation, U.S. antitrust enforcement issues and, 73
Monoeconomics, 36, 43
Monopolies and Restrictive Trade Practices (MRTP) Commission and Act, in India, 59, 62, 250–256, 303n8, 304nn28,29, 305n46; definitions of "group" and "acquisition," 267–268, 307nn102,112; economics of merger control and corporate lobbying, 258–265, 260t; jurisdictional monetary

thresholds and, 260–265, 260t; merger precedents and, 265–270
Monti, Mario, 100

National Association of Attorneys General (United States), 73
National competition agency (NCA), characteristics of competition law and, 121–122, 286n22
National Competition Policy (NCP), in Australia, 193–198
Nationality principle, jurisdiction and, 15–16
Nehru, Jawaharlal, 42, 252
Neoclassical economists. See Development economics, tension with competition economics
Netherlands, 128, 143
Network benefits, of convergence strategy, 19, 21–22, 24–27
Neutrality, convergence strategy and, 25–26
New International Economic Order, 42
New York Diamond Dealers' Club (DDC), 159–164
New Zealand, 124, 128
Ng, Wendy: essay by, 182–198; references to, 9
NHK Automotive, 266, 269
North, Douglass, 155, 156, 157
Norway, 124
Nurske, Ragnar, 40–41

Office of Fair Trading, of United Kingdom, 102–104, 103t, 244–245
Olson, Mancur, 45–46
Opportunity costs, of convergence strategy, 23, 31–32
Optimal competition policy: enhanced societal welfare and, 84–85, 89; implementation, 87–89; principles of, 85–87
Organisation for Economic Co-operation and Development (OECD), 81–82, 139–140, 209; Competition Assessment Toolkit of, 196–198; South Africa and, 231
Ostrom, Elinor, 158

Pareto efficient equilibrium, development economics and, 37–38
Park, W. G., 223
Partial equilibrium theory, 38
Patent-antitrust interface, 212–227; country-specific approach to, 224–225; development concerns and, 213–214, 219–221; foreign inventor issues, 217–219; industry-specific approach to, 225–227; innovative capacity issues, 215–217;

Patent-antitrust interface (*continued*)
   technological capacity issues, 220,
   221–224
Peltzman, Sam, 98–99
Penubarti, Mohan, 222, 223
Per capita income, patent-antitrust interface
   and, 222–224
Peru, 86
Pharmaceutical industry, India and, 249, 261
Phelps, Edmund, 45
Poland: competition agency statistics, 102,
   105, 105*t*, 106*t*, 107, 109–110, 110*t*, 111*t*,
   285n14; GDP and enforcement in, 128
Posner, Richard, 55, 61
Poverty: competition law and priorities of
   alleviation, 62–64; patent protection in
   China and, 219–220
Prebisch, Raúl, 41, 42
Predictability, convergence strategy and,
   25–27
Prescriptive/legislative jurisdiction, conver-
   gence strategy and, 15, 271n11
Priest, George L.: essay by, 79–89; references
   to, 7, 35–36
Primi, Annalisa, 223, 224
Private treble damages. *See* United States,
   export of antitrust remedies
Procedural competition law, 121
Process-based incentives, convergence strategy
   and, 18–19, 20–23
Procurement. *See* Bid rigging, domestic
   anticartel enforcement and
Procurement-related conditions, South
   African competition and, 239–243
Production capacity, patent-antitrust interface
   and, 216
Protected firms, convergence strategy and, 29
Public administration, enforcement limitations
   and efficiencies and, 115–136
Public choice theory, 43
Puttitanun, Thitima, 222–223

Raghavan, S. V. S., 256
Raghavan Committee, in India, 256–257,
   259
Rao, Narasimha, 304n28
Raslan, Azza: essay by, 35–51; references to, 6
Rationality, convergence strategy and, 25–26
Regime I, of law enforcement: defined, 119,
   286n20; policy implications, 134
Regime II, of law enforcement, 132; defined,
   119; policy implications, 134–135
Regime III, of law enforcement, 132; defined,
   120; policy implications, 135; threshold
   for, 125

Remedies, private and public. *See* United
   States, export of antitrust remedies
Richman, Barak D.: essay by, 155–166;
   references to, 9
Robinson-Patman Act (United States), 54
Rosenstein-Rodan, Paul N., 40, 41
Rostow, Walt Whitman, 40
Russia, 184, 224

Salamao, Calixto, 82
Schankerman, Mark, 118
Scherer, F. M., 219
Schumpeter, Joseph, 38, 47–48, 273n9,
   275n68
Scitovsky, Tibor, 43
Scott, Maurice, 43
Sen, Amartya, 4, 63
Shapiro, Helen, 44
Sherman Act (United States), 54, 69–71, 80,
   87, 251, 281nn55,62; history of private
   damages and incarceration in the United
   States, 168–170
Shleifer, Andrei, 116, 119
Siemens, 267, 308n117
Singapore: competition agency and, 91, 112;
   competition law history, 58; democracy
   and enforcement in, 132
Singer, Hal, 41, 42
Singh, Ajit, 49
Singh, Rahul: essay by, 249–270; references to,
   10–11
Slovakia, 128, 132
Slovenia, 123
Small and medium enterprises (SMEs),
   convergence strategy and, 29–30
Smith, Adam, 36–37, 41
Sokol, D. Daniel: essay by, 137–154; references
   to, 8
South Africa, 64, 118; antitrust remedies,
   171*t*, 172, 172*t*, 173*t*, 175*t*, 178, 178*t*;
   competition advocacy and, 186–187;
   competition agency statistics, 102, 105*t*,
   106*t*, 107, 109–110, 110*t*, 111*t*; development economics and, 49; GDP and
   enforcement in, 128; patent-antitrust
   interface and, 224
South Africa, embedding of competition
   culture in, 228–249; creation of
   competition culture in, 230–233;
   government, industrial policy, and
   deterioration of competition culture,
   235–239; industrial policy and black
   economic empowerment aspects,
   233–235; market mechanism dominance
   and, 228–230; Walmart/Massmart and

employment- and procurement-related issues, 239–243; Walmart/Massmart and government intervention in and hostility to foreign mergers, 186–187, 244–247; Walmart/Massmart and industrial policy goals, 243

South African Communist Party, 233

South Korea, 64, 147–148; antitrust remedies, 171t, 172t, 173t, 175t, 176, 178t; competition advocacy and, 192; competition law history, 58

Spain, 123

Stages of Growth: A Non-Communist Manifesto, The (Rostow), 40

Standardization-based claims, for convergence strategy, 18–19, 21

Status benefits, convergence strategy and, 22

Stephan, Andreas: essay by, 137–154; references to, 8

Stewart, Taimoon, 83–84

Stiglitz, Joseph, 44

Substantive competition law, 120

Supreme Court (U.S.): private damage remedies and, 169; weaknesses of U.S. competition law and, 66–78, 283n97, 284n106

Suslow, Valerie Y., 138

Switzerland, 220–221

Tacit collusion, 148–150, 153

Taiwan: competition agency statistics, 102, 105t, 106t, 109–110, 110t, 111t; competition law history, 58

Tata Oil Mills Company Limited (TOMCO), 254–255

Technological capacity, patent-antitrust interface and, 216, 220, 221–224

Territoriality principle, jurisdiction and, 15–16

Thailand, 58

Trade-Related Aspects of Intellectual Property Rights (TRIPS), of WTO, 24, 63–64; patent-antitrust interface and, 214, 215, 221, 227

Transfer of wealth, domestic and cross-border, 119–211; cross-border setting, 202–204; domestic setting, 200–202, 298nn3,4, 299n11; externality and cooperation and, 204–206, 299nn24,25; implications for small and developing economies, 206–210

Treaty of Rome, 251

Treaty on the Functioning of the European Union (TFEU), 57

Trebilcock, Michael, 156–157

Trusts and cartels, United States and, 69–70, 74–75, 283n85

Turkey: competition agency statistics, 104–105, 105t, 106t, 107, 109, 285n14; democracy and enforcement in, 132; GDP and enforcement in, 128; patent-antitrust interface and, 224

Tybout, James, 48, 118

Unilever, 254–255

United Kingdom: antitrust remedies, 171, 171t, 172t, 173t, 174, 175t, 178, 178t; cartel deterrence and, 143; competition agency statistics, 102–105, 103t, 105t, 106t, 107, 109–110, 110t, 111t; competition law history, 55–56; Office of Fair Trading, 102–104, 103t, 244–245; U.S. free riding in the nineteenth century, 220

United Nations Conference on Trade and Development (UNCTAD), 139–140, 209, 210

United States, 66–78; cartel deterrence and, 139; competition agency independence, 100–101; competition law, 13, 271n3; competition law history, 54–55, 64, 67–70, 278n34; convergence strategy and, 17; current decentralized, fragmented, and political nature of law enforcement in, 70–74, 76; current performance of law, 74–77; free riding in the nineteenth century, 220; GDP and enforcement in, 128; optimal competition law and, 87–88; WTO and competition law, 16–17, 272n15

United States, export of antitrust remedies, 77–78, 167–181; conclusions and caveats, 179–181; history of private damages and incarceration in the United States, 168–170; private damages and incarceration spread outside the United States, 170–179, 171t, 172t, 173t, 175t, 178t

United States v. Trans-Missouri Freight Association, 54

Uruguay, 128

UTV Software Communications Limited, 268

van Reenen, John, 48

Venezuela, 86, 128

Vested interests. *See* Enforcement, limitations and efficiencies of

Vietnam, 58

Wallace Act, Canada, 53

Walmart and Massmart, in South Africa: employment- and procurement-related issues, 239–243; government intervention in and hostility to foreign mergers,

Walmart and Massmart, in South Africa
    (*continued*)
    186–187, 244–247; industrial policy goals,
    243
Washington Consensus, 43, 44, 274nn40,41;
    optimal competition law and, 81, 83,
    87
Welfare economics, 38–39, 43, 56
Whistleblowers, anticartel enforcement and,
    145–148, 288nn33,38
Wilks, Stephen, 56
Williamson, John, 274n40

Wockhardt EU Operations Swiss AG, 266
Wood Pulp case, 149
Workhardt Limited, 266
World Bank, 43, 81
World Trade Organization (WTO): Agree-
    ment on Trade-Related Aspects of
    Intellectual Property Rights (TRIPS), 24,
    63–64, 214, 215, 221, 227; competition
    law and, 16–17, 272n15

Zambia, 64
Zimbabwe, 86

Global Competition Law and Economics

Thomas K. Cheng, Ioannis Lianos, and D. Daniel Sokol, editors

Competition law and economics—known in the United States as
antitrust—is an area of cutting-edge academic work with significant policy
implications. Once confined to the United States and a few other countries,
antitrust has taken off as an area of study in a relatively short period of time.
More than 100 jurisdictions now have competition laws. Increasingly,
enforcement activities abroad have far-reaching implications for
any antitrust regime. Moreover, developments in economic thinking have
helped to reformulate attitudes in both academic and policy circles.
This book series is at the forefront of the development of new ideas
and approaches within the field.

The Global Limits of Competition Law
Ioannis Lianos and D. Daniel Sokol
2012